WORKSHOP
MATH

Robert Scharff

BARNES
&NOBLE
BOOKS
NEW YORK

Library of Congress Cataloging-in-Publication Data
Scharff, Robert.
    [Math for construction, workshop, and the home]
    Workshop math / Robert Scharff.
       p.   cm.
    Reprint. Originally published: Math for construction, workshop,
and the home. [New York?] : Grolier Book Clubs, 1979.
    Includes index.
    ISBN 0-8069-5802-2
    1. Shop mathematics.   2. Mathematics.   I. Title.
[TJ1165.S26   1989]
601'.513—dc20   89-33753
                                                     CIP

Published in 1989 by Sterling Publishing Co., Inc.
387 Park Avenue South, New York, N.Y. 10016
The material in this book was originally
published in hardcover by Grolier Book
Clubs, Inc., in "Math for Construction, Workshop
and the Home" copyright © by Robert Scharff
Distributed in Canada by Sterling Publishing
% Canadian Manda Group, P.O. Box 920, Station U
Toronto, Ontario, Canada M8Z 5P9
Distributed in Great Britain and Europe by Chrysalis Books
64 Brewery Road, London N7 9NT
Distributed in Australia by Capricorn Link (Australia) Pty. Ltd.
P.O. Box 704, Windsor, NSW 2756 Australia
Manufactured in the United States of America
All rights reserved

Sterling ISBN 0-8069-5802-2 Paper
ISBN 0-7607-4684-2 Hardcover

CONTENTS

ACKNOWLEDGMENTS

Thanks to A.J. Hand for writing the chapter on energy savings and for updating the chapter on heating, cooling, and plumbing.

For text and data reprinted in this book, special thanks go to the following organizations:

Air-conditioning and Refrigeration Institute; American Society of Heating, Refrigeration, and Air Conditioning Engineers; American Standard Inc.; Brick Institute of America; California Redwood Association; General Drafting Company Inc.; Home Ventilating Institute; *Homeowners How to* magazine; National Bureau of Standards; National Paint and Coating Company; Pennsylvania State Extension Service; *Popular Science* magazine; Portland Cement Association; Rockwell International Inc.; Sears, Roebuck & Co.; Stanley Tools, Division of Stanley Works Inc.; L.S. Starrett Company; Texas Instruments Inc.; Tile Council of America; U.S. Bureau of Naval Personnel; U.S. Department of Agriculture; Wallcovering Institute; Western Wood Products Association.

Robert Scharff

1

MATH FOR CONSTRUCTION LAYOUT AND ESTIMATING

THE STEEL SQUARE

Among all the tools used by the professional carpenter or the do-it-yourselfer there is perhaps none so useful, simple, and indispensable as the modern steel square (often called the carpenter's, framing, or rafter square). No other tool may be so readily applied to the quick solution of the many difficult problems of laying out work. In the right hands, the square becomes a simple calculating device of wonderful capacities. In fact, the problems that can be solved with the square are so many and varied that whole books have been written on the square. Only a few of the more common uses of the square are presented here. (Note: Upcoming pages cover uses of squares imprinted with numerous tables and scales. Simpler "homeowner squares" lack some of these references.)

The steel square forms a right angle—that is, its body (blade) and tongue make an angle of 90 degrees, which is a right angle.

Refer to the diagram in **Figure 1-1.** Note that if we connect points A and C by drawing a straight line we have the triangle ABC, and since the angle

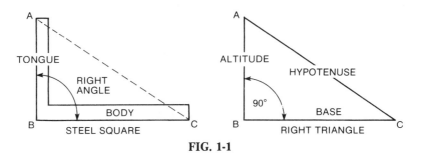

FIG. 1-1

1

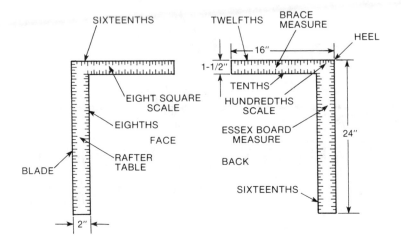

FIG. 1-2

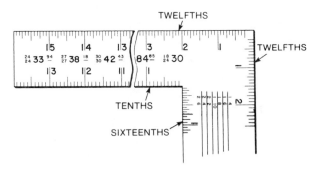

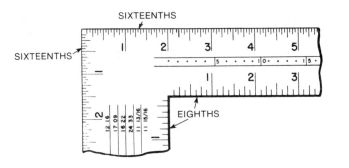

FIG. 1-3

B on the square is a right angle, the triangle is considered a right triangle. Therefore the steel square is based on the principles of a right triangle.

Again, the steel square **(Figure 1-2)** consists of a wide and long member called the body (or blade) and a narrower and shorter member called the tongue. The face of the square is the side you see when the square forms a reversed number seven (⌐); the manufacturer's name is usually stamped on the face. The back of the square is the side you see when the square forms a seven (⌐). The body is usually 24 inches long and 2 inches wide, and the tongue varies from 14 inches to 18 inches long and is $1\frac{1}{2}$ inches wide, as measured from the heel, the outer corner where the body and the tongue meet. Of course, one of the easiest ways to distinguish the body and tongue is to associate the square with the human figure; the body is longer than the tongue.

The outer and inner edges of the tongue and the body, on both face and back, are graduated in inches. The first thing you must remember is the manner in which the inch is subdivided in the scales on the back of the square. In the scales on the face, the inch is usually subdivided in the units of carpenter's measure of eighths or sixteenths of inches **(Figure 1-3)**. On the back of the square, however, the outer edge of the body and outer edge of the tongue are often graduated in inches and twelfths of inches; the inner edge of the tongue is graduated in inches and tenths of inches; and the inner edge of the body on most squares is graduated in inches and sixteenths of inches.

Common uses of the twelfths and tenths scales on the back of the framing square will be described a bit later.

SOLVING BASIC PROBLEMS USING THE STEEL SQUARE

The steel square is often used to find the length of the hypotenuse (longest side) of a right triangle when the lengths of the other two sides are known. For example, this is the basic problem involved in determining the length of a roof rafter, a brace, or any other member which forms the hypotenuse of an actual or an imaginary right triangle, as shown earlier in **Figure 1-1**.

Figure 1-4 shows how to use the steel square to determine the length of the hypotenuse of a right triangle with other sides each 12 inches long. Plane a true, straight edge on a board, and set the square on the board so as to bring the 12-inch mark on the tongue and the 12-inch mark on the body even with the edge of the board. Draw the pencil marks shown in the second view. The distance between these marks, as measured along the edge of the board, is the

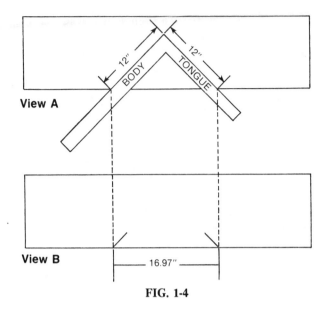

View A

View B |—— 16.97" ——|

FIG. 1-4

length of the hypotenuse of a right triangle with other sides each 12 inches long. You will find that the distance, which is called the *bridge measure,* measures just a shade under 17 inches. To be exact, it is 16.97 inches, as shown in the drawing, but for practical purposes 16.97 inches may be rounded off to 17 inches.

Unit and Total Run and Rise

In **Figure 1-4** the length of the hypotenuse could be determined with a single set (called a cut) of the steel square, because the dimensions of the triangle in question lie within the dimensions of the square. Now suppose that you are trying to find the length of the hypotenuse of a right triangle with the two known sides, each 48 inches long. Let us assume that the unknown length is the brace shown in **Figure 1-5.** The total run of this brace is 48 inches, and the total rise is also 48 inches.

To figure the length of the brace, you first reduce the triangle in question to a similar triangle which is within the dimensions of the framing square. The length of the vertical side of this triangle is called the *unit of rise,* and the length of the horizontal side is called the *unit of run.* In carpentry, unit of run is always taken as 12 inches, and measured on the tongue of the framing square. Now, if the total run is 48 inches, the total rise 48 inches, and the unit of run 12 inches, what is the unit of rise? Well, since the sides of similar triangles are

4

proportional, the unit of rise must be the value of x in the proportional expression $48 : 48 :: 12 : x$ or $^{48}/_{48} = {}^{12}/_x$. In this case, then, the unit of rise is obviously 12 inches.

Many calculations with the steel square involve such proportional expressions, or ratios. The example here is so simple the value of x is obvious, but in case you've forgotten how to deal with ratios, here is how it's done.

The proportion $48 : 48 :: 12 : x$ is equivalent to the equation

$$\frac{48}{48} = \frac{12}{x}$$

First multiply both sides of the equation by x:

$$\frac{48x}{48} = \frac{12x}{x}$$

In this case simplifying is easy:

$$\frac{48x}{48} = \frac{12x}{x} \; ; x = 12$$

To get the length of the brace, set the steel square to the unit of run (12 inches) on the tongue and to the unit of rise (also 12 inches) on the body as shown in **Figure 1-5** and then "step off" this cut as many times as the unit of run (12 inches) can be divided into the total run (48 inches). In this case that is $48 \div 12$ equals 4 times, as shown in the drawing.

In the above example the total run and total rise were the same, from which it followed that the unit of run and unit of rise were also the same. Suppose now that you want to know the length of a brace with a total run of 60 inches and a total rise of 72 inches. Since the unit of run is 12 inches, the unit of rise must be the value of x in the proportional equation $60 : 72 :: 12 : x$.

$$\frac{60}{72} = \frac{12}{x} \; ; \frac{60x}{72} = \frac{12x}{x} = 12$$

$$60x = 12 \times 72 = 864$$

$$x = 864 \div 60 = 14.4$$

Thus the unit of rise is 14.4 inches. For all building applications this is near enough to $14\frac{3}{8}$ inches to serve any practical purpose.

To lay out the full length of the brace, you set the square to the unit of rise ($14\frac{3}{8}$ inches) and the unit of run (12 inches), as shown in **Figure 1-6,** and then "step off" this cut as many times as the unit of run goes into the total run (in this case $60 \div 12$ or $^{60}/_{12}$, or 5 times). This will always work out to be a whole number of times (3, 4, 5, etc.) with no remainder.

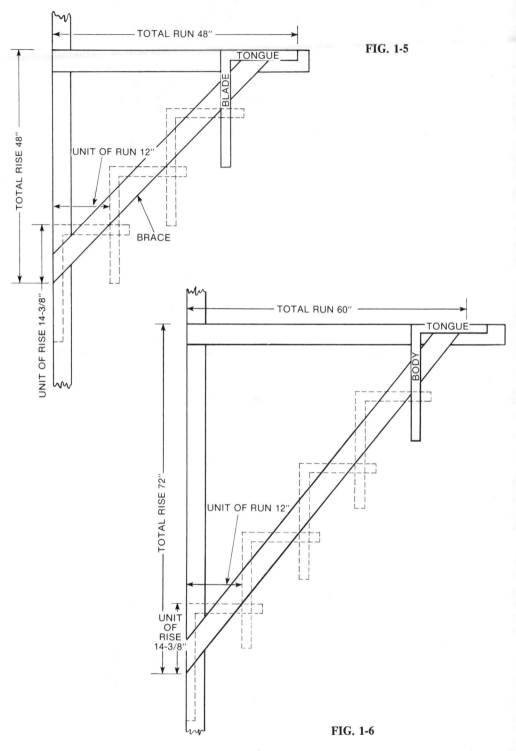

TOTAL RUN 48″

TONGUE

FIG. 1-5

BLADE

TOTAL RISE 48″

UNIT OF RUN 12″

BRACE

UNIT OF RISE 14-3/8″

TOTAL RUN 60″

TONGUE

BODY

TOTAL RISE 72″

UNIT OF RUN 12″

UNIT OF RISE 14-3/8″

FIG. 1-6

Line Length

If you do not go through the procedure of "stepping off," you can figure the total length of the member in question by first determining the bridge measure. The line length is the length of the hypotenuse of a right triangle with the other sides equal to the unit of run and the unit of rise. Take the situation shown in **Figure 1-6,** for example. The unit of run here is 12 inches, and the unit of rise is 14⅜ inches. Set the square to this cut as shown in **Figure 1-7,** and mark the edges of the board as shown. If you measure the distance between the marks, you will find that it is 18¾ inches.

To get the total length of the member, simply multiply the bridge measure by the number of times that the unit of run goes into the total run. Since that is 5 in this case, the total length of the member is 18¾ × 5, or 93¾ inches. Actually, the length of the hypotenuse of a right triangle with the other sides 60 and 72 inches long is between 93.72 and 93.73 inches, but 93¾ inches is close enough for any practical purpose. (If you were to use math rather than the steel square here, the formula would be hypotenuse² = sides a² + b².)

Once you have determined the total length of the member, all you need to do is measure it off and make the end cuts. To make these cuts at the proper angles, simply set the square to the unit of run on the tongue and unit of rise on the body and draw a line for the cut along the body (lower end cut) or the tongue (upper end cut).

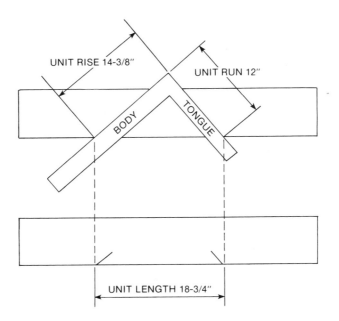

FIG. 1-7

Using the Twelfths Scale

The graduations in inches and twelfths of inches on the back of the square, along the outer edges, make up the twelfths scale. The chief purpose of the twelfths scale is to provide various shortcuts in problem-solving with the square. Since the scale is graduated in inches and twelfths of inches, dimensions in feet and inches can be reduced to one-twelfth of size by simply allowing each graduation on the twelfths scale to represent 1 inch. For example, $2\%_{12}$ ($2\frac{1}{2}$) inches on the twelfths scale may be taken to represent 2 feet 6 inches (2 $\frac{1}{2}$ feet).

Here are a few examples to show you how the twelfths scale is used. Suppose you want to know the total length of a rafter with a total run of 10 feet and a total rise of 6 feet 5 inches. Set the square on a board with the twelfths scale on the body at 10 inches and the twelfths scale on the tongue at $6\frac{5}{12}$ inches, and make the usual marks. If you measure the distance between the marks, you will find it to be $11\frac{11}{12}$ inches. The total length of the rafter, then, is 11 feet 11 inches.

Suppose now that you know the unit of run, unit of rise, and total run of

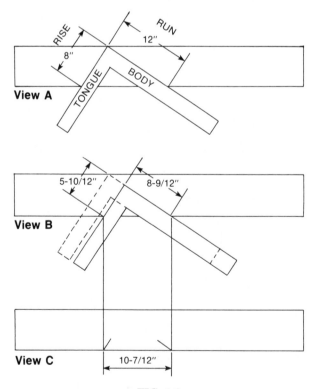

FIG. 1-8

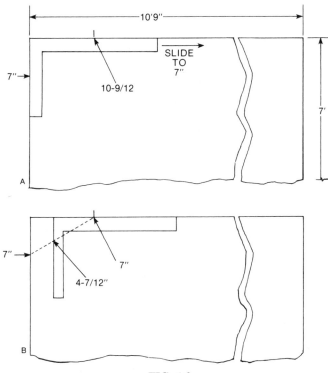

FIG. 1-9

a rafter and you want to find the total rise and the total length. Let us say that unit of run and unit of rise are 12 inches and 8 inches, respectively, and that total run is 8 feet 9 inches. Set the square to the unit rise on the tongue and unit run on the body, as shown in the first view of **Figure 1-8.** Then, as in the second view, slide the square down and rightward until the $8\frac{9}{12}$ inches mark on the body (representing the total run of 8 feet 9 inches) comes even with the edge of the board. The figure of $5\frac{10}{12}$ inches which is now indicated on the tongue is one-twelfth of the total rise. The total rise is therefore 5 feet 10 inches. The distance between pencil marks ($10\frac{7}{12}$ inches) drawn along the tongue and the body is one twelfth of the total length. The total length is therefore 10 feet 7 inches.

The twelfths scale may also be used to determine dimensions by inspection for proportional reductions or enlargements. For example, suppose that you have a panel 10 feet 9 inches long by 7 feet wide, and you want to cut a panel 7 feet long with the same proportions. Set the square as shown in **Figure 1-9,** but with the body at $10\frac{9}{12}$ inches and the tongue at 7 inches. Then slide the body to 7 inches and read the figure indicated on the tongue, which will be $4\frac{7}{12}$ inches. The smaller panel, then, should be 4 feet 7 inches wide.

9

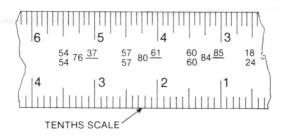

FIG. 1-10

Using the Tenths Scale

The scale along the inner edge of the back of the tongue, which is graduated in inches and tenths of inches, is called the tenths scale **(Figure 1-10)**. This scale can be used along with the scale along the inner edge of the back of the body (which is graduated in inches and sixteenths of inches) to determine various proportions. Suppose that a crew can excavate 44 linear feet of trench in 8 hours. How many feet can they excavate in $3\frac{1}{4}$ hours? As shown in **Figure 1-11,** set the square on a board with the tenths scale on the tongue at the 4.4-inch mark and the scale on the inner edge of the body at the 8-inch mark. Then slide the body down to the $3\frac{1}{4}$-inch mark. The reading on the tenths scale will now be 1.8 inches. Since you took 4.4 to represent 44, 1.8 must represent 18, and the crew should therefore be able to excavate about 18 linear feet in $3\frac{1}{4}$ hours.

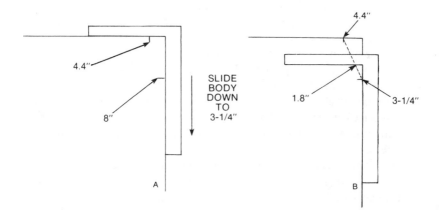

FIG. 1-11

10

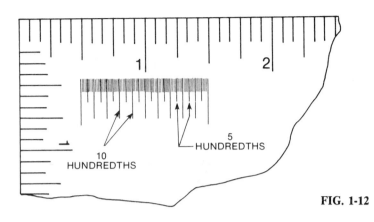

FIG. 1-12

Using the Hundredths Scale

The hundredths scale is on the back of the tongue, in the corner of the square, near the brace table **(Figure 1-12)**. This scale is called the hundredths scale because one inch is divided into one hundred parts. The longer lines indicate 10 hundredths, while the next shorter lines indicate 5 hundredths, etc. By using dividers, you can easily obtain a fraction of an inch.

The inch is graduated in twelfths, and located below the hundredths scale; therefore, the conversion from hundredths to twelfths can be made at a glance without the use of dividers simply by eyeballing or lining up the two scales with your finger. This can be a great help when determining rafter lengths, using the figures of the rafter tables where hundredths are given.

Using the Octagon Scale

The octagon scale (sometimes called the 8-square scale) is located in the middle of the face of the tongue. The octagon scale is used to lay out an octagon (8-sided figure) in a square of given even-inch dimensions. The procedure is as follows.

Suppose you want to cut an 8-inch octagonal piece for a stair newel. First square the stock to 8 by 8 inches, square and smooth the end section, and draw crossed center lines on the end section as shown in **Figure 1-13.** Then set a pair of dividers to the distance from the first to the eighth dot on the octagon scale, and lay off this distance on either side of the center lines on the 4 slanting sides of the octagon.

When you use the octagon scale, set one leg of the dividers on the first dot and the other leg on the dot whose number corresponds to the width in inches of the square from which you are cutting the piece. This distance amounts to one-half the length of a side of the octagon.

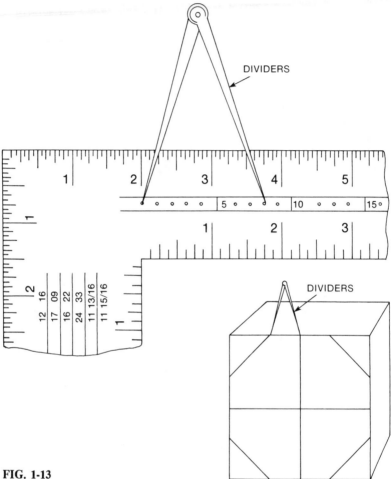

FIG. 1-13

Using the Framing Tables on the Steel Square

There are three tables on the steel square, as follows: (1) the *unit length rafter table,* located on the face of the body; (2) the *brace table,* located on the back of the tongue; and (3) the *Essex board measure table,* located on the back of the body. Before you can use the unit length rafter table, you must be familiar with the different types of rafters and with the methods of framing them. Consequently, the use of the unit length rafter table and methods of laying out stairs with a steel square are discussed in Chapter 2. Yet, as to the uses of the two other tables—which are covered in this chapter—let us see how the steel square can help lay out cuts for the sawhorse shown in **Figure 1-14.**

The first layout problem is laying off the end cuts for the legs. If you think about it for a moment while examining the drawing, you will see that there is a right triangle involved here, with a total rise of 24 inches (vertical height of the sawhorse) and a total run of 4 inches (amount that the top of the leg is set away from the end of the top). To get the correct end cuts, then, you set the square to 4 inches on the tongue and 24 inches on the body, as shown in **Figure 1-15.** How long a piece will you need to start with? Well, if you measure the hypotenuse, as shown in the figure, you will find that the length of the finished piece will be a little more than 24$\frac{1}{4}$ inches. Since you'll be cutting ends, start with a board at least 26 inches long.

Mark the left-hand end cut along the tongue, and mark the point where the end of the body contacts the edge of the piece at the opposite end. Then turn the square over and end for end and mark the opposite end cut as shown. Saw off the ends and use the piece as a pattern for laying out the end cuts on the other three legs.

Next problem is to lay off the side cuts on the legs, as shown in **Figure 1-16.** Once again there is a right triangle involved, and once again the total rise is 24 inches (vertical height of the sawhorse). The total run is a little harder to figure. If you study **Figure 1-16** closely, you will see that the total run must amount to one-half the span of the legs (15 inches divided by 2, or 7$\frac{1}{2}$ inches) minus the horizontal thickness of the leg (you can call that $\frac{3}{4}$ inch), and minus one-half the *actual* width of the top (a 2-by-4 is usually only about 3$\frac{1}{2}$ inches wide, and half of that is 1$\frac{3}{4}$ inches), less the width of the top of the gain, which is shown in the drawing to be $\frac{3}{8}$ inch.

If you cannot quite see why this is so, study the simplified drawing in **Figure 1-16** where the basic triangle you are solving is shaded in. If you work out the arithmetic in the previous paragraph, you will find that the total run is 5$\frac{1}{4}$ inches. To lay off the side cuts for the legs, then, you set the square to 5$\frac{1}{4}$ inches on the tongue and 24 inches on the body, on the edge of a leg, as shown in **Figure 1-17.** Mark a line along the tongue, carry the line across the face of the piece, parallel to the line of the end cut, and bevel the end down to the line with a plane.

To lay out the gain on the side of the top, first set the top of a leg in place against the side, 4 inches from the end, as shown in **Figure 1-18, view A,** and draw the lines for the sides of the gain. Then mark a line $\frac{3}{8}$ inch from the edge of the top, and chisel out the gain as indicated in **view B.**

The set of the square for the edges of the 1 $\times$ 10 end pieces is the same as the set for the side cuts of the legs; study **Figure 1-16** to see why. Select a piece that is *actually* 10 inches wide, and lay off the line for one of the edges as shown in **Figure 1-19.** Since you will not be able to end-for-end the square to get the line for the other edge in this case, the best way to lay that line off is to set a T-bevel to the other line, measure off the prescribed 9$\frac{1}{2}$ inches along the bottom, reverse the T-bevel, set it to the mark, and lay off the line as indicated in **Figure 1-19.**

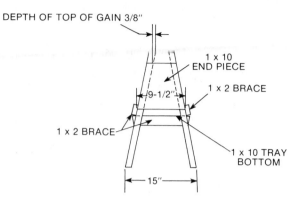

DEPTH OF TOP OF GAIN 3/8"

1 x 10 END PIECE

1 x 2 BRACE

9-1/2"

1 x 2 BRACE

1 x 10 TRAY BOTTOM

15"

FIG. 1-14

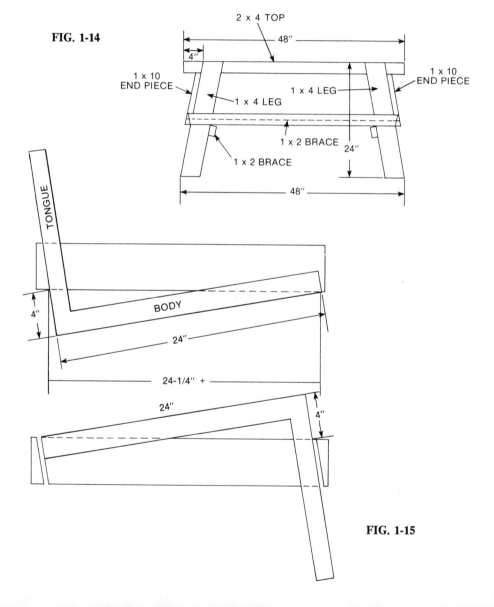

2 x 4 TOP

48"

4"

1 x 10 END PIECE

1 x 4 LEG

1 x 4 LEG

1 x 10 END PIECE

1 x 2 BRACE

1 x 2 BRACE

24"

48"

TONGUE

BODY

4"

24"

24-1/4" +

24"

4"

FIG. 1-15

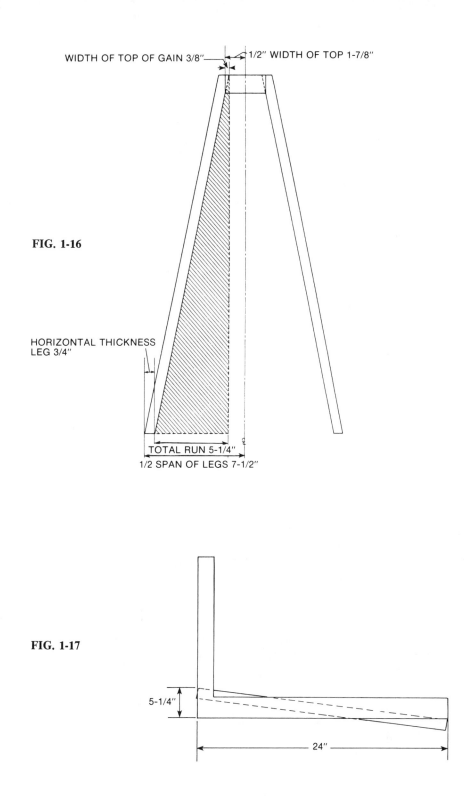

WIDTH OF TOP OF GAIN 3/8″

1/2″ WIDTH OF TOP 1-7/8″

FIG. 1-16

HORIZONTAL THICKNESS
LEG 3/4″

TOTAL RUN 5-1/4″

1/2 SPAN OF LEGS 7-1/2″

FIG. 1-17

5-1/4″

24″

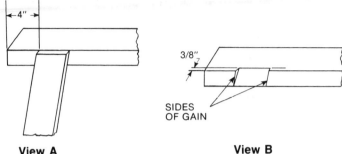

View A   View B

FIG. 1-18

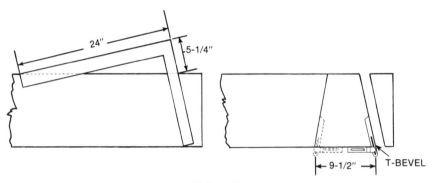

FIG. 1-19

The set of the framing square for the edge cuts for the 1 × 10 tray is also 5½ inches on the tongue and 24 inches on the body, but the best way to fit the tray is to set it in place and mark it after the top, legs, and end pieces have been assembled. Use 8-penny coated nails to nail the pieces together.

Using the Brace Table

The brace table sets forth a series of equal runs and rises for every 3-unit interval from $^{24}/_{24}$ to $^{60}/_{60}$, together with the brace length, or length of the hypotenuse, for each given run and rise. The table can be used to determine by inspection the length of the hypotenuse of a right triangle with equal shorter sides of any length given in the table.

For example, in the segment of the brace table shown in **Figure 1-20,** you can see that the length of the hypotenuse of a right triangle with two sides 24 units long is 33.94 units; with two sides 27 units long, 38.18 units; with two sides 30 units long, 42.43 units, and so on.

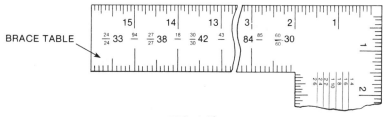

FIG. 1-20

By applying simple arithmetic, you can use the brace table to determine the hypotenuse of a right triangle with equal sides of practically any even-unit length. Suppose, for example, that you want to know the length of the hypotenuse of a right triangle with two sides each 8 inches long. The brace table shows that a right triangle with two sides 24 inches long has a hypotenuse 33.94 inches long. Since 8 amounts to 24 ÷ 3, a right triangle with two shorter sides 8 inches long must have a hypotenuse 33.94 ÷ 3, or 11.31 inches long.

Suppose you want to find the length of the hypotenuse of a right triangle with two sides 40 inches each. The sides of similar triangles are proportional, and any right triangle with two equal sides is similar to any other right triangle with two equal sides. The brace table shows you that a right triangle with the two shorter sides being 30 inches each in length has a hypotenuse 42.43 inches long. The length of the hypotenuse of a right triangle with the two shorter sides being 40 inches each in length must be the value of x in the proportional equation

$$30 : 42.43 :: 40 : x$$

which is

$$30x = 40 \times 42.43$$

$$30x = 1697.20$$

$$x = 56.57 \text{ inches}$$

Notice that the last item in the brace table (the one farthest to the right in **Figure 1-20**) gives you the hypotenuse of a right triangle with the other sides 18 and 24 units long respectively. The proportions 18 : 24 : 30 are those of the most common type of unequal-sided right triangle, which is called the 3-4-5 right triangle. Any triangle with sides in the proportions of 3 : 4 : 5 must be a right triangle.

Using the Essex Board Measure Table

Board measure is a method of measuring lumber in which the basic unit is an abstract volume 1 foot long by 1 foot wide by 1 inch thick. This abstract volume or unit is called a board foot. Sizes of softwood or building construction lumber are standardized for convenience in ordering and handling. Building materials sizes run 8, 10, 12, 14, 16, 18, and 20 feet in length, 2, 4, 6, 8, 10, and 12 inches in width, and 1, 2, and 4 inches in thickness. The actual width and thickness of dressed lumber are considerably less than the standard, or quoted, width and thickness. For instance, a green, rough-sawed board 1 inch thick is actually $\frac{3}{4}$ inch thick if dry and dressed; it is $\frac{25}{32}$ inch thick if it is green (above 19 percent moisture content) and dressed. If the lumber is grade-marked, the stamp will indicate whether the piece was green or dry when it was dressed to size. For the relative difference between standard, or nominal, sizes and actual sizes of softwoods or construction lumber, see **Table 1-1.** Hardwoods, which have no standard lengths or widths, usually run $\frac{1}{4}$, $\frac{1}{2}$, 1, $1\frac{1}{4}$, $1\frac{1}{2}$, 2, $2\frac{1}{2}$, 3, and 4 inches in thickness.

The Essex board measure table is a quick aid in computing board feet. In using the board measure table, all computations are made on the basis of 1-inch thickness. A segment of the table is shown in **Figure 1-21.** The inch graduations above the table (1, 2, 3, 4, and so on) represent the width in inches of the piece to be measured. The figures shown under the 12-inch graduation (8,

TABLE 1-1:
NOMINAL AND ACTUAL SIZES OF SOFTWOOD LUMBER

	Thicknesses			Face widths	
	Actual (inches)			Actual (inches)	
Nominal size*	Minimum dry**	Dressed green	Nominal size	Minimum dry**	Dressed green
1	$\frac{3}{4}$	$\frac{25}{32}$	2	$1\frac{1}{2}$	$1\frac{9}{16}$
$1\frac{1}{4}$	1	$1\frac{1}{32}$	3	$2\frac{1}{2}$	$2\frac{9}{16}$
$1\frac{1}{2}$	$1\frac{1}{4}$	$1\frac{9}{32}$	4	$3\frac{1}{2}$	$3\frac{9}{16}$
2	$1\frac{1}{2}$	$1\frac{9}{16}$	5	$4\frac{1}{2}$	$4\frac{5}{8}$
$2\frac{1}{2}$	2	$2\frac{1}{16}$	6	$5\frac{1}{2}$	$5\frac{5}{8}$
3	$2\frac{1}{2}$	$2\frac{9}{16}$	7	$6\frac{1}{2}$	$6\frac{5}{8}$
$3\frac{1}{2}$	3	$3\frac{1}{16}$	8	$7\frac{1}{4}$	$7\frac{1}{2}$
4	$3\frac{1}{2}$	$3\frac{9}{16}$	9	$8\frac{1}{4}$	$8\frac{1}{2}$
			10	$9\frac{1}{4}$	$9\frac{1}{2}$
			11	$10\frac{1}{4}$	$10\frac{1}{2}$
			12	$11\frac{1}{4}$	$11\frac{1}{2}$

*Thickness sometimes is expressed as $\frac{4}{4}$, $\frac{5}{4}$, etc.
**Dry lumber has been seasoned to a moisture content of 19 percent or less.

FIG. 1-21

9, 10, 11, 13, 14, and 15, arranged in column) represent lengths in feet. Thus they can be used only for lumber 8 to 11 feet, and 13 to 15 feet, inclusive. The figure 12 itself, at the 12-inch graduation, represents a 12-foot length. The column headed by the figure 12 is the starting point for all calculations.

To use the table, run down the figure-12 column to the figure that represents the length of the piece of lumber in feet. Then run horizontally to the figure which is directly below the inch mark that corresponds to the width of the stock in inches. The figure you find will be the number of board feet and twelfths of board feet in a 1-inch-thick piece of the given length and width.

For example, suppose you want to figure the board measure of a piece 10 feet long by 9 inches wide by 1 inch thick. Run down the column headed by the 12-inch graduation to 10, and then run horizontally to the left to the figure directly below the 9-inch graduation. You will find the figure to be 7.6 or 7 $^{6}/_{10}$ board feet.

What do you do if the piece is more than 1 inch thick? All you have to do is multiply the result obtained for a 1-inch piece by the actual thickness of the piece in inches. For example, if the board described in the preceding paragraph were 5 inches thick instead of 1 inch thick, you would follow the procedure described and then multiply the result by 5.

As noted earlier, the board measure scale can be read only for pieces from 8 to 15 feet in length, inclusive. If your piece is longer than 15 feet, you can proceed in one of two ways. If the length of the piece is evenly divisible by one of the tabulated lengths in the table, you can read for that length and multiply the result by the number of times that the tabulated length goes into the length of the piece. For example, suppose you want to find the number of board feet in a piece 33 feet long by 7 inches wide by 1 inch thick. Since 33 is evenly divisible by 11, run down the 12-inch column to 11 and then move left to the 7-inch column. The figure given there (which is $6^{5}/_{12}$ board feet) is one-third of the number of board feet in a piece 33 feet long by 7 inches wide by 1 inch thick. The total number of board feet, then, is $6^{5}/_{12} \times 3$, or $19^{3}/_{12}$ board feet.

If the length of the piece is not evenly divisible by one of the tabulated lengths, you can divide it into two tabulated lengths, read the table for these two, and add the results together. For example, suppose you want to find the board measure of a piece 25 feet long by 10 inches wide by 1 inch thick. This length can be divided into 10 feet and 15 feet. The table shows that the 10-foot length contains $8\frac{4}{12}$ board feet and the 15-foot length $12\frac{6}{12}$ board feet. The total length, then, contains $8\frac{4}{12}$ plus $12\frac{6}{12}$, or $20\frac{10}{12}$ board feet.

Other Methods of Calculating Board Feet

In addition to the steel square method just described, there are two other methods of determining lumber board feet: the arithmetic method and the tabular method.

Arithmetic Method

To determine the number of board feet in one or more pieces of lumber, the following formula is used:

$$\text{pieces} \times \text{thickness in inches} \times \text{width in inches} \times \frac{\text{length in feet}}{12}$$

EXAMPLE 1: Find the number of board feet in a piece of lumber 2 inches thick, 10 inches wide, and 6 feet long **(Figure 1-22).**

$$\frac{1 \times 2 \times 10 \times 6}{12} = 10 \text{ board feet}$$

EXAMPLE 2: Find the number of board feet in 10 pieces of lumber 2 inches thick, 10 inches wide, and 6 feet long.

$$\frac{10 \times 2 \times 10 \times 6}{12} = 100 \text{ board feet}$$

If all three dimensions are in inches, divide by 144 instead of 12.

EXAMPLE 3: Find the number of board feet in a piece of lumber 2 inches thick, 10 inches wide, and 18 inches long.

$$\frac{1 \times 2 \times 10 \times 18}{144} = 2\frac{1}{2} \text{ board feet}$$

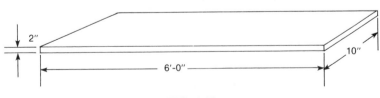

FIG. 1-22

20

Rapid Estimation of Board Feet by Use of
Tables

Estimation of board feet can be done rapidly by use of **Table 1-2** or **Table 1-3.**

Lumber is usually quoted at a specified price per M (1,000) board feet. To find the cost of a given quantity of lumber, you first must find the total number of board feet. Then divide this by 1,000 and multiply by the cost per 1,000 board feet. For example, if you need 20 pieces of yellow pine lumber measuring 2 inches by 8 inches by 20 feet and it was quoted at $220 per M board feet, the cost would be:

$$\frac{2 \times 8 \times 20 \times 20}{12} = 533.3 \text{ feet board measure (fbm)}$$

$$\frac{533.3}{1000} \times 220 = \$117.33$$

If the price is quoted in terms of one board foot, multiply the number of board feet required by the cost per board foot. The cost of a 2-by-4 12 feet long, if the quote is 22 cents per board foot, would be:

$$\frac{2 \times 4 \times 12}{12} = 8 \text{ board feet}$$

$$8 \text{ board feet} \times .22 = \$1.76$$

Lumber less than 4 inches wide and of any thickness is frequently sold by the linear foot. Thus an order for a board 10 feet long would specify 10 linear feet. Plywood, hardboard, insulating board, particleboard, and other similar panel materials are sold by the square foot. For example, if a 4×8 panel of $\frac{1}{4}$-inch plywood sells for 36 cents a square foot, the cost would be:

$$4 \times 8 = 32 \text{ square feet}$$

$$32 \times 0.36 = \$11.52 \text{ per plywood panel}$$

TABLE 1-2:
RAPID CALCULATION OF BOARD MEASURE

Width	Thickness	Board feet
3"	1" or less	¼ of the length
4"	1" or less	⅓ of the length
6"	1" or less	½ of the length
9"	1" or less	¾ of the length
12"	1" or less	Same as the length
15"	1" or less	1 ¼ of the length

TABLE 1-3:
BOARD FEET

Nominal size (in.)	Actual length in feet								
	8	10	12	14	16	18	20	22	24
1 × 2		1 2/3	2	2 1/3	2 2/3	3	3 1/3	3 2/3	4
1 × 3		2 1/2	3	3 1/2	4	4 1/2	5	5 1/2	6
1 × 4	2 3/4	3 1/3	4	4 2/3	5 1/3	6	6 2/3	7 1/3	8
1 × 5		4 1/6	5	5 5/6	6 2/3	7 1/2	8 1/3	9 1/6	10
1 × 6	4	5	6	7	8	9	10	11	12
1 × 7		5 5/6	7	8 1/6	9 1/3	10 1/2	11 2/3	12 5/6	14
1 × 8	5 1/3	6 2/3	8	9 1/3	10 2/3	12	13 1/3	14 2/3	16
1 × 10	6 2/3	8 1/3	10	11 2/3	13 1/3	15	16 2/3	18 1/3	20
1 × 12	8	10	12	14	16	18	20	22	24
1 1/4 × 4		4 1/6	5	5 5/6	6 2/3	7 1/2	8 1/3	9 1/6	10
1 1/4 × 6		6 1/4	7 1/2	8 3/4	10	11 1/4	12 1/2	13 3/4	15
1 1/4 × 8		8 1/3	10	11 2/3	13 1/3	15	16 2/3	18 1/3	20

		10 5/12	12 1/2	14 7/12	16 2/3	18 3/4	20 5/6	22 11/12	25
1 1/4 × 10		10 5/12	12 1/2	14 7/12	16 2/3	18 3/4	20 5/6	22 11/12	25
1 1/4 × 12		12 1/2	15	17 1/2	20	22 1/2	25	27 1/2	30
1 1/2 × 4	4	5	6	7	8	9	10	11	12
1 1/2 × 6	6	7 1/2	9	10 1/2	12	13 1/2	15	16 1/2	18
1 1/2 × 8	8	10	12	14	16	18	20	22	24
1 1/2 × 10	10	12 1/2	15	17 1/2	20	22 1/2	25	27 1/2	30
1 1/2 × 12	12	15	18	21	24	27	30	33	36
2 × 4	5 1/3	6 2/3	8	9 1/3	10 2/3	12	13 1/3	14 2/3	16
2 × 6	8	10	12	14	16	18	20	22	24
2 × 8	10 2/3	13 1/3	16	18 2/3	21 1/3	24	26 2/3	29 1/3	32
2 × 10	13 1/3	16 2/3	20	23 1/3	26 2/3	30	33 1/3	36 2/3	40
2 × 12	16	20	24	28	32	36	40	44	48
3 × 6	12	15	18	21	24	27	30	33	36
3 × 8	16	20	24	28	32	36	40	44	48
3 × 10	20	25	30	35	40	45	50	55	60
3 × 12	24	30	36	42	48	54	60	66	72
4 × 4	10 2/3	13 1/3	16	18 2/3	21 1/3	24	26 2/3	29 1/3	32
4 × 6	16	20	24	28	32	36	40	44	48
4 × 8	21 1/3	26 2/3	32	37 1/3	42 2/3	48	53 1/3	58 2/3	64
4 × 10	26 2/3	33 1/3	40	46 2/3	53 1/3	60	66 2/3	73 1/3	80
4 × 12	32	40	48	56	64	72	80	88	96

ESTIMATING MATERIAL AND COSTS

One of the best uses for math is to estimate the materials needed and cost of a given project. In this and subsequent chapters, we tell how to estimate specific jobs. However, bear in mind that material and equipment prices as well as labor rates will vary considerably over time and from one section of the country to another. For this reason when preparing an estimate of any job be sure to ascertain the local prices for materials, equipment, and labor. The purpose of this text is to teach math methods and procedures, not instill exact prices in anyone's mind.

Once the project plan has been established, a bill of materials can be drawn up. This bill of materials is a list of all materials needed to complete a project. It includes item number, name, description, unit of measure, quantity, and—where called for—the stock size and number.

Bills of materials are generally based on takeoffs and estimates of the materials needed. In professional circles, they are usually made up by the draftsman when the original drawings are prepared; the builder simply uses them when ordering materials. However, the do-it-yourselfer must make up his own bills of materials. Fortunately, some of the better magazines and books catering to the do-it-yourselfer provide bills of materials for their projects, as shown in **Figure 1-23.**

If a prepared bill of materials is not available, the first step in undertaking such a bill is to prepare a *materials takeoff list.* This is an individual listing of all parts of the project, "taken off" the plans, usually by an actual tally and checkoff of the items shown, noted, or specified on the drawings and specifications. Both architectural and engineering plans provide the names and sizes of the various items to be listed.

Figure 1-24, views A and **B,** show the plan for the substructure of a 20-foot-wide building. **Table 1-4** is a materials takeoff list prepared for those plans. This list contains all parts of the building, starting with its bottom and working upward until all its parts are listed. See page 28.

Look at the first item on the materials takeoff list as an example. The item number is followed by the name of the item. Next is the total number of pieces needed to make up the item. In the example there are 15 posts in a 20-by-40-foot building. With 3 pieces needed for each footer, a total of 45 pieces are needed. The length in place is the actual length of the member after it has been cut and is ready to be nailed in place. The length in place of the footer is 1 foot 5 inches. The size refers to the quoted size of the lumber, such as 2-by-4 or 2-by-6. Since 2-by-6 stock is being used in the example, the dimension 2 × 6 is put into the size column. The commercial length refers to the standard lengths available from the lumberyard, such as 8, 10, and 12 feet.

It must be decided which length is the most economical to use in making the footers, which are built from 45 pieces of 2-by-6, each 1 foot 5 inches long.

24

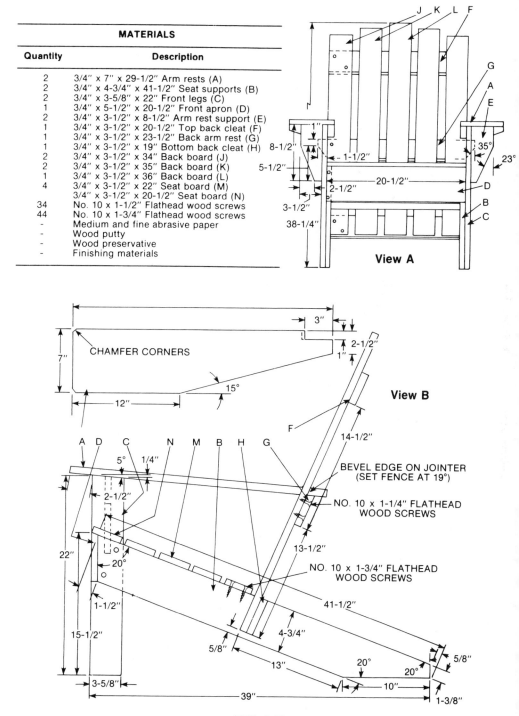

MATERIALS

Quantity	Description
2	3/4" x 7" x 29-1/2" Arm rests (A)
2	3/4" x 4-3/4" x 41-1/2" Seat supports (B)
2	3/4" x 3-5/8" x 22" Front legs (C)
1	3/4" x 5-1/2" x 20-1/2" Front apron (D)
2	3/4" x 3-1/2" x 8-1/2" Arm rest support (E)
1	3/4" x 3-1/2" x 20-1/2" Top back cleat (F)
1	3/4" x 3-1/2" x 23-1/2" Back arm rest (G)
1	3/4" x 3-1/2" x 19" Bottom back cleat (H)
2	3/4" x 3-1/2" x 34" Back board (J)
2	3/4" x 3-1/2" x 35" Back board (K)
1	3/4" x 3-1/2" x 36" Back board (L)
4	3/4" x 3-1/2" x 22" Seat board (M)
	3/4" x 3-1/2" x 20-1/2" Seat board (N)
34	No. 10 x 1-1/2" Flathead wood screws
44	No. 10 x 1-3/4" Flathead wood screws
-	Medium and fine abrasive paper
-	Wood putty
-	Wood preservative
-	Finishing materials

View A

CHAMFER CORNERS

View B

BEVEL EDGE ON JOINTER
(SET FENCE AT 19°)

NO. 10 x 1-1/4" FLATHEAD
WOOD SCREWS

NO. 10 x 1-3/4" FLATHEAD
WOOD SCREWS

FIG. 1-23

25

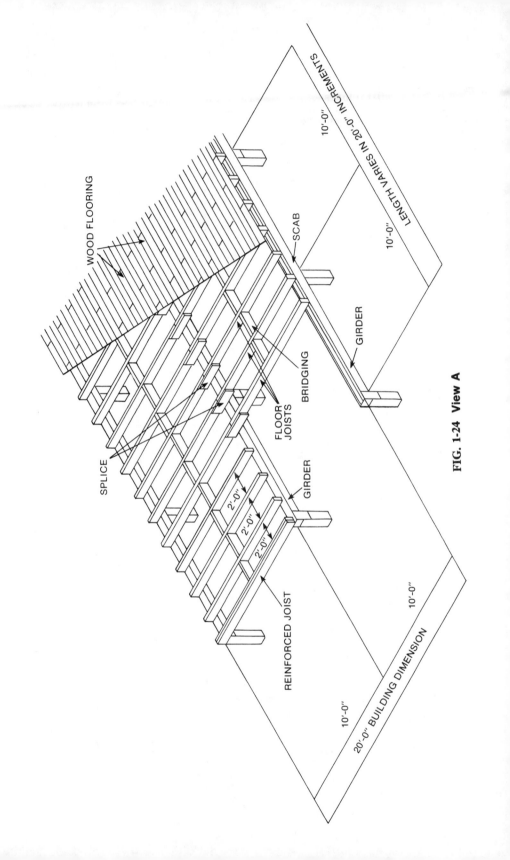

FIG. 1-24 View A

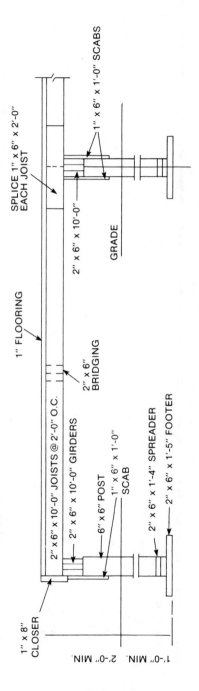

1" x 6" x 1'-0" SCABS

SPLICE 1" x 6" x 2'-0" EACH JOIST

2" x 6" x 10'-0"

GRADE

1" FLOORING

2" x 6" BRIDGING

2" x 6" x 10'-0" JOISTS @ 2'-0" O.C.

2" x 6" x 10'-0" GIRDERS

6" x 6" POST

1" x 6" x 1'-0" SCAB

2" x 6" x 1'-4" SPREADER

2" x 6" x 1'-5" FOOTER

1" x 8" CLOSER

1'-0" MIN.   2'-0" MIN.

FIG. 1-24   View B

TABLE 1-4:
MATERIALS TAKEOFF LIST FOR 20-FOOT BUILDING

Item name or use of piece	No. of pieces	Unit	Length in place	Size	Length	No. per length	Quantity
1. Footers	45	Pc	1'-5"	2×6	10'	7	7
2. Spreaders	30	Pc	1'-4"	2×6	8'	6	5
3. Foundation post	15	Pc	3'-0"	6×6	12'	4	4
4. Scabs	20	Pc	1'-0"	1×6	8'	8	3
5. Girders	36	Pc	10'-0"	2×6	10'	1	36
6. Joists	46	Pc	10'-0"	2×6	10'	1	46
7. Joist splices	21	Pc	2'-0"	1×6	8'	4	6
8. Block bridging	40	Pc	1'-10 ⅜"	2×6	8'	4	10
9. Closers	12	Pc	10'-0"	1×8	10'	1	12
10. Flooring	800	BF	RL	1×6	RL	—	—

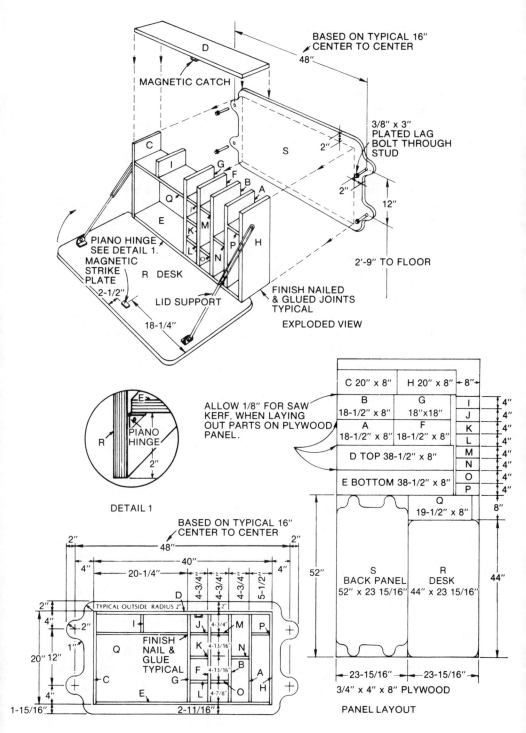

FIG. 1-24 (Cutting Diagram)

If the standard lengths of 8, 10, and 12 feet are changed to 96, 120, and 144 inches, the length in place can be divided into the commercial lengths in inches. This will give the number of pieces that can be obtained from each commercial length, plus the amount of waste per commercial length. For example, the length in place of the footers is 1 foot 5 inches, or 17 inches. Dividing 17 inches into 96 inches, the 8-foot commercial length, we find we can get 5 pieces with 11 inches waste. In a 10-foot piece, dividing 17 inches into 120 inches gives 7 pieces with 1 inch waste. When there is only 1 inch waste or no waste at all, that commercial length can be used without going further. Since 7 pieces 1 foot 5 inches long are obtained from each 10-foot length of stock and since 45 pieces are needed, 7 10-foot 2-by-6s are ordered to give the required 45 pieces 1 foot 5 inches long. This is actually enough for 49 pieces, so there will be some leftover 2-by-6, but it may be used elsewhere on the job. Frequently, especially in smaller jobs and when working on panel materials such as plywood, it is wise to make a cutting diagram such as shown on page 29.

The materials estimate list puts into a shorter form the information on the materials takeoff list, adds an allowance for waste and breakage, and makes an estimate of quantities of materials which are known to be necessary but which may not have been placed on the drawings, such as nails, cement, concrete-form lumber and tie wire, temporary bracing or scaffold lumber, and so on.

The first step in preparing the materials estimate list **(Table 1-5)** is to consolidate the information on the takeoff list. This means to group all pieces of the same size and length in a logical order. For example, start with the largest-size lumber that can be found on the materials takeoff list. Add together all the pieces of that same size and length that appear anywhere on the list. This gives the total number of pieces of that particular size and length that will be needed for the project. Continue in this way with the next smaller size of lumber, and work down to the smallest size and length of material.

To each total number of pieces of one length and size, the waste factor must be added. For flooring, sheathing, and other 1-inch material, add a waste allowance of 20 percent to the total number of pieces. For all other materials 2 inches and larger, add 10 percent to the total number. In the next column, estimate the amount of additional requirements for materials not shown on the plans. Add up the total quantity for each size and length of material, and then convert it to board feet, using one of the three methods given earlier in this chapter.

The sizes and pounds of nails needed should be added to the list. To estimate the number of pounds of each size of nail needed, the following formula should be used:

$$\text{number of pounds} = \frac{d}{4} \times \frac{\text{board measure (bm)}}{100}$$

30

TABLE 1-5:
MATERIALS ESTIMATE LIST

Item	Size & length	Unit	Takeoff quantity	Waste allowance	Additional requirements	Total quantity	Board measure (b.m.)
1	6 × 6 × 12	Pc	4	1	None	5	180
2	2 × 6 × 10	Pc	89	9	None	98	980
3	2 × 6 × 8	Pc	15	2	3 for temporary bracing	20	160
4	1 × 8 × 10	Pc	12	2	None	14	91
5	1 × 6 × 8	Pc	9	2	2 for batter boards	13	52
6	1 × 6 × RL	BF	800	160	None	960	960
7	16d	lb	—	—	36 nails, framing	36	—
8	8d	lb	—	—	23 nails, flooring	23	—

TABLE 1-6:
BILL OF MATERIALS

Item	Quantity	Unit	Size & length	b.m.	Description or where used
1.	5	Pc	6″ × 6″ × 12′	180	Posts
2.	98	Pc	2″ × 6″ × 10′	980	Footing, girder, joist
3.	20	Pc	2″ × 6″ × 8′	160	Spreader, bridging
4.	14	Pc	1″ × 8″ × 10′	94	Closers
5.	13	Pc	1″ × 6″ × 8′	52	Scabs, splices
6.	960	BF	1 × 6 × RL	960	Flooring
7.	36	lb	16d	—	Nails, framing
8.	23	lb	8d	—	Nails, area coverage

The actual bill of materials is the final step. Although the materials estimate list contains all of the information on all the materials needed for the project, it contains much information of little interest to lumberyard personnel, so it is simplified into the bill of materials format shown in **Table 1-6.** This is the document submitted to the building supply dealer to order the materials. The rest of the building would be analyzed in the same way.

Another order form for lumber and similar materials is shown in **Figure 1-25.** A form for other supplies, fasteners, and hardware is illustrated in **Figure 1-26.** The advantage of these bills of materials is that they leave space for the

LUMBER AND MATERIAL ORDER LIST

No. of Pieces or Units	Dimensions			Type of Material	Number of: Bd. Ft. Line. Ft. or Sq. Ft.	Cost per: Bd. Ft. Line. Ft. or Sq. Ft.	Total Cost
	T	W	L				

FIG. 1-25

SUPPLIES, FASTENERS AND HARDWARE ORDER LIST

Quantity	Item	Size	Unit Cost	Total Cost

FIG. 1-26

total cost of an item. Speaking of costs, be sure to include *everything* that goes into or is necessary to complete the project. Small items such as glue, sandpaper, and staples should be added to the cost.

MATH AND BACKYARD ENGINEERING*

Any job takes planning, and math will be a great aid in planning almost any project. Do you want to lay out a tennis or badminton court in your backyard? Extend your patio? Provide better drainage? Put down a concrete apron for a storage building or a place to park your new car?

Where do you start? Of course, you can go out and simply "eyeball" the situation and start digging. Some people do just that. But you may end up doing twice the work and only getting a less than satisfactory result.

You will save yourself a lot of sweat if you do some planning on paper beforehand, and then take the time to stake out the job. The odds are high that any backyard project will require some digging, and it may require considerable grading or even importation of fill. All of this comes under the heading of "backyard engineering."

That word "engineering" may sound highflown, but all engineering means is planning precisely and then proceeding in the most efficient and economical way. We have engineers build bridges because they are experts in providing safe structures at the least cost. The fact is, just about anybody could build a bridge—if he had unlimited money and materials. You will need to know the way the land lies for any kind of walk, paving, foundation, flight of steps, or

*This section originally appeared in slightly altered form in the May–June 1979 issue of *Homeowners How to* under the title "Fun and Good Sense of Backyard Engineering." It is here reprinted with permission of its author, John Robinson, and *Homeowners How to*.

other structure. You will want the finished project to be set level, except that paved areas should have a little pitch to drain correctly ($\frac{1}{4}$ inch to the foot should be adequate). Check, too, to see that fill around the house and lawns tilts at least that much to carry water away. And when you are ready to start, you will also want to know how much dirt you will have to move, how deep to dig, how much space to allow.

You will not need a lot of engineering equipment and math to get these answers, but when you have questions, it is a good idea to first put things on paper. You won't need an expensive drafting set. You can get by with a compass, a ruler, and a big sheet of paper. Wrapping paper will be fine—in fact, more durable. But use a large piece, 30 inches or 3 feet square at least —otherwise you will be forced to work on such small scale that your plan will be virtually useless to you.

An easy way to get started is to find the plot plan from your property deed, if it has one, or get a copy from the county recorder. It will give you the dimensions of your lot, which you can convert to a more workable scale— somewhere between $\frac{1}{2}$ and $\frac{1}{16}$ inch to the foot, depending upon the size of your property and paper.

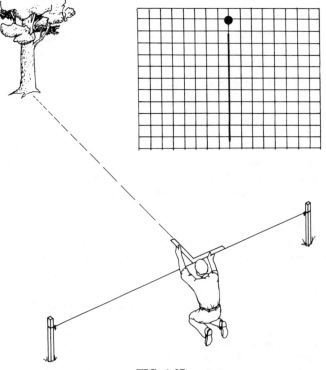

FIG. 1-27

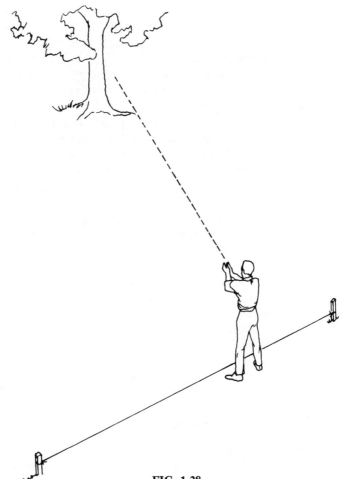

FIG. 1-28

If it is a contractor's or architect's plot plan, perhaps it will show the location of your house. But if you live in a tract, look carefully at indicated positions of houses—many tract builders only roughly locate the houses—and, if in doubt, check by actual measurement.

Your plan should show your house's entries, windows, and overhang, if appreciable. Also locate trees, patios, paths, driveway, any outbuildings, and other permanent features. If you have a septic tank, mark it and its drain field. Show young trees with their estimated overhang and height at least 10 years hence, and the expected height of all large shrubs, as well as the height of any existing or proposed buildings and fences, so shadows at various seasons can be taken into account. It is important when drawing a plan of your property on which you want to locate an object exactly, such as a tree, that a base line

35

be established with two known points. Then establish an imaginary line at right angles, marking where it intersects the base **(Figure 1-27)**. To sight at a right angle from the base line, stand so legs or toes are touching the line, hold your hands out, palms together, fingertips touching evenly. Sight between your thumbs **(Figure 1-28)**. Or align the body of a steel square on the base line and sight along the tongue. Also, it is a good idea to include at least one compass reference point on your drawing plan.

It will be worth your while to spend a few patient hours of work on this drawing, for you will be mapping your property for future reference, as well as for any immediate uses. The map will save you a lot of thoughtless mistakes, such as running a path through an area you might better save for vegetables, or locating a sports court where missed balls would be a nuisance to people on the patio.

The future value of the plan is that you will be able to tell in a minute or two where space might be available for horseshoes or tetherball or for a concealed service yard, instead of going out and looking things over and measuring off the distance. You will probably save yourself money and worry if you lightly pencil in the location of all your proposed projects. You may decide there is no room for some of them.

If your land has much gradient, mark a few plus and minus ground elevations relative to some arbitrary point—perhaps your patio. This will also help in a number of ways in future planning, not the least of which is knowing how your land naturally drains. If you feel like getting fancy, you can mark elevations for the whole area and connect equal points with contour lines.

Measuring Elevations

The elevation of any object is its vertical distance above or below an established height on the earth's surface. This established height is referred to as a *reference plane,* or simple *reference.* The most commonly used reference plane for elevations is *mean* (or average) *sea level,* which has been assigned an assumed elevation of 000.0 feet. However, the reference plane for a construction project is usually the height of some permanent or semipermanent object in the immediate vicinity, such as the rim of a manhole cover, a road, or the finish floor of an existing structure. This object may be given its relative sea-level elevation, if that happens to be known. Or it may be given a convenient, arbitrarily assumed elevation, usually a round number such as 100.0 feet. An object of this type, with a given, known, or assumed elevation which is to be used in determining the elevations of other points, is called a *bench mark.*

The most common procedure for determining elevations in the field, or for locating points at specified elevations, is known as *differential leveling.* This procedure, as its name implies, is nothing more than finding the vertical

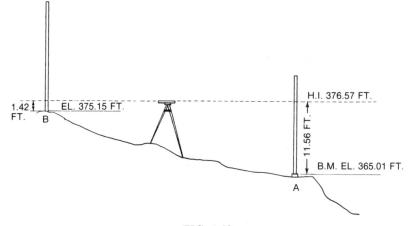

FIG. 1-29

difference between the known or assumed elevation of a bench mark and the elevation of the point in question. Once the difference is measured, it can be added to, or subtracted from (depending on the circumstances), the bench mark elevation to determine the elevation of the new point.

Figure 1-29 illustrates the principle of differential leveling. The instrument shown in the center represents an engineer's level. This optical instrument (described in more detail below) provides a perfectly level line of sight through a telescope which can be trained in any direction. Point A in the figure is a bench mark (B.M.) having a known elevation of 365.01 feet. (It could be a concrete monument, a wooden stake, a sidewalk curb, or any other of a variety of objects.) Point B is a ground surface point whose elevation is desired.

The first step in finding the elevation of point B is to determine the elevation of the line-of-sight of the instrument. This is known as the height of instrument (H.I.). To determine H.I. you would take a backsight on a level rod held vertically on the bench mark (B.M.), as shown, by a rodman. A backsight (B.S.) is always taken after a new instrument setup by sighting back to a known elevation in order to get the new H.I. A leveling rod is a rod which is graduated upward from 0 at its base with appropriate subdivisions of feet.

In **Figure 1-29,** the backsight reading is 11.56 feet. It follows, then, that the elevation of the line-of-sight (that is, the H.I.) must be 11.56 feet greater than the bench mark elevation, point A. Therefore, the H.I. is 365.01 feet + 11.56 feet, or 376.57 feet, as indicated.

Next, you would aim the instrument ahead on another rod (or more usually on the same rod carried ahead) held vertically on B. This is known as taking a foresight. After reading a foresight (F.S.) of 1.42 feet on the rod, it follows that the elevation at point B must be 1.42 feet lower than the H.I. Therefore, the elevation of point B is 376.57 feet − 1.42 feet, or 375.15 feet.

SPIRIT LEVEL

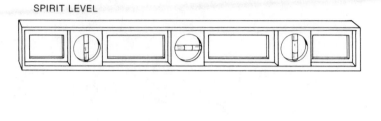

LINE LEVEL

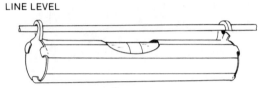

FIG. 1-30

There are various other measuring levels in addition to the engineer's type that may be used. Actually, the fact is that after thousands of years of experience in building, man still largely depends on the phenomenon of water finding its own level. That is the principle behind what is called a *spirit level* (**Figure 1-30**), and for short distances, a reliable spirit level taped onto a straight 2-by-4 does quite a good job. By carefully staking as you go, you can use a homemade rig over distances of 50 feet or so and get fairly accurate results—but eventually, cumulative error can throw you off.

More convenient to use over longer distances is the *line level* (**Figure 1-30**). This is just the working part of a spirit level, with a hook arrangement, so you

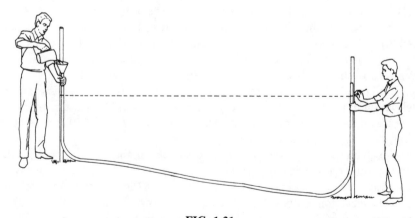

FIG. 1-31

38

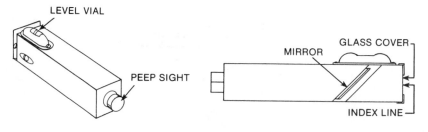

LEVEL VIAL

MIRROR

GLASS COVER

PEEP SIGHT

INDEX LINE

HAND-SIGHTING LEVEL

FIG. 1-32

can hang it on a chalk line or other sturdy cord. Since any dip in the line obviously will throw measurements off, the cord must be taut for satisfactory results.

One of the best and most accurate devices for finding points at equal elevation over short distances is an ordinary garden hose. It also operates on the principle that water will find its own level **(Figure 1-31).** For accurate results, fasten one end of the hose (open end up, of course) to a stake at a mark indicating a known elevation. For convenience, it is better to work with "plus 3 feet" grades or thereabouts, so you do not have to spend time on your knees peering into the hose. Pour water into one end, until it runs out the other. Once the hose is full, all you have to do to find equal levels is adjust the movable end until the hose stays full of water, with none running out either end. This system works better if you have a helper. There is an inexpensive kit you can buy for a few dollars at hardware and building-supply stores that facilitates the operation; it includes short, transparent extensions you screw into the hose.

When looking at levels and such in retail hardware outlets, you may see a *hand-sighting level* **(Figure 1-32),** which you use as its name implies. It is a small, telescopelike instrument with a visible bubble inside the viewer and a crosshair. By sighting through it and lining up the bubble across the hair line, you get a fairly good reading of whether a point is higher or lower than your eye level. After some practice, if you brace yourself against a building or post or use a rest, you can probably achieve accuracy within an inch or so over a 25-foot distance; but over longer distances, error builds up. For practical application you will need a helper holding a marker stake like a surveyor's rod.

The *surveyor's transit,* often referred to as a type of engineer's level **(Figure 1-33),** has a number of advantages. It uses line-of-sight to extend its imaginary plane outward from its own elevation, which eliminates the need for extending a board or cord or hose or whatever from point to point. Because it is telescopic (usually 20-power), you can see distant points much more clearly, which greatly extends its range as well as its accuracy. Comparable levels can be

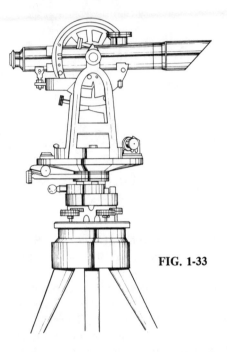

FIG. 1-33

checked by the fine vertical and horizontal crosshairs etched on the glass. And the instrument rotates on its base so you can compare points in various directions (and at various distances too, of course).

The surveyor's transit used by engineers and surveyors pivots up and down vertically as well, with a scale for measuring these angles, from which, by trigonometry, the relative elevation of high and low spots can be computed if distance is known.

In general, run-of-the-mill constructions, a less-expensive version—the *builder's* or *Dumpy level*—is commonly used. It will rotate but does not elevate or depress. A builder's level would be helpful if you were putting in a foundation for a guesthouse, for instance. You should be able to rent one inexpensively, complete with tripod and rod.

If you rent one, get full instructions, since the various makes vary a bit in design and operation. Be sure to ask for a tripod with adjustable legs.

Whichever of the various devices you use to find elevations, they are not much value to you unless you record the results. The time-honored method is with stakes. You will also measure the distances involved, which will probably include the intervals between the stakes.

In the old days, surveyors developed the chain as a flexible measuring tool, relatively unaffected by temperature changes and moisture. Many old land deeds are still so recorded, but today we have excellent metal tapes that are much more suitable for use in the backyard. If you do not have a 50- or 100-foot tape, borrow or rent one.

Unless distances are very short, trying to measure on the ground with an ordinary 6-foot tape will get you into all kinds of trouble. You will waste a lot of time, have difficulty with laps, and find it awkward to follow a straight line unless you stretch a cord.

Where absolute accuracy is not vital, learn to pace—another old-fashioned but handy method—since you always have your legs with you. To find your natural pace, measure the distance you cover with ten natural steps. Get an average. Do this two or three times as a check. Unless you are a giant, you will find your natural step is somewhat less than 3 feet.

You can accept whatever distance you cover in your average pace—probably around 30 to 33 inches—and use that figure in your estimates. Or do as the old-timers did—practice stretching your stride a bit so that when you need to you can make measured steps of 36 inches consistently.

For recording the levels and distances information you obtain, you should have handy a supply of stakes to use as you go. They are simple to make from conventional 1-inch scrap board. Cut the boards into pieces all the same length —18 or 24 inches or whatever size you want to use—and split them about 2 inches wide, putting a point on one end. You will probably want a few 3 to 4 feet long, too.

When staking out your property, use a finishing nail and a $1/4$-inch hole to keep the 2-by-4 from falling off one stake while you position the next (**Figure 1-34, view A**). The stakes should show plus or minus zero (level) for earth moving (**Figure 1-34, view B**). To "eyeball" an acceptable curve, use a flexible hose, then stake it (**Figure 1-34, view C**). For short distances, a "surveyor's rod" can be made with dressmaker's tape stapled to a 1-by-2 (**Figure 1-34, view D**). Setting stakes alone? A roofing nail will hold your tape ring when you measure (**Figure 1-34, view E**). Some pros mark their stakes a short distance from the top with a reference line. But unless your ground is very hard so that the tops get battered pounding them into the ground, you will find it simpler to use the tops of the stakes for reference. (Of course, they will ordinarily be a foot above base level, or whatever consistent distance you decide on.)

Plotting Areas

When the location and alignment of a building have been determined, a rectangle corresponding to the exterior dimensions of the structure is staked out. If the building is other than rectangular, a rectangle corresponding to the major outline of the irregular structure is staked out and the irregularities are plotted and proved by smaller rectangles inside or outside the basic form.

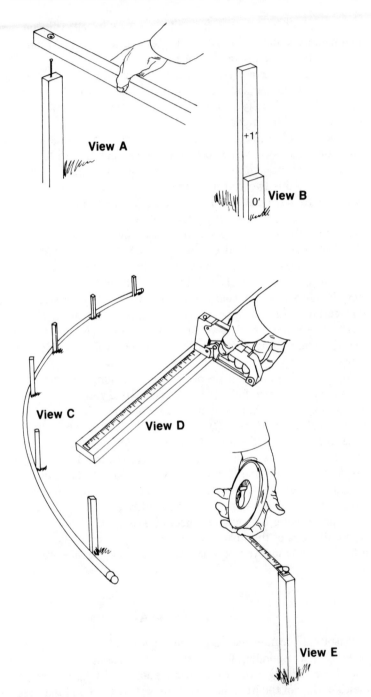

FIG. 1-34

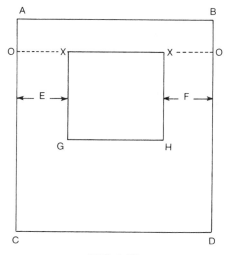

FIG. 1-35

Without Transit

If the construction is parallel to an identifiable guideline, staking-out may be accomplished without a builder's transit. If there is a clearly defined line or reference points available that are parallel to the construction (AB in **Figure 1-35**) and the maximum outer perimeter of the building area (AC, CD, DB) is known, proceed in the following manner:

1. Measure away from the front line (AB) along the side lines (AC and BD) the distances (AO and BO) desired to the dimension of the project that is to run parallel to the front line.
2. Stretch a line tightly from point O to O. This line will mark out what will be frontage of the project.
3. Measure in from lines AC and BD along line OO, one-half the difference between the length of OO and the desired length of the project. The points (X and X) will constitute the front corners of the project.
4. The two distances OX and XO establish the distance E and F. Extending lines from the two front corners, X and X, parallel to AC and BD at the distances established as E and F for the required depth of the project provides the side lines of the project, XG and XH.
5. Joining the extreme ends of side lines XG and XH will provide the rear line of the project.
6. After the four corners (X, X, G, and H) have been located, drive stakes at each corner. Batter boards may be erected at these points either after all the stakes have been set or while they are being set. Dimensions are determined accurately during each step.

7. If the building is not rectangular, several lines such as OO may be run and appropriate adjacent rectangles constructed from these lines in the same fashion as indicated above.

With Transit or Leveling Instrument

When laying out a simple rectangle with an engineer's transit or leveling instrument, proceed as follows:

1. Working from an established line **AB** (**Figure 1-36**) such as a road or street line, property line, or an established reference line, select a point to represent the lateral limit for a front corner of the project.
2. Set up the engineer's transit at point C and establish point D, a front corner of the project.
3. Set up the engineer's transit at a point E a greater distance along line AB from point C than the intended length of the project. Set a stake at F, the same distance from AB as D. CD and EF are equal.
4. Establish the front line of the project by marking off the length of the project DG along the established line DF. The two front corners of the project will be located at D and G.
5. With engineer's transit at point C, shoot E and then swing the transit 90 degrees and sight along this position to establish H, the rear corner of the project.
6. With the engineer's transit set up at G, sight D and swing the transit sight tube 90 degrees and shoot I, the other rear corner of the project.
7. To prove the work, set up the transit at I and take a sighting on H. If IH is equal to DG, the work is correct. If it is not, the work must be repeated until correct.

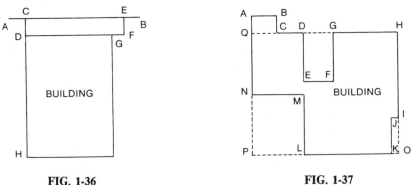

FIG. 1-36   **FIG. 1-37**

Typical rectangular space allowances for some backyard games are as follows:

BADMINTON. Official court is 38 × 17 (unless otherwise specified, all dimensions are in feet), plus necessary end and side space. Usually, however, home badminton is played wherever there's room.

CROQUET. Official layout requires 85 × 37½, but most home layouts are fitted into available space.

DECK TENNIS. Official court is 40 × 18 for doubles, 40 × 12 for singles, plus necessary surround.

HORSESHOES. Stakes should be 40 feet apart for men, 30 for women. If boxes are provided around stakes, they should be 6 feet square.

SAND BOX. Minimum is about 6 × 10, but be prepared for scatterings of sand several feet around.

SHUFFLEBOARD. Allow minimum of 10 × 57, with centered 6 × 52 board.

TABLE TENNIS. Official table size is 5 × 9, but minimum 11 × 20 space should be provided for recovering balls, wide shots, etc.

TENNIS. Few backyards can accommodate. A full, official doubles court is 78 × 36, but fence should enclose total space of at least 120 × 60.

VOLLEYBALL. With an official 30 × 60 court, plus side clearance and 15 to 20 feet at either end for long shots, this is also a space eater. But volleyball, like croquet and badminton, is often played anywhere there is room to put up the equipment.

When laying out an irregularly shaped project where the outline of the building is not a rectangle, the procedure in establishing each point is the same as described above, but more points have to be located and the final proving of the work is more likely to reveal a small error. It is usually advisable with an irregularly shaped building to lay out first a large rectangle which will comprise the entire building or the greater part of it. This is shown in **Figure 1-37,** as the rectangle HOPQ. Once this rectangle is established accurately, the remaining portion of the layout will consist of small rectangles, each of which can be laid out and proved separately. The other rectangles are illustrated in **Figure 1-37** as LMNP, ABCQ, DEFG, and IJKO.

45

Grading and Excavating

The term "grade" is used in several different senses in construction. In one sense it refers to the steepness of a slope; a slope, for example, which rises 3 vertical feet for every 100 horizontal feet has a grade of 3 percent. Although the term "grade" is commonly used in this sense, the more accurate term for indicating steepness of slope is "gradient."

In another sense the term "grade" simply means surface. On a wall section, for example, the line which indicates the ground surface level outside the building is marked "grade" or "grade line."

The elevation of a surface at a particular point is a grade elevation. A grade elevation may refer to an existing, natural earth surface or a hub or stake used as a reference point, in which case the elevation is that of existing grade or existing ground; or it may refer to a proposed surface to be created artificially, in which case the elevation is that of prescribed grade, plan grade, or finished grade.

Grading and excavating can either be done by hand or with earth-moving equipment. The latter is usually rented or hired with an operator on an hourly or job basis. However, if you properly lay out the grading and/or excavating job for the earth-moving operator you can save yourself some money.

Grading

Grade elevations of the surface area around a structure are indicated on the plot plan. Because a natural earth surface is usually irregular in contour, existing grade elevations on such a surface are indicated by contour lines on the plot plan—that is, by lines which indicate points of equal elevation on the ground. Contour lines which indicate existing grade are usually made dotted; however, contour lines on maps are sometimes represented by solid lines. If the prescribed surface to be created artificially will be other than a horizontal-plane surface, prescribed grade elevations will be indicated on the plot plan by solid contour lines.

On a level, horizontal-plane surface the elevation is, of course, the same at all points. Grade elevation of a surface of this kind cannot be indicated by contour lines, because each contour line indicates an elevation different from that of each other contour line. Therefore, a prescribed level surface area, to be artificially created, is indicated on the plot plan by outlining the area and inscribing inside the outline the prescribed elevation, such as "First Floor Elevation 127.50."

The first earth-moving operations for a structure usually involve the artificial creation of a level area of prescribed elevation at and adjacent to the place where the structure will be built. This grading operation involves removing earth from areas which are higher than the prescribed elevation (cut) and filling earth into areas which are below the prescribed elevation (fill).

46

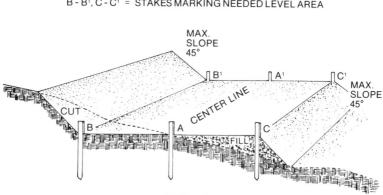

A - A¹ = CENTER LINE GUIDE STAKES
B - B¹, C - C¹ = STAKES MARKING NEEDED LEVEL AREA

FIG. 1-38

To guide the earth-moving operator, a sufficient number of grade stakes must be driven in the area **(Figure 1-38),** the number depending mainly on how irregular the existing surface is. Grade stakes usually consist of about 18-inch lengths (depending on the amount to be cut) of 1-by-2s, marked on the side with lumber crayon (called *keel* by the surveyors), as follows:

A stake driven at a point where the elevation of existing grade coincides with that of prescribed grade is simply marked GRD (for grade), indicating to the earth-moving crew that the surface here is already at prescribed grade elevation, and no cut or fill is required. A stake driven at a point where the elevation of existing grade is greater than that of prescribed grade is marked with a C (for cut), followed by a figure indicating the difference between the two elevations. In writing this figure it is customary to indicate decimal subdivisions of feet not by a decimal point, but by raising and underlining the figures which indicate the decimal subdivisions. For example, for a cut of 6.25 feet you should write C 6 $\underline{25}$, not C 6.25. A stake driven at a point where the elevation of prescribed grade is greater than that of existing grade is marked with an F (for fill), followed by the figures which indicate the difference between the two elevations.

The elevation of prescribed grade at each point where a grade stake will be driven is obtained from the plot plan. Once this is known, all you need to know to mark the stake correctly is the elevation of existing ground at that point. You may have studied in the preceding section how to determine this by differential leveling, using the engineer's or builder's level. However, in setting grade stakes you often set a number of stakes from a single instrument setup, and in such a case you speed up the calculations by applying values called *grade rod* and *ground rod* **(Figure 1-39).**

47

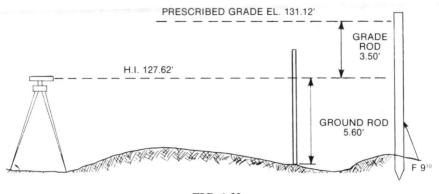

FIG. 1-39

Grade rod is simply the difference between the prescribed elevation of the point and the H.I. (height of instrument). If you are setting stakes for a level surface area, grade rod will be the same for all points sighted from the same instrument setup point. This will not be the case, of course, if the prescribed elevation differs at different points. Once you have determined the H.I., grade rod can be calculated in advance for all points to be sighted from a particular instrument setup point.

Ground rod is simply the rod reading you get on a particular point. When you know the grade rod (difference between plan elevation and H.I.) and the ground rod (read on a rod set on the point) for a particular point, you can rapidly determine the mark for the stake by applying rules as follows:

The H.I. is always greater than the elevation of existing ground at the point (if it were less, you could not read a rod on the point from that particular setup), but it may be greater or less than the elevation of prescribed grade. If the H.I. is less than the elevation of prescribed grade (see **Figure 1-39**), the difference in elevation between existing ground and prescribed grade (which is what you need to know to mark the stake) amounts to the sum of grade rod and ground rod and the stake should be marked with an F (meaning Fill).

For example, in **Figure 1-39,** the elevation of the prescribed grade is 131.12 feet, and the H.I. is 127.62 feet. The grade rod is therefore 131.12 − 127.62, or 3.50 feet, and the H.I. is less than prescribed grade elevation. You can see that fill must be put in at this point, and that the vertical depth of fill equals the sum of ground rod plus grade rod, or 5.60 feet + 3.50 feet, or 9.10 feet. Therefore you would mark the stake F 9$^{\underline{10}}$.

If the H.I. is greater than the prescribed grade elevation (see **figures 1-40** and **1-41**), the difference in elevation between existing and prescribed grade (that is, the vertical depth of cut or fill) equals the difference between ground

48

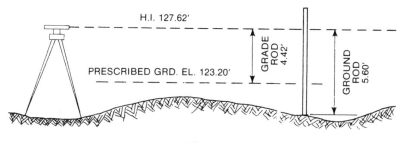

FIG. 1-40

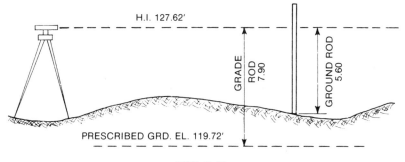

FIG. 1-41

rod and grade rod. Whether the stake should be marked with a C (Cut) or an F (Fill) depends upon which of the two, ground rod or grade rod, is the larger.

If ground rod is larger than grade rod **(Figure 1-40),** the stake takes an F (Fill). Here the difference between existing ground elevation and prescribed grade elevation equals the difference between ground rod and grade rod, or 5.60 − 4.42, or 1.18. Ground rod is larger than grade rod, and you can see that fill is required to bring the ground line up to grade. Therefore, you would mark this stake F 1^{18}.

If grade rod is larger than ground rod **(Figure 1-41),** the stake takes a C (Cut). Here again the difference between existing ground elevation and prescribed grade elevation equals the difference between grade rod and ground rod, or 7.90 − 5.60, or 2.30 feet. Grade rod is larger than ground rod, and you can see that cut is required to bring the ground line down to grade. Therefore you would mark this stake C 2^{30}.

To estimate the number of cubic yards to be cut from a square parcel of land

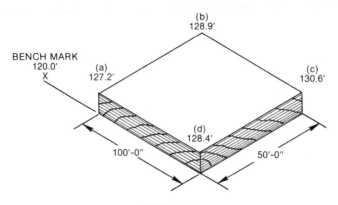

FIG. 1-42

50 × 100 feet with the station elevations as shown above the grade bench mark in **Figure 1-42,** proceed as follows:

STEP 1: From the given bench mark, estimate the average height of the stations:

$$\frac{7.2 + 8.9 + 10.6 + 8.4}{4} = \frac{35.1}{4} = 8.78 \text{ average height}$$

STEP 2: Multiply the area of the land in square feet by the average height of the stations in feet:

$$50 \times 100 \times 8.78 = 43{,}900 \text{ cubic feet}$$

STEP 3: Since grading and excavating is reckoned in cubic yards (3 × 3 × 3 = 27 cu. ft.), the estimate would be:

$$\frac{43900}{27} = 1{,}625.9 \text{ cubic yards}$$

Excavating

Grading means, generally speaking, the earth moving required to create a surface of desired grade elevation at and adjacent to the place where a structure will be erected. After this has been accomplished, further earth moving is usually required. If the structure is to have a below-grade basement, for example, earth lying within the building lines must be removed down to the prescribed finished basement floor elevation, less the thickness of the basement floor paving and subfill. After this earth is removed, further earth may have to be removed for footings under the foundation walls. This type of earth removal is generally known as *excavating*.

Before foundation and footing excavation for a building can begin, the building lines must be laid out to determine the boundaries of the excavations. Points shown on the plot plan (such as building corners) are located at the site from a system of horizontal control points. This system consists of a framework of stakes, driven pipes, or other markers, located at points of known horizontal location. A point in the structure (such as a building corner) is located on the ground by reference to one or more nearby horizontal control points.

We cannot describe here all the methods of locating a point with reference to a horizontal control point of known horizontal location. We will just use as an example the situation shown in **Figure 1-43, view A,** which shows two horizontal control points, consisting of monuments A and B. The term "monument," incidentally, doesn't necessarily mean an elaborate stone or concrete structure. In layout, it simply means any relatively permanently located object, either artificial (such as a driven length of pipe) or natural (such as a tree), of known horizontal location.

In **Figure 1-43, view A,** the line from A to B is a control base line, from which the building corners of the structure can be located. Corner E, for example, can be located by first measuring 15 feet along the base line from A to locate point C; then measuring off 35 feet on CE, laid off at 90 degrees to (that is, perpendicular to) AB. By extending CE another 20 feet, you can locate building corner F. Corners G and H can be similarly located along a perpendicular run from point D, which is itself located by measuring 55 feet along the base line from A.

The easiest and most accurate way to locate points on a line or to turn a given angle (such as 90 degrees) from one line to another is by the use of a transit. However, if you do not have a transit, you can locate the corner points by tape measurements by applying the Pythagorean theorem (in a right triangle, the square of the hypotenuse is equal to the sum of the squares of the other two sides, **Figure 1-43, view B**).

$$c^2 = a^2 + b^2$$

First stretch a cord from monument A to monument B, and locate points C and D by tape measurements from A. If you examine **Figure 1-43, view A,** you will observe that straight lines connecting points C, D, and E would form a right triangle with one side 40 feet long and the adjacent side 35 feet long. Using the Pythagorean theorem, the length of the hypotenuse of this triangle (the line ED) would equal the square root of $35^2 + 40^2$, which is about 53.1 feet. (For a refresher on calculating square roots, refer to Chapter 11.) Because the figure EGCD is a rectangle, the diagonals both ways (ED and CG) are equal; therefore, the line from C to G should also measure 53.1 feet. If you have one man hold the 53.1 foot mark of a tape on D, have another hold the

51

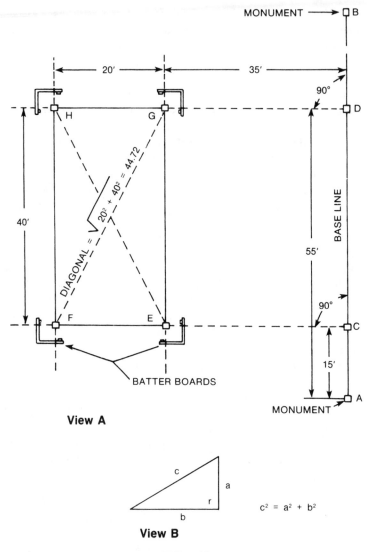

View A

View B

$$c^2 = a^2 + b^2$$

FIG. 1-43

35-foot mark of another tape on C, and have a third man walk away with the joined 0-feet ends, when the tapes come taut the joined 0-feet ends will lie on the correct location for point E. The same procedure, but this time with the 53.1-foot length of tape running from C and the 35-foot length running from D, will locate corner point G. Corner points F and H can be located by the same process, or by extending CE and DG 20 feet.

52

If you would rather avoid the square-root calculations, you can use a simpler method based on the fact that any triangle with sides in the proportions of 3 : 4 : 5 is a right triangle. In locating point E (for example), you know that this point lies 35 feet from C on a line perpendicular to the base line. You also know that a triangle with sides 30 and 40 feet long and a hypotenuse 50 feet long is a right triangle.

To get the 40-foot side, you would measure off 40 feet from C along the base line; in **Figure 1-43, view A,** the segment from C to D happens to measure 40 feet. If you run a 50-foot tape from D and a 30-foot tape from C, the joined ends will lie on a line perpendicular from the base line, 30 feet from C. Drive a stake at this point, and extend the line to E (5 more feet) by stretching a cord from C across the mark on the hub.

You always check a rectangular layout for its accuracy by "checking the diagonals." The diagonals of any rectangle are equal. You check the layout by tape-measuring the diagonals—if the layout is correct, the two diagonals will measure the same (or very nearly the same) distance. If you wish to know the value of the correct diagonal length, you may compute it by using the Pythagorean theorem ($c^2 = a^2 + b^2$); as you can see, the diagonals for the structure shown in **Figure 1-43, view A,** should measure 44.72 feet.

Batter Boards

Stakes driven at the exact locations of building corners will, of course, be disturbed as soon as excavation for foundations begins. To preserve the corner locations, and also to provide a reference for measurement down to prescribed elevations, batter boards are erected outside the foundation, as shown in **Figure 1-44.**

Each pair of boards is nailed to three 2-by-4 corner stakes, as shown. The stakes are driven far enough outside the building lines so that they will not be disturbed during excavating. The top edges of the boards are located at a specific elevation, usually some convenient number of whole feet above a significant prescribed elevation (such as that of the top of the foundation). Cords located directly over the lines through corner hubs (placed by holding plumb bobs on the hubs) are nailed to the batter boards. **Figure 1-44** shows how a corner point can be located in the excavation by dropping a plumb bob from the point of intersection between two cords.

In addition to their function in horizontal control, batter boards are also used for vertical control. As stated, the top edge of a batter board is placed at a specific elevation. Elevations of features in the structure (such as foundations, floors, and the like) may be located by measuring downward or upward from the cords stretched between the batter boards.

You should always make sure that you have complete information as to exactly what lines and elevations are indicated by the batter boards.

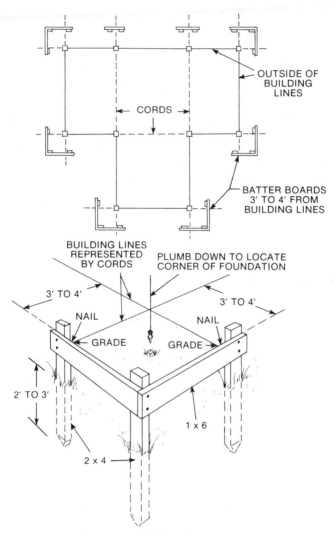

FIG. 1-44

Dimensions of Excavations

With regard to the dimensions of basement excavations, for example, the specifications usually say something like the following: "Excavations shall extend 2 feet 0 inch outside of all basement wall planes and to 9 inches below finished planes of basement floor levels."

The 2-foot space is the customary allowance made for working space outside the foundation walls. It is a space which must be backfilled after the founda-

54

tions have set. The 9 inches below finished planes of basement floor levels is the usual allowance for basement floor thickness (usually about 3 inches plus about 6 inches of cinder or other fill placed under the basement floor).

The actual depth below grade to which a basement excavation must be carried is determined by study of a wall section like the one shown in **Figure 1-45.** This section shows that the depth of the basement excavation below grade would in this case equal 8 feet 0 inch (vertical distance between basement and first floor finished planes), minus 1 foot 6 inches (vertical distance between surface grade and first floor finished plane), plus 9 inches (3 inches pavement floor plus 6 inches cinder fill), or 7 feet 3 inches.

The top of the footing comes level with the top of the 6 inches of cinder fill.

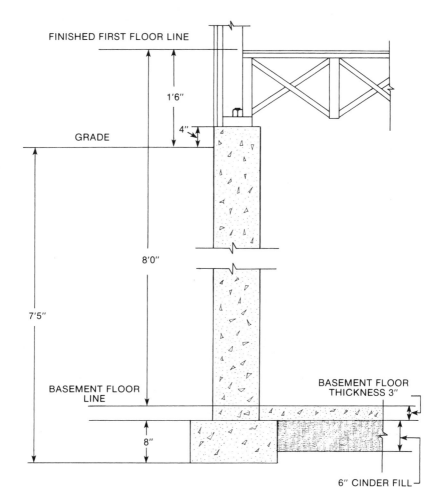

FIG. 1-45

However, the footing is 2 inches deeper than the fill. Therefore, the footing excavation would be carried 2 inches lower than the basement floor elevation, or to 7 feet 5 inches below grade.

If a specific elevation was prescribed for the finished first floor line, then the basement floor and footing excavation would be carried down to the corresponding elevation, without reference to surface grade. Suppose, for example, that the specified elevation for the finished first floor line was 163.50 feet. Obviously, the elevation to which the basement floor elevation would be carried would be 163.50 − (8 feet + 3 inches + 6 inches), or 163.50 − (8 feet + 0.25 feet + 0.50 feet), or 154.75 feet. The elevation to which the footing excavation would be carried would be 2 inches deeper, or 163.50 feet − (8 feet + 0.25 feet + 0.67 feet), or 154.58 feet. Suppose the batter-board cords were at elevation 165.00 feet. Then the vertical distance from the cords to the bottom of the basement floor excavation would be 165.00 feet − 154.75 feet, or 10.25 feet, or 10 feet 3 inches. The vertical distance from the cords to the bottom of the footing excavation would be 165.00 − 154.58, or 10.42 feet, or 10 feet 5 inches.

Excavations should never be carried below the proper depths. If a basement floor or footing excavation is by mischance so carried, however, the error should not ordinarily be corrected by refilling because it is almost impossible to attain the necessary load-bearing density by compacting the refill unless special, carefully controlled procedures are used. For a basement floor excavation a relatively small error should be corrected by increasing the vertical or height dimension of the subfloor fill by the amount of the error. For a footing excavation the error should be corrected by increasing the vertical dimension of the footing by the amount of the error. Of course both of these mean additional expense for the extra material.

To avoid slides or cave-ins, the sides of excavations 4 feet or more in depth should be supported by substantial and adequate sheathing, sheet piling, bracing, shoring, etc., or else the sides should be sloped to the angle of repose. The angle of repose is the angle, measured from the horizontal, of the natural slope of the side of a pile of granular material formed by pouring grains or particles through a funnel, practically without impact. The angle of repose varies with the moisture content and the type of earth or other material. For ordinary earth, the angle of repose varies from about 20 to 45 degrees, corresponding to vertical slopes of from about 2.8 : 1 to 1 : 1. The sides of an excavation do not consist of poured particles, however; many types of earth, because of their cohesive qualities, will stand vertically without failure. But because of the nonuniformity of most soils, the times and places of local and intermittent cave-ins and slides cannot ordinarily be predicted. Therefore, it is conservative and safe to require laying the bank back to the angle of repose, or natural slope, of the material being excavated.

Even in shallow excavations, the angle of repose must be considered. Unless you are putting in retaining walls, you will need to make slopes of at least 45 degrees both above and below such a cut for stability. If your soil is fine and mucks up easily, you will probably need a gentler slope, so it will not slump the first time it rains. It helps to sow some cheap grass seed on such slopes and sprinkle them gently until the seeds sprout.

Actually, you can use your engineering math to determine how to plant the grass area. Should you seed, or use plugs of grass? Cost may be a determining factor and the cost for seed versus plugs will vary with the content of seed in a package. Often, too, your final decision may depend on the type of terrain to be covered. You will have to measure the area by any of the methods described, or can use a fast method as follows:

Take a known length of ground, 10 or 20 yards, and pace its length, counting your strides. Perhaps you took 14 steps to cover 10 yards. Then you know that each of your steps is $^{10}/_{14}$ths of a yard. Now pace off your lawn. If one side took 42 steps, then its length is $42 \times {}^{10}/_{14} = 30$ yards, or, multiplying by 3 feet per yard, 90 feet. Measure the other side similarly and multiply to find square yards or square feet. Another way to measure is to put stakes in the ground and string them, measuring the length of the string.

Once you know the square footage to be covered, you can figure the cost by multiplying square footage with the amount of seed or plugs needed, then multiply the price for each. For every 100 square feet you will need about half a pound of grass seed. Or, for every 100 square feet, you will need about 7,200 plugs.

Foundations

Foundations vary according to their use, the bearing capacity of the soil, and the type of material available. The material may be cut stone, brick, concrete, wood, or masonry block, depending upon the weight which the foundation is to support. Foundations may be classified as wall, slab, column, or pier foundations **(Figure 1-46).**

Wall foundations are built solid for their total length when heavy loads are to be carried or where the earth has low supporting strength. These walls may

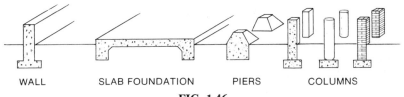

WALL　　　　SLAB FOUNDATION　　　PIERS　　　COLUMNS

FIG. 1-46

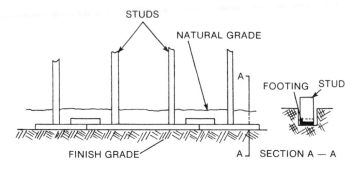

FIG. 1-47

be made of masonry block, concrete, rock, brick, or cut stone, with a footing at the bottom **(Figure 1-47)**.

Column or pier foundations save time and labor. They may be constructed from masonry or wood. The piers or columns are spaced according to the weight to be carried. In most cases, the spacing is from 6 to 10 feet.

The remainder of this chapter will consider the mathematics of using poured concrete, brick, and concrete and stone masonry.

MATH FOR CONCRETE WORK

Concrete, as you probably know, is an artificial stone made by mixing cement and sand with gravel, broken stone, or other aggregate. These materials must be mixed with sufficient water to cause the cement to set and bind the entire mass.

There are various types of concrete used during construction operations, such as precast, prestressed, and many others. No matter how the concrete is expected to be used, the makeup is basically the same the world over. That is, concrete is a synthetic construction material made by mixing *cement, fine aggregate* (usually sand), *coarse aggregate* (usually gravel or crushed stone), and water together in proper proportions. The product is not concrete unless all four of these ingredients are present. A mixture of cement, sand, and water, without coarse aggregate, is not concrete but *mortar* or *grout.* Many people mistakenly call a *concrete* wall or floor a *cement* wall or floor. There is no such thing as a cement wall or floor.

The fine and coarse aggregates in a concrete mix are called the *inert* ingredients; the cement and water are the *active* ingredients. The inert ingredients and the cement are thoroughly mixed together first. As soon as the water is added, a chemical reaction between the water and the cement begins, and it is this reaction (which is called *hydration*) that causes the concrete to harden.

Remember that the hardening process is caused by hydration of the cement by the water, not by drying out of the mix. Instead of being dried out, the concrete must be kept as moist as possible during the initial hydration process. Drying out would cause a drop in water content below the amount required for satisfactory hydration of the cement. In fact, concrete will harden just as well underwater as it will in the air.

In mixing concrete, the most important proportion to remember is that between cement and water. As long as a mix is workable, the amount of aggregate may be varied considerably. However, for a given strength of concrete, the ratio between cement and water is *fixed*. The relationship between strength of concrete and the relative quantities of water and cement is expressed more definitely by concrete experts:

For given materials and conditions of handling, the strength of the concrete is determined primarily by the ratio of the volume of the mixing water to the volume of cement as long as the mixture is plastic and workable.

In other words, if 6 gallons of water are used for each sack of cement in a mixture, the strength of the concrete at a certain age is already determined. The only extra provisions are that the mixture be plastic and workable and that the aggregates be strong, clean, and made up of sound particles. More water will mean less strength and less water greater strength.

Following this principle, modern practice is to state the amount of mixing water for each sack of cement to produce "pastes" of different strengths. Common combinations are 5-gallon paste, 6-gallon paste, and 7-gallon paste, to be selected according to the type of work to be done.

To help you choose pastes and make trial mixes for different types of jobs, **Table 1-7** shows proportions recommended by the Portland Cement Association. See page 60.

Choosing and Mixing Materials

Portland cement is sold in sacks of 94 pounds each, or 1 cubic foot in volume. It should be free from all lumps when used. If it contains lumps that cannot be pulverized between thumb and finger, don't use it.

Water should be clean, and free of oil, acid, or alkali. As a general rule, you can use any water that is fit to drink.

TABLE 1-7:
HOW TO SELECT PROPER CONCRETE MIX

Kinds of work	Add U.S. gallons of water to each sack batch if sand is			Suggested mixture for trial batch*			Materials per cu. yd. of concrete*		
	Very wet	Wet (average sand)	Damp	Cement, sacks	Aggregates Fine cu. ft.	Aggregates Coarse cu. ft.	Cement, sacks	Aggregates Fine cu. ft.	Aggregates Coarse cu. ft.
5-gallon paste for concrete subjected to severe wear, weather, or weak acid and alkali solutions									
One-course industrial, creamery, and dairy plant floors, etc.	3 ½	4	4 ½	Maximum size aggregate ¾ in. 1	2	2 ¼	7 ¾	15 ½	17 ½
6-gallon paste for concrete to be watertight or subjected to moderate wear and weather									
Watertight floors, such as industrial plant, basement, dairy barn; watertight foundations; driveways, walks, tennis courts, swimming and wading pools, septic tanks, storage tanks, structural beams, columns, slabs, residence floors, etc.	4 ¼	5	5 ½	Maximum size aggregate 1 ½ in. 1	2 ½	3 ½	6	15	21
7-gallon paste for concrete not subjected to wear, weather, or water									
Foundation walls, footings, mass concrete, etc., for use where watertightness and abrasion resistance are not important	4 ¾	5 ½	6 ¼	Maximum size aggregate 1½ in. 1	3	4	5	15	20

*Mixes and quantities are based on wet (average) aggregates and medium consistencies. Actual quantities will vary according to the grading of aggregate and the workability that is desired for each job.

Aggregates are classified as fine or coarse. Fine aggregate consists of sand or other solid and clean fine material, including rock screenings. Suitable sand will contain particles ranging uniformly in size from very fine up to $\frac{1}{4}$ inch.

Coarse aggregate consists of gravel, crushed stone, or other materials up to about $1\frac{1}{2}$ inches in size. Material that is sound, hard, durable, and free from foreign matter is best for making concrete.

The maximum size of coarse aggregate depends on the kind of work for which the concrete is to be used. Aggregate up to $1\frac{1}{2}$ inches, for example, may be used in a thick foundation wall or heavy footing. In ordinary walls, the largest pieces should never be more than one-fifth the thickness of the finished wall section. For slabs the maximum size should be approximately one-third the thickness of the slab. Coarse aggregate is well graded when particles range uniformly from $\frac{1}{4}$ inch up to the largest that may be used on the kind of work to be done.

Allowance for Moisture in the Aggregates

Most sand or fine aggregates contain some water. Allowance must therefore be made for this moisture in determining the amount of water to be added to the mix. You can easily determine whether sand is damp, wet, or very wet by pressing some together in your hand. If the sand falls apart after your hand is opened, it is damp; if it forms a ball that holds its shape, it is wet; if the sand sparkles and wets your hand, it is very wet. If the sand is bone dry—an unusual condition—you should use the full 5, 6, or 7 gallons of water called for in the table.

Measuring Materials

All materials, including water, should be accurately measured. For measuring water, a pail marked on the inside to indicate quarts and gallons will prove handy. On small jobs a pail may also be used for measuring cement, sand, and pebbles. In mixing 1-sack batches, merely remember that 1 sack holds exactly 1 cubic foot. Sand and pebbles are then conveniently measured in bottomless boxes made to hold exactly 1 cubic foot, or other volumes desired.

How to Obtain a Workable Mixture

A workable mixture is one of such wetness and plasticity that it can be placed in the forms readily and with light spading and tamping will result in a dense concrete. There should be enough portland cement mortar to give good dense surfaces, free from rough spots, and to hold pieces of coarse aggregate within the mass so that they will not separate out in handling. In other words, the cement-and-fine-aggregate mortar should completely fill the spaces between the coarse aggregate and ensure a smooth, plastic mix. Mixtures lacking sufficient mortar will be hard to work and difficult to finish. Too much fine aggregate increases porosity and reduces the amount of concrete obtainable from a sack of cement.

A workable mix for one type of work may be too stiff for another. Concrete that is placed in thin sections must be more plastic than concrete used for massive construction.

Mixing and Placing the Concrete

Mixing should continue until every piece of coarse aggregate is completely coated with a thoroughly mixed mortar of cement and fine aggregate. Machine mixing is preferable, if you have the equipment available, and should continue for at least 1 minute after all the materials have been placed in the mixer.

The concrete should be placed in the forms within 45 to 60 minutes after mixing. It should be tamped or spaded as it goes into the form. This forces the coarse aggregate back from the face or surface, making a dense concrete surface.

Estimating Material

Table 1-8 gives the approximate quantities required for 100 square feet of concrete at various thicknesses. Actual quantities used may vary 10 percent, depending upon the aggregate used. It is good practice to provide 10 percent more fine and coarse aggregates than estimated, to allow for waste.

When tables such as Table 1-8 are not available for determining quantities of material required for 1 cubic yard of concrete, a rule known as the $\frac{3}{2}$s rule

TABLE 1-8:
ESTIMATING MATERIALS FOR CONCRETE

		Proportions								
		1:2:2 ¼ mix			1:2 ½:3 ½ mix			1:3:4 mix		
Thickness of concrete, in.	Amount of concrete, cu. yd.	Cement, sacks	Aggregate Fine, cu. ft.	Coarse, cu. ft.	Cement, sacks	Aggregate Fine, cu. ft.	Coarse, cu. ft.	Cement, sacks	Aggregate Fine, cu. ft.	Coarse, cu. ft.
3	0.92	7.1	14.3	16.1	5.5	13.8	19.3	4.6	13.8	18.4
4	1.24	9.6	19.2	21.7	7.4	18.6	26.0	6.2	18.6	24.8
5	1.56	12.1	24.2	27.3	9.4	23.4	32.8	7.8	23.4	31.2
6	1.85	14.3	28.7	32.4	11.1	27.8	38.9	9.3	27.8	37.0
8	2.46	19.1	38.1	43.0	14.8	36.9	51.7	12.3	36.9	49.3
10	3.08	23.9	47.7	53.9	18.5	46.2	64.7	15.4	46.2	61.6
12	3.70	28.7	57.3	64.7	22.2	55.5	77.7	18.5	55.5	74.0

may be used for rough approximation. The rule states that to produce a given volume of concrete, the combined amounts of cement, sand, and gravel are 1 $\frac{1}{2}$ (that is, $\frac{3}{2}$) times the volume of the concrete pour. Since the void spaces between the coarse aggregate are filled with sand particles, and the voids between the sand particles are similarly filled with cement, the total volume occupied by the three components will be less than the sum of their individual volumes. Normally, a mix ratio of 1 : 2 : 3 is assumed when using the $\frac{3}{2}$s rule. This means that of a total volume, 1 part will be cement, 2 parts will be sand, and 3 parts will be gravel. The amount of water is roughly established by assuming a ratio that assures watertightness—6 gallons per sack. Additional water will be needed for wetting down forms and subgrade, washing tools, and curing the concrete. When computing quantities of concrete, the space occupied by embedded objects or steel reinforcement is ignored.

By using the $\frac{3}{2}$s rule, we will determine the amount of cement, sand, and gravel required to construct a 45 $\times$ 10 $\times$ 2-foot retaining wall. Assume a mix ratio of 1 : 2 : 3.

Volume of concrete required:

$$45 \times 10 \times 2 = 900 \text{ cubic feet} = 33.3 \text{ cubic yards}$$

Applying the $\frac{3}{2}$s rule and allowing 10 percent handling loss, the total volume required is 33.3 $\times$ 1.10 $\times$ $\frac{3}{2}$, or 55 cubic yards.

The required volumes needed are:

$$\text{Cement: } \frac{1}{6} \times 55 = 9.17 \text{ cubic yards}$$

$$\text{Sand: } \frac{2}{6} \times 55 = 18.33 \text{ cubic yards}$$

$$\text{Gravel: } \frac{3}{6} \times 55 = 27.50 \text{ cubic yards}$$

Since cement is usually obtained in sacks, you should multiply the volume by 27 and round it to the next larger number.

$$9.17 \times 27 = 247.59 \text{ cubic feet, or 248 sacks}$$

There are other interesting rules regarding the measuring of cement. Since it is known that a bag of cement contains 94 pounds by weight and about 1 cubic foot by loose volume, a batch formula for bagged cement is usually based upon the highest even number of bags that will produce a batch within the capacity of the men (hand mixing) or the machine (machine mixing).

Rules 38, 41, and 42

You can use rules 38, 41, and 42 for calculating the amount of material needed for the mix without a great deal of paperwork. These so-called "rule numbers" have been set by Portland Cement Association and the numbers are only for identification. For instance, rule 38 is used in the mixing of mortar. Rule 41 is used in calculating the quantities of materials for concrete when the size of the coarse aggregate is not over 1 inch. Rule 42 is used when the size of the coarse aggregate is not over 2½ inches. (Coarse aggregates over 1 inch in size are termed *rock* in concrete work.) These three calculating rules will not give the accurate amount of required materials for large construction jobs; you will have to use the absolute volume or weight formulas. However, in most cases you can use these rules of thumb to calculate the quantities of required materials.

It has been found that it takes about 38 cubic feet of raw materials to make 1 cubic yard of mortar. In using rule 38 for calculating mortar, take the rule number and divide it by the sum of the quantity figures specified in the mix. For example, let us assume that the building specifications call for a 1:3 mix for mortar. 1 + 3 = 4; dividing 38 by 4, we get 9½. You will then need 9 ½ bags or 9½ cubic feet of cement. In order to calculate the amount of fine aggregates (sand), you simply multiply 9½ by 3. The product, 28½ cubic feet, is the amount of sand you need to mix one cubic yard of mortar using a 1 : 3 mix. The sum of the two required quantities should equal the rule number, 38. Therefore, you can always check in order to see if you are using the correct amounts. In the above example, 9½ bags of cement plus 28½ cubic feet of sand equal 38 cubic feet.

Rules 41 and 42, for calculating the amount of raw materials needed to mix 1 cubic yard of concrete, are worked in the same manner. For example, let us assume that the specifications call for a 1 : 2 : 4 mix with 2-inch coarse aggregates:

1 + 2 + 4 = 7; 42 ÷ 7 = 6 bags or cubic feet of cement

6 × 2 = 12 cubic feet of sand

6 × 4 = 24 cubic feet of coarse aggregates

6 + 12 + 24 = 42 (the rule number), so your calculations have been proved correct.

Frequently, it will be necessary to convert these volumes in cubic feet to weights in pounds. These conversions are easy. Multiply the required cubic feet of cement by 94 pounds, remembering that 1 cubic foot or a standard bag of cement weighs 94 pounds. The average weight of dry-compacted, fine aggregate or gravel is 105 pounds per cubic foot. The average weight of dry-compacted, coarse aggregate over 1 inch in size—termed rock—is 100 pounds. Therefore, you multiply the quantity of coarse gravel in cubic feet by 105 when using rule 41 for coarse gravels or aggregates. When the calculating rule 42 is used, multiply the cubic feet of required rock by 100 in order to figure the amount of needed rock in pounds.

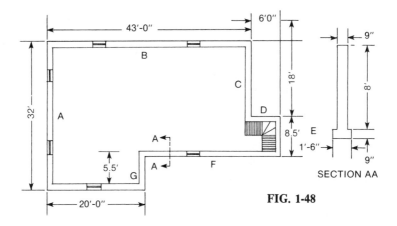

FIG. 1-48

Estimating Ready-Prepared Concrete

When using ready-prepared concrete (only water need be added to already mixed ingredients), simply follow the manufacturer's suggestions (usually found on the bag) as to the amount you will need for a given job.

To estimate the amount of transit-mixed concrete (ready-mixed concrete delivered by a truck) needed for a given job, proceed as follows:

1. Find the number of cubic yards (the volume in cubic yards) of concrete that will be required.
2. Round off to the nearest whole unit (cubic yards).

To find how many cubic yards of transit mix should be ordered to build the foundation shown in **Figure 1-48,** proceed as follows:

1. First, find the total number of square feet in the foundation wall:

$$\text{length} \times \text{height} = \text{square feet}$$

(A) $32 \times 8 = 256$

(B) $43 \times 8 = 344$

(C) $18 \times 8 = 144$

(D) $6 \times 8 = 48$

(E) $8.5 \times 8 = 68$

(F) $49 \times 8 = 392$

(G) $5.5 \times 8 = 44$

Total $= 1,296$ square feet (no deduction for openings is necessary)

2. To find the cubic feet needed, multiply by the thickness of the wall:

$$1{,}296 \times \frac{9}{12} \text{ or } 0.75 = 972 \text{ cubic feet}$$

3. To find the cubic yards needed, divide by 27:

$$\frac{972}{27} = 36 \text{ cubic yards for walls}$$

4. To find the amount needed for the footing, multiply the total length by the width by the thickness and divide by 27.

$$32 + 43 + 18 + 6 + 8.5 + 49 + 5.5 = 162 \text{ total length}$$

$$162 \times 0.75 \times 1.5 = 182.25 \text{ square feet}$$

$$\frac{182.25}{27} = 6.75$$

5. The total number of cubic yards of concrete needed for the foundation is:

$$36 + 6.52 = 42.52 \text{ or } 43 \text{ yards of transit-mixed concrete}$$

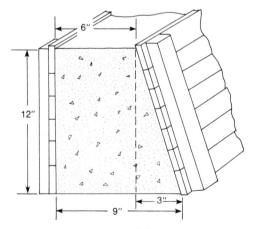

FIG. 1-49

Often, the object to be made of concrete is irregular in shape. To find the volume of such a form, first find the cross-sectional area and multiply this area by the length. To get workable shapes for calculations, you can usually break up the cross-sectional area into squares, rectangles, triangles, trapezoids, and circles. To find the cubic yards of concrete necessary for the 200-foot-long curbing shown in **Figure 1-49,** divide the cross-sectional area into a 12 × 6-inch rectangle and 12 × 3-inch right triangle:

$$12 \times 6 = 72 \text{ square inches (rectangle)}$$

$$\frac{1}{2} \text{ (base} \times \text{height)} = \frac{1}{2} (3 \times 12) = 18 \text{ square inches (triangle)}$$

$$\text{total square inches} = 90 \text{ square inches or } 0.625 \text{ square feet}$$

$$0.625 \times 200 = 125 \text{ cubic feet}$$

$$\frac{125}{27} = 4.63 \text{ cubic yards or 5 cubic yards needed}$$

At a cost of $21.60 per cubic yard of ready-mixed concrete, the cost would be:

$$21.60 \times 5 = \$108.00$$

When ordering transit-mixed concrete, it may pay you to figure your job so you use enough concrete to get the best price. In some areas, 2 yards bought separately cost a trifle more than 3 yards taken at one crack, which works out to an appealing 33 percent discount on the latter.

Form Lumber and Other Expenses

With any concrete job, the cost of equipment—trowels, floats, mixer rental, etc.—as well as reinforcing steel rods, which are sometimes needed, must be figured in the overall expense. In addition, while some soils are sufficiently rigid to permit their use as forms for the concrete, most require the installation of special forms. These forms may be fabricated from lumber or plywood **(Figure 1-50),** or you can rent ready-made ones of steel and aluminum. A typical footing form such as in **Figure 1-51** consists of 1-inch-thick lumber planks, which are cleated together, side by side, in the correct width. These planks are designated as sheathing. The sheathing is held in place by 2-by-4 studs and braces, spaced about 18 inches apart around the outside of the forms.

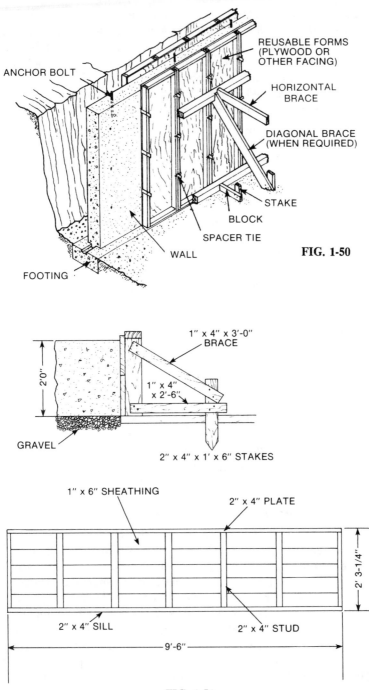

ANCHOR BOLT

REUSABLE FORMS
(PLYWOOD OR
OTHER FACING)

HORIZONTAL
BRACE

DIAGONAL BRACE
(WHEN REQUIRED)

STAKE

BLOCK

SPACER TIE

WALL

FOOTING

FIG. 1-50

1" x 4" x 3'-0"
BRACE

2'0"

1" x 4"
x 2'-6"

GRAVEL

2" x 4" x 1' x 6" STAKES

1" x 6" SHEATHING

2" x 4" PLATE

2' 3-1/4"

2" x 4" SILL

2" x 4" STUD

9'-6"

FIG. 1-51

68

The quantity of lumber in feet board measure (fbm) required to build one 9½-foot section of this typical form would be:

Sheathing, 5 pc, 1 in. × 6 in. × 10 ft. 0 in. =   25 bm

Plates, 2 pc, 2 in. × 4 in. × 10 ft. 0 in. =   14 bm

Studs, 7 pc, 2 in. × 4 in. × 2 ft. 0 in. =   10 bm

Stakes, 7 pc, 2 in. × 4 in. × 1 ft. 6 in. =   7 bm

Braces, 7 pc, 1 in. × 4 in. × 3 ft. 0 in. =   7 bm

Braces, 7 pc, 1 in. × 4 in. × 2 ft. 6 in. =   6 bm

Total lumber =   69 bm

Lumber per sq. ft. of surface, 69 ÷ 19 (9.5 × 2) =   3.6 bm

Nails, 69 fbm @ 10 pounds per M fbm =   0.7 pounds

If the lumber needed for the form averaged at $190 per M board feet, the cost of the lumber for *one* section would be:

$$\frac{69}{1000} \times \$190 = \$13.11$$

plus nails and oil used to keep the concrete from sticking to the form

To find the total cost of the forms, multiply the cost of the single form by the number of forms needed for the job. This cost, as well as that of equipment needed, must be included to obtain the complete expense of any concrete job.

MATH FOR BRICK MASONRY

Brick masonry is that type of construction in which units of baked clay or shale of uniform size, small enough to be placed with one hand, are laid in courses with mortar joints to form walls of virtually unlimited length and height. Bricks are kiln-baked from various clay and shale mixtures. The chemical and physical characteristics of the ingredients vary considerably; these and the kiln temperatures combine to produce brick in a variety of colors and hardnesses. In some regions, pits are opened and found to yield clay or shale which, when ground and moistened, can be formed and baked into durable brick; in other regions, clays or shales from several pits must be mixed.

The dimensions of a U.S. standard building brick are 2½ × 3¾ × 8 inches. The actual dimensions of brick may vary a little because of shrinkage during burning.

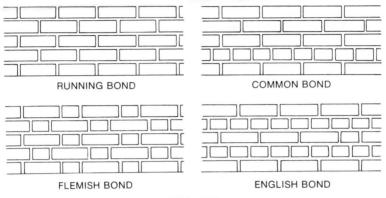

RUNNING BOND

COMMON BOND

FLEMISH BOND

ENGLISH BOND

FIG. 1-52

Brick Quantity Estimate

There are several ways of estimating the number of bricks in a wall. One method is to determine the number of bricks in a square foot and then multiply this number by the total square feet required. This will give the number of bricks for a wall of one-brick thickness, which for a standard-size brick is 4 inches. The quantity of brick in a wall 8 inches thick would be twice this number, the quantity in a wall 12 inches thick would be three times the number in the 4-inch wall, and so on.

The size of the mortar joint has quite a lot of influence on the number of bricks required. As mentioned above, the standard brick is $2\frac{1}{4} \times 3\frac{3}{4} \times 8$ inches, with the $2\frac{1}{4} \times 8$ inch dimension visible in the wall. With a $\frac{1}{4}$-inch joint the number of bricks in a square foot would be $144 \div (2\frac{1}{2} \times 8\frac{1}{4}) = 7$ (approximately). In an 8-inch wall the number would be $2 \times 7 = 14$. In a 12-inch wall the number would be $3 \times 7 = 21$, and so on. Most walls are of standard brick with $\frac{1}{4}$-inch mortar joints. For the different-size joints using standard brick the number of bricks per square foot in a 4-inch-thick wall will be:

Joint sizes:	¼ inch	⁵⁄₁₆ inch	⅜ inch	½ inch	⅝ inch	¾ inch
Bricks per square feet:	7	6.75	6.55	6.15	5.80	5.50

If the bricks are laid in a bond or pattern (**Figure 1-52**), if half bricks are used, and if no headers are required, then the quantities suggested will be adequate. However, if header courses are required, then the number of bricks per square foot will have to be increased. After the required number of bricks is determined the amount should be increased by 3 to 5 percent to allow for waste and breakage.

To find how many bricks are needed to construct a wall 1 foot thick and 6 feet high around a plot of ground measuring 50 by 125 feet, proceed as follows:

Find the total number of square feet in the wall.

$$50 \times 6 = 300$$
$$125 \times 6 = 750$$
$$750 + 750 + 300 + 300 = 2{,}100 \text{ square feet of wall}$$

Since the wall is 12 inches thick, 21 bricks are needed per square foot. Therefore,

$$21 \times 2{,}100 = 44{,}100 \text{ bricks plus 4 percent waste} =$$
$$44{,}100 + 1{,}764 = 45{,}864 \text{ bricks to be ordered}$$

If the bricks are sold at $42 per thousand, the cost of the bricks for the wall would be $44.2 \times 42 = \$1{,}856.40$.

To this cost you must add the equipment that is needed for laying brick, which will consist of such things as mortar boxes, hand tools, mortar mixers, manual hoists, shovels, scaffolding, etc.

The cost of common and face brick will be influenced by the required texture, finish, size, and shape of the brick. However, none of these will affect the cost as much as the requirements of a modular size permitting no variations in dimensions such as the number of bricks required to lay up a brick-and-block wall in which three brick layers with the required joint size will exactly match the nominal height of the block. Of course, walls are frequently erected with a 4-inch-thick veneer of face bricks, while the balance of the wall thickness is obtained with common bricks. If a common bond is used, it is customary to lay face bricks as headers every sixth course for bond purposes. As a header course will require twice as many face bricks as a stretcher course, the total number of face bricks required must be increased over the number that would be required for a uniform 4-inch thickness. This is equivalent to one extra stretcher course in six courses, amounting to an increase of $16\frac{2}{3}$ percent in the number of face bricks required. The number of common bricks may be reduced in an amount equal to the increase in the number of face bricks.

For face brick showing $8 \times 2\frac{1}{4}$ inches on the face, with $\frac{3}{8}$-inch mortar joints, it takes slightly more than $6\frac{1}{2}$ bricks to cover 1 square foot of wall. Consequently, to determine face brick requirements, you multiply the net area of wall to be faced by $6\frac{1}{2}$, and add a few over, depending on the size of the area. Face brick quantities should be subtracted, of course, from the total brick requirements found as described.

Sometimes it is more convenient to compute the number of bricks by the cubical content. An average number of bricks per cubic foot of masonry for the standard size of brick is:

Joint sizes:	¼ inch	5/16 inch	3/8 inch	½ inch
Bricks per cubic feet:	21	20	19	17.5

TABLE 1-9:
MATERIAL FOR 100 SQUARE FEET OF ½-INCH-JOINT BRICK WALL

Character of construction	Thickness of wall (in.)	Number of bricks	Mortar (cu. ft.)
Basement walls, solid:			
Outer 4-inch thickness laid with all joints filled. Other brick laid on full bed of mortar, touching end to end. Vertical space between 4-inch thicknesses filled with mortar. Every fifth course headers	8 12 16	1,271 1,926 2,580	19.5 31.4 43.3
Walls above grade, solid:			
Same construction, but vertical space between 4-inch thickness left open	8 12 16	1,271 1,925 2,580	13.5 19.5 25.5
Walls above grade, solid:			
Outer 8-inch thickness laid with as many as possible vertical joints parallel with face of wall left open. Other brick in thicker walls laid on full mortar bed but with brick touching end to end and vertical space between 4-inch thickness left open	8 12 16	1,233 1,887 2,541	19.5 25.5 31.4
Walls above grade, solid:			
All joints filled with mortar	4 8 12 16	617 1,233 1,849 2,465	7.6 19.5 31.4 43.3

Using our previously given example (a 6-foot-high wall around a 50 × 125 plot), the total cubic footage of wall is 2,100:

2,100 cubic feet × 21.0 bricks = 44,100 bricks total needed

Another popular method of counting bricks is to first calculate the *net* surface area by deducting the total area of all openings. **Table 1-9** shows the material requirements for 100 square feet of ½-inch-joint brick wall under ordinary conditions. **Table 1-10** shows the material requirements for brick-work footings and piers.

Suppose you need to know the number of bricks required for 35 square feet of 8-inch-thick basement wall. **Table 1-9** indicates that it takes 1,271 bricks to make 100 square feet of wall this type. If it takes 1,271 bricks to make 100 square feet, it takes x bricks to make 35 square feet and your equation reads:

$$1,271 : 100 :: x : 35$$

$$\frac{1271}{100} = \frac{x}{35}$$

Consequently, $100x = (35 \times 1,271)$, or 44,485, and $x = 44,485 \div 100$. How do you divide anything by 100? Simply by moving the decimal point two spaces to the left. The number of bricks required for 35 square feet of wall in this case is, therefore, 444.9.

TABLE 1-10:
MATERIAL FOR BRICKWORK FOOTINGS AND
PIERS

Construction	Number of bricks	Mortar (cu. ft.)
Footings: quantities for 100 linear feet		
8-inch wall	2,272	39
12-inch wall	2,812	48
16-inch wall	4,592	78
Piers: quantities for 10-foot height		
8 × 12-inch solid	124	2.25
12 × 12-inch solid	185	3.25
12 × 16-inch solid	247	4.50
10 ¾-inch × 10 ¾-inch hollow brick laid on edge	113	1.00

TABLE 1-11:
ESTIMATING LABOR FOR LAYING BRICK

Type of work	Mason hours per 1,000 bricks*
Common brick walls (finished one side)	5–12
Common brick walls (finished two sides)	6–14
Face brick walls	10–20
Firebrick walls	18–32

*For other than common or running bond, increase labor by 10 to 15 percent. For house chimneys, double the man-hours in this table.

If windows or doors are to be installed in the wall, openings are left for them as the bricklaying proceeds. The height to the top of one full course should be exactly the height of the windowsill or doorsill. When the distance from the foundation to the bottom of the windowsill is known, the number of courses that are required to bring the wall up to sill height can be determined. If the sill of a window, for example, is to be 4 feet $4\frac{1}{4}$ inches above the foundation and $\frac{1}{2}$-inch mortar joints are to be used, 19 courses will be required. (Each brick plus its mortar joint is $2\frac{1}{4} + \frac{1}{2} = 2\frac{3}{4}$ inches. One course is thus $2\frac{3}{4}$ inches high. 4 feet $4\frac{1}{4}$ inches divided by $2\frac{3}{4}$ is 19, the number of courses required.) In the case of face brick backed up by common brick or block, add 1.5 face bricks per linear foot of openings around windows and around doors except at bottoms of doors. In the case of brick veneer, add 5 bricks per foot at tops of windows and doors for soldier course and 5 bricks per foot at bottoms of windows for rowlock course. Bricks are usually quoted in prices of so much per 1,000 units.

To give you some idea as to the time required to lay brick, **Table 1-11** gives the average time taken by a *professional* mason.

Brick Mortar

Ingredient amounts required per cubic yard of mortar will depend upon the mix formula of the mortar. Proportions of cement, lime, and sand in mortar range from 1 : 0.05 : 2 all the way to 1 : 2 : 9. It takes 13 sacks of cement, 26 pounds of lime, and 0.96 cubic yards of sand to make a cubic yard of 1 : 0.05 : 2 mortar. It takes 3 sacks of cement, 240 pounds of lime, and 1 cubic yard of sand to make a cubic yard of 1 : 2 : 9 mortar.

For most brick and concrete masonry use around the home, you can use rule 38 (mentioned earlier in the chapter) for calculating the amount of raw materials needed to mix 1 yard of mortar without a great deal of paperwork. That is, builders have found that it takes about 38 cubic feet of raw materials to make 1 cubic yard of mortar. In using the 38 calculating rule for mortar, take the rule number and divide it by the sum of the quantity figures specified in

TABLE 1-12:
QUANTITY OF MATERIAL PER CUBIC FOOT OF MORTAR

Cement sack (1 cu. ft.)	Mortar mixes		Quantities			
	Hydrated lime or lime putty, cu. ft.	Sand,* cu. ft.	Masonry cement, sack	Portland cement, sack	Hydrated lime or lime putty, cu. ft.	Sand,* cu. ft.
1 masonry cement	—	3	0.33	—	—	0.99
1 portland cement	1	6	—	0.16	0.16	0.97
1 masonry cement plus	—	6	0.16	0.16	—	0.97
1 portland cement						
1 portland cement	¼	3	—	0.29	0.07	0.86

*Sand in damp, loose condition.

the mix. For example, let us assume that the building specifications call for a 1 : 3 mix for mortar. $1 + 3 = 4$, and $38 \div 4 = 9\frac{1}{2}$. You will then need 9 $\frac{1}{2}$ sacks or $9\frac{1}{2}$ cubic feet of cement. In order to calculate the amount of fine aggregates (sand), you simply multiply $9\frac{1}{2}$ by 3. The product, $28\frac{1}{2}$ cubic feet, is the amount of sand you need to mix 1 cubic yard of mortar using a 1 : 3 mix. The sum of the two required quantities should always equal the calculating rule number, 38. Therefore, you can always check in order to see if you are using the correct amounts. In the above example, $9\frac{1}{2}$ sacks of cement plus $28\frac{1}{2}$ cubic feet of sand equal 38. See **Table 1-12** (page 75) for the exact quantities of materials per cubic foot of mortar.

MATH FOR CONCRETE AND STONE MASONRY

Concrete masonry has become increasingly important as a construction material. Important technological developments in the manufacture and utilization of the units have accompanied the rapid increase in the use of concrete masonry. Concrete masonry walls properly designed and constructed will satisfy varied building requirements including fire resistance, safety, durability, economy, appearance, utility, comfort, and acoustics.

Concrete building units are made in sizes and shapes to fit different construction needs. Units are made in full-length and half-length sizes, as shown in **Figure 1-53.** Concrete unit sizes are usually referred to by their nominal

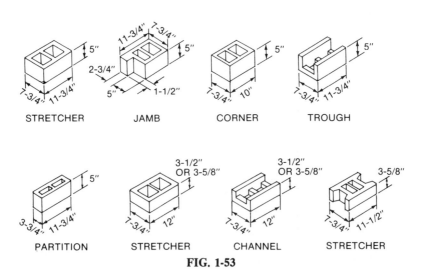

STRETCHER   JAMB   CORNER   TROUGH

PARTITION   STRETCHER   CHANNEL   STRETCHER

FIG. 1-53

76

FIG. 1-53 (Cont.)

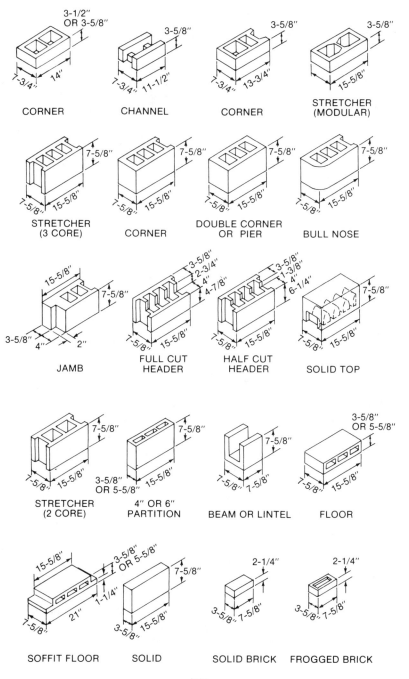

CORNER

CHANNEL

CORNER

STRETCHER
(MODULAR)

STRETCHER
(3 CORE)

CORNER

DOUBLE CORNER
OR PIER

BULL NOSE

JAMB

FULL CUT
HEADER

HALF CUT
HEADER

SOLID TOP

STRETCHER
(2 CORE)

4" OR 6"
PARTITION

BEAM OR LINTEL

FLOOR

SOFFIT FLOOR

SOLID

SOLID BRICK

FROGGED BRICK

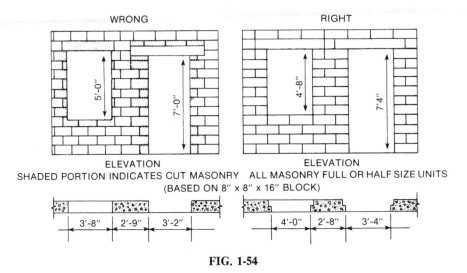

FIG. 1-54

dimensions. A unit measuring $7\frac{5}{8}$ inches wide, $7\frac{5}{8}$ inches high, and $15\frac{5}{8}$ inches long is referred to as an $8 \times 8 \times 16$-inch unit. When it is laid in a wall with $\frac{3}{8}$-inch mortar joints, the unit will occupy a space exactly 16 inches long and 8 inches high. Besides the basic $8 \times 8 \times 16$ units, the illustration shows a smaller partition unit and other units which are used much as cut bricks are in brick masonry.

The corner unit is, of course, laid at a corner or at some similar point where a smooth rather than a recessed end is required. The header unit is used in a backing course placed behind a brick face-tier header course. Part of the block is cut away to admit the brick headers. The uses of the other special shapes shown are self-evident. Besides the shapes shown in **Figure 1-53,** a number of smaller shapes for various special purposes are available. Units may be cut to desired shapes with a bolster or, more conveniently and accurately, with a power-driven masonry saw.

Concrete masonry walls should be laid out to make maximum use of full- and half-length units, thus minimizing cutting and fitting of units on the job. Length and height of wall, width and height of openings, and wall areas between doors, windows, and corners should be planned to use full-size and half-size units which are usually available **(Figure 1-54).** This procedure assumes that window and door frames are of modular dimensions which fit modular full- and half-size units. Then, all horizontal dimensions should be in multiples of nominal full-length masonry units, and both horizontal and vertical dimensions should be designed to be in multiples of 8 inches. **Table 1-13** lists nominal length of concrete masonry walls by stretchers, and **Table**

TABLE 1-13:
NOMINAL LENGTH OF
CONCRETE MASONRY WALLS BY STRETCHERS

Actual length of wall is measured from outside edge to outside edge of units and is equal to the nominal length minus ⅜″ (one mortar joint).

No. of stretchers	Nominal length of concrete masonry walls	
	Units 15 ⅝″ long and half units 7 ⅝″ long with ⅜″ -thick head joints	*Units 11 ⅝″ long and half units 5 ⅝″ long with ⅜″ -thick head joints*
1	1′ 4″	1′ 0″
1 ½	2′ 0″	1′ 6″
2	2′ 8″	2′ 0″
2 ½	3′ 4″	2′ 6″
3	4′ 0″	3′ 0″
3 ½	4′ 8″	3′ 6″
4	5′ 4″	4′ 0″
4 ½	6′ 0″	4′ 6″
5	6′ 8″	5′ 0″
5 ½	7′ 4″	5′ 6″
6	8′ 0″	6′ 0″
6 ½	8′ 8″	6′ 6″
7	9′ 4″	7′ 0″
7 ½	10′ 0″	7′ 6″
8	10′ 8″	8′ 0″
8 ½	11′ 4″	8′ 6″
9	12′ 0″	9′ 0″
9 ½	12′ 8″	9′ 6″
10	13′ 4″	10′ 0″
10 ½	14′ 0″	10′ 6″
11	14′ 8″	11′ 0″
11 ½	15′ 4″	11′ 6″
12	16′ 0″	12′ 0″
12 ½	16′ 8″	12′ 6″
13	17′ 4″	13′ 0″
13 ½	18′ 0″	13′ 6″
14	18′ 8″	14′ 0″
14 ½	19′ 4″	14′ 6″
15	20′ 0″	15′ 0″
20	26′ 8″	20′ 0″

TABLE 1-14:
NOMINAL HEIGHT OF CONCRETE MASONRY WALLS BY COURSES

For concrete masonry units 7 ⅝″ and 3 ⅝″ in height laid with ⅜″ mortar joints. Height is measured from center to center of mortar joints.

No. of courses	Nominal height of concrete masonry walls	
	Units 7 ⅝″ high and ⅜″-thick bed joint	Units 3 ⅝″ high and ⅜″-thick bed joint
1	8″	4″
2	1′ 4″	8″
3	2′ 0″	1′ 0″
4	2′ 8″	1′ 4″
5	3′ 4″	1′ 8″
6	4′ 0″	2′ 0″
7	4′ 8″	2′ 4″
8	5′ 4″	2′ 8″
9	6′ 0″	3′ 0″
10	6′ 8″	3′ 4″
15	10′ 0″	5′ 0″
20	13′ 4″	6′ 8″
25	16′ 8″	8′ 4″
30	20′ 0″	10′ 0″
35	23′ 4″	11′ 8″
40	26′ 8″	13′ 4″
45	30′ 0″	15′ 0″
50	33′ 4″	16′ 8″

1-14 lists nominal height of concrete masonry walls by courses. When 8 × 4 × 16 units are used, the horizontal dimensions should be planned in multiples of 8 inches (half-length units) and the vertical dimensions in multiples of 4 inches. If the thickness of the wall is greater or less than the length of a half unit, a special-length unit is required at each corner in each course.

Blocks are generally laid in running bond or stacked or in some similar pattern with the 8 × 16-inch face showing. With a ⅜-inch joint the number of blocks required per square foot of wall would be 144 ÷ (8 × 16) = 1.125 or 1⅛ blocks. For different-size joints the procedure would be the same, giving approximately 1⅐ blocks for ¼-inch joints and 1.1 blocks for ½-inch joints. To these quantities should be added 2 to 4 percent for waste and breakage.

In estimating the number of blocks required in a wall laid up in running bond, subtract the area for openings from the overall area to get the net area to be covered by the block. Next compute the number of lintel blocks, jamb blocks, half-length jamb blocks, steel sash blocks, half-length steel sash blocks,

TABLE 1-15:
CONCRETE MASONRY ESTIMATING GUIDE*

	Concrete blocks needed		Mortar needed	
Block size	Blocks per 100 sq. ft. of wall	Size	For 100 sq. ft. of wall area	Per 100 blocks
4×4×16	225	4″ high	13 ½ cu. ft.	6 cu. ft.
6×4×16	225	8″ high	8 ½ cu. ft.	7 ½ cu. ft.
8×4×16	225			
4×8×16	112 ½			
6×8×16	112 ½			
8×8×16	112 ½			
12 ×8×16	112 ½			

*Cinder blocks, which are basically the same size as concrete masonry units, can be estimated by using this guide.

half-length regular blocks, and other special blocks called for on plans. To obtain the actual number of regular blocks required, compute the number of blocks needed to fill up the net area and then subtract the number of special blocks which will be used in the wall. In running bond, vertical lines through the joints will cut every other course of blocks at its midpoint of length. Therefore half-length blocks are needed at every other course to end the wall in a flush line. Add 3 to 5 percent to cover breakage. **Table 1-15** will serve as a guide to estimate the number of blocks and the amount of mortar needed.

Table 1-16 shows the average time taken by a professional mason to lay 100 blocks, including pointing and cleaning. Remember that as in the case of brick the complexity of the work will affect the time necessary to lay blocks.

TABLE 1-16:
ESTIMATING LABOR FOR LAYING BLOCKS

Block size	Mason hours per 100 blocks
2 × 8 × 16	3.0–3.5
4 × 8 × 16	3.5–4.0
6 × 8 × 16	4.0–4.5
8 × 8 × 16	4.7–5.2
10 × 8 × 16	6.0–6.5
12 × 8 × 16	7.0–7.5

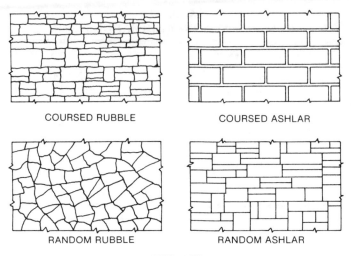

COURSED RUBBLE   COURSED ASHLAR

RANDOM RUBBLE   RANDOM ASHLAR

FIG. 1-55

Stone Masonry

Several kinds of stone, both natural and artificial, are used in structures such as buildings, walls, and piers. Natural stones used for construction include stones such as sandstone, limestone, dolomite, slate, granite, and marble. Artificial limestone is available in many areas.

Each kind of stone and work should be estimated separately. The cost of stone in place may be estimated by the cubic yard, ton, cubic foot, square foot, or linear foot. Because of the various methods of pricing stonework, you should be very careful to see that you use the correct method in preparing your estimate.

Figure 1-55 illustrates the more common bonds for stone masonry. Rubble masonry is formed of stones of irregular shapes which are laid either in regular courses or at random with mortar joints. Ashlar masonry is formed of stones cut with rectangular faces. The stones may be laid in courses or at random with mortar joints.

The mortar used for setting stones may be similar to that used for brick masonry. Sometimes special nonstaining white or stone-set cement may be specified instead of gray portland cement. Frequently, hydrated lime is added to improve the working properties of the mortar. The quantity of mortar required for joints will vary considerably with the type of bond, the thickness of the joints, and the size of stones used. **Table 1-17** gives representative quantities of mortar required per cubic yard of stone.

The cost of stone varies so much with the kind of stone, the extent of cutting done at the quarry, and the location where it will be used that no estimate

82

TABLE 1-17:
QUANTITIES OF MORTAR
REQUIRED PER CUBIC YARD OF
STONE MASONRY

Type of bond	Quantity of mortar, cu. ft.
Coursed rubble	6.5–8.5
Random rubble	7.5–9.5
Cobblestone	6.5–9.5
Coursed ashlar, ¼″ joints	1.5–2.0
Random ashlar, ¼″ joints	2.0–2.5
Coursed ashlar, ½″ joints	3.0–4.0
Random ashlar, ½″ joints	4.0–5.0

which requires accurate pricing should be made without obtaining current prices for the particular stone. The cost of freight to the destination must be added to the cost at the source in order to determine the cost at the job.

Stones suitable for rubble masonry may be priced by the ton for the specified kind of stone and sizes of pieces. Stones may be purchased at a quarry in large rough-cut blocks, hauled to the job, and then cut to the desired sizes and shapes. The cost of such blocks may be based on the volume, with the largest dimensions used in determining the volume, or the cost may be based on the weight of the stone. Weight of common building stones is given in **Table 1-18**.

Stones used for ashlar masonry may be priced by the ton, cubic foot, or square foot of wall area for a specified thickness. A gray limestone frequently used for random ashlar construction, for instance, is available in such sizes as 4 inches thick, 2 to 10 inches or more in height in steps of 2 inches, and random

TABLE 1-18:
WEIGHTS OF BUILDING STONES

Stone	Weight, lb. per cu. ft.
Dolomite	155–175
Granite	165–175
Limestone	150–175
Marble	165–175
Sandstone	140–160
Slate	160–180

TABLE 1-19:
STONE COSTS

Item	Cost, including 7% waste	
	Per cu. ft.	*Per sq. ft.*
Stone, for job	$9.00	$3.00
Cutting end joints	3.60	1.20
Total cost	$12.60	$4.20

lengths. The top and bottom beds and the back side will be sawed at the quarry, with the end joints to be sawed at the job, using a power-driven abrasive wheel. The exposed face may be left rough. The cost of this stone will vary, running upwards of $125.00 per ton delivered to a job. It weighs about 140 pounds per cubic foot. Thus a ton will produce 2,000 ÷ 140 = 14.3 cubic feet. If the stones are 4 inches thick, the wall area per ton will be 3 × 14.3 = 43 square feet gross. Considering waste and breakage, the net area should be about 40 square feet per ton.

If the stone costs $120.00 per ton, for a job, the cost of stone only in a wall, requiring a 4-inch thick facing, should be about as given in **Table 1-19.**

MATH FOR
ROUGH CARPENTRY

The mathematics of house carpentry is a lengthy subject. It involves every aspect of building and remodeling a home. To simplify the subject, we have divided it into two chapters, one on rough carpentry (Chapter 2) and the other on interior finishing (Chapter 3).

FLOOR FRAMING AND COVERING

The floor framing in a wood-frame house consists specifically of the posts, beams (girders), sill plates, joists, and subfloor. When these elements are assembled properly on a foundation, they form a level anchored platform for the rest of the house (**Figure 2-1**). The posts and beams that support the inside ends of the joists are sometimes replaced by a wood-frame or masonry wall when the basement area is divided into rooms. Wood-frame houses may also be constructed on a concrete floor slab.

One of the important factors in the design of a wood floor system is to equalize shrinkage and expansion of the wood framing at the outside walls and at the center beam. This is usually accomplished by using approximately the same total depth of wood at the center beam as the outside framing. Thus, as beams and joists approach moisture equilibrium (the moisture content they reach in service), there are only small differences in the amount of shrinkage. This will minimize plaster cracks, sticking doors, and other inconveniences. Thus if there is a total of 12 inches of wood at the foundation wall (including joists and sill plate), this should be balanced with about 12 inches of wood at the center beam.

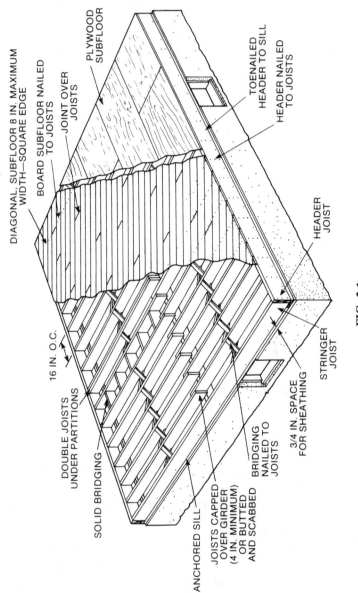

PLYWOOD SUBFLOOR

DIAGONAL, SUBFLOOR 8 IN. MAXIMUM WIDTH—SQUARE EDGE

BOARD SUBFLOOR NAILED TO JOISTS

JOINT OVER JOISTS

TOENAILED HEADER TO SILL

HEADER NAILED TO JOISTS

HEADER JOIST

16 IN. O.C.

DOUBLE JOISTS UNDER PARTITIONS

SOLID BRIDGING

ANCHORED SILL

JOISTS CAPPED OVER GIRDER (4 IN. MINIMUM) OR BUTTED AND SCABBED

BRIDGING NAILED TO JOISTS

3/4 IN. SPACE FOR SHEATHING

STRINGER JOIST

FIG. 2-1

86

The principal loads present in every structure are classified as *dead loads* and *live loads*. The dead load is the weight of the structure itself, which increases gradually as the structure is being built and then remains constant, in most cases, once it has been completed. It must be remembered, however, that if any modifications are made to the structure, their effect on the existing load-bearing members must be considered. In some cases, the addition of partitions or heating and air-conditioning equipment, not anticipated in the original design, might require the relocation or addition of load-bearing members. The weight of all structural members plus floors, walls, heating equipment, and all other nonmovable items in a building is considered its dead load.

Live load is the weight of movable objects in the building or forces acting on its exterior. It includes people and furniture in a building and external forces such as wind, snow, ice, wave action, etc., outside.

Beams

If a building is wider than 14 or 15 feet, it is generally desirable and often necessary to introduce additional support near the center to avoid the need for excessively heavy floor joists. To save expense and to eliminate partitions in the basement, it has become common practice to introduce beams resting on posts or columns. These beams and their supporting posts carry a relatively large part of the weight of the building. Because it is often necessary for you to decide upon their size and type, you should be well informed on their design.

In determining the number and location of beams, you must consider the permissible length of joists to the room arrangement, and to the location of bearing partitions.

In most houses one girder will suffice; but if joist span with a single girder exceeds 14 or 15 feet, for which a 2-by-10 joist is usually required, considerable increase in joist size becomes necessary, which makes adding another girder advisable.

To illustrate this point, suppose a building is to be 17 feet 4 inches between inner faces of bearing walls. If no girder is used, with some species of wood and grades of lumber, 2-by-14 or 3-by-10 joists will be required. On the other hand, if a girder is used at the center of the building, the joist span will be only half of 17 feet 4 inches, or 8 feet 8 inches, for which in most species of lumber 2-by-6 joists can be used. Furthermore, since joists over 14 or 16 feet long require two rows of bridging, it is additionally economical to keep joist lengths under 14 feet. In general, it is desirable to place the girders as close together as will not unduly increase the cost of foundation work. From 8 to 14 feet is usually an economical spacing for girders.

Room arrangements usually affect the location of beams, since locating a girder directly or approximately under a bearing partition avoids the necessity of additional or larger joists.

Strength of Beams

The beam should be strong enough for its load, but any size larger than needed is waste. There are three principal factors that must be understood before attempting to determine the size of a wood beam: (1) the effect of length on strength; (2) the effect of width on strength; and (3) the effect of depth on strength.

LENGTH. If an 8-foot plank is supported at its ends on sawhorses and loads are evenly distributed throughout its length, the plank will tend to bend. If the plank is 16 feet instead of 8 feet long, with the same load per foot of length, it will bend more and will be likely to break. It may seem logical to think that if the length is doubled, the safe load the plank can carry per foot will be reduced one-half, but experience and the theory of mechanics have shown that the safe load is reduced much more. Instead of carrying safely half the load, the double-length plank is good for only one-quarter the load per foot.

This principle applies to planks or beams carrying a load distributed uniformly along their entire lengths and to all joists and beams. The reason is that for each foot of length added to the beam, another foot of load is also added. (If you put a single concentrated load at the center, however, increasing the span does not increase the load; hence in this case doubling the length decreases the safe load by only one-half.)

Consequently, the greater the unsupported length or span, the greater the need for strength in the beam. The strength can be increased in two ways—by using a stronger material or by using a beam of greater width, depth, or both.

WIDTH. If the width is doubled, the strength is doubled, as is shown by many tests. This is made clearer by considering two beams, each of which will carry the same load. If they are combined, side by side, to become a beam of double width, they together will carry a double load. The load is the same whether the beam is in two pieces or one.

DEPTH. Doubling the depth of a beam much more than doubles the carrying capacity. Actually the increase is fourfold. In other words, a beam 3 inches wide and 12 inches deep will carry 4 times as much as one 3 inches wide and 6 inches deep. Therefore, as a general principle in the efficient use of material, it is better to increase the depth of a beam than the width.

On the other hand, it is well to keep down the height of horizontal material in members such as beams and joists. Too much depth in a beam, especially one placed under the joists, decreases headroom in the basement. It is desirable, therefore, to adopt any of the following courses rather than increase the beam depth to more than 10 inches or 12 inches.

- Increase the width.
- Use a stronger material. (Thoroughly dry lumber should always be used, especially if the beam is under joists.)
- Put in additional supports to reduce the beam span and permit a smaller beam.

Determining the Size of Beams

To determine the size of a beam, seven steps are necessary:

1. Find the beam length between supports.
2. Find the "half-widths."
3. Find the floor load per square foot carried by joists and bearing partitions to the beam.
4. Find the load per linear foot on the beam.
5. Find the total load on the beam.
6. Select the material for the beam.
7. Find the proper size of the beam in the material chosen.

1. LENGTH OF BEAM. Before it is possible to determine the beam size, the length of the beam between supports must be settled upon. This length will be determined by the spacing of the supporting posts. These posts must be spaced according to some suitable division of the total length of the beam between walls, with due regard to the avoidance of excessive spans. For an example of the method, see **Figure 2-2**, which is a building 35 feet wide by 31 feet 8 inches deep, with a first-floor arrangement as shown.

In such an arrangement, the partition between the living room and the dining room, with its extension between the front hall and kitchen, would probably be used as a bearing partition. The beam should be located directly or nearly under it. The total length is 33 feet 8 inches between basement walls. This can be divided into two, three, or four approximately equal parts of about 17 feet, 11 feet, or 8 feet 5 inches each, respectively.

As posts carry a relatively large part of the weight, and it is well to use short spans as a means of reducing the size of beams, it will be better in this case to use three posts, thus fixing the span at about 8 feet 5 inches center to center of posts.

Having determined the location of supports, the next step is to find out what proportion of the joist load the beam must carry. This involves the determination of what in **Table 2-1** is called the half-width. See page 91.

89

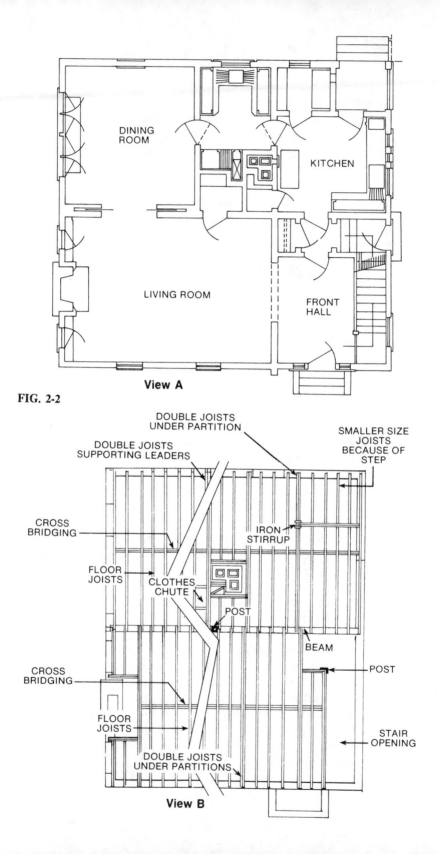

DINING ROOM

KITCHEN

LIVING ROOM

FRONT HALL

View A

FIG. 2-2

DOUBLE JOISTS UNDER PARTITION

DOUBLE JOISTS SUPPORTING LEADERS

SMALLER SIZE JOISTS BECAUSE OF STEP

CROSS BRIDGING

IRON STIRRUP

FLOOR JOISTS

CLOTHES CHUTE

POST

BEAM

CROSS BRIDGING

POST

FLOOR JOISTS

STAIR OPENING

DOUBLE JOISTS UNDER PARTITIONS

View B

TABLE 2–1:
BEAM LOADS PER LINEAR FOOT

This table gives loads per linear foot on beams for various half-widths and types of buildings, as explained earlier in this chapter. In the left-hand column are figures for various total loads per square foot. Each column is for a different half-width. The table shows the total load per linear foot on the beam, the figures being the product of the total square foot load by the half-width.

Total square-foot floor load	Total beam load per linear foot by half-widths										
	5	6	7	8	9	10	12	14	16	18	20
10	50	60	70	80	90	100	120	140	160	180	200
20	100	120	140	160	180	200	240	280	320	360	400
30	150	180	210	240	270	300	360	420	480	540	600
40	200	240	280	320	360	400	480	560	640	720	800
50	250	300	350	400	450	500	600	700	800	900	1,000
60	300	360	420	480	540	600	720	840	960	1,080	1,200
70	350	420	490	560	630	700	840	980	1,120	1,260	1,400
80	400	480	560	640	720	800	960	1,120	1,280	1,440	1,600
90	450	540	630	720	810	900	1,080	1,260	1,440	1,620	1,800
100	500	600	700	800	900	1,000	1,200	1,400	1,600	1,800	2,000
110	550	660	770	880	990	1,100	1,320	1,540	1,760	1,980	2,200
120	600	720	840	960	1,080	1,200	1,440	1,680	1,920	2,160	2,400
130	650	780	910	1,040	1,170	1,300	1,560	1,820	2,080	2,340	2,600
140	700	840	980	1,120	1,260	1,400	1,680	1,960	2,240	2,520	2,800
150	750	900	1,050	1,200	1,350	1,500	1,800	2,100	2,400	2,700	3,000
160	800	960	1,120	1,280	1,440	1,600	1,920	2,240	2,560	2,880	3,200
170	850	1,020	1,190	1,360	1,530	1,700	2,040	2,380	2,720	3,060	3,400
180	900	1,080	1,260	1,440	1,620	1,800	2,160	2,520	2,880	3,240	3,600
190	950	1,140	1,330	1,520	1,710	1,900	2,280	2,660	3,040	3,420	3,800
200	1,000	1,200	1,400	1,600	1,800	2,000	2,400	2,800	3,200	3,600	4,000
210	1,050	1,260	1,470	1,680	1,890	2,100	2,520	2,940	3,360	3,780	4,200
220	1,100	1,320	1,540	1,760	1,980	2,200	2,640	3,080	3,520	3,960	4,400

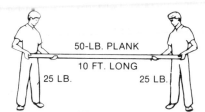

FIG. 2-3

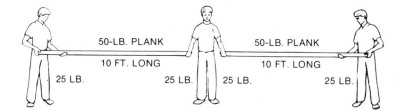

FIG. 2-4

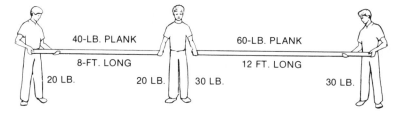

FIG. 2-5

2. HALF-WIDTHS. Consider two men carrying a plank 10 feet long, weighing 5 pounds for each foot of length, or 50 pounds in all. The two, bearing the total weight between them, would each be lifting 25 pounds (**Figure 2-3**). Then suppose one of the men holding the first plank is carrying one end of a second 10-foot plank of the same weight, and a third person is at its other end (**Figure 2-4**). You can see that the man in the center carries half the weight of both planks and that the other two men divide the balance between them. In other words, the man at the center carries half the weight of each plank and each one at the end supports half a plank. A single beam running through the center of a building and supporting the inner ends of floor joists is in a position similar to that of the center person; it will take half the weight of every joist resting upon it. Thus the beam carries half the weight of the floor. The foundation walls, supporting the outer ends of the joists, divide the other half between them.

However, support doesn't always lie halfway between the outer walls. Assume in our example that one plank is 8 feet long, and the other is 12 feet long (**Figure 2-5**), and that each weighs 5 pounds per foot. The total length of the two planks will be the same as before, or 20 feet, and the combined weight will be the same, or 100 pounds, with the 8-foot plank weighing 40 pounds and the 12-foot plank weighing 60 pounds. It should be clear that the men at the outer ends of the planks will carry half the weight of their planks, or 20 pounds for the short plank and 30 pounds for the longer. On the other hand, the man near the center will carry half the weight of each plank, or 20 pounds plus 30 pounds, a total of 50 pounds, which is the same as the previous illustration, in which the planks were of equal length. So the following general statement may be made:

A single beam running through a building, whether or not it is at the center, will carry half the weight of the load between it and the adjacent walls or beams.

This statement, modified slightly to include such conditions ordinarily met with, as two or more beams, becomes the following:

General rule for half-widths
A beam carries the weight of the load on each side to the midpoint of the joists that rest upon it.

This statement assumes that the joists are joined end to end without overlapping over the beam supporting them. Fully loaded, they tend to sag between supports, as shown in exaggerated fashion in **Figure 2-6**. Under such conditions there is little resistance to the joists' bending over the beam because they are merely butted (joined end to end), or at best lapped and spiked. Suppose, however, they were continuous. Under load they would tend to assume the shape indicated in **Figure 2-7**. Being in one piece, they would resist bending

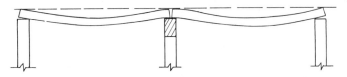

FIG. 2-6

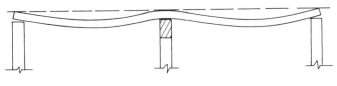

FIG. 2-7

over the center support; the beam would be able to carry a larger proportion of the load than if the joists were cut. The proportion of extra-load capability can be found through engineering formulas. But the computation involves complicated math. The results may be stated as follows:

If the beam is at the midpoint of continuous joists, it will take five-eighths instead of one-half the load.

If the beam is not located midway between end supports, determining its load is further complicated. Here, as the beam support moves toward the end support of the shorter span, the proportion of the longer-span load carried by the beam support decreases from five-eighths toward one-half. Since it is usually most economical to place the beam near the center of continuous joists, all beams supporting continuous joists should be designed to support five-eighths of the total load of adjacent spans and the five-eighths width formula rather than half-width formula applies. In other words, use the half-width formula for all cut joists and the five-eighths formula for continuous joists.

The following may be used as a working rule for half-widths. To ascertain the half-width for a beam, find the distance from the centerline of the beam to the nearest joist support on one side; this distance is generally known as the *joist span*. Add to this figure the corresponding span from the beam to the nearest beam or wall support. One-half of the total corresponds to the half-width, provided the joists are lapped or butted over the beam. If the joists are continuous, five-eighths of the total corresponds to the half-width.

To show the application of this rule, the following examples are given:

1. This is the simplest case (**Figure 2-8**). There is a single beam (heavy line) running the length of the building. The light lines running at right angles to the beam are the joists that rest upon it. The joist spans, that is, the distances to the nearest joist supports on either side of this beam, are 7 and 13 feet, a total of 20 feet. Half of this total, or 10 feet, is the half-width for this beam, if the joists are cut. If the joists are continuous, the half-width is five-eighths of 20 feet, or 12½ feet.
2. Here the problem is complicated by the presence of two beams (**Figure 2-9**). In such cases, each beam must be considered separately. Applying the rule to beam A, the joist spans on either side are 13 and 7 feet, for a total of 20 feet. If the joists are cut, the half-width for beam A is 10 feet.

   In the case of beam B, the joist spans are 7 and 11 feet, or a total of 18 feet. If the joists are cut, the half-width for beam B is 9 feet.

94

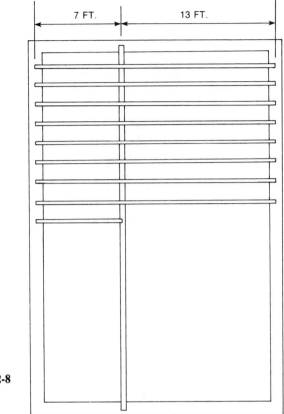

FIG. 2-8

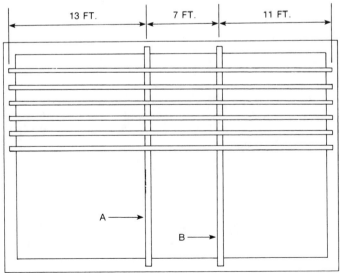

FIG. 2-9

3. TOTAL FLOOR LOAD. The method for calculating the total floor load per square foot carried by joists and bearing partitions to the beam is illustrated in **Figure 2-10**. The live loads specified also determine the size of joists. Although it may be possible that the maximum live load provided for will never be applied, consideration must be given to the possibility of crowded rooms and unusual loading situations, as when furniture is moved to the center of the room to permit painting or papering. When calculating loads for small-house framing, you will find the information here valuable.

Assume that **Figure 2-10** represents a side view of the building shown earlier in **Figure 2-2**. The beam carries the first-floor joist load.

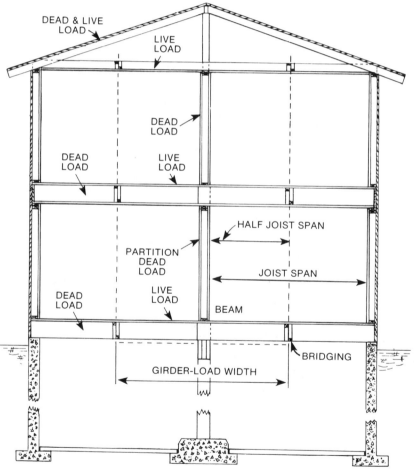

FIG. 2-10

The bearing partition above, which rests directly upon the beam, carries the second-floor joist load down to the beam. Hence, the beam carries the weight of the second floor in addition to the first. Similarly, a bearing partition on the second floor carries the second-floor ceiling, attic, and roof loads. Thus the beam must carry not only the first floor, but the second floor, attic, and roof. (In some buildings the roof is framed so that the roof loads are carried entirely by the outside walls. In that case, no allowance would be made for roof loads when calculating total floor load to be carried by the beam. For this reason a plan should be carefully studied, and framing methods analyzed, to determine just what loads are carried through the bearing partitions to the beam.)

Using the live and dead load figures given, the combined square foot floor load to be carried by the beam in **Figure 2-10** may be represented as follows:

	lb. per sq. ft.
Dead load of first floor	10
Live load on first floor	40
Dead load of first-floor partitions	10
Dead load of second floor	20
Live load on second floor	40
Dead load of second-floor partitions	10
Live load on attic floor	20
Dead load of attic floor	10
Dead and live load of light roof	20
Total	180

The minimum floor load to be allowed for the beam is 180 pounds per square foot, assuming that there is no attic flooring and that the ceiling of the basement is not plastered.

4. LOAD PER LINEAR FOOT ON THE BEAM. To arrive at the load per linear foot of beam, the total live and dead load per square foot is multiplied by the half-width.

For a half-width of 15 feet and a total square-foot floor load of 180 pounds, the load on the beam would be 2,700 pounds per foot of length.

Table 2-1 provides beam load figures only for beams of even lengths such as 12, 14, and 16 feet. To arrive at the load for an odd length,

97

such as 15 feet in the example, add half the difference of beam loads for 14- and 16-foot half-widths to the 14-foot figure:

$$2,880 - 2,520 = 360 \times \frac{1}{2} = 180$$

$$2,520 + 180 = 2,700$$

In this case, the load represents the combined weights of imaginary strips of the first, second, and attic floors measured 1 foot long along the beam and 15 feet across it, carried by each foot of the beam.

5. TOTAL LOAD ON THE BEAMS. If the load upon a beam is 2,700 pounds for each foot of length, the total load the beam must carry is the pounds per square foot multiplied by the distance in feet between beam supports. The total load per foot (in this case, 2,700 pounds) multiplied by the length of the beam, or 8 feet 5 inches if the posts are equidistant, is approximately 22,750 pounds. This is the total load that the beam must carry. Since this load does not occur at any one point, but is, for all practical purposes, spread equally over the whole length, it is what is termed a uniformly distributed load.

6. MATERIAL FOR THE BEAM. At this point we must decide whether the beam is to be of wood or steel. If the beam is to be wood, then species is a consideration. Also we must decide whether to use a built-up or a solid member.

Table 2-2 shows a list of various softwoods used in building construction, with allowable unit working stresses for each species and grade. (A stress is the internal resistance that balances an external force applied to a member. A unit stress is the force per unit of area.) The species mentioned in the list are manufactured in several structural grades, as shown. Manufacturers have assigned working stresses to all of these grades.

Under the heading "Extreme fiber in bending" are measurements of a beam's resistance to sagging. The first column gives working stresses in bending for joists up to 4 inches in thickness. The second column shows stresses for timbers 5 inches and over in thickness. After choosing the species to be used, pick out the corresponding bending stress.

Table 2-3 gives the total safe loads for different solid-wood girder sizes and spans, with working stresses of 1,200 pounds per square inch. Where beams larger than those shown in the table are needed, it's wise to consult a civil engineer or architect. When the depth of the beam is greater than one-twelfth of the span, the assumption is that loads will be limited by horizontal shear strength instead of bending strength.

TABLE 2-2:
ALLOWABLE UNIT STRESSES FOR STRUCTURAL LUMBER AND TIMBER

(All Sizes, Dry Locations)

Species of timber	Grade	Allowable unit stress (lb./in.^{2})	
		Extreme fiber in bending	
		Joist and planks 4 in. and less thick	Beams 5 in. and thicker
Douglas fir, West Coast	Dense superstructural	2,000	2,000
	Superstructural and dense structural	1,800	1,800
	Structural	1,600	1,600
	Common structural	1,200	1,400
Douglas fir, inland empire	Dense superstructural*	2,000	2,000
	Dense structural*	1,800	1,800
Larch, western	No. 1 common dimension and timbers	1,135	1,135
	No. 1 common dimension and timbers	1,135	1,135
Pine, southern yellow	Extra dense select structural	2,300	2,300
	Select structural	2,000	2,000
	Extra dense heart	2,000	2,000
	Dense heart	1,800	1,800
	Structural square edge and sound	1,600	1,600
	Dense No. 1 common	1,200	1,200
Redwood	Superstructural	2,133	1,707
	Prime structural	1,707	1,494
	Select structural	1,280	1,322
	Heart structural	1,024	1,150

*When graded the same as corresponding grade of coast region Douglas fir.

TABLE 2-3:
SOLID WOOD BEAMS AND GIRDERS. ALLOWABLE FIBER STRESS 1,200

Solid dressed sizes	Span (ft.)														
	4, 5, 6	7	8	9	10	11	12	13	14	15	16	17	18	19	20
2 × 6	1,127	961	837	738	660	595	541	494	454	419	388	360	335	312	292
3 × 6	1,820	1,552	1,351	1,192	1,065	960	872	796	731	675	625	580	539	502	469
4 × 6	2,514	2,144	1,866	1,647	1,471	1,327	1,206	1,102	1,012	933	864	802	747	697	650
6 × 6	3,650	3,111	2,708	2,389	2,134	1,924	1,747	1,597	1,467	1,352	1,252	1,161	1,081	1,007	941
2 × 8	1,605	1,605	1,503	1,331	1,191	1,075	980	898	827	766	712	662	619	580	544
3 × 8	2,580	2,580	2,414	2,135	1,911	1,726	1,572	1,439	1,325	1,225	1,139	1,060	990	927	870
4 × 8	3,570	3,570	3,340	2,953	2,643	2,388	2,175	1,993	1,836	1,700	1,590	1,472	1,375	1,288	1,210
6 × 8	5,420	5,420	5,064	4,481	4,011	3,625	3,300	3,025	2,786	2,579	2,396	2,232	2,086	1,953	1,834
8 × 8	7,390	7,390	6,905	6,110	5,464	4,941	4,500	4,125	3,799	3,516	3,265	3,043	2,845	2,664	2,500
2 × 10	2,020	2,020	2,020	2,020	1,912	1,730	1,578	1,449	1,336	1,238	1,153	1,077	1,009	946	891
3 × 10	3,255	3,255	3,255	3,255	3,088	2,792	2,546	2,336	2,152	1,997	1,859	1,735	1,624	1,525	1,435
4 × 10	4,500	4,500	4,500	4,500	4,267	3,864	3,520	3,230	2,981	2,763	2,572	2,402	2,249	2,113	1,988
6 × 10	6,830	6,830	6,830	6,830	6,473	5,860	5,341	4,902	4,524	4,193	3,904	3,647	3,416	3,206	3,020
8 × 10	9,320	9,320	9,320	9,320	8,827	7,980	7,284	6,685	6,179	5,719	5,324	4,972	4,657	4,374	4,116
10 × 10	11,795	11,795	11,795	11,795	11,181	10,110	9,226	8,468	7,815	7,245	6,744	6,299	5,900	5,540	5,215
2 × 12	2,435	2,435	2,435	2,435	2,435	2,435	2,328	2,136	1,973	1,832	1,708	1,597	1,497	1,410	1,328
3 × 12	3,920	3,920	3,920	3,920	3,920	3,920	3,754	3,446	3,183	2,953	2,752	2,572	2,413	2,269	2,138
4 × 12	5,430	5,430	5,430	5,430	5,430	5,430	5,191	4,766	4,393	4,087	3,809	3,553	3,341	3,143	2,964
6 × 12	8,250	8,250	8,250	8,250	8,250	8,250	7,870	7,232	6,682	6,202	5,781	5,407	5,072	4,770	4,499
8 × 12	11,240	11,240	11,240	11,240	11,240	11,240	10,733	9,862	9,111	8,456	7,783	7,374	6,916	6,506	6,134
10 × 12	14,250	14,250	14,250	14,250	14,250	14,250	13,597	12,491	11,541	10,711	9,985	9,338	8,760	8,240	7,769
12 × 12	17,240	17,240	17,240	17,240	17,240	17,240	16,460	15,121	13,960	12,967	12,086	11,304	10,605	9,974	9,404
2 × 14	3,065	3,065	3,065	3,065	3,065	3,065	3,065	3,065	2,729	2,534	2,366	2,212	2,076	1,954	1,845
3 × 14	4,600	4,600	4,600	4,600	4,600	4,600	4,600	4,600	4,412	4,097	3,825	3,577	3,358	3,161	2,984
4 × 14	6,340	6,340	6,340	6,340	6,340	6,340	6,340	6,340	6,102	5,668	5,288	4,950	4,648	4,377	4,132
6 × 14	9,630	9,630	9,630	9,630	9,630	9,630	9,630	9,630	9,258	8,601	8,020	7,511	7,054	6,642	6,270
8 × 14	13,140	13,140	13,140	13,140	13,140	13,140	13,140	13,140	12,628	11,730	10,942	10,244	9,619	9,058	8,552
10 × 14	16,640	16,640	16,640	16,640	16,640	16,640	16,640	16,640	16,002	14,854	13,860	12,975	12,183	11,472	10,830
12 × 14	20,140	20,140	20,140	20,140	20,140	20,140	20,140	20,140	19,167	17,982	16,780	15,706	14,748	13,887	13,110
14 × 14	23,640	23,640	23,640	23,640	23,640	23,640	23,640	23,640	22,742	21,120	19,690	18,440	17,310	16,370	15,388

For built-up girders multiply above figures by 0.897 when 4-in. girder is made up of two 2-in. pieces.
0.887 when 6-in. girder is made up of three 2-in. pieces.
0.867 when 8-in. girder is made up of four 2-in. pieces.
0.856 when 10-in. girder is made up of five 2-in. pieces.

Built-up girders of dressed lumber will carry somewhat smaller loads than solid girders, that is, two 2-in. dressed planks will equal only 3 ¼ in., whereas dressed 4-in. lumber will equal 3 ⅝ in. It is, therefore, necessary to multiply by the above figures in order to compute the loads for built-up girders.

For example, if No. 1 common southern yellow pine is to be used, the value given under "Extreme fiber in bending" is 1,200 pounds per square inch. Hence, use **Table 2-3**, which is based on 1,200 pounds per square inch. Similarly, if a structural grade of Douglas fir is to be used with a bending stress of 1,800 pounds per square inch, a table like **Table 2-3** but based on 1,600 pounds per square inch should be used.

7. SIZE OF WOOD BEAM. If you know the total load on the beam, the span, and the strength of allowable working stress of the lumber to be used, it is possible by engineering formulas to compute the necessary size of the beam. Alternately, tables can show the maximum allowable loads on beams of different sizes for various spans. The size needed will naturally vary with the species and grade used. The beam may be one solid timber or built up of several pieces spiked together. If you use a built-up beam, you must take care to use the percentage figures applying to built-up beams, which allow for the lesser thickness of dressed material. A built-up beam is as satisfactory as a solid one. In fact, a built-up beam may be better, since it affords an opportunity to select and arrange the material for the best possible results.

Table 2-3 shows a zigzag line starting at the top left and ending at the bottom right. Loads represented by figures given on the right of this line cause bending (usually downward) in timbers of indicated size and span greater than $\frac{1}{360}$ of the span. This is the limit usually set for deflection of beams and joists, lest wall cracks, sticking doors, and other difficulties occur. Loads represented to the left of the line do not cause serious deflection.

In most cases the lumber used for framing floors is southern yellow pine or Douglas fir. The zigzag line applies only to grades of these two species, even though the working stresses for lower grades are less than those given at the top of the table. When other species of lower strength (working stress) are used, the larger sizes of timbers required will usually give a stiffer beam or joist. The joist and beam table show that it is usually possible to use either of two timbers, one of which is 2 inches deeper than the other. For example, **Table 2-3** shows that either a 10-by-10 or an 8-by-12 will safely support a load of 10,000 pounds over an 11-foot span. The deeper size is nearly always preferable. In this example the 8-by-12 is both stronger and stiffer.

If, in the house depicted in **Figure 2-2**, a No. 1 common grade of southern yellow pine is to be used, refer to **Table 2-3**. There you'll see that for a span of 8 feet 5 inches a solid beam of dressed material 14 by 14 inches will carry 23,640 pounds, or more than the 22,750-pound load to be carried on this beam (as we computed earlier in paragraph 5, "Total load on the beams"). Although this beam is large for small-house work, it is nevertheless required to carry safely the loads expected.

The house plans in **Figure 2-2** show on both sides of the beam a wide span that approaches the usual maximum total of half-widths. If wood beams are used, it would probably be advisable either to put in extra posts to reduce the beam span to about 5 feet, thus reducing the load to 13,500 pounds, for which a 10-by-14-inch timber of No. 1 common southern pine would suffice, or to use a high-grade dense structural timber, for which much higher stresses are allowable. Closer spacing of columns would materially reduce the load on columns and improve the arrangement.

Columns/Posts

A bearing post or column is a vertical member designed to carry a superimposed vertical load. A foundation supports it either directly or indirectly. In light-frame construction the post or column in the basement supports the beam. As pointed out above, a supporting post or column in a house that is approximately square and large enough to require a beam, supported at the center, may carry one-fourth of the entire weight of the building. Therefore, the utmost care should be exercised in deciding upon the size, type, and material of the column and in ensuring that the column is properly seated on an adequate foundation.

Again, great distances between posts should be avoided both to avoid heavy concentration of weight on one footing, and to avoid the use of very large beams.

In general, it is wise to limit spans to between 8 and 10 feet. For spans over 12 feet in a two-story house, the beams required must be deep and consequently they will also reduce basement headroom, will be heavier and harder to handle, will naturally increase the cost, and will concentrate heavy loads on post footings. If in addition to long beam spans the joist spans are also long, the disadvantages are even more noticeable.

Columns/Posts

Before we discuss the determination of column/post size, let's consider the function a post serves. For this purpose, consider a 2 × 6-inch post about 2 feet long securely fastened in an upright position. You would not hesitate to rest your whole weight upon it. Suppose, however, it projected 20 feet above its support. You would now be reluctant to put any weight upon it. Were it any thinner, it might not stand up under its own weight. The first post is rigid because it is short; the other one bends because it is too long in proportion to its sectional area. Bending occurs most readily across the narrowest dimension.

Tests show that the smaller dimension in any relatively long post is the principal factor limiting its capacity for support. Tests further show that if a wood column is more than 50 times as long as its smallest dimension, it is quite unsafe. Thus a dressed 2-by-6 or 2-by-4 longer than about 7 feet is unsafe as a post, unless it is braced sideways. For this reason, all strength tables for columns show decreased bearing capacity with increase in length.

Determining the Size of Columns/Posts

The first step in determining the size of a column is to find the load it must carry. Since a column in a normal dwelling supports a beam, it must carry the weight brought to it by the beam. The general rule giving the proportion of the joist load carried by the beam may be reworded slightly and used to show the proportion of the beam load supported by a column:

As a general rule, a post carries the load on the beam to the midpoint of the beam span on both sides.

In computing post loads, the following procedure should be carried out:

1. Find the span in feet from the center of the post to the nearest beam support on one side.
2. Multiply this span in feet by the beam load per linear foot, using the method suggested in computing the beam size for this span.
3. Find the span in feet from the center of the post to the nearest beam support on the other side.
4. Multiply this span by the beam load per linear foot.
5. Find the load on the post by considering which type of construction is used. For this purpose, consider the following examples, which illustrate the types of construction commonly encountered.

EXAMPLE 1: Here the beam is cut over the post in question and over the two nearest supports (**Figure 2-11**). In this instance, post B takes one-half the total beam load on each side, so that the load on the post is one-half the beam weight itself and one-half the load carried by each length of beam.

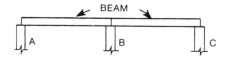

FIG. 2-11

103

EXAMPLE 2: The beam is continuous over the post in question but cut over the support on each nearest support (**Figure 2-12**). In this instance, post B carries approximately five-eighths of the load on the beam from A to C.

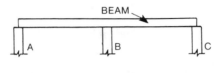

FIG. 2-12

EXAMPLE 3: **Figure 2-13** shows a continuous beam with two equidistant intermediate supports. Remember that when more than one post is used, each post must be considered separately. Although not exact in all cases, the following rules are reliable enough for this type of construction. Post B can be assumed to take five-eighths of the beam load from A to B and one-half the beam load from B to C. In a similar manner post C may be considered to take five-eighths of the beam load from C to D and one-half of the beam load from C to B.

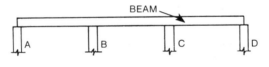

FIG. 2-13

EXAMPLE 4: In **Figure 2-14** a single beam is supported at five points. The three center posts are equidistant and divide the beam into four equal parts. As mentioned earlier, we must consider each post separately and note whether the beam is cut or continuous over the post in question. We must also consider whether the beam is cut or continuous over the nearest supports on both sides of the post in question.

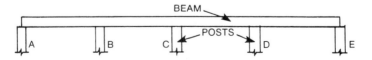

FIG. 2-14

104

Post C will carry one-half of the load between C and B and C and D. Post B will carry one-half the load between B and C and five-eighths of the load between B and A. In a similar manner post D will carry one-half the beam load between D and C and five-eighths of the beam load between D and E.

Having determined the load on each post, we find the size required, which depends on the material and type selected.

Other things being equal, round steel-pipe posts or square timber posts are preferred over other shapes, because they give equal strength in two directions and provide greater strength for the same area than any other cross-sectional shape. In order to determine the size of timber post required, refer to **Tables 2-4** and **2-5**. To determine the size of steel-pipe post required, refer to **Table 2-6.** See pages 106–108.

For example, determine the size required for a basement post 6 feet 6 inches high for a house 17 feet wide with a load on the beam of 2,700 pounds per linear foot and a single center post.

You will recall (Example 1) that where the beam is cut over the center post the post will carry one-half of the total beam load. If the beam span is 8 feet 5 inches on either side of the post, the total load on the post will consequently be approximately 22,750 pounds.

The following sizes and materials will be adequate **(Tables 2-3 to 2-5)**.

- *No. 1 common Douglas fir* (West Coast), 6-by-6, dressed size, will carry 29,300 pounds.
- *No. 2 common eastern hemlock,* 6-by-8, dressed size, will carry 22,700 pounds.
- *Steel-pipe,* 7 feet long and 3 inches in diameter, will carry 26,300 pounds.

Any of the foregoing could be used for this building. Which would be best depends upon availability and cost.

From this you might mistakenly conclude that a timber column smaller than 4 by 6 inches or 5 by 5 would be satisfactory for a small house. However, no post smaller than 4 by 6 inches, and preferably 6 by 6 inches, should be used in a basement because of the possibility of damage from a severe blow.

Joists

Joists are those members which actually carry the floors and ceilings between supports. The principles governing size of joists are the same as those for beams. The first consideration, of course, is that there be ample strength.

TABLE 2-4:
MAXIMUM LOAD ALLOWANCE IN POUNDS FOR LUMBER COLUMNS OF DOUGLAS FIR, SOUTHERN PINE, AND NORTH CAROLINA PINE, NO. 1 COMMON GRADE

Nominal size (in.)	3 × 4	4 × 4	4 × 6	6 × 6	6 × 8	8 × 8
Actual size (in.)	2 ⅝ × 3 ⅝	3 ⅝ × 3 ⅝	3 ⅝ × 5 ⅝	5 ½ × 5 ½	5 ½ × 7 ½	7 ½ × 7 ½
Area (in.²)	9.51	13.14	20.39	30.25	41.25	56.25
Height of column (ft.)						
4	8,720	12,920	19,850	30,250	41,250	56,250
5	7,430	12,400	19,200	30,050	41,000	56,250
6	5,630	11,600	17,950	29,500	40,260	56,250
6 ½	4,750	10,880	16,850	29,300	39,950	56,000
7	4,130	10,040	15,550	29,000	39,600	55,650
7 ½		9,300	14,400	28,800	39,000	55,300
8		8,350	12,950	28,150	38,300	55,000
9		6,500	10,100	26,850	36,600	54,340
10				24,670	33,600	53,400
11				22,280	30,380	52,100
12				19,630	26,800	50,400
13				16,920	23,070	47,850
14				14,360	19,580	44,700

TABLE 2-5:
MAXIMUM LOAD ALLOWANCE IN POUNDS FOR LUMBER COLUMNS OF EASTERN HEMLOCK, WESTERN RED CEDAR, WHITE FIR, WHITE PINES, AND SPRUCES, NO. 1 COMMON GRADE

Nominal size (in.)	3 × 4	4 × 4	4 × 6	6 × 6	6 × 8	8 × 8
Actual size (in.)	2 ⅝ × 3 ⅝	3 ⅝ × 3 ⅝	3 ⅝ × 5 ⅝	5 ½ × 5 ½	5 ½ × 7 ½	7 ½ × 7 ½
Area (in.²)	9.51	13.14	20.39	30.25	41.25	56.25
Height of column (ft.)						
4	4,950	7,280	11,300	16,940	23,100	31,500
5	4,380	7,100	11,000	16,900	23,060	31,500
6	3,460	6,650	10,300	16,700	22,850	31,500
6 ½	2,960	6,320	9,800	16,600	22,700	31,400
7		5,960	9,270	16,400	22,400	31,300
7 ½		5,630	8,720	16,200	22,100	31,100
8		5,160	7,930	15,950	21,800	31,000
9		4,060	6,300	15,350	20,950	30,640
10				14,400	19,600	30,240
11				13,350	18,200	29,650
12				12,200	16,600	28,800
13				10,500	14,350	27,700
14				8,950	12,200	26,300

TABLE 2-6:
STEEL-PIPE COLUMNS. STANDARD PIPE SAFE LOADS IN THOUSANDS OF POUNDS

Nominal size (in.)	6	5	4 ½	4	3 ½	3	2 ½	2	1 ½
External diameter (in.)	6.625	5.563	5.000	4.500	4.000	3.500	2.875	2.375	1.900
Thickness (in.)	0.280	0.258	0.247	0.237	0.226	0.216	0.203	0.154	0.145
Effective length (ft.)									
5	72.5	55.9	48.0	41.2	34.8	29.0	21.6	12.2	7.5
6	72.5	55.9	48.0	41.2	34.8	28.6	19.4	10.6	6.0
7	72.5	55.9	48.0	41.2	34.1	26.3	17.3	9.0	5.0
8	72.5	55.9	48.0	40.1	31.7	24.0	15.1	7.4	4.2
9	72.5	55.9	46.4	37.6	29.3	21.7	12.9	6.6	3.5
10	72.5	54.2	43.8	35.1	26.9	19.4	11.4	5.8	2.7
11	72.5	51.5	41.2	32.6	24.5	17.1	10.3	5.0	
12	70.2	48.7	38.5	30.0	22.1	15.2	9.2	4.1	
13	67.3	46.0	35.9	27.5	19.7	14.0	8.1	3.3	
14	64.3	43.2	33.3	25.0	18.0	12.9	7.0		
Area (in.^{2})	5.58	4.30	3.69	3.17	2.68	2.23	1.70	1.08	0.80
Weight (lb./ft.)	18.97	14.62	12.54	10.79	9.11	7.58	5.79	3.65	2.72

Allowable fiber stress per square inch: 13,000 lb. for lengths of 60 radii or under, reduced for length over 60 radii.

Many times, however, a joist that is strong enough may still permit a noticeable bending or vibration from walking. This not only is annoying but also may be sufficient to crack the ceiling below. Stiffness, therefore, is also a consideration. In **Table 2-7** the recommended joist sizes are adequate to carry the loads and are also designed to give sufficient stiffness to prevent vibration harmful to plaster. **Table 2-8** gives joist sizes suitable for light-frame structures in which jarring can be permitted. In order to use the tables, you need only to know the anticipated live load, span, spacing between centers of joists required, whether or not the ceiling is to be plastered, and the unit fiber-bending stress for the species and grades of wood to be used.

EXAMPLE 1: The live load in a certain house is 40 pounds per square foot. The joist span on both floors is 15 feet, spaced 16 inches on center. For common structural West Coast Douglas fir with a fiber stress of 1,200 pounds to the square inch, use **Table 2-7** to determine the size. By following to the right on the line of 40 pounds and using the 16-inch spacing, you will find that 15 feet 3 inches is the maximum permissible span for 2-by-10 joists. Therefore, the correct size joist for both the first and second floors of this house will be common structural West Coast Douglas fir, 2 by 10 inches.

EXAMPLE 2: To determine the size of the attic joists for the same house, if common structural Douglas fir (West Coast) is used, consult **Table 2-7** again. The live load will be 20 pounds per square foot. For 16-inch spacing, a 2-by-10-inch joist will provide a maximum span of 17 feet 6 inches. A 2-by-8-inch joist would not be suitable for spans over 13 feet 11 inches.

Note that the tables do not cover each and every species and grade of lumber that you may encounter. However, they do represent the more common species and grades. Should you need information on other species and grades, consult the appropriate references in a public library.

Floor joists are generally doubled under a wall partition that runs parallel to the joists and at headers around stairwells and other openings in the floor. Take these steps to find the number of joists:

1. Take three-quarters of the floor length perpendicular to the joists and add one joist.
2. Add one joist for each partition parallel to the joists and one for each header.

TABLE 2-7:
MAXIMUM SPANS FOR JOISTS (UNIFORMLY LOADED) WITH PLASTERED CEILINGS BELOW. FIBER STRESS: 1,200 Pounds per Square Inch

Live load (lb./ft.²)	Spacing (in. center to center)	Joist 2 in. ×					Joist 3 in. ×				
		6	8	10	12	14	6	8	10	12	14
10	12	12-9	16-9	21-1	24-0		14-7	19-3	24-0		
	16	11-8	15-4	19-4	23-4	24-0	13-6	17-9	22-2	24-0	
	24	10-3	14-6	17-3	20-7	24-0	11-11	15-9	19-10	23-9	24-0
20	12	11-6	15-3	19-2	23-0	24-0	13-3	17-6	21-9	24-0	
	16	10-5	13-11	17-6	21-1	24-0	12-0	16-1	20-2	24-0	
	24	9-2	12-3	15-6	18-7	21-9	10-6	14-2	17-10	21-6	24-0
30	12	10-8	14-0	17-9	21-4	24-9	12-4	16-4	20-5	24-5	
	16	9-9	12-11	16-3	19-6	22-9	11-4	14-11	18-9	22-7	26-4
	24	8-6	11-4	14-4	17-3	20-2	10-0	13-2	16-8	19-11	23-4
40	12	10-0	13-3	16-8	20-1	23-5	11-8	15-4	19-3	23-1	26-11
	16	9-1	12-1	15-3	18-5	21-5	10-8	14-0	17-8	21-3	24-10
	24	7-10	10-4	13-1	15-9	18-5	9-4	12-4	15-7	18-9	22-1
50	12	9-6	12-7	15-10	19-1	22-4	11-0	14-7	18-4	22-0	25-8
	16	8-7	11-6	14-7	17-6	20-5	10-0	13-4	16-10	20-3	23-8
	24	7-3	9-6	12-1	14-7	17-0	8-10	11-9	14-10	17-10	20-10
60	12	9-0	12-0	15-2	18-3	21-4	10-6	14-0	17-7	21-1	24-7
	16	8-1	10-10	13-8	16-6	19-3	9-7	12-10	16-1	19-4	22-7
	24	6-8	8-11	11-3	13-7	15-11	8-5	11-5	14-1	17-0	20-0
70	12	8-7	11-6	14-6	17-6	20-6	10-1	13-5	16-11	20-5	23-9
	16	7-8	10-2	12-10	15-6	18-3	9-3	12-3	15-5	18-7	21-10
	24	6-5	8-5	10-7	12-9	15-0	8-0	10-7	13-4	16-1	18-10

TABLE 2-8:
MAXIMUM SPANS FOR JOISTS (UNIFORMLY LOADED) WITH NO PLASTERED CEILINGS BELOW. FIBER STRESS: 1,200 Pounds per Square Inch

Live load (lb./ft.²)	Spacing (in. center to center)	Joist 2 in. ×					Joist 3 in. ×				
		6	8	10	12	14	6	8	10	12	14
30	12	13–5	17–8	22–2	24–0		16–8	21–10	24–0		
	16	11–9	15–6	19–5	23–3	24–0	14–7	19–3	24–0		
	24	9–8	12–10	16–2	19–5	22–6	12–1	16–0	20–1	24–0	
40	12	12–0	15–11	19–11	23–11		15–0	19–8	24–0		
	16	10–6	13–11	17–4	20–11	21–0	13–1	17–4	21–8	24–0	
	24	8–7	11–5	14–5	17–5	20–3	10–10	14–4	18–0	21–8	24–0
50	12	10–11	14–5	18–2	21–11	24–0	13–8	18–0	22–6	24–0	
	16	9–6	12–7	15–10	19–1	22–3	11–11	15–9	19–9	23–9	24–0
	24	7–10	10–4	13–1	15–9	18–5	9–9	13–0	16–5	19–9	23–0
60	12	10–0	13–4	16–10	20–2	23–6	12–7	16–8	20–11	24–0	24–0
	16	8–9	11–8	14–8	17–8	20–7	11–0	14–6	18–4	22–0	21–4
	24	7–3	9–6	12–1	14–7	17–0	9–0	12–0	15–2	18–3	24–0
70	12	9–5	12–5	15–8	18–11	22–0	11–10	15–7	19–7	23–6	24–0
	16	8–1	10–10	13–8	16–6	19–3	10–4	13–7	17–1	20–7	19–11
	24	6–8	8–11	11–3	13–7	15–11	8–5	11–3	14–1	17–1	24–0
80	12	8–9	11–8	14–9	17–9	20–10	11–1	14–9	18–6	22–3	24–0
	16	7–8	10–2	12–10	15–6	18–3	9–9	12–10	16–3	19–6	22–9
	24	6–5	8–5	10–7	12–9	15–0	8–0	10–7	13–4	16–1	18–10

For example, a building with a floor 16½ feet wide and 48 feet long is to have joists spaced 16 inches on center spanning the width. How many joists will be required, if there are 7 points at which they must be doubled up?

$$\text{joists required} = \text{length in feet} \times \tfrac{3}{4} + 1 + \text{no. of doublings}$$

$$\text{joists required} = 48 \times \tfrac{3}{4} + 1 + 7 = 36 + 1 + 7 = 44$$

In your figuring, allow 5 percent for waste. In the above case, you would most likely have to order joists that were 18 feet long and cut them to length.

Bridging

When joists are used over a long span, they have a tendency to sway and deflect from side to side. Bridging is used to stiffen the floor frame, to prevent unequal deflection of the joists, and to enable an overloaded joist to receive some upward support from the joists on either side.

Bridging is of two types **(Figure 2-15)**: horizontal (or solid) bridging, and cross bridging, composed of diagonal braces. Cross bridging is the one most generally used; it is very effective and requires less material and labor than horizontal bridging. If the joists have a span of more than 10 feet, at least one row of bridging should be used. For spans greater than 14 or 16 feet, two rows of bridging are necessary, since they should be spaced 5 to 8 feet apart. For joists on 16-inch centers, bridging can be figured as 18-inch lengths of 1-by-4 lumber. Allow 5 percent for waste.

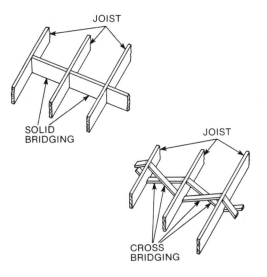

FIG. 2-15

112

Subfloors

Subflooring is used over the floor joists to form a working platform and base for finish flooring. It usually consists of (1) square-edge or tongue-and-groove boards no wider than 8 inches and not less than $\frac{3}{4}$ inch thick or (2) plywood $\frac{1}{2}$ to $\frac{3}{4}$ inch thick, depending on species, type of finish floor, and spacing of joists.

Boards

Subflooring may be applied either diagonally (most common) or at right angles to the joists, using 1-by-6-inch or 1-by-8-inch boards. When subflooring is placed at right angles to the joists, the finish floor should be laid at right angles to the subflooring. Diagonal subflooring permits finish flooring to be laid either parallel or at right angles (most common) to the joists. End joints of the boards should always be made directly over the joists. Subfloor is nailed to each joist with two 8d nails for widths under 8 inches and three 8d nails for 8-inch widths.

To determine the amount of subflooring needed to cover a given space, first find the area (length $\times$ width). Since most board subflooring is 1-inch lumber, the result is the number of board feet of subflooring needed. To this figure, however, add 15 percent for waste if the subfloor is laid at right angles to the joists, and 20 percent if it is laid diagonally. Of course, where there are bay windows or other projections, allow for additional subflooring.

Plywood

Plywood can serve as combined plywood subfloor and underlayment, eliminating separate underlayment because the plywood functions as both structural subfloor and as a good substrate. The spacing and thickness should be as follows:

1. For species such as Douglas fir (West Coast) and southern pine: $\frac{1}{2}$ inch minimum thickness for 16-inch joist spacing, $\frac{5}{8}$ inch for 20-inch joist spacing, and $\frac{3}{4}$ inch for 24-inch joist spacing.
2. For species such as western hemlock, western white pine, and ponderosa pine: $\frac{5}{8}$ inch minimum thickness for 16-inch joist spacing, $\frac{3}{4}$ inch for 20-inch joist spacing, and $\frac{7}{8}$ inch for 24-inch joist spacing.

Plywood should be installed with the grain direction of the outer plies at right angles to the joists and should be staggered so that end joints in adjacent panels break over different joists. Plywood should be nailed to the joist at each bearing with 8d common or 7d threaded nails for plywood $\frac{1}{2}$ to $\frac{3}{4}$ inch thick. Space nails 6 inches apart along all edges and 10 inches apart along intermediate members. When plywood serves as both subfloor and underlayment, nails may be spaced 6 to 7 inches apart at all joists and blocking.

WALL FRAMING

Wall platform framing (**Figure 2-16**) is composed of regular studs, diagonal bracing, trimmers, headers, and fire blocks and is supported by the floor soleplate. The vertical members of the wall framing are the studs, which support the top plates and all of the weight of the upper part of the building,

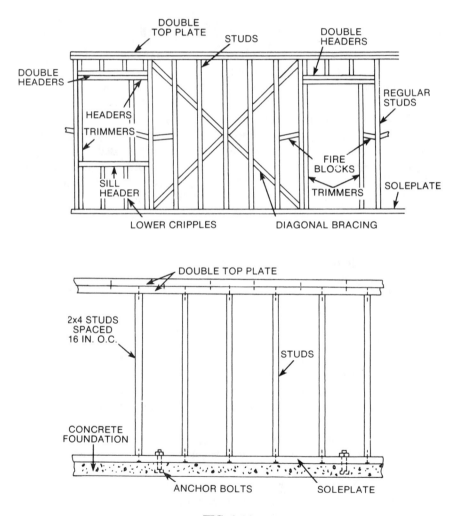

FIG. 2-16

that is, everything above the top plate line. They provide the framework to which the wall sheathing is nailed on the outside and which supports the wall covering and insulation on the inside.

The top plate of wall platform framing serves two purposes. It ties the studding together at the top and forms a finish for the walls. Also, it supports the lower ends of the rafters, which hold up the roof. The top plate connects the wall and the roof, just as the sills and girders connect the floors and the walls. The plate is made up of one or two pieces of lumber the same size as the studs. (The studs at the ends of some buildings extend to the rafters, and no plate is used.) When the top plate is used on top of partition walls, it is sometimes called the cap. Where the plate is doubled, the first plate, or bottom section, is nailed with 16d or 20d nails to the top of the corner posts and to the studs; the connection at the corner is made as shown in **Figure 2-17**. After the single plate is nailed securely and the corner braces are nailed into place, the top part of the plate is then nailed to the bottom section by means of 16d or 20d nails either over each stud, or spaced with two nails every 2 feet. The edges of the top section should be flush with the bottom section, and the corner joints should be lapped as shown in **Figure 2-17.**

All partition walls and outside walls rise from the soleplate, which is usually 2-by-4-inch lumber. This member, laid flat on the floor joists, carries the bottom end of the studs. The soleplate should be nailed with two 16d or 20d nails at each joist that it crosses. If it is laid lengthwise on top of a beam or joist, it should be nailed with two nails every 2 feet.

The wall-framing members used in conventional platform framing construc-

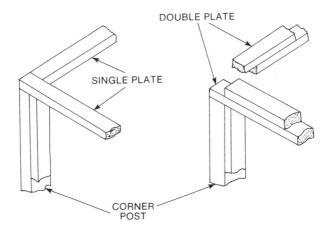

FIG. 2-17

115

tion are generally nominal 2-by-4-inch studs spaced 16 inches on center. Depending on the thickness of the covering material, 24-inch spacing might be used. Top plates and soleplates are also nominal 2 by 4 inches in size. Headers over doors or windows in load-bearing walls consist of doubled 2-by-6-inch and deeper members, depending on the span of the opening.

Partitions

Partition walls divide the inside space of a building. These walls in most cases are framed at the same time exterior walls are. In cases where floors are to be installed after the outside of the building is completed, the partition walls are left unframed. There are two types of partition walls: bearing and nonbearing. Bearing walls support ceiling joists; nonbearing walls, supporting only themselves, can be put in at any time after the other framework is installed. Only one cap or plate is used. A soleplate should be used in every case, to distribute the load over a larger area.

Window and Door Framing

The members used to span over window and door openings are called *headers,* or *lintels.* In exterior walls and load-bearing partitions, headers are supported at the ends by the inner studs, called trimmers, that often are joined to studs.

On load-bearing partitions the header should be doubled, even over narrow openings, especially if a short stud occurs near the header center **(Figures 2-18**

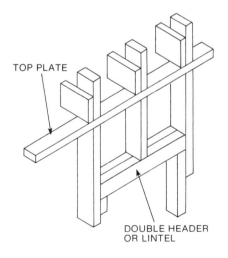

TOP PLATE

DOUBLE HEADER
OR LINTEL

FIG. 2-18

116

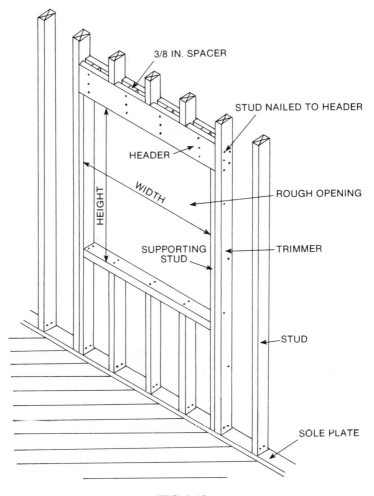

3/8 IN. SPACER

STUD NAILED TO HEADER

HEADER

WIDTH

HEIGHT

ROUGH OPENING

SUPPORTING STUD

TRIMMER

STUD

SOLE PLATE

FIG. 2-19

and **2-19**). The header should rest on the studs and trimmers as shown. If the 2-by-4s placed over the opening are placed one above the other, they should be thoroughly spiked together in order to support the load. If they are placed side by side, spiking will not be quite as important, since each piece will offer greater resistance to bending than when laid flat. Note that the two 2-by-4s laid on edge will together measure only 3 inches instead of $3\frac{1}{2}$ inches when laid flat. Consequently, it will be necessary to insert small pieces of lath between the 2-by-4s in order to make the header line up with the studs.

If the opening is more than 3 feet in width, the header will need additional strength to carry the weight imposed upon it from above. To gain additional

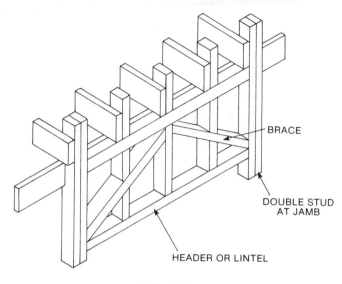

BRACE

DOUBLE STUD
AT JAMB

HEADER OR LINTEL

FIG. 2-20

strength, use material of greater depth or cross section than 2-by-4s. For openings ranging from 3 to 6 feet, use 2-by-4s to form a truss. A truss over an opening in light-frame construction is in general a triangular arrangement of 2-by-4s forming a rigid framework for the support of weight above (**Figure 2-20**). Theoretically the only stresses placed on a truss are compression and tension.

For distances over 6 feet, or where unusually heavy weights must be supported, use a beam. You can use the discussion and tables on beams and columns earlier in this chapter to determine sizes and materials.

In normal light-frame construction, two headers of wood species normally used for floor joists are usually appropriate. **Table 2-9** shows header sizes for varying spans.

**TABLE 2-9:
HEADER SIZES FOR VARYING
SPANS**

Maximum span, ft.	Header size, in.
3 ½	2 × 6
5	2 × 8
6 ½	2 × 10
8	2 × 12

For other than light-frame construction, other design may be necessary. Wider openings often require trussed headers.

Location of the studs, headers, and sills around window openings should conform to the rough opening sizes recommended by the manufacturers of the millwork. The framing height to the bottom of the window and door headers should be based on the door heights, normally 6 feet 8 inches for the main floor. Thus to allow for the thickness and clearance of the head casing of window and door frames and the finish floor, the bottoms of the headers are usually located 6 feet 10 inches to 6 feet 11 inches above the subfloor, depending on the type of finish floor used.

Rough opening sizes for exterior door and window frames vary slightly among manufacturers, but the following allowances should be made:

Double-Hung Window (Single Unit)

rough opening width = glass width + 6 inches

rough opening height = total glass height + 10 inches

For example, **Table 2-10** illustrates several glass and rough opening sizes for double-hung windows:

TABLE 2-10:
GLASS SIZE AND ROUGH FRAME OPENING

Window glass size (each sash)		Rough frame opening	
Width, in.	Height, in.	Width, in.	Height, in.
24	16	24 + 6 = 30	42 = 16 × 2 + 10
28	20	28 + 6 = 34	50 = 20 × 2 + 10
32	24	32 + 6 = 38	58 = 24 × 2 + 10
36	24	36 + 6 = 42	58 = 24 × 2 + 10

Casement Window (One Pair, Two Sashes)

rough opening width = total glass width + $11\frac{1}{4}$ inches

rough opening height = total glass height + $6\frac{3}{8}$ inches

Doors

rough opening width = door width + $2\frac{1}{2}$ inches

rough opening height = door height + 3 inches

119

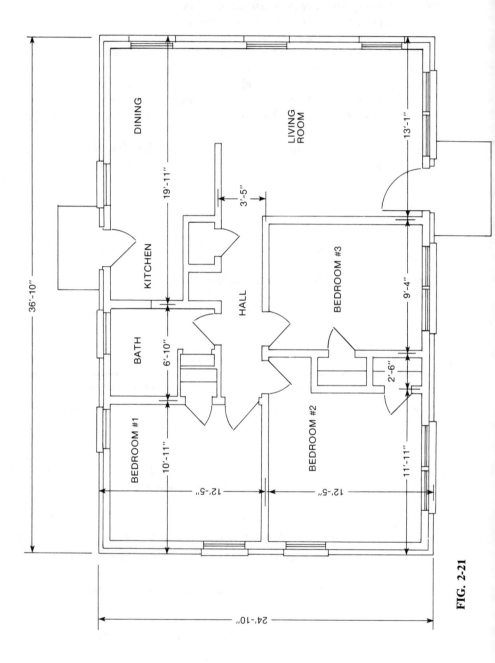

FIG. 2-21

Number of Studs Needed

Use this helpful rule for finding the number of wall and partition studs and also plates and caps when the spacing is 16 inches on center:

1. Take three-quarters of the total lengths in feet of all walls and partitions.
2. Add for plates and caps three times the total length of all walls and partitions divided by the length of the studs.
3. Add one stud for each length of wall.
4. Add one stud where an exterior wall is intersected by a partition.
5. Add one stud for each intersection of partitions.
6. Add one stud for each length of partition.
7. Add two studs for each exterior wall opening and two for each partition opening.
8. Allow 5 percent for waste.

To estimate the approximate number of 2 × 4s needed for the walls and partitions of floor plan shown in **Figure 2-21**, proceed, using the above procedure, as follows:

1.	¾ × 236′ 8″	=	177′ 6″		
2.	177′ 6″ × 3 ÷ 8	=	66′ 8″		
3.	18 × 8′	=	144′		
4.	6 × 8′	=	48′		
5.	17 × 8′	=	136′		
6.	15 × 8′	=	120′		
7.	10 × 8′ × 2	=	160′		
	Subtotal studs	=	852′ 2″ ÷ 8	=	107
8.	107 × 5% =	Total studs needed	=	113	

CEILING JOISTS

After exterior and interior walls are plumbed and braced and top plates are added, ceiling joists can be positioned and nailed in place. They are normally placed across the width of the house, as are the rafters. The partitions of the house are usually located so that ceiling joists of even lengths (10, 12, 14, and 16 feet or longer) can be used without waste to span from exterior walls to load-bearing interior walls. The sizes of the joists depend on the span, wood species, spacing between joists, and load on the second floor or attic. The correct sizes can be found in much the same manner as sizes for floor joists are, as discussed earlier. The method for figuring the number needed is also the same as that for floor joists. While ceiling joists are used to support ceiling finishes, they often also act as floor joists for second and attic floors and as ties between exterior walls and interior partitions. Since ceiling joists also serve as tension members to resist the thrust of the rafters of pitched roofs, they must be securely nailed to the plate and outer and inner walls. They are also nailed together, directly or with wood or metal cleats, where they cross or join at a load-bearing partition **(Figure 2-22, view A)**, and to the rafters at exterior walls **(Figure 2-22, view B)**. Further, they are toenailed—joined by a nail at an angle —at each wall.

Whenever it is necessary to cut regular joists to provide an opening as, for example, at a stairwell, it is necessary to provide auxiliary joists (headers) at right angles to the regular joists, to carry the ends of the cut joists, which are called *tail beams* **(Figure 2-23)**. The headers, in turn, are supported by double or triple joists called *trimmers*. Whatever its strength requirements, a header cannot be of greater depth than the joists, except perhaps on the first floor,

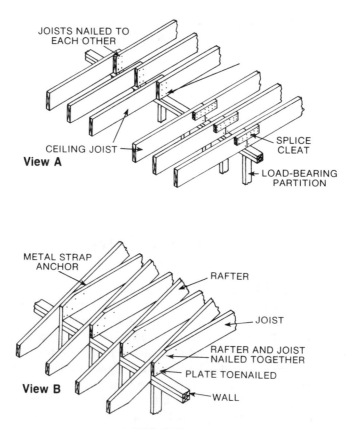

FIG. 2-22

122

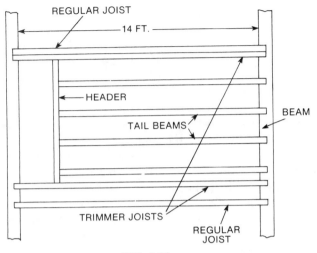

REGULAR JOIST

14 FT.

HEADER

BEAM

TAIL BEAMS

TRIMMER JOISTS

REGULAR JOIST

FIG. 2-23

where projection below the ceiling line of the basement is not objectionable. The sizes of headers and trimmers should be determined by the loads to be carried. Custom has usually decreed the doubling of all headers and trimmers. In many cases, however, it is unnecessary to double. On the other hand, there are cases in which doubling of headers may be insufficient.

A header is similar to a beam in that it carries the end of certain floor joists. Before you can determine the load on the trimmer, you must determine the load carried by the header. To do this, use the methods outlined earlier for beams. As a matter of convenience, however, the general rule for beams may be modified for headers as follows: The header will carry the weight of the floor to the midpoint of the tail beams that rest upon it. Therefore, the load on the header is: Length of tail beam multiplied by length of header multiplied by floor load (both live and dead) in pounds per square foot divided by 2. For example, if the tail beam is 12 feet long, the header 6 feet long, and the floor load 50 pounds to the square foot, the total header load is

$$\frac{12 \times 6 \times 50}{2} = 1,800 \text{ pounds}$$

Two supporting trimmers divide the total header load. To summarize: The header takes half the floor load on the tail beams, and the trimmers each take half of the header load, so the trimmer carries one-fourth of the floor load carried by the tail beams. The following rule may therefore be formulated:

trimmer load = ¼ (length of header ×
length of tail beams × total floor load)

123

Table 2-11: Table for Use in figuring Header and Trimmer Loads

Length of tail beams	4	5	6	7	8	10	12	14	16	18	20
Total live and dead loads per square foot:											
10	20	25	30	35	40	50	60	70	80	90	100
30	60	75	90	105	120	150	180	210	240	270	300
40	80	100	120	140	160	200	240	280	320	360	400
50	100	125	150	175	200	250	300	350	400	450	500
60	120	150	180	210	240	300	360	420	480	540	600
70	140	175	210	245	280	350	420	490	560	630	700
80	160	200	240	280	320	400	480	560	640	720	800
90	180	225	270	315	360	450	540	630	720	810	900
100	200	250	300	350	400	500	600	700	800	900	1000

The figures in **Table 2-11** are arranged according to total floor load (live plus dead) and length of tail beams. These figures multiplied by the length of the header will give the total uniformly distributed load on the header. Half this amount gives the concentrated load on each trimmer corresponding to the foregoing formula.

The next step in determining the trimmer load is to note the point of application of the header load and to ascertain its effect upon the trimmer. Nearly all tables for beams are based on uniformly distributed loads. Earlier we noted that a concentrated load of 1,000 pounds applied at the center of a span produces the same effect as a uniformly distributed load of twice the amount, or 2,000 pounds. The beam tables will give the proper size of beams required for any such concentrated load for any span or material. Merely double the load and treat it as is uniformly distributed. If the relation found between the bending effect of a concentrated load at points other than the center and a corresponding uniformly distributed load of equal bending effect, the size of the beam may be quickly found from the tables by using the equivalent uniformly distributed load. This relationship is shown in **Table 2-12**. The concentrated load multiplied by the proper factor (determined by position of load) from **Table 2-12** gives the uniform load, which you can use to select from the tables of maximum spans the necessary size of joist or trimmer. Here's an example:

Assume you want to build a hearth 6 feet long in a living room 14 feet wide. The header is to be 2 feet from one end of the trimmer (**Figure 2-24**). The tail beams, therefore, are 12 feet long. Assume the usual live load of 40 pounds per square foot and a dead-load allowance for the weight of the floor of 10 pounds per square foot.

Table 2-12: Relationship Between Bending Effect of Concentrated and Uniformly Distributed Loads

Load	Position of load	Factor
Concentrated	Applied at center of span	Multiply by 2
"	Applied at one-third of span	Multiply by 1¾
"	Applied at one-fourth of span	Multiply by 1½
"	Applied at one-fifth of span	Multiply by 1¼
"	Applied at one-seventh of span	Multiply by 1
"	Applied at one-eighth of span	Multiply by ⅞
"	Applied at one-tenth of span	Multiply by ¾

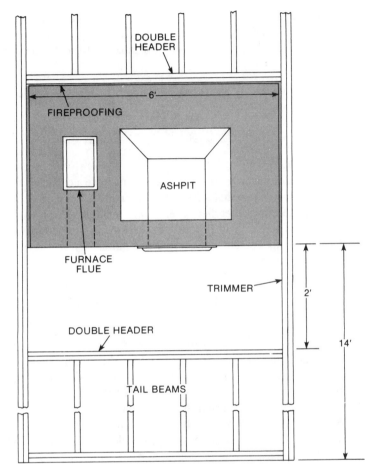

FIG. 2-24

According to the tables, the joists, if of No. 1 common southern pine, are 2-by-10s; hence, the header and trimmer depth is limited to 10 inches. The load on the header, according to **Table 2-11**, is 300 × 6 = 1,800 pounds. Beam tables show that a 2-by-10 of 6-foot span, for example, will carry 2,020 pounds. Therefore, it is not necessary to double the header.

The load on the trimmer is one-half the header load, or 900 pounds. This load is applied 2 feet from one end of the trimmer, so it is one-seventh of the span from one end. According to **Table 2-12**, this is equivalent in bending effect to an equal load of 900 pounds distributed over the whole beam. Beam tables show that a 2-by-10 of common structural Douglas fir with a 14-foot span will carry 1,336 pounds. This is ample to carry the header.

If the regular joist is used as a trimmer also, it must support the header load in addition to its share of the floor load, which it is seldom able to do. In such

125

instances the joist must carry a strip of floor 16 inches wide with a combined live and dead load of 50 pounds per square foot. The total load on the joist would be given by the sum of the joist load and the header load:

$$
\begin{aligned}
\text{total} &= \text{joist length} \times \text{spacing} \times \text{load} + \text{header load} \\
&= 14 \times 1\frac{1}{3} \times 50 + 900 \\
&= 932 + 900 = 1{,}832 \text{ pounds}
\end{aligned}
$$

The trimmer joist to carry both loads must have a capacity of 1,832 pounds. The beam tables show that a 2-by-10 of Douglas fir has a capacity of only 1,336 pounds, as determined earlier. Therefore, if a single piece is to act as both joist and trimmer, its size will have to be increased to 3 × 10 inches, which for a 1,200-pound fiber stress will carry 2,152 pounds.

WALL SHEATHING

Wall sheathing covers the wall framework of studs, plates, and window and door headers and forms a flat base to which the exterior finish can be applied. Certain types of sheathing and methods of application can lend great rigidity to a house and eliminate the need for corner bracing. Sheathing also minimizes air infiltration and, in certain forms, insulates.

Some sheet materials serve both as sheathing and as siding. Sheathing is sometimes eliminated from houses in the mild climates of the South and West. Among the many forms in which it occurs are, most commonly, boards, plywood, structural insulating board, and gypsum.

Wood Sheathing

Wood sheathing is usually of nominal 1-inch boards in a shiplap, tongue-and-groove, or square-edge pattern. Resawn $^{11}/_{16}$-inch boards are also allowed under certain conditions. The requirements for wood sheathing are that it be easy working and easy nailing, and that it shrink only moderately. Common widths are 6, 8, and 10 inches. Sheathing may be applied horizontally or diagonally.

Plywood Sheathing

Plywood, used extensively for wall sheathing, is applied vertically, normally in 4 × 8-foot and longer sheets. This sheathing eliminates the need for diagonal corner bracing, but, like all sheathing materials, it should be well nailed.

Insulating Board Sheathing

Insulating board sheathing is coated or impregnated with asphalt or other material to become water-resistant. Occasional wetting and drying that occur during construction do not damage this sheathing much.

The three common types of insulating board (structural fiberboards) used for sheathing are regular-density, intermediate-density, and nail-base. Regular-density sheathing is manufactured in $\frac{1}{2}$- and $\frac{25}{32}$-inch thicknesses and in sizes of 2 × 8, 4 × 8, and 4 × 9 feet. Intermediate-density and nail-base sheathing are denser products than regular-density. They are regularly manufactured only in $\frac{1}{2}$-inch thickness and in sizes of 4 × 8 and 4 × 9 feet. While 2 × 8-foot sheets with matched edges are used horizontally, 4 × 8-foot and longer sheets are usually installed with the long dimension vertical.

Gypsum Sheathing

Gypsum sheathing is $\frac{1}{2}$ inch thick, 2 × 8 feet in size, and is applied horizontally for stud spacing of 24 inches or less. It is composed of treated gypsum filler faced on two sides with water-resistant paper. Often one edge is grooved, and the other has a matched V edge. This makes application easier, adds a small amount of tie between sheets, and provides some resistance to air and moisture penetration.

The method of figuring the amount of sheathing needed to cover the studs is basically the same as that for determining subflooring: Find the area in square feet, then divide by the area of a single sheet of material. For example, if a wall 8 × 28 feet (224 square feet) is to be sheathed with 4 × 8-foot plywood (each sheet 32 square feet), you need 224 ÷ 32 = 7 sheets of plywood.

Since wood sheathing is nominally 1 inch in thickness, you would need 224 board feet. To be on the safe side, forget about all openings in figuring the material needed and consider that the extra quantity will adequately compensate for waste.

ROOF FRAMING

The primary object of a roof in any climate is to keep out the rain, snow, and wind. The roof must be sloped to shed water. Where heavy snows cover the roofs for long periods, roofs must be constructed to bear the extra weight. They must also be strong enough to withstand high winds. The most commonly used types of roof construction include the gable, the lean-to or shed, the hip, and the gable and valley.

The *gable roof* (**Figure 2-25**) has two roof slopes meeting at the center, or ridge, to form a gable. This form of roof is popular because it is simple in

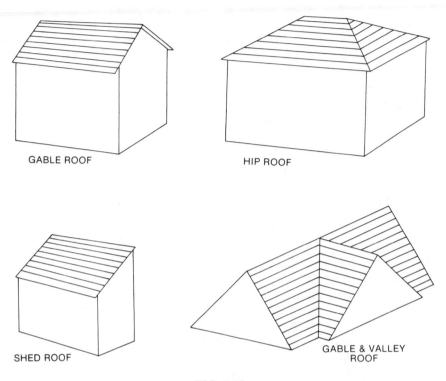

GABLE ROOF

HIP ROOF

SHED ROOF

GABLE & VALLEY
ROOF

FIG. 2-25

design, economical to construct, and may be used on any type of structure.

The *lean-to* or *shed roof* is a near-flat roof and is used where large buildings are framed under one roof, where hasty or temporary construction is needed, and where sheds or additions to buildings are erected. The pitch of the roof is in one direction only. The roof is held up by the walls or posts on four sides; one wall or the posts on one side are at a higher level than those on the opposite side.

The *hip roof* consists of four sides or slopes running toward the center of the building. Rafters at the corners extend diagonally to meet at the center, or ridge. Into these rafters, other rafters are framed.

The *gable and valley roof* is a combination of two gable roofs intersecting each other. The valley is that part where the two roofs meet, each roof slanting in a different direction. This type of roof is more complicated than the others to construct.

The *pitch* or *slope* of a roof is the angle that the roof surface makes with

128

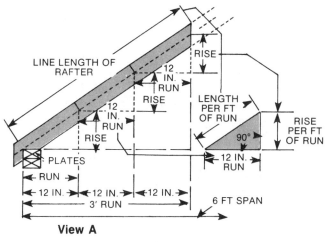

FIG. 2-26

a horizontal plane. The surface may vary from absolutely flat to steep. The usual way to express roof pitch is by pairs of numbers, for example, 8 and 12, 8 being the rise and 12 the run. On drawings, roof pitch is shown as in **Figure 2-26, view A**. Pitches are determined as shown in **Figure 2-26, view B**.

The *span* (**Figure 2-27, view A**) of any roof is the shortest distance between the two opposite rafter seats. Stated in another way, it is the distance between the outside plates, measured at right angles to the direction of the ridge of the building.

Total rise (**Figure 2-27, view A**) is the vertical distance from the plate to the top of the ridge. (See page 130.)

Total run is the horizontal distance over which any rafter passes. For the ordinary rafter, it is one-half the span.

Since the unit of measurement—feet—is the same for the roof as for any other part of the building, the framing square can be employed in laying out large roofs.

Rise in inches is the number of inches that a roof rises for every foot of run.

The *cut* of a roof is the rise in inches per foot of run (**Figure 2-27, view B**).

Plumb and *level lines* refer to the direction of an edge of a rafter. Any line that is vertical when the rafter is in its proper position is called a plumb line. Any line that is horizontal when the rafter is in its proper position is called a level line (**Figure 2-27, view B**).

Line length is the hypotenuse of a triangle whose base is the total run and whose altitude is the total rise (**Figure 2-27, view A**).

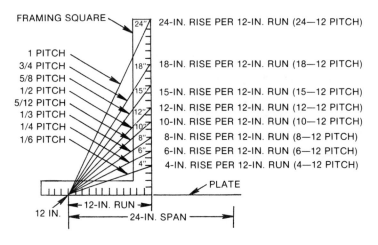

FIG. 2-26   **View B**

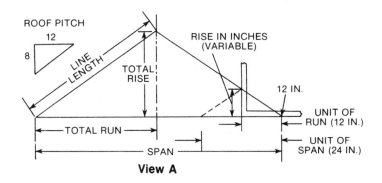

View A

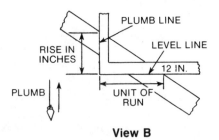

View B

FIG. 2-27

130

Rafters

The main body of the framework of a roof is the rafters. They do for the roof what joists do for a floor and what studs do for a wall. Rafters are inclined members, spaced from 16 to 48 inches apart, which vary in size, depending on their length and the distance between them. The bottoms of the rafters rest on the plate member, which connects the wall and roof and is really a functional part of both. The structural relationship between rafters and wall is the same in all types of roofs. The rafters are not framed into the plate but are simply nailed to it, some being cut to fit the plate while others, in hasty construction, are merely laid on top of the plate and nailed in place. Rafters may extend a short distance beyond the wall to form the eaves and protect the sides of the building.

The various roof-framing members are shown in **Figure 2-28**.

A *ridge board* is the horizontal member that holds rafters where they peak.

Common rafters extend from plate to ridge board at right angles to both.

Hip rafters extend diagonally from the outside corners formed by perpendicular plates to the ridge board.

Valley rafters extend from the plates to the ridge board along the lines where two roofs intersect.

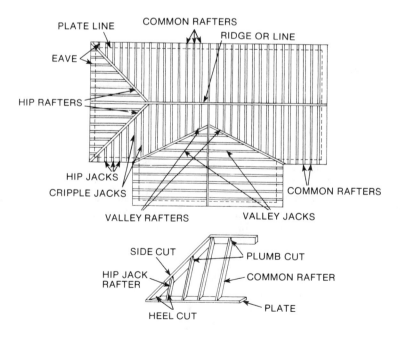

FIG. 2-28

131

Jack rafters, or *jacks,* never extend the full distance from plate to ridge board. They are subdivided into *hip jacks,* whose lower ends rest on the plate and whose upper ends rest against the hip rafters; *valley jacks,* whose lower ends rest against the valley rafters and whose upper ends rest against the ridge board; and *cripple jacks* which are nailed between hip and valley rafters.

The *top* or *plumb cut* is the cut made at the end of the rafter to be placed against the ridge board or, if the ridge board is omitted, against the opposite rafter.

The *seat, bottom,* or *heel cut* is the cut made at the end of the rafter which is to rest on the plate.

The *side* or *cheek cut* is a bevel cut on the side of a rafter to fit it against another frame member.

The *rafter length* is the shortest distance between the outer edge of the plate and the center of the ridge line.

The *eave* or *tail* is the portion of the rafter extending beyond the outer edge of the plate.

The *measure line* is an imaginary reference line down the middle of the face of a rafter. If a portion of a roof is represented by a right triangle (**Figure 2-29**), the measure line corresponds to the hypotenuse, the rise to the leg, and the run to the base.

Common Rafter Layout

Rafters must be laid out and cut with slope, length, and overhang exactly right so that they will fit when placed in the position they will occupy in the finished roof.

The builder first determines the length of the rafter and the length of the piece of lumber from which the rafter may be cut. A set of plans which includes a roof plan provides the rafter lengths and the width of the building. If no plans are available, the width of the building may be measured with a tape. To determine the rafter length, first find one-half of the distance between the outside plates. This distance is the horizontal distance that the rafter will cover. Next consider the amount of rise per foot. If, for example, the rise per foot is 8 inches, to determine the approximate overall length of a rafter, measure on the steel square the distance between 8 on the tongue and 12 on the body, because 8 is the rise and 12 is the unit of run. This distance, $14^5/_{12}$ inches, represents the line length of a rafter with a total run of 1 foot and a rise of 8 inches. If the building is 20 feet wide, the run of the rafter is 10 feet. Multiply by 10 the line length for 1 foot. The result is $144\,^2/_{12}$ inches, or 12 feet and $^1/_6$ inch. The amount of overhang, normally 1 foot, must be added if an overhang is to be used. This makes a total of 13 feet for the length of the rafter, but since 13 feet is an odd length for lumber, a 14-foot length is used.

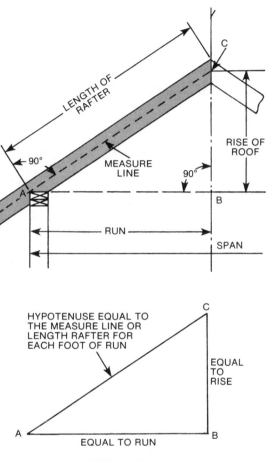

FIG. 2-29

After determining length, lay the piece of lumber on sawhorses with the crown or bow (if any) as the top side of the rafter. If possible, select a straight piece for this first, pattern, rafter. If a straight piece is not available, have the crown toward the person laying off the rafter. Hold the square with the tongue in the right hand, the body in the left, the heel away from you, and place the square as near the upper end of the rafter as possible. In this case, the numbers 8 on the tongue and 12 on the body are placed along the edge of timber that is to be the top edge of the rafter, as shown in **Figure 2-30A**. Mark along the tongue edge of the square, which will be the plumb cut at the ridge. Since the length of the rafter is known to be 12 feet $\frac{1}{6}$ inch, measure the distance from the top of the plumb cut and mark it on the lumber. Hold the square in the same manner with the 8 mark on the tongue directly over the 12-foot-and-

133

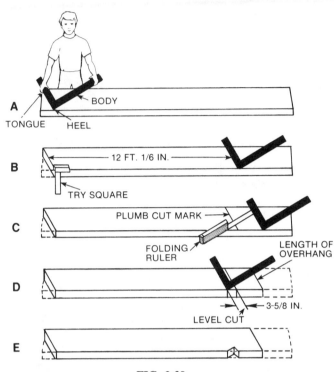

FIG. 2-30

$\frac{1}{6}$-inch mark. Mark along the tongue of the square to give the plumb cut for the seat (**Figure 2-30B**). Next measure off, perpendicular to this mark, the length of overhang along the lumber and make a plumb cut mark in the same manner, keeping the heel of the square on the same edge of the lumber (**Figure 2-30C**). This will be the tail cut of the rafter; often the tail cut is made square across the timber.

The level cut or width of the seat is the width of the plate, measured perpendicular to the plumb cut, as shown in **Figure 2-30D**. Using the try square, square lines down on the sides from all level and plumb cut lines. Now the rafter is ready to be cut, as shown in **Figure 2-30E**.

If a building is 20 feet 8 inches wide, the run of the rafter is 10 feet 4 inches, or half the span. Instead of using the above method, the rafter length may be determined by "stepping it off" by successive steps with the square as shown in **Figure 2-31**. Stake the same number of steps as there are feet in the run, which leaves 4 inches over 1 foot. This 4 inches is taken care of in the same manner as the full foot run; that is, with the square at the last step position, make a mark on the rafters at the 4-inch mark on the tongue. Then move the

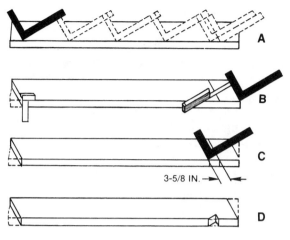

FIG. 2-31

square along the rafter until the tongue rests at the 4-inch mark. Holding the square for the same cut as before, make a mark along the tongue. This is the line length of the rafter. The seat cut and hangover are made as noted above. When laying off rafters by any method, be sure to recheck the work carefully. When two rafters have been cut, it is best to put them in place to see if they fit. Minor adjustments can be made at this time without serious damage or waste of material.

Table Method—Using the Rafter Table on the Framing Square

The rafter table, located on the square's body, gives both the line length of any pitch or rafter per foot of run and the line length of any hip or valley rafter per foot of run. The table also shows the difference in length of the jack rafters spaced 16 or 24 inches on center (o.c.). Where the jack, hip, or valley rafter requires side cuts, the cut is given in the table.

The table **(Figure 2-32)** appears on the face of the body. It is used to

FIG. 2-32

135

determine the length of the common, valley, hip, and jack rafters, and the angles at which they must be cut to fit at the ridge and plate. The row of numbers in the first line represents the length of common rafters per foot of run, as the title indicates at the left-hand end of the body. Each set of numbers under each inch division mark represents the length of rafter per foot of run with a rise corresponding to the number of inches over the number. For example, under the 18-inch mark appears the number 21.63 inches. This number equals the length of a rafter with a run of 12 inches and a rise of 18 inches. Under the 9-inch mark appears the number 15.00, which is the rafter length for a 12-inch run and a 9-inch rise. We will disregard the other five lines of figures in the table because they are seldom useful.

To use the table for laying out rafters, you must first know the width of the building. Suppose the building is 20 feet 8 inches wide, and the rise of the rafters is to be 8 inches per foot of run. The total run of the rafter will be 10 feet 4 inches. Look in the first line of figures. Under the 8-inch mark appears the number 14.42, which is the length in inches of a rafter with a run of 1 foot and a rise of 8 inches. To find the line length of a rafter with a total run of 10 feet 4 inches, multiply 14.42 inches by $10\frac{1}{3}$ and divide by 12 to get the answer in feet. 14.42 inches $\times$ $10\frac{1}{3}$ = 149.007 inches = $12\frac{5}{12}$ feet. Therefore 12 feet 5 inches is the line length of the rafter.

When the roof has an overhang the rafter can be cut square to save time. When the roof has no overhang, the rafter cut is plumb, but no notch is cut in the rafter for a seat. The level cut is made long enough to extend across the plate and the wall sheathing. This type of rafter saves material, although little protection is given to the side wall.

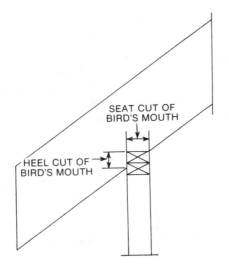

FIG. 2-33

136

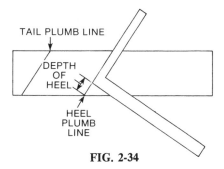

FIG. 2-34

Bird's Mouth

A rafter with a projection has a notch in it called a *bird's mouth,* as shown in **Figure 2-33**. The plumb cut of the bird's mouth, which bears against the side of the rafter plate, is called the *heel cut*; the level cut, which bears on the top of the rafter plate, is called the *seat cut.*

The size of the bird's mouth is usually stated in terms of the depth of the heel cut rather than in terms of the width of the seat cut. You lay out the bird's mouth in about the same way you lay out the seat on a rafter without a projection. Measure off the depth of the heel on the heel plumb line, set the square as shown in **Figure 2-34**, and draw the seat line along the body. For the roof surface, *all rafters* should be exact. Therefore, the amount above the seat cut, rather than the bottom edge of the rafters, is the important measurement. Suppose that on a hip roof, or an intersecting roof, the hips or valley rafters are 2-by-6s and the common rafters 2-by-4s. The amount above the seat cut should be such as to adequately support the overhang of the roof, plus people working on the roof. The width of the seat cut is important as a bearing surface. The maximum width of the common rafter should not exceed the width of the plate.

Determining the number of rafters needed when the spacing is 16 inches on center is achieved in the same manner as is the number of joists: take three-quarters of the length in feet perpendicular to the rafters and add one rafter. Allow for the extra length due to the slope of the roof and for any overhang. Also allow for 5 percent waste.

Hip Roof Layout

Most hip roofs are *equal-pitch*: The slope on the roof end or ends is the same as the slope on the sides. Unequal-pitch hip roofs do exist, but they are quite rare, and they require special layout methods. The unit-length rafter table on the framing square applies only to equal-pitch hip roofs. In the following

137

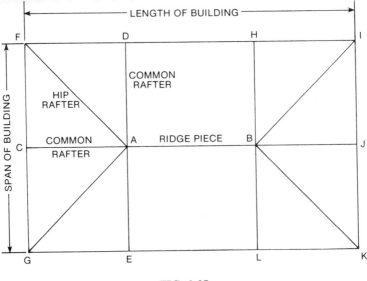

FIG. 2-35

discussion of hip roof framing, assume that in every case the roof is an equal-pitch hip roof. The length of a hip rafter, like the length of a common rafter, is calculated on the basis of the bridge measure (distance from plate line to ridge piece) times the unit of run. For a common rafter, use any of the methods previously described. However, some of the basic data for a hip rafter are different.

Figure 2-35 shows part of a roof framing diagram for an equal-pitch hip roof. A roof framing diagram may be included among working drawings for a building; if it is not, you should lay one out for yourself.

In an equal-pitch hip roof framing diagram the lines that indicate the hip rafters (FA, GA, IB, and KB in **Figure 2-35**) form 45-degree angles with the building lines. The points where they meet the ridge piece centerline are the *theoretical* ends. The ridge-end common rafters CA, DA, EA, HB, JB, and LB join the ridge at the same points, A and B.

A line that indicates a rafter in the roof framing diagram is equal in length (to scale, of course) to the total run of the rafter it represents. You can see from the diagram that the total run of a hip rafter (represented by lines FA, GA, IB, and KB) is the hypotenuse of a right triangle whose shorter side equals the total run of a common rafter. You know the total run of a common rafter: It is one-half the span, or one-half the width, of the building. Knowing this, you can find the total run of a hip rafter by applying the Pythagorean theorem.

Here's how:

Let us suppose that the span of the building is 30 feet. Then one-half the span, which is the same as the total run of a common rafter, is 15 feet. Using the Pythagorean theorem and computing square root, the total run of a hip rafter is

$$\text{hypotenuse}^2 = 15^2 + 15^2$$
$$\text{hypotenuse}^2 = 225 + 225 = 450$$
$$\text{hypotenuse} = 21.21$$

What is total rise? Since a hip rafter joins the ridge at the same height as a common rafter, the total rise for a hip rafter is the same as the total rise for a common rafter, which we know how to figure out. If this roof has a unit run of 12 and a unit rise of 8, since the total run of a common rafter in the roof is 15 feet, the total rise of a common rafter is the value of x in the proportion $12 : 8 :: 15 : x$.

$$\frac{12}{8} = \frac{15}{x} ; \frac{12x}{8} = 15; \ 12x = 15 \times 8 = 120; \ x = 10$$

Thus the total rise is 10 feet. Knowing this and knowing the total run of the hip rafter (21.21 feet), you can figure the line length by applying the Pythagorean theorem. The line length is the square root of $(21.21^2 + 10^2)$, or 23.44 feet, or about 23 feet $5\frac{1}{4}$ inches.

To find the length of a hip rafter on the basis of bridge measure, you must first determine the bridge measure. As with a common rafter, the bridge measure of a hip rafter is the length of the hypotenuse of a triangle whose shorter sides equal the unit run and unit rise of the rafter. The unit rise of a hip rafter is always the same as that of a common rafter, but *the unit run of a hip rafter is different.* The unit run of a hip rafter in an equal-pitch hip (hip rafters are same length) roof is the hypotenuse of a right triangle whose shorter sides each equal the unit run of a common rafter. Since the unit run of a common rafter is 12, the unit run of a hip rafter is the square root of $(12^2 + 12^2)$, or 16.97.

If the unit run of the hip rafter is 16.97 and the unit rise (in this particular case) is 8, the unit length of the hip rafter must be the square root of $(16.97^2 + 8^2)$, or 18.76. This means that for every 16.97 units of run, the rafter

139

has 18.76 units of length. Since the total run of the rafter is 21.21 feet, the length of the rafter must be the value of x in the proportion $16.97 : 18.76 :: 21.21 : x$.

$$\frac{16.97}{18.76} = \frac{21.21}{x}$$

$$\frac{16.97x}{18.76} = 21.21$$

$$16.97x = 21.21 \times 18.76 = 397.8996$$

$$x = 23.45 \text{ ft.}$$

Like the unit length of a common rafter, the bridge measure of a hip rafter may be obtained from the unit-length rafter table on the framing square. If you turn back to **Figure 2-32**, you will see that the second line in the table is headed "Length hip or valley rafters per foot run." This means "per foot run of a common rafter in the same roof." Actually, the unit length given in the tables is the unit length for every 16.97 units of run of the hip rafter itself. If you run across to the unit length given under 8, you will find the same figure, 18.76, calculated above.

An easy way to calculate the length of an equal-pitch hip roof rafter is to multiply the bridge measure by the number of feet in the total run of a common rafter, which is the same as the number of feet in one-half of the span of the building. One-half of the span of the building in this case is 15 feet. The length of the hip rafter is therefore 18.76×15, or 281.40 inches, which is 23.45 feet. Note that when you use this method you get a result in inches, which you must convert to feet. The slight difference of 0.01 feet between this result and the one previously obtained amounts to less than $\frac{1}{8}$ inch, and may be ignored.

You step off the length of an equal-pitch hip roof rafter just as you do the length of a common rafter, except that you set the square to a unit of run of 16.97 inches instead of to a unit of run of 12 inches. Setting the square to a unit of run of 17 inches is close enough for most practical purposes. Bear in mind that, for any plumb cut line on an equal-pitch hip roof rafter, you set the square to the unit rise of a common rafter and to a unit run of 17.

You step off the same number of times as there are feet in the total run of a common rafter in the same roof; however, the size of each step is different. For every 12-inch step in a common rafter, a hip rafter has a 17-inch step. In the roof on which we are working, since the total run of a common rafter is exactly 15 feet, you would step off the hip rafter cut (17 inches and 8 inches) exactly 15 times.

Suppose, however, that there is an odd unit in the common rafter total run, for example, that the total run of a common rafter is 15 feet $10\frac{1}{2}$ inches. How would you make the odd fraction of a step on the hip rafter?

You remember that the unit run of a hip rafter is the hypotenuse of a right triangle whose other sides each equal the unit run of a common rafter. This being the case, the run of the odd unit on the hip rafter must be the hypotenuse of a right triangle whose other sides each equal the odd unit of run of the common rafter, which in this case is $10\frac{1}{2}$ inches. You can figure this by using the Pythagorean theorem—that is, finding the square root of $(10.5^2 + 10.5^2)$ —or you can set the square to $10\frac{1}{2}$ inches on the tongue and $10\frac{1}{2}$ inches on the body and measure the distance between the marks on a true edge. It comes to 14.84 inches, which rounded off to the nearest sixteenth inch equals $14\frac{13}{16}$ inches.

To lay off the odd unit, set the tongue of the framing square to the plumb line for the last full step made and measure off $14\frac{13}{16}$ inches along the body. Place the tongue of the square at the mark, set the square to the hip rafter plumb cut of 8 inches on the tongue and 17 inches on the body, and draw the line length cut line.

Hip-Shortening Allowance

As with a common rafter, the line length of a hip rafter does not take into account the thickness of the ridge piece. The size of the ridge-end shortening allowance for a hip rafter depends upon the manner in which the ridge end of the hip rafter is joined to the other structural members. The ridge end of the hip rafter may be framed against the ridge piece **(Figure 2-36)** or against the ridge-end common rafters **(Figure 2-37)**. If the hip rafter is framed against the ridge piece, the shortening allowance is one-half of the 45-degree thickness

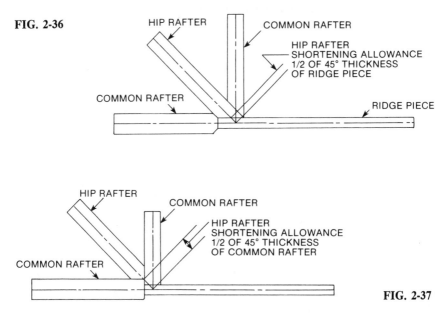

FIG. 2-36

HIP RAFTER COMMON RAFTER

HIP RAFTER
SHORTENING ALLOWANCE
1/2 OF 45° THICKNESS
OF RIDGE PIECE

COMMON RAFTER

RIDGE PIECE

HIP RAFTER

COMMON RAFTER

HIP RAFTER
SHORTENING ALLOWANCE
1/2 OF 45° THICKNESS
OF COMMON RAFTER

COMMON RAFTER

FIG. 2-37

of the ridge piece. The 45-degree thickness of stock is the length of a line laid at 45 degrees across the thickness dimension of the stock. If the hip rafter is framed against the common rafters, the shortening allowance is one-half of the 45-degree thickness of a common rafter. To lay off the shortening allowance, set the tongue of the framing square to the line length ridge cut line, measure off the shortening allowance along the body, set the square at the mark to the cut of the rafter (8 inches and 17 inches), and draw the actual ridge plumb cut line.

Hip Rafter Projection

A hip rafter projection, like a common rafter, is figured as a separate problem. The run of a hip rafter projection is not the same as the run of a common rafter projection in the same roof (**Figure 2-38**). The run of the hip rafter projection, as you can see, is the hypotenuse of a right triangle whose shorter sides each equal the run of a common rafter projection. If the run of the common rafter overhang is 18 inches, the run of the hip rafter is the square root of ($18^2 + 18^2$), or 25.45 inches. Since the rafter rises 8 units for every 17 units of run, the total rise of the projection is the value of x in the proportion $17 : 8 :: 25.45 : x$, or 11.9 inches. If the total run is 25.45 inches and the total rise 11.9 inches, the length of the projection is the square root of ($25.45^2 + 11.9^2$), or about 28 inches.

Hip Rafter Side Cuts

Since a common rafter runs at 90 degrees to the ridge, the ridge end of a common rafter is cut square to the narrower dimension. A hip rafter, however, joins the ridge, or the ridge ends of the common rafters at an angle. The ridge end of a hip rafter must therefore be cut to a corresponding angle, called a

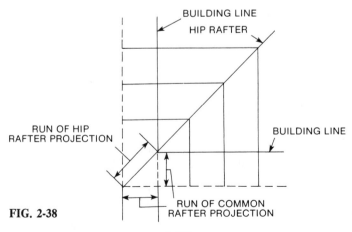

FIG. 2-38

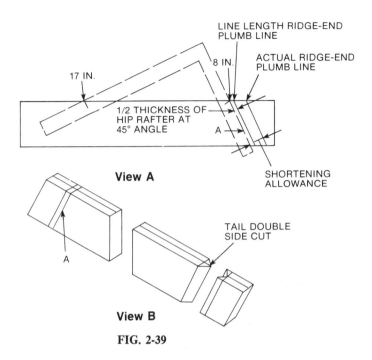

View A

View B

FIG. 2-39

side cut. The angle of the side cut is more acute for a high unit rise than it is for a low one.

The angle of the side cut is laid out as shown in **Figure 2-39**. Place the tongue of the framing square along the ridge cut line, as shown in view A, and measure off one-half the thickness of the hip rafter along the body of the square. Shift the tongue to the mark, set the square to the cut of the rafter (17 inches and 8 inches), and draw the plumb line marked A in the figure. Then turn the rafter edge-up, as shown in view B, and draw an edge centerline. Then draw in the angle of the side cut as shown. For a hip rafter to be framed against the ridge there will be only a single side cut; for one to be framed against the ridge ends of the common rafters there will be a double side cut, as shown. The tail of the rafter must have a double side cut at the same angle, but in the reverse direction.

The angle of the side cut on a hip rafter may also be laid out by referring to the unit length rafter table on the framing square. If you turn back to **Figure 2-32**, you will see that the bottom line in the table is headed "SIDE CUT HIP OR VALLEY USE." If you follow this line rightward to the column under the number 8 (for a unit rise of 8), you will find the number $10\frac{7}{8}$. If you place the framing square face up on the rafter edge, with the tongue on the ridge-end cut line, and set the square to a cut of $10\frac{7}{8}$ inches on the body and 12 inches on the tongue, you can draw the correct side-cut angle along the tongue.

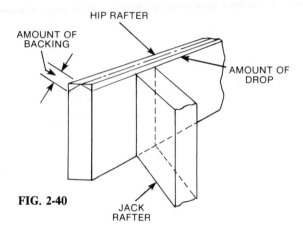

FIG. 2-40

HIP RAFTER

AMOUNT OF
BACKING

AMOUNT OF
DROP

JACK
RAFTER

If the bird's mouth on a hip rafter had the same depth as the bird's mouth on a common rafter, the edges of the hip rafter would extend above the upper ends of the jack rafters, as shown in **Figure 2-40**. This can be corrected by either backing or dropping the hip rafter. Backing means beveling the upper edge of the hip rafter. As shown in **Figure 2-40**, the amount of backing is taken at the right angle to the roof surface or the top edge of the hip rafter. Dropping means deepening the bird's mouth to bring the top edge of the hip rafter down to the upper ends of the jacks. The amount of drop is taken on the heel plumb line.

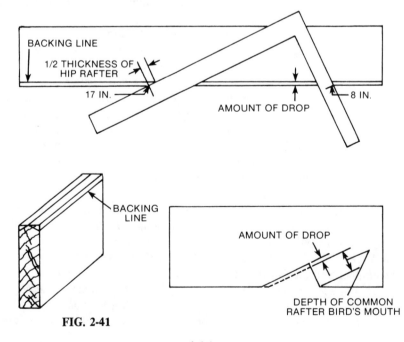

BACKING LINE

1/2 THICKNESS OF
HIP RAFTER

17 IN.

AMOUNT OF DROP

8 IN.

BACKING
LINE

AMOUNT OF DROP

DEPTH OF COMMON
RAFTER BIRD'S MOUTH

FIG. 2-41

The amount of backing or drop required is calculated as shown in **Figure 2-41**. Set the framing square to the cut of the rafter (8 inches and 17 inches) on the upper edge, and measure off one-half the thickness of the rafter from the edge along the body of the square. If the rafter is to be backed, a line drawn through this mark, parallel to the edge, will indicate the bevel angle as shown. The perpendicular distance between the line and the edge of the rafter will be the amount of drop, meaning the amount that the depth of the hip rafter bird's mouth should exceed the depth of the common rafter bird's mouth.

Valley Rafter Layout

A valley rafter lies in the intersection between a main roof surface and a gable roof addition or a gable roof dormer surface. Most roofs that contain valley rafters are equal-pitch roofs: the pitch of the addition or dormer roof is the same as the pitch of the main roof. There are unequal-pitch valley rafter roofs, but they are quite rare and require relatively complicated framing methods. In the discussion that follows, it will be assumed that the roof is an equal-pitch roof, so the unit of run and unit of rise of an addition or dormer common rafter will be the same as the unit of run and unit of rise of a main roof common rafter. In an equal-pitch roof the valley rafters always run at 45 degrees to the building lines and the ridge pieces.

Figure 2-42 shows an equal-span framing situation in which the span of the addition is the same as the span of the main roof. Since the pitch of the addition roof is the same as the pitch of the main roof, equal spans bring the ridge pieces to equal heights. If you look at the roof framing diagram in the figure, you will see that the total run of a valley rafter (AB and AD) is the hypotenuse of a right triangle whose shorter sides each equal the total run of a common rafter in the main roof. The unit run of a valley rafter is therefore the same as the unit run for a hip rafter. It follows that figuring the length of an equal-span valley rafter is the same as figuring the length of an equal-pitch hip roof hip rafter.

However, a valley rafter does not require backing or dropping. The projection, if any, is figured just as it is for a hip rafter. Side cuts are laid out as they are for a hip rafter; the valley rafter tail has a double side cut, like the hip rafter tail, but in the reverse direction, since the tail cut on a valley rafter must form an inside rather than an outside corner. As indicated in **Figure 2-43**, the ridge-end shortening allowance in this framing situation amounts to one-half of the 45-degree thickness of the ridge.

Figure 2-44 shows a framing situation in which the span of the addition is shorter than the span of the main roof. Since the pitch of the addition roof is the same as the pitch of the main roof, the shorter span of the addition brings the addition ridge down to a lower level than that of the main roof ridge. There are two ways of framing an intersection of this type. By the method

145

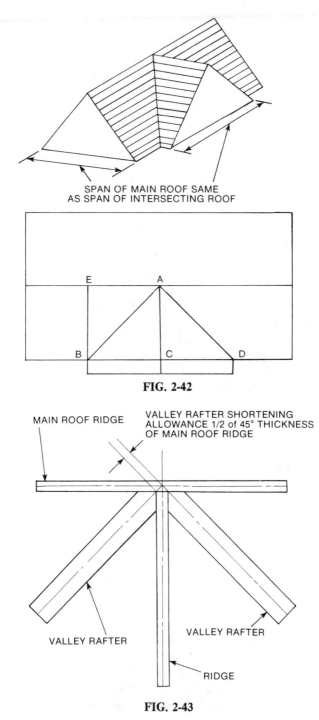

SPAN OF MAIN ROOF SAME
AS SPAN OF INTERSECTING ROOF

FIG. 2-42

MAIN ROOF RIDGE

VALLEY RAFTER SHORTENING
ALLOWANCE 1/2 of 45° THICKNESS
OF MAIN ROOF RIDGE

VALLEY RAFTER

VALLEY RAFTER

RIDGE

FIG. 2-43

146

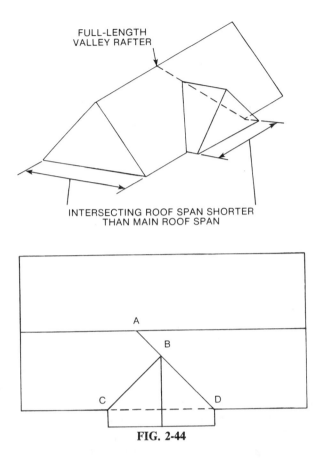

FULL-LENGTH
VALLEY RAFTER

INTERSECTING ROOF SPAN SHORTER
THAN MAIN ROOF SPAN

A

B

C   D

FIG. 2-44

shown in **Figure 2-44**, a full-length valley rafter (AD) is framed between the rafter plate and the ridge piece, and a shorter valley rafter (CB) is then framed to the longer one. If you study the framing diagram, you will see that the total run of the longer valley rafter is the hypotenuse of a right triangle whose shorter sides each equal the total run of a common rafter in the main roof. The total run of the shorter valley rafter, on the other hand, is the hypotenuse of a right triangle whose shorter sides each equal the total run of a common rafter in the addition. The total run of a common rafter in the main roof is equal to one-half the span of the main roof; the total run of a common rafter in the addition is equal to one-half the span of the addition.

Knowing the total run of a valley rafter (or of any rafter, for that matter), you can always find the line length by multiplying the bridge measure times the total run. Suppose that the span of the addition in **Figure 2-44** is 30 feet and that the unit rise of a common rafter in the addition is 9. The total run of the shorter valley rafter is the square root of ($15^2 + 15^2$), or 21.21 feet. If you refer back to the unit length rafter table in **Figure 2-32**, you will see that

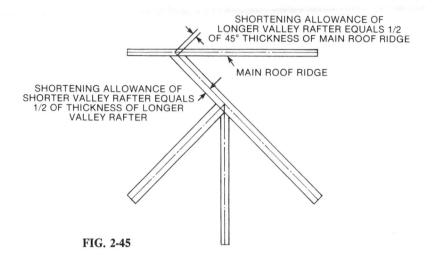

FIG. 2-45

the bridge measure for a valley rafter in a roof with a common rafter unit rise of 9 is 19.21. Since the unit run of a valley rafter is 16.97 and the total run of this rafter is 21.21 feet, the line length must be the value of x in the proportion 16.97 : 19.21 :: 21.21 : x, or 24.01 feet.

An easier way to find the length of a valley rafter is simply to multiply the bridge measure by the number of feet in one-half the span of the roof to which the valley rafter belongs. The length of the longer valley rafter in **Figure 2-44,** for example, is 19.21 times one-half the span of the main roof. The length of the shorter valley rafter is 19.21 times one-half the span of the addition. Since one-half the span of the addition is 15 feet, the length of the shorter valley rafter is 15 × 19.21, or 288.15 inches, which is 288.15/12, or 24.01 feet. Note again that when you use this method you get a result in inches, which you must change to feet.

Figure 2-45 shows the long and short valley rafter shortening allowances. Note that the long valley rafter has a single side cut for framing to the main roof's ridge piece, while the short valley rafter is cut square to the smaller dimension for framing to the addition ridge.

Figure 2-46 shows another method of framing an equal-pitch unequal-span addition, the suspended-ridge method. In this method the inboard end of the addition ridge is nailed to a piece that hangs from the main roof ridge. As shown in the framing diagram, this method calls for two short valley rafters, each of which extends from the rafter plate to the addition ridge. The framing diagram shows that the total run of each of these valley rafters is the hypotenuse of a right triangle whose shorter sides each equal the total run of a common rafter in the addition.

As indicated in **Figure 2-47** the shortening allowance of each of the short

148

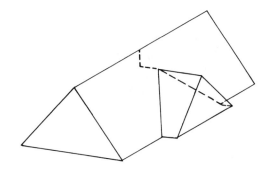

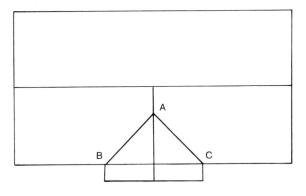

FIG. 2-46

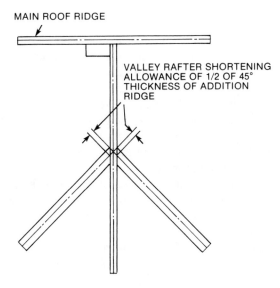

MAIN ROOF RIDGE

VALLEY RAFTER SHORTENING
ALLOWANCE OF 1/2 OF 45°
THICKNESS OF ADDITION
RIDGE

FIG. 2-47

149

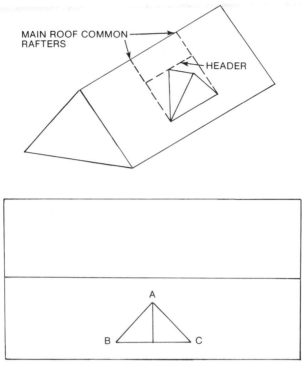

FIG. 2-48

valley rafters is one-half of the 45-degree thickness of the addition ridge. Each rafter is framed to the addition ridge with a single side cut.

Figure 2-48 shows a method of framing a gable dormer without side walls. The dormer ridge is framed to a header set between a couple of doubled main-roof common rafters. The valley rafters are framed between this header and a lower header. As indicated in the framing diagram, the total run of a valley rafter is the hypotenuse of a right triangle whose shorter sides each equal the total run of a common rafter in the dormer.

Figure 2-49 shows the arrangement and names of framing members in this type of dormer framing. This figure also shows that the upper edges of the headers must be beveled to the cut of the main roof. **Figure 2-50** shows that, in this method of dormer framing, the shortening allowance for the upper end of a valley rafter is one-half of the 45-degree thickness of the inside member in the upper doubled header. There is also a shortening allowance for the lower end, consisting of one-half of the 45-degree thickness of the inside member of the doubled common rafter. The figure also shows that each valley rafter has a double side cut at the upper end and a double side cut at the lower end.

150

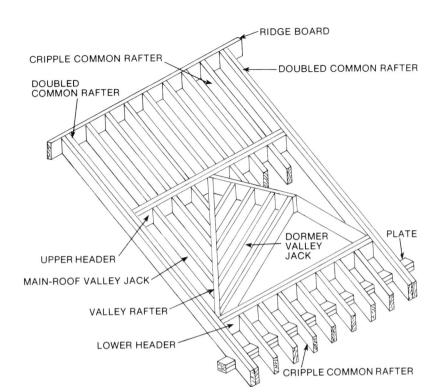

FIG. 2-49

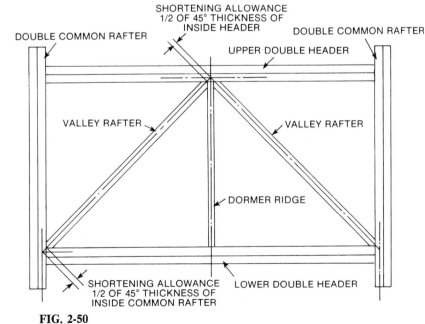

FIG. 2-50

151

Figure 2-51 shows a method of framing a gable dormer with side walls. As indicated in the framing diagram, the total run of a valley rafter is again the hypotenuse of a right triangle whose shorter sides each equal the run of a common rafter in the dormer. You figure the lengths of the dormer corner posts and side studs just as you do the lengths of gable-end studs, and you lay off the lower-end cut-off angle by setting the square to the cut of the main roof.

Figure 2-52 shows the valley-rafter shortening allowances for this method of framing a dormer with side walls.

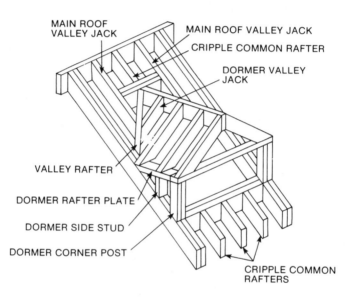

MAIN ROOF VALLEY JACK

MAIN ROOF VALLEY JACK

CRIPPLE COMMON RAFTER

DORMER VALLEY JACK

VALLEY RAFTER

DORMER RAFTER PLATE

DORMER SIDE STUD

DORMER CORNER POST

CRIPPLE COMMON RAFTERS

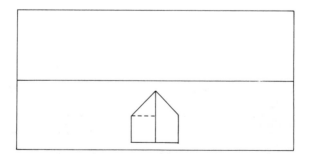

FIG. 2-51

152

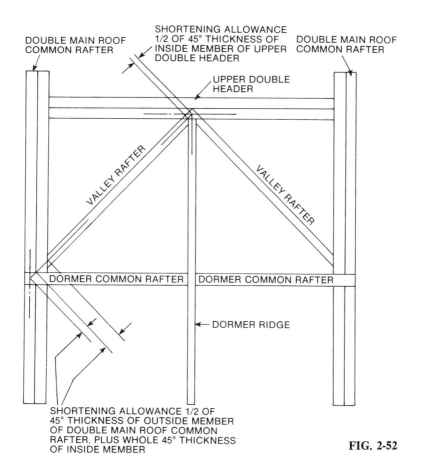

DOUBLE MAIN ROOF
COMMON RAFTER

SHORTENING ALLOWANCE
1/2 OF 45° THICKNESS OF
INSIDE MEMBER OF UPPER
DOUBLE HEADER

DOUBLE MAIN ROOF
COMMON RAFTER

UPPER DOUBLE
HEADER

VALLEY RAFTER

VALLEY RAFTER

DORMER COMMON RAFTER

DORMER COMMON RAFTER

DORMER RIDGE

SHORTENING ALLOWANCE 1/2 OF
45° THICKNESS OF OUTSIDE MEMBER
OF DOUBLE MAIN ROOF COMMON
RAFTER, PLUS WHOLE 45° THICKNESS
OF INSIDE MEMBER

FIG. 2-52

Jack Rafter Layout

A *jack rafter* is a part of a common rafter, shortened for framing to a hip rafter, a valley rafter, or both. This means that in an equal-pitch framing situation the unit rise of a jack rafter is always the same as the unit rise of a common rafter. A *hip jack* (**Figure 2-28**) is one that extends from a hip rafter to a rafter plate. A *valley jack* is one that extends from a valley rafter to a ridge. A *cripple jack* is one that contacts neither a rafter plate nor a ridge. A *valley cripple jack* is one that extends between two valley rafters in the long-and-short valley rafter method of addition framing. A *hip-valley cripple jack* is one that extends from a hip rafter to a valley rafter. All types of jacks except cripple jacks are shown in **Figure 2-53**. A valley cripple jack and a couple of hip-valley cripple jacks are shown in **Figure 2-54**.

153

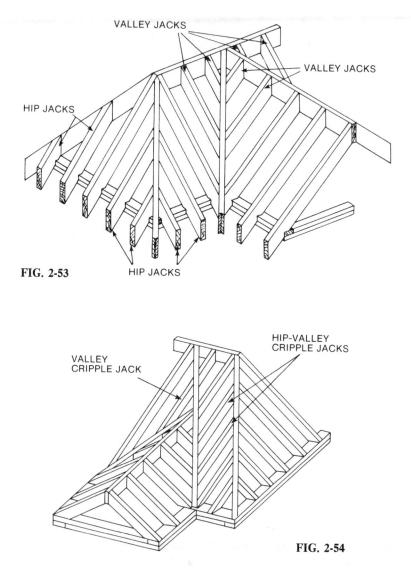

VALLEY JACKS

VALLEY JACKS

HIP JACKS

FIG. 2-53

HIP JACKS

HIP-VALLEY
CRIPPLE JACKS

VALLEY
CRIPPLE JACK

FIG. 2-54

Length of Hip Jack

Figure 2-55 shows a roof-framing diagram for a series of hip jack rafters. The jacks are always on the same spacing on center as the common rafters. Suppose that the spacing in this instance is 16 inches. You can see that the total run of the shortest jack is the hypotenuse of a right triangle whose shorter sides are each 16 inches long. The total run of the shortest jack is therefore the square root of ($16^2 + 16^2$), or 22.62 inches.

154

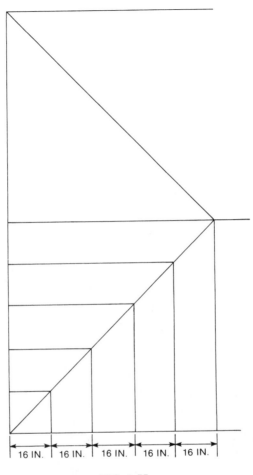

16 IN. | 16 IN. | 16 IN. | 16 IN. | 16 IN.

FIG. 2-55

Suppose that a common rafter in this roof has a unit rise of 8. Since the jacks, as you know, have the same unit rise as common rafters, the unit length of a jack in this roof is the square root of $(12^2 + 8^2)$, or 14.42. This means that a jack is 14.42 units long for every 12 units of run. The length of the shortest hip jack in this roof is therefore the value of x in the proportion $12 : 14.42 :: 16 : x$, or 19.23 inches. This is always the length of the shortest hip jack when the jacks are spaced 16 inches on center and the common rafter in the roof has a unit rise of 8. It is also the common difference of jacks: the next hip jack will be 2×19.23 inches long, the next, 3×19.23 inches long, and so on.

The common difference for hip jacks spaced 16 inches on center and also for hip jacks spaced 24 inches on center is given in the unit length rafter table

155

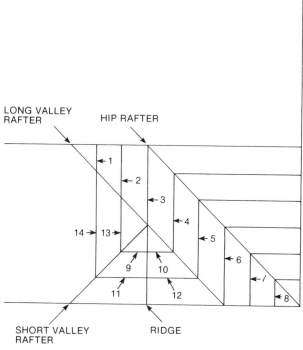

FIG. 2-56

on the framing square for unit rises ranging from 2 to 18 inclusive. **Figure 2-32** shows a segment of the unit length rafter table. If you follow the third line in the table, which reads "DIFF. IN LENGTH OF JACKS 16 INCHES CENTERS," to the number under 8 (for a unit rise of 8), you will find the same unit length (19.23 inches) that you worked out above.

The best way to figure the length of a valley jack or a cripple jack is to apply the bridge measure to the total run. The bridge measure of any jack is the same as the bridge measure of a common rafter having the same unit of rise as the jack. Suppose, for example, that the jack has a unit rise of 8. In **Figure 2-32**, look along the line on the unit length rafter tables headed "LENGTH COMMON RAFTERS PER FOOT RUN" for the figure in the column under 8, and you will find a unit length of 14.42.

The best way to figure the total runs of valley jacks and cripple jacks is to lay out a framing diagram and study it to determine what these runs must be. **Figure 2-56** shows part of a framing diagram for a main hip roof with a long-and-short valley rafter gable addition. By studying the diagram you can figure the total runs of the valley jacks and cripple jacks as follows:

The run of valley jack 1 is obviously the same as the run of hip jack 8, which is the run of the shortest hip jack. The length of valley jack 1 is therefore equal to the common difference of jacks.

The run of valley jack 2 is the same as the run of hip jack 7, and the length is therefore twice the common difference of jacks.

The run of valley jack 3 is the same as the run of hip jack 6, and the length is therefore three times the common difference of jacks.

The run of hip-valley cripple 4 and that of hip-valley cripple 5 is the same as the run of valley jack 3.

The run of valley jack 9 and that of valley jack 10 is equal to the spacing of jacks on center. Therefore, the length of one of these jacks is equal to the common difference of jacks.

The run of valley jacks 11 and 12 is twice the run of valley jacks 9 and 10, and the length of one of these jacks is therefore twice the common difference of jacks.

The run of valley cripple 13 is twice the spacing of jacks on center, and the length is therefore twice the common difference of jacks.

The run of valley cripple 14 is twice the run of valley cripple 13, and the length is therefore 4 times the common difference of jacks.

Jack Rafter Shortening Allowances

A hip jack has a shortening allowance at the upper end consisting of one-half of the 45-degree thickness of the hip rafter. A valley jack has a shortening allowance at the upper end consisting of one-half of the thickness of the ridge and another at the lower end consisting of one-half of the 45-degree thickness of the valley rafter. A hip-valley cripple has a shortening allowance at the upper end consisting of one-half of the 45-degree thickness of the hip rafter and another at the lower end consisting of one-half of the 45-degree thickness of the valley rafter. A valley cripple has a shortening allowance at the upper end consisting of one-half of the 45-degree thickness of the long valley rafter and another at the lower end consisting of one-half the 45-degree thickness of the short valley rafter.

Jack Rafter Side Cuts

The side cut on a jack rafter can be laid out by the method illustrated in **Figure 2-39** for laying out the side cut on a hip rafter. Another method is to use the fifth line of the unit length rafter table, which is headed "SIDE CUT OF JACKS USE" (**Figure 2-32,** page 135). If you follow that line to the number under 8 (unit rise of 8), you will see that the figure given is 10. To lay out the side cut on a jack, set the square face-up on the edge of the rafter to 12 inches on the tongue and 10 inches on the body, and draw the side-cut line along the tongue.

A jack rafter is a shortened common rafter; consequently, the bird's mouth and projection on a jack rafter are laid out just as they are on a common rafter.

157

Ridge Layout

Laying out the ridge for a gable roof presents no particular problem, since the line length of the ridge is equal to the length of the building. The actual length includes any overhang. For a hip roof, however, the ridge layout requires a certain amount of calculation.

As previously mentioned, in an equal-pitch hip roof the line length of the ridge equals the length of the building minus twice the total run of a common rafter. The *actual* length, however, depends upon the way the hip rafters are framed to the ridge.

As indicated in **Figure 2-57**, the line length ends of the ridge are at the points where the ridge centerline and the hip rafter centerlines cross. In **Figure 2-57, view A**, the hip rafter is framed against the ridge; in this method of framing the actual length of the ridge exceeds the line length, at each end, by one-half of the thickness of the ridge plus one-half of the 45-degree thickness of the hip rafter. In **Figure 2-55, view B**, the hip rafter is framed between the common rafters; in this method of framing the actual length of the ridge exceeds the line length, at each end, by one-half of the thickness of a common rafter.

Figure 2-58, view A, shows that the length of the ridge for an equal-span addition is equal to the length of the addition rafter plate, plus one-half the

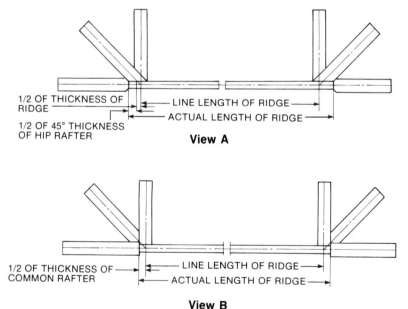

1/2 OF THICKNESS OF RIDGE
1/2 OF 45° THICKNESS OF HIP RAFTER
— LINE LENGTH OF RIDGE —
— ACTUAL LENGTH OF RIDGE —

View A

1/2 OF THICKNESS OF COMMON RAFTER
— LINE LENGTH OF RIDGE —
— ACTUAL LENGTH OF RIDGE —

View B

FIG. 2-57

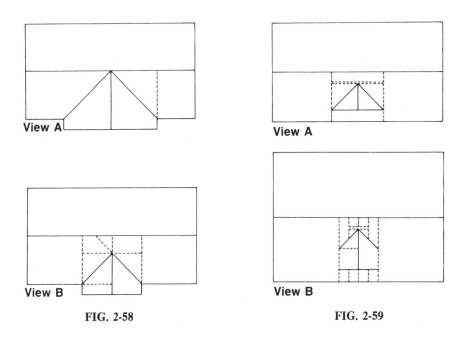

View A

View A

View B

View B

FIG. 2-58

FIG. 2-59

span of the building, minus the shortening allowance at the main roof ridge; the shortening allowance amounts to one-half of the thickness of the main roof ridge. **Figure 2-58, view B,** shows that the length of the ridge for an unequal-span addition varies with the method of framing the ridge. If the addition ridge is suspended from the main roof ridge, the length is equal to the length of the addition rafter plate plus one-half the span of the building. If the addition ridge is framed by the long-and-short valley rafter method, the length is equal to the length of the addition rafter plate, plus one-half of the span of the addition, minus a shortening allowance, consisting of one-half of the 45-degree thickness of the long valley rafter. If the addition ridge is framed to a double header set between a couple of double main roof common rafters, the length of the ridge is equal to the length of the addition side-wall rafter plate, plus one-half the span of the addition, minus a shortening allowance, consisting of one-half the thickness of the inside member of the double header.

 Figure 2-59, view A, shows that the length of the ridge on a dormer without side walls is equal to one-half of the span of the dormer, less a shortening allowance consisting of one-half the thickness of the inside member of the upper double header. **Figure 2-59, view B,** shows that the length of the ridge on a dormer with side walls amounts to the length of the dormer rafter plate, plus one-half the span of the dormer, minus a shortening allowance consisting of one-half the thickness of the inside member of the upper double header.

Shed Roof Framing

Again, a shed (or single-pitch) roof is essentially one-half of a gable (or double-pitch) roof. Like the full-length rafters in a gable roof, the full-length rafters in a shed roof are common rafters. Note, however, that as shown in **Figure 2-60**, the total run of a shed roof common rafter is equal to the span of the building *minus the width of the rafter plate on the higher rafter end wall.* Note also that the run of the projection on the higher wall is measured from the inner edge of the higher rafter plate. To this must be added the width of the plate and the length of the overhang or projection at the top. Shed-roof common rafters are laid out like gable-roof common rafters. A shed-roof common rafter has two bird's mouths, but they are laid out just like the bird's mouth on a gable-roof common rafter. **Figure 2-60** also shows that the height of the higher rafter end wall must exceed the height of the lower by an amount equal to the total rise of a common rafter.

Figure 2-61 shows a method of framing a shed dormer. There are three layout problems to be solved here: (1) determining the total run of a dormer rafter, (2) determining the angle of cut on the inboard ends of the dormer rafters, and (3) determining the lengths of the dormer side-wall studs.

To determine the total run of a dormer rafter, divide the height of the dormer side or end wall, in inches, by the difference between the unit rise of the dormer roof and the unit rise of the main roof. Take the dormer shown in **Figure 2-62**, for example. The height of the dormer end wall is 9 feet, or 108 inches. The unit rise of the main roof is 8; the unit rise of the dormer roof is $2\frac{1}{2}$; the difference between them is $5\frac{1}{2}$. The total run of a dormer rafter is

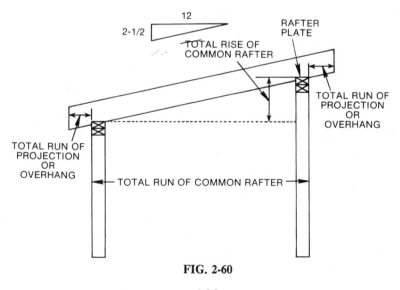

FIG. 2-60

160

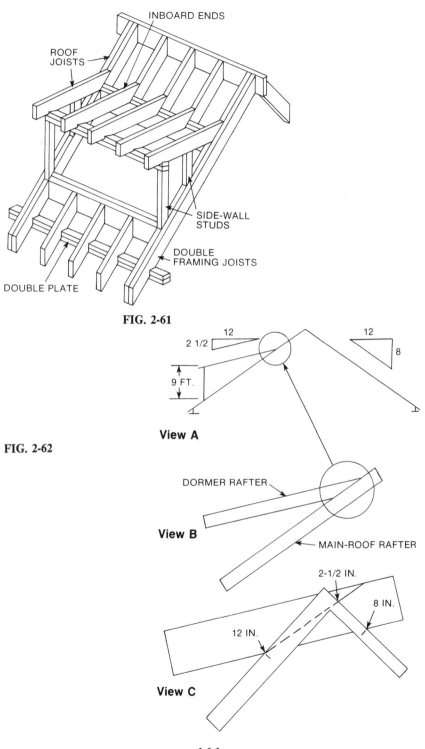

INBOARD ENDS

ROOF JOISTS

SIDE-WALL STUDS

DOUBLE FRAMING JOISTS

DOUBLE PLATE

FIG. 2-61

FIG. 2-62

12

2 1/2

9 FT.

12

8

View A

DORMER RAFTER

View B

MAIN-ROOF RAFTER

2-1/2 IN.

8 IN.

12 IN.

View C

161

therefore 108 divided by $5\frac{1}{2}$, or 19.63 feet. Knowing the total run and the unit rise, you can figure the length of a dormer rafter by any of the methods already described.

As indicated in **Figure 2-62, view B**, the inboard ends of the dormer rafters must be cut to fit the slope of the main roof. To get the angle of this cut, set the square on the rafter to the cut of the main roof, as shown in **Figure 2-62, view C**; measure off the unit rise of the dormer roof from the heel of the square along the tongue as indicated, and make a mark at this point; draw the cutoff line through this mark from the 12-inch mark.

Figure the lengths of the side-wall studs on a shed dormer as follows:

In the roof shown in **Figure 2-62**, a dormer rafter rises $2\frac{1}{2}$ units for every 12 units of run, and a main-roof common rafter rises 8 units for every 12 units of run. If the studs were spaced 12 inches on center, the length of the shortest stud (which is also the common difference of studs) would be the difference between 8 and $2\frac{1}{2}$ inches, or $5\frac{1}{2}$ inches. This being the case, if the stud spacing is 16 inches, the length of the shortest stud is the value of x in the proportion $12 : 5\frac{1}{2} :: 16 : x$, or $7\frac{5}{16}$ inches. The shortest stud, then, will be $7\frac{5}{16}$ inches long, the next stud will be $2(7\frac{5}{16})$ inches long, and so on. To get the lower-end cutoff angle for studs, set the square on the stud to the cut of the main roof; to get the upper-end cutoff angle you set it to the cut of the dormer roof.

Rafter Location Layout

Rafter locations are laid out on plates, ridge boards, and other rafters in pencil or chalk. For a gable roof the rafter locations are laid out on the rafter plates first, and the locations are then transferred to the ridge by matching the ridge against a rafter plate.

The rafter plate locations of the ridge-end common rafters in an equal-pitch hip roof measure one-half of the span (or the run of a main roof common rafter) away from the building corners. These locations, plus the rafter plate locations of the rafters lying between the ridge-end common rafters, can be transferred to the ridge by matching the ridge against the rafter plates.

The locations of addition ridge and valley rafters can be determined as indicated in **Figure 2-63**. In an equal-span situation (illustrated in **Figure 2-63, views A and B**), the valley rafter locations on the main roof ridge lie alongside the addition ridge location. In **Figure 2-63, view A**, the distance between the ends of the main roof ridge and the addition ridge is equal to distance A plus distance B, distance B being one-half the span of the addition. In **Figure 2-63, view B**, the distance between the line length end of the main roof ridge and the end of the addition ridge is the same as distance A. In both cases the line length of the addition ridge is equal to one-half the span of the addition plus the length of the addition side-wall rafter plate.

162

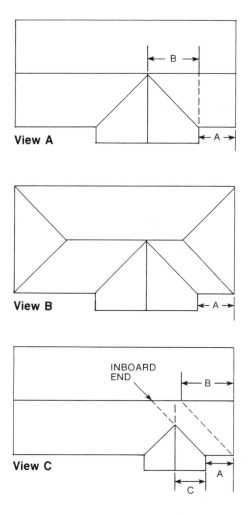

View A

View B

INBOARD
END

View C

FIG. 2-63

Figure 2-63, view C, shows an unequal-span situation. If framing is by the long-and-short valley rafter method, the distance from the end of the main roof ridge to the upper end of the longer valley rafter is equal to distance A plus distance B, distance B being one-half of the span of the main roof. The location of the inboard end of the shorter valley rafter on the longer valley rafter can be determined as follows:

First calculate the unit length of the longer valley rafter, or obtain it from the unit length rafter tables. Let us suppose that the common rafter unit rise is 8; in that case the unit length of a valley rafter is 18.76.

163

The total run of the longer valley rafter between the point where the shorter rafter joins it and the rafter plate is the hypotenuse of a right triangle whose other sides each equal one-half of the span of the addition. Suppose the addition is 20 feet wide; then the total run in question is the square root of $(10^2 + 10^2)$, or 14.14 feet.

You know that the valley rafter is 18.76 units long for every 16.97 units of run. The length of rafter for 14.14 feet of run must therefore be the value of x in the proportion 16.97 : 18.76 :: 14.14 : x, or 15.63 feet. The location for the inboard end of the shorter valley rafter on the longer valley rafter, then, will be 15.63 feet, or 15 feet 7⅝ inches, from the heel plumb cut line on the longer valley rafter. The length of the addition ridge will be equal to one-half the span of the addition, plus the length of the addition side-wall rafter plate, minus a shortening allowance equal to one-half of the 45-degree thickness of the longer valley rafter.

If framing is by the suspended-ridge method, the distance between the suspension point on the main roof ridge and the end of the main roof ridge is equal to distance A plus distance C; distance C is one-half of the span of the addition. The distance between the point where the inboard ends of the valley rafters (both short in this method of framing) tie into the addition ridge and the outboard end of the ridge is equal to one-half the span of the addition plus the length of the addition side-wall rafter plate. The length of the addition ridge is equal to one-half the span of the main roof plus the length of the addition side-wall rafter plate.

Roof Truss

A wood truss is an assembly of members forming a rigid framework of triangular shapes capable of supporting loads over long spans without intermediate support. Its members are connected only at their intersections in such a way that when loads are applied at these intersections, the stress in each member is in the direction of its length. Wood trusses, greatly refined during their development over the years, are being used extensively in light-frame construction.

The common W-type truss **(Figure 2-64, view A)** for moderate spans requires less material than the conventional joist-and-rafter framing system, since the members are usually only 2-by-4s for spans of 24 to 32 feet. The king-post truss **(Figure 2-64, view B)** for spans of 20 to 26 feet uses even less material than the W-truss, but is perhaps more suitable for light to moderate roof loads. In addition to lowering material costs, the truss has the advantage of permitting freedom in location of interior partitions because only the side walls carry the ceiling and roof loads. The principal parts of a truss are the

164

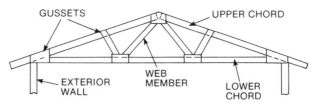

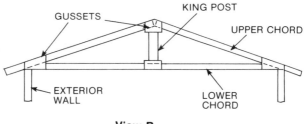

FIG. 2-64

upper chord (consisting of rafters), the lower chord (corresponding to a ceiling joist), various diagonal and/or vertical bracing members known collectively as the web members, and the connecting members, called gussets

The roof sheathing, trim, roofing, interior ceiling finish, and type of ceiling insulation used do not vary a great deal between the truss and conventional roof systems. For plywood or lumber sheathing, 24-inch spacing for truss and joist-rafter construction is considered a normal maximum. Greater spacing can be used, but this usually requires a thicker roof sheathing and application of wood stripping on the underside of the ceiling joists and trusses to furnish a support for ceiling finish. Thus, most W-trusses are designed for 24-inch spacing, and joist-rafter construction is usually used for 24- or 16-inch spacing. Trusses generally require a higher grade of material than the joist-and-rafter roof. However, specific details of the roof construction are usually covered in the working drawings for each structure. Additional information concerning the mathematics of design and construction details for other types of wood trusses is available from several sources, including the American Plywood Association at P. O. Box 11700, Tacoma, WA 98411. Remember, however, the design of a truss must allow for snow and wind loads as well as the weight of the roof itself. Design must also take into account the slope of the roof. Generally, the flatter the slope, the greater the stresses. This results in the need for larger members and also stronger connections.

165

Collar Tie

Gable or double-pitch roof rafters are often reinforced by horizontal members called *collar ties* (**Figure 2-65**).

In a finished attic the ties may also function as ceiling joists.

To find the line length of a collar tie, divide the amount of drop of the tie in inches by the unit of rise of the common rafter. This will equal one-half the length of the tie in feet. Double the result for actual length. The formula is:

drop in inches × 2 ÷ unit of rise = length in feet

The length of the collar tie depends on whether the drop is measured to the top edge or bottom edge of the collar tie (**Figure 2-66**). The tie must fit the slope of the roof. To obtain this angle, use the framing square. Mark and cut the collar tie on the run side (**Figure 2-66**).

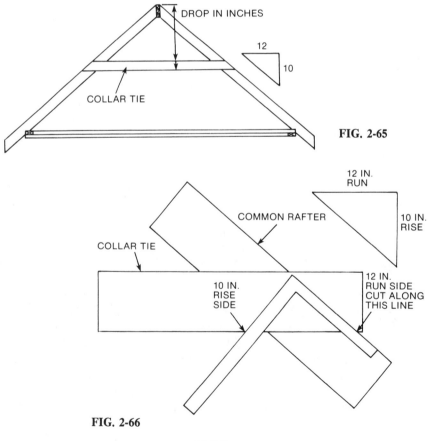

FIG. 2-65

FIG. 2-66

Roof Sheathing

The lower layer of roof covering is called the *roof sheathing*; the upper layer is called the *roof covering,* or the *roofing.* Roof sheathing, like wall sheathing and subflooring, is a structural element and therefore a part of the framing. The roof covering or roofing is a part of the exterior finish. Roof sheathing is usually laid across the rafters. Plywood sheathing may also be used.

You can figure the amount of roof sheathing needed in the same manner as you would estimate subfloor or wall sheathing. Find the total number of square feet needed and multiply it by the wastage percentage, which with most sheathing is 15 percent. **Table 2-13** and **Figure 2-67** show how to find the areas of various types of roofs. Measure dimensions A, B, C, and L in feet. By substituting these numbers in the following formulas, you can obtain the actual areas in square feet.

For example, suppose a gable roof is 30 feet long and A is 18 feet 6 inches. The area of this roof is $2 \times 30 \times 18\frac{1}{2} = 1,100$ square feet.

To find the amount of 1-inch wood sheathing needed for the job, add 15 percent: $1,100 \times 1.15 = 1,266.5$ board feet.

When it is necessary to find the area of a hip roof on a square building, the space could be considered four triangles. From geometry, the area of a triangle is equal to one-half the length of its base multiplied by its height ($A = \frac{1}{2}bh$). In the triangles forming this roof, the distance A is equal to 13 feet 8 inches or to $13\frac{2}{3}$ feet. Hence the area of one triangle is

$$\frac{26 \times 13\frac{2}{3}}{2} = 178 \text{ square feet}$$

The area of the entire roof is $4 \times 178 = 712$ square feet.

If it is impossible to measure the distances on the roof, we still can calculate the area. With a gable roof, for example, the slope can be calculated and

TABLE 2-13:
FORMULAS FOR ROOF AREA

Roof type	Formula for area
Shed	$A \times L$
Gable	$2 \times A \times L$
Hip (square bldg.)	$2(A \times L)$ or $2(A' \times L')$
Hip (rectangular bldg.)	$(A \times L') + C(L+B)$
Mansard	$C'(L'+A) + C(L+B) + (A \times B)$
Gambrel	$2 \times L \times (A+B)$
Gothic	$2 \times A \times L$

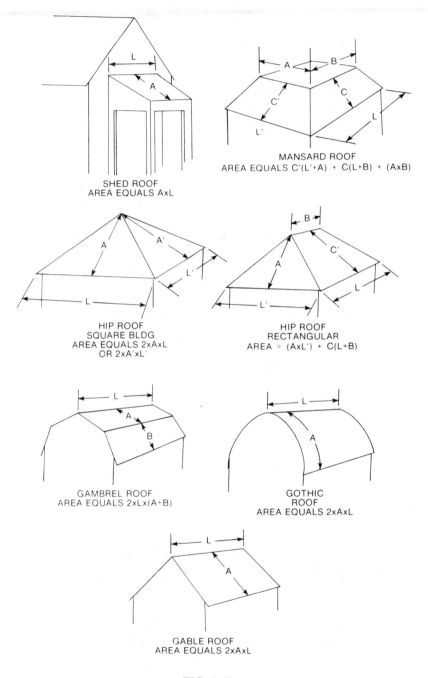

SHED ROOF
AREA EQUALS AxL

MANSARD ROOF
AREA EQUALS C'(L'+A) + C(L+B) + (AxB)

HIP ROOF
SQUARE BLDG.
AREA EQUALS 2xAxL
OR 2xA'xL'

HIP ROOF
RECTANGULAR
AREA = (AxL') + C(L+B)

GAMBREL ROOF
AREA EQUALS 2xLx(A+B)

GOTHIC
ROOF
AREA EQUALS 2xAxL

GABLE ROOF
AREA EQUALS 2xAxL

FIG. 2-67

TABLE 2-14:
SLOPE FACTORS FOR COMPUTING
ROOF AREA FROM
GROUND AREA

Slope	Multiplying factor
$2/12$	1.11
$3/12$	1.13
$4/12$	1.15
$5/12$	1.18
$6/12$	1.22
$8/12$	1.30
$10/12$	1.40
$12/12$	1.51
$16/12$	1.72
$18/12$	1.90

expressed in inches. As we already know, the slope equals the rise (the distance from the attic joists to the ridge) divided by the run (half the distance between the front and back walls of the house), assuming the roof peaks at the midpoint. For example, if the house measures 36 feet between the front and back walls, the run is 18. If the ridge is 12 feet above the joists, the rise is 12. The slope equals 12 feet divided by 18 feet, which reduces to 8 inches in a foot, or an 8/12 slope.

Then, to determine the area of the roof, calculate the ground area of the house, including eave and cornice overhang. Then, multiply that total by the factor shown below for the slope of your roof (**Table 2-14**).

If the example house is 42 × 36 feet, the roof area is 36 × 42 × 1.3 = 1,965.6 square feet.

WALL AND ROOF COVERING

Finish siding and roofing are applied, respectively, over wall and roof sheathing, to protect interiors from the weather.

Exterior Walls

Many materials are used to cover exterior walls: siding, boards placed horizontally; shingles, surfaces of wood, asphalt, or asbestos that overlap; panels of plywood, fiberboard, or metal; and masonry or stucco. Many prefinished sidings are available. Coatings and films applied to several types of base materials presumably eliminate the need of refinishing for many years.

169

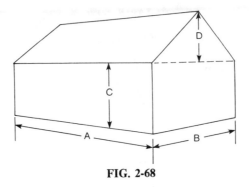

FIG. 2-68

Siding

Accurate estimates of the amount of material needed for siding jobs—whether the material be wood, aluminum, or vinyl—can easily be determined by measuring the length (A), the width (B), the height of your home to the eaves (C), and the height of the gable (D) (**Figure 2-68**). The total area to be sided will be

$$2(A \times C) + 2(B \times C) + 2(\tfrac{1}{2} B \times D)$$

Using the same method, measure the remaining walls, offsets, and so forth. Do not deduct for door and window openings or add for waste. These two items will offset each other in conventionally built homes.

To find the amount of vinyl siding needed for a rectangular home 35 feet long by 25 feet with a height to the eaves of 9 feet and a height of the gable end of 8 feet, compute as follows:

$$2(A \times C) + 2(B \times C) + 2(\tfrac{1}{2} B \times D)$$
$$= 2(35 \times 9) + 2(25 \times 9) + 2(\tfrac{1}{2} 25 \times 8)$$
$$= 630 + 450 + 200 = 1{,}280 \text{ square feet}$$

If the siding is 1 inch thick, the number of board feet of wood siding is the figure calculated above.

When installing any type of bevel siding, allow about equal width exposure above and below the sill. Here is one method of accomplishing this: Divide the overall height of the window frame by the approximate recommended exposure distance for the siding used (4 for 6-inch-wide siding, 6 for 8-inch siding, 8 for 10-inch siding, and 10 for 12-inch siding). This will yield the number of courses between the top and bottom of the window. For example, the overall height of a window from the top of the drip cap to the bottom of the sill is 61 inches. If 12-inch siding is used, the number of courses is $61/10 = 6.1$, or six courses. To obtain the exact exposure distance, divide 61 by 6 to get $10\frac{1}{6}$ inches. The next step is to determine the exposure distance from the bottom of the sill to just below the top of the foundation wall. If this is 31 inches, three courses at $10\frac{1}{3}$ inches each would be used. Thus, the exposure distance above and below the window would be almost the same.

Wood Shingles

Wood shingles are available in three standard lengths, 16, 18, and 24 inches. The 16-inch length is perhaps the most popular. Its thickness, measured as a number of butts (thick ends) in a number of inches, is 5 butt thicknesses per 2 inches when green (designated as 5/2). These shingles are packed in bundles with 20 courses on each side. Four bundles will cover 100 square feet (called a *square*) of wall or roof, with an exposure of 5 inches. The 18- and 24-inch-length shingles have thicker butts, 5 in $2\frac{1}{4}$ inches for the 18-inch shingles and 4 in 2 inches for the 24-inch lengths.

Shakes are usually available in several types, the most popular being those split and resawn. The sawed face is used as the back face. The butt thickness of each shake ranges between $\frac{3}{4}$ and $1\frac{1}{2}$ inches. They are usually packed in bundles (20 square feet), 5 bundles to the square.

If the house in the previous example, requiring 1,280 square feet of siding, was to be shingled with wood shakes, the number of bundles necessary would be $1,280 \div 20 = 64$ bundles.

In figuring the square footage, do not deduct for window and door openings; these openings will usually compensate for wastage.

Plywood and Other Sheet Siding

Exterior-grade plywood, paper-overlaid plywood, and similar sheet materials are available in 4-foot widths and 8-, 9-, and 10-foot lengths. They are usually installed vertically. The total number of sheets needed is obtained by dividing total square feet in a wall by the square feet of a sheet and rounding off to next full sheet. In our example house, for instance, the number of 4×9-foot sheets required to do one of the long walls (35×9 feet) is given by dividing the wall area ($35 \times 9 = 315$) by the area of a sheet ($4 \times 9 = 36$). Since $315 \div 36 = 8.75$, the wall will require 9 sheets.

Other Siding Materials

Fascias, friezes, corner boards, and other trim materials are sold by the linear foot. Measure with a rule and multiply the cost per foot.

Roofing

Most roofing materials—wood, slate, asbestos, and asphalt—are sold by the square (100 square feet). To find the number needed divide the total roof area by 100. Add 10 percent to the area you have calculated to allow for waste, mistakes, and unusual roof features. Then add 1 square of roofing for each 100 linear feet of valley to determine the total number of squares of roofing needed.

If, in our example house, the combined valley length is 20 feet, the total amount of shingles is given in the following:

Roof area:	1,970
Add for waste:	197
	2,167 or 2,170
Divide by 100:	21.7
Round to next whole number:	22
Add for valley length:	+1
Total:	23 squares of shingles

From the roof's area in squares you can also figure the number of rolls of 15-pound felt underlayer you will need. This special asphalt-saturated roofer's felt is recommended for use under all asphalt or asbestos cement shingles. It minimizes condensation problems. Do not use heavier vapor-barrier material in place of roofer's felt. The underlayer not only protects the roof deck from any wind-driven rain that might work in under the shingles, but it also protects the shingles from contact with resinous spots in the deck, which because of chemical incompatibility might damage the shingles. A standard No. 15 roll contains 432 square feet (it is 36 inches wide and 144 feet long) but because it must be lapped will cover only 400 square feet. The number 15 applies to the number of pounds per square, i.e., per 100 square feet. Therefore, since a roll covers 400 square feet, the total weight of the roll is 60 pounds. To find the number of rolls needed for the roof, divide the total square footage of the roof by 400. This allows for lappage, which is 32 square feet. In our example, we would need 2,170 ÷ 400 = 5.425, or 6 rolls of No. 15 felt.

Other Roofing Materials

The quantity of other materials you'll need will depend upon the roof and the roofing material applied. Usually metal or vinyl drip strips should be used along the roof's eaves, and also, unless the roof has wood drip or fascia strips, along the rakes to cover the edges of the sheathing (**Figure 2-69**). Along the

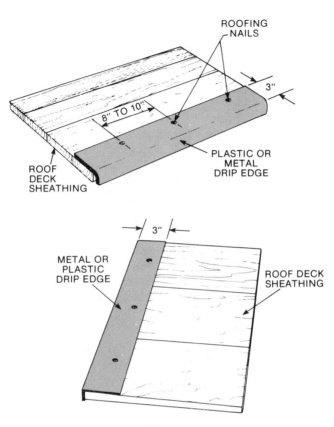

ROOFING NAILS

3"

8" TO 10"

ROOF DECK SHEATHING

PLASTIC OR METAL DRIP EDGE

3"

METAL OR PLASTIC DRIP EDGE

ROOF DECK SHEATHING

FIG. 2-69

eaves, install the drip strip under the underlayer. Along the rake, nail it over the underlayer. Measure the number of linear feet of roof edge to figure the number of lengths needed.

The material needed for valley linings depends on the valley treatment used. Use the valley treatment the roofing manufacturer recommends unless you are an experienced roofer. Most manufacturers of asphalt strip shingles now recommend "closed" valleys, with the courses of shingles laid right across the valley on a 90-pound roll roofing lining. A woven valley offers the advantage of adding extra thicknesses of roofing in the valley, which is the roof's most vulnerable point. But these extra layers of roofing form noticeable humps along the valley. Some roofers find these objectionable and prefer traditional open valleys—open valley flashing can be either doubled 90-pound roll roofing, painted galvanized sheet metal, or sheet copper.

Most asphalt shingle manufacturers make special shingles for capping hips

173

and ridges that match their standard shingles. Hot-dip galvanized roofing nails used should be long enough to penetrate the deck's sheathing. You will need about 2½ pounds of 1½-inch nails per square of roofing, together with a few pounds of 1-inch nails for the 15-pound felt underlayer.

The cost of materials for a plain roof whose area is 1,550 square feet is based on the following:

1. 1 square of 3-tab asphalt strip shingles costs $10.25.
2. 1 roll 15-pound roofing felt costs $4.75.
3. 1 pound of galvanized iron roofing nails costs $0.40.

1. Since the roof area is 1,550 square feet and 1 square of roofing covers 100 square feet, we will need 1,550 ÷ 100 = 15.5, or 16 squares of shingles.
2. One roll of 15-pound roofing felt will cover 400 square feet. We will need 1,550 ÷ 400 = 3.88, or 4 rolls of roofing felt.
3. Allowing 2 pounds of nails per roofing square, we will need 2 × 16 = 32 pounds of nails.

Using the above unit prices, the cost of the required materials will be

1. 16 squares of 3-tab asphalt strip shingles at $10.25 per square = $164.00
2. 4 rolls of 15-pound roofing felt at $4.75 per roll = 19.00
3. 32 pounds of nails at $0.40 per pound = 12.80
   Total cost = $195.80

If two carpenters were employed to install the roof, what would be their wages for the work? Allowing 2 hours per square for each carpenter, each should be able to install 4 squares in an 8-hour day. For two carpenters, 8 squares per day should be installed, which means 16 squares would take the men 2 days. The labor cost is, then, at $10.00 per hour, 2 × 2 × 8 × $10.00 = $320.00. The total cost of the roof is then:

Materials	= $195.80
Labor	= $320.00
Total	= $515.80

Most other roof materials—ridge strips, gutters, downspouts, gravel stops, and so on—are sold by the linear foot. Metal flashing—copper and aluminum —is sold by the square foot.

MATH FOR
INTERIOR FINISHING

Interior finish of a house or an addition consists of the finish covering applied to rough walls, ceiling, and floors as well as to inside door frames, doors, window sashes, and stairs. Here is the usual order of new construction for the interior finish:

1. Ceiling covering
2. Wall covering
3. Stairs
4. Finish flooring
5. Inside door frames and casings and inside window casings, stools, and aprons
6. Baseboards
7. Molding trim
8. Painting or wallcovering

The math of interior finish also applies to all interior remodeling projects. Now let's look at various items involved in interior finish.

CEILING TILES

While many of the products mentioned later in this chapter as wall materials —plywood, hardboard, gypsum wallboard—may be used on ceilings, the material most popular with do-it-yourselfers is ceiling tiles, often called "acoustical" or sound-conditioning tiles. There are three popular ways to tile a ceiling: (1) fastening the tiles directly to the ceiling or to furring strips nailed across it; (2) attaching a grid system directly to the exposed beams; and (3) suspending the new ceiling from a grid that will drop it below the existing one.

The first method is the one most often employed for installing a new ceiling in an existing room. If the old ceiling is in fairly good condition, the tiles can be fastened directly to it with adhesive. If the ceiling is in poor shape, furring, a framework of thin wood or metal strips, must be used. The use of grids, either fastened directly to the beams or suspended below them, offers many interesting ceiling treatments, including some with invisible seams.

The materials available for covering ceilings range in size from 12 × 12-inch tiles to 4 × 10-foot panels. The most popular sizes for direct application are 12 × 12-inch and 12 × 24-inch while those for suspended ceilings are 2 × 2-foot and 2 × 4-foot.

The math of installation of tiles begins with measuring and drawing a plan of the ceiling. Measure the length of each wall at the height of your new ceiling and mark it on grid or graph paper in which each square will represent a square foot of the ceiling area. Write down measurements you obtain. Once the room dimensions are charted on your plan, measure and mark the positions of lighting fixtures, alcoves, columns, ducts, or any other items that will require special cutting or additional materials. Also measure and mark areas to be left uncovered, such as skylights, attic doors, recessed lighting units, and vents.

For best appearance, plan your ceiling so that border tiles or suspended panels at opposite sides of the ceiling are of equal width or length and more than half their original measurement. This is easily accomplished by shifting tiles or suspended panels by one-half their width (or length) in either direction. For example, when 12 × 12-inch ceiling tile is used, a room 15 feet 6 inches long will take 14 rows of 12-inch tiles plus border tiles at opposite walls trimmed uniformly to 9 inches **(Figure 3-1)**. If the room is 12 feet 4 inches wide, it will take across its width 11 rows of 12-inch tiles plus border tiles along opposite walls trimmed uniformly to 8 inches.

This means that the corner tiles for the room would be trimmed to measure 9 × 8 inches. The total number of tiles required is

Whole tiles	14 × 11	=	154
8 × 12-inch border tiles (short walls)	11 × 2	=	22
9 × 12-inch border tiles (long walls)	14 × 2	=	28
9 × 8-inch corner tiles	1 × 4	=	4
"Alibi," or extra, tiles			10
Total quantity of tiles			218

If the unit cost of the 12 × 12-inch tiles you select is 48 cents, the total cost of the ceiling material is $0.48 × 218 = $104.64.

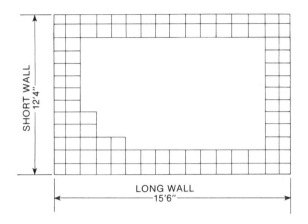

FIG. 3-1

Sometimes ceiling tiles are sold by the carton. An average carton of 12 × 12-inch tiles contains 60 tiles. Since buying tiles by the carton is frequently cheaper than buying them individually, it is wise to check that possibility.

Special alcoves or vertical applications over boxed ductwork will require extra tiles to be added to the total quantity of tiles needed. On the other hand, subtract tiles eliminated by skylights, columns, large recessed lighting fixtures, and attic doors. If your room is irregular in shape, plan to arrange your tiles for the best appearance in the largest ceiling area. If you plan to install a recessed lighting fixture between joists, make allowances for it on your plan.

When the ceiling tile is applied directly to the ceiling, a tile adhesive or cement must be used. To determine the number of gallons needed for a given ceiling, divide the ceiling area by the coverage of 1 gallon.

When applying ceiling tiles to a badly cracked or broken plaster ceiling or over exposed ceiling joists, a series of parallel 1 × 3-inch wood furring strips must be applied as a base for the staples used to hold the panels. The furring strips should run perpendicular to the joists and be nailed at each joist. Joists are usually 16 inches apart on center, so once you have located one joist you can just space the nails 16 inches apart. The first furring strip is applied flush where the wall and ceiling meet. The location of the second furring strip is determined by the width of the border tile that you decided on in planning your ceiling layout. Space this second strip so that the stapling edge of the border tile will be centered on it. Work across the ceiling from the second strip, installing furring strips parallel to it on 12-inch centers for 12 × 12-inch and 12 × 24-inch tiles. The next-to-the-last strip will be the same distance from the wall as the second strip, and the last strip is nailed flush against the wall. Your layout plan will help you to determine the linear feet of furring needed for the job. Of course, the cost of furring and staples must be added to that of the ceiling tiles for the complete cost of your new ceiling.

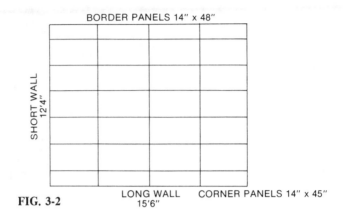

FIG. 3-2

If you use 2 × 4-foot panels suspended from a grid, you must add the cost of the grid and its hangers. The suspended ceiling should be planned so that the main runners are placed at right angles to ceiling joists and at 4-foot intervals. Using a room layout plan, draw lines perpendicular to the direction of the joists (usually parallel to the long wall) to represent the position of main runners, spaced 4 feet on centers (see **Figure 3-2**). Draw lines for cross tees between main runners and at 4-foot intervals parallel to the joists, if the long edges of panels are to run perpendicular to joists. If you want the long edges of panels to run parallel to joists, revise your drawing and border panel measurements to fit. Here, the main runners must be positioned so that border panels will be the same length on each side; all cross tees will run parallel to

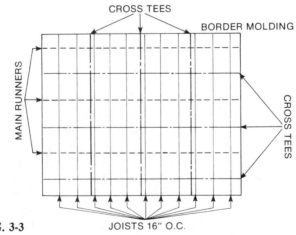

FIG. 3-3

178

joists between main runners, and they will be spaced 2 feet apart (see **Figure 3-3**). Once your suspended ceiling system is determined, it will be helpful to stretch reference strings between walls to indicate positions of main runners and cross tees. Once your plan is complete, add up the quantity of grid materials you require, as follows:

1. Wall angle molding (add up wall lengths)
2. Main runners (according to plan)
3. Cross tees (according to plan)

When figuring the materials needed for a suspended ceiling you will also need eye rings and wire, grid hangers, or grip clips, depending on the type of grid being used. The number of hanging devices needed will depend on the grid arrangement. Your local lumberyard or home center dealer will be able to help you to purchase the correct amount needed for the installation.

WALL CONSTRUCTION MATERIALS

There are two basic types of wall construction: dry-wall and lath-and-plaster. Lath-and-plaster finish is presently employed to a very limited degree in home construction; dry-wall materials are more popular today. A dry-wall finish, as the name implies, uses a material that requires little, if any, water for application. More specifically, dry-wall finishes include plywood, hardboard, insulation board (fiberboard), gypsum wallboard, and similar sheet materials, as well as wood paneling in various thicknesses and forms. The thickness of the finish material is determined partly by the spacing of the framing to which it is to be attached, as shown in **Table 3-1**.

TABLE 3-1:
MINIMUM THICKNESS OF MATERIALS USED FOR INTERIOR
WALL COVERINGS

Framing spaced (in.)	Thickness (in.)		
	Plywood and hardboard	Gypsum board	Wood paneling
16	$\frac{1}{4}$	$\frac{3}{8}$	$\frac{3}{8}$
20	$\frac{1}{4}$	$\frac{1}{2}$	$\frac{1}{2}$
24	$\frac{5}{16}$ or $\frac{3}{8}$	$\frac{1}{2}$	$\frac{25}{32}$

Solid Wood Paneling

Various types and patterns of woods are available as paneling. Knotty pine, redwood, whitepocket Douglas fir, sound wormy chestnut, and pecky cypress, finished natural or stained and varnished, may be used to cover one or more sides of a room. Such desirable hardwoods as red oak, pecan, elm, walnut, white oak, and cherry are fancier. Most types of paneling come in thicknesses that range around $^{25}/_{32}$ inch; widths vary from 4 to 8 inches, lengths from 3 to 10 feet.

In a wood-paneled room boards of random widths call more attention to a wall than do equal-width boards. Small rooms can be given the illusion of increased size with paneling applied horizontally. Of course, paneling can be applied vertically, horizontally, diagonally, or in combined directions.

To estimate quantities needed of board paneling, measure and multiply the dimensions of the areas to be paneled. Deduct for major openings (doors, fireplaces, etc.). Then add 10 to 20 percent for waste in fitting, lap of boards, if any, and the difference of rough width from finished width. In a room 14 feet 6 inches wide, 17 feet 3 inches long, and 8 feet high, with major openings totaling 78 square feet, the amount of paneling needed would be:

$$2(14\frac{1}{2} \times 8) + 2(17\frac{1}{4} \times 8) = 232 + 276 = 508 \text{ square feet}$$

$$508 - 78 = 430 \text{ square feet after deduction for opening}$$

$$430 \times 15\% \text{ (for waste)} = 64\frac{1}{2} \text{ square feet}$$

$$64\frac{1}{2} + 430 = 494\frac{1}{2} \text{ square feet}$$

Since most solid wood paneling is nominally 1 inch thick, the square foot and board foot totals are the same. If knotty pine is selling for $150 per 100 board feet, the cost of paneling would be 4.95 × $150 = $742.50.

Solid wood is subject to shrinkage and swelling, even if kiln-dried. After delivery, therefore, stack the lumber inside the house at a temperature as close to room temperature as possible. The paneling should never be stored where it will be exposed to weather or to excessive moisture. The building or room in which the wood planking is to be installed should be completely closed in and dry before installation begins. Masonry and other work involving moisture should be completed and dried. A moisture barrier such as polyethylene plastic sheeting (4 mils thick) should be provided behind paneling where any danger of moisture penetration exists—especially on outside walls and on all concrete or masonry walls. Also, if you intend to install paneling over a masonry wall that is often damp, it is a good idea to apply a wood preservative containing pentachlorophenol to the back of each panel nailed to the furring strips. Use 8d nails for $^{3}/_{4}$-inch boards when face-nailing, 6d for blind-nailing. Use proportionately smaller nails for thinner panels. If face-nailing is used, set the nails

$\frac{1}{32}$ inch below the surface and fill the resulting holes with colored filler or stick putty. When solid wood paneling is to be applied horizontally on an existing wall that is reasonably sound and true, furring strips are not usually required.

Plywood

Plywood panels come with faces—outer plies—ranging from richly figured oak, mahogany, birch, and walnut to fir and pine. Often the face is scored to resemble planks. The variety in style and range in price are extensive. They can be applied effectively to either traditional or modern interiors.

One outstanding advantage of plywood for interiors is the elimination of the need for periodic patching of cracks. Plywood walls are kickproof, puncture-proof, and crackproof. The only upkeep required is an occasional waxing. The large sheets, 4 feet wide, 8 feet long, and $\frac{1}{4}$ inch thick, can be erected quickly and easily with ordinary hand tools.

A rough pencil drawing of walls to be paneled will help you design the best arrangement for a room. Always plan to let the joints between the panels follow the pattern set by the vertical joints at door and window openings. This helps to maintain a pleasing symmetrical design.

When mounting plywood, start paneling at the openings, with vertical joints, and then divide the plain space in an orderly pattern, placing the panels in a reasonably balanced horizontal or vertical arrangement. Place vertical joints at each side of the top of doors and at the top and bottom of window openings. If the width of the door or window opening is more than 4 feet, most designers do not hesitate to place panels horizontally. Remember, vertical arrangements increase visual height and horizontal paneling appears to widen a space. Both can be combined in the same room with a pleasing effect. In certain woods, panels 9 or 10 feet long are available to solve special paneling problems.

To estimate the number of panels required, measure the perimeter of the room—that is, the total of the widths of each wall. If the room is not higher than 8 feet, divide the perimeter footage by the width of a panel, 4 feet.

For example, if your height is 8 feet and your walls measure 14 + 16 + 14 + 16 feet, the perimeter equals 60 feet and 15 panels are required. To allow for areas such as windows, doors, fireplaces, etc., use the following deductions:

Door	$\frac{1}{2}$ panel
Window	$\frac{1}{4}$ panel
Fireplace	$\frac{1}{2}$ panel

Thus, the actual number of panels for this room would be 13 (15 − 2 total deductions). If the final figure falls in between whole numbers of panels, use the higher whole number. For walls over 8 feet high, select a paneling which has V grooves and that will "stack," allowing panel grooves to line up perfectly from floor to ceiling.

For most wall paneling, $\frac{1}{4}$-inch plywood sheets are used. Of course, $\frac{3}{8}$- and $\frac{3}{4}$-inch panels may be applied with good results, but they are more expensive. The latter thickness may be used as a partition without framing. For special designs, such as patterns made of small panels, 16- to 24-inch diamonds, squares, etc., it is best first to sheathe the walls with $\frac{5}{16}$-inch plywood sheathing and then to apply the finish panels as desired.

Plywood paneling is sometimes sold by the square foot but is usually sold by the sheet. To figure the total panel cost, just multiply the number of panels by their single unit cost. When figuring the cost of panels by the square foot, multiply the unit square foot price times the number of square feet in a panel times the number of panels required.

To the total paneling cost, the installation items (nails, adhesives, molding, stick putty, furring strips, etc.) must be added to obtain the total cost of the job.

Hardboard

Hardboard is made by subjecting wood fibers to heat and high pressure. The result is a dense, hard board that is resistant to stains, scrubbing, and moisture, as well as to dents, mars, and scuffs. It may be smooth-surfaced or random-grooved. In most cases, the material is prefinished in wood grains such as walnut, cherry, birch, oak, teak, and pecan, in a variety of shades. Finishes also include marble reproductions, plain colors, speckled colors, simulated tile, lace prints, wallpaper textures, and murals. In addition there are decorative and work-saving plastic-surfaced hardboards that resist water, stains, and household chemicals exceptionally well. Most hardboard is sufficiently dense and moisture-resistant for use in bathrooms, kitchens, and laundry rooms.

Hardboards vary from $\frac{1}{12}$ inch to $\frac{3}{4}$ inch thick. One can use $\frac{1}{4}$-inch or $\frac{5}{16}$-inch board thicknesses for structural wall members. Use $\frac{3}{16}$-, $\frac{1}{4}$-, and $\frac{5}{16}$-inch hardboards over open framing. All panel edges should be backed. Studs or framing members should be spaced no more than 16 inches on center. Hardboards $\frac{1}{8}$ and $\frac{3}{16}$ inch thick should be applied over solid backing. Boards $\frac{1}{4}$ inch thick may be applied directly over studding or stripping not over 16 inches on center.

Since hardboard is usually available in 4 × 8-foot panels, costs—both paneling and total job—may be figured in the same way as they are for plywood panels. Hardboard panels may be installed with either nails or a special type of adhesive. The label on the adhesive can states the amount of coverage for the glue.

Gypsum Wallboard

Gypsum wallboard, also called plasterboard, Sheetrock, gypsumboard, and wallboard, is low-cost, durable, and easy to handle when installing. It is

182

TABLE 3-2:
MAXIMUM MEMBER SPACING FOR
VARIOUS THICKNESSES OF GYPSUM WALLBOARD

Install long direction of sheet	Minimum thickness (in.)	Maximum spacing of supports (in. o.c.)	
		Walls	Ceilings
Parallel to	3/8	16	16
framing members	1/2	24	16
	5/8	24	16
Perpendicular to	3/8	16	16
framing members	1/2	24	24
	5/8	24	24

composed of a gypsum filler faced with paper. Sheets are normally 4 feet wide and 8 long, but can be obtained in lengths up to 16 feet. The edges along the length are usually tapered, although some types are tapered on all edges, which allows a filled and taped joint. This material may also be obtained with a foil back, which serves as a vapor barrier on exterior walls. It is also available with vinyl or other prefinished or predecorated surfaces. In new construction, a $\frac{1}{2}$-inch thickness is recommended for single-layer application. In laminated two-ply applications, two $\frac{3}{8}$-inch-thick sheets are used. (Sheets can be specially ordered $\frac{5}{8}$ inch thick.) The $\frac{3}{8}$-inch thickness, while considered minimum for 16-inch stud spacing in single-layer applications, is normally specified for repair and remodeling work **(Table 3-2)**.

When the single-layer system is used, 4-foot-wide gypsum sheets are applied vertically or horizontally on the walls after the ceiling has been covered. Applied vertically, each sheet covers three stud spaces when studs are spaced 16 inches on center, and two when spacing is 24 inches. Edges should be centered on studs, and only moderate contact should be made between edges of sheets.

Although long panels are priced slightly higher than those 8 feet long, it is wise to order the longest panel you can use; the difference in price is worth it because the panel covers a larger area with less time and reduces the number of joints that must be taped. (But remember that smaller boards are much easier for one person to handle.) If, for instance, the wall to be wallboarded is 21 feet long, it would be better to use one 4 × 12 panel and one 4 × 10 panel rather than three 4 × 8 panels for each horizontal course. Not only would there be a smaller amount of waste, there would be one less joint to tape. In such a case, the little extra cost of the large sheets and the effort needed to handle them would be justified in the time saved and neatness of the finished job.

TABLE 3-3:
RECOMMENDED SIZES AND QUANTITIES OF NAILS REQUIRED PER
1,000 SQUARE FEET OF GYPSUM WALLBOARD

Thickness (in.)	Nail size	Quantity of nails (lb.)	
		Spacing of studs or joists	
		16 in.	24 in.
¼	4d	4	3
⅜	4d	4	3
½	5d	6	4
⅝	6d	7	5

When gypsum board is installed, nail heads should be driven about $\frac{1}{16}$ inch below the face of the board; this set can be obtained by using a crowned hammer. The indentations around the nails away from the edges are concealed by applying joint cement or spackle. The nail indentations along the edges are concealed with a perforated fiber joint tape set in joint cement. The edges are slightly recessed to bring the tape flush with the faces. Besides concealing the nail indentations, the tape and cement also conceal the joint when the surface is sanded flush.

The cost of the joint tape, spackle, sandpaper, and nails must be added to job. Incidentally, the nails used to fasten gypsum board are of the plasterboard type—4d, 5d, or 6d—with $\frac{5}{16}$- or $\frac{3}{8}$-inch heads, depending on the thickness of the board. Recommended nail spacings are 8 inches for wall and 7 inches for ceiling installation **(Table 3-3)**.

TABLE 3-4:
MAN-HOURS IN INSTALLING GYPSUM WALLBOARD

Operation	Unit	Spacing of studs or joists (man-hours)	
		16 in.	24 in.
Install wallboard			
Large spaces	100 sq. ft.	1.5	1.2
Medium-size rooms	100 sq. ft.	2.5	2.0
Small rooms	100 sq. ft.	3.5	3.0
Install perforated tape and sand surface	100 ft	4.0	4.0

184

The labor time required to install gypsum wallboard varies considerably with the size and complexity of the area to be covered. For large wall or ceiling areas, which require little or no cutting and fitting of boards, two professional carpenters should install a board 4 feet wide and 8 to 9 feet long in about 10 to 15 minutes. This is equivalent to 1 to $1\frac{1}{2}$ man-hours per 100 square feet. However, when an area contains numerous openings and it is necessary to mark the boards and cut them to fit the openings, the labor required may be as high as 3 to 4 man-hours per 100 square feet. Cutting is done by scoring one side of a board with a curved knife, which is drawn along a straightedge. A slight bending force will break the board along the scored line. **Table 3-4** gives representative man-hours required by professionals to install gypsum wallboard and perforated-tape joints. It can be used as a guide to time needed by you to install gypsum board.

Ceramic Tiles

There are many types of ceramic tiles, including glazed wall tiles, ceramic mosaics, quarry tiles, and specialty tiles. Tiles range in size from 1-inch-square mosaics to 12-inch squares and are available in high- or low-relief designs with colorful glazes or multicolored patterns. There are also handsome contoured tiles. Along with hexagons, octagons, and rectangles, there are curvilinear shapes inspired by historic Moorish, Norman, and Florentine designs. Many of these are quarry tiles, which are now offered in a large range of natural colors as well as durable glazes. Because of its many practical and decorative virtues, tile has a place in any room in your home.

In the past, tile could be installed only by highly skilled professionals since the only setting material available was cement, which is difficult to work with. Today, as a result of the development of new setting techniques and materials, it is possible to install your own tile.

To estimate the number of tiles required, add the length and width of a room, multiply by 2, then multiply this answer by the height of the wall to cover. This will give you the square footage of the area to be tiled. For example, for an 8 × 12-foot room, add 8 and 12 (20) and multiply by 2 (40). If the wall is to be tiled up to 5 feet in height, multiply 40 by 5. This gives a total of 200 square feet to be tiled. If you plan to use common 4 $\frac{1}{4}$-inch square tiles, figure that eight tiles will cover a square foot of surface; then 200 × 8, or 1,600, tiles are needed. The factor of 8 already takes into account waste and allowances for doors and windows.

When buying tiles, it is always a good idea to get a few more than you actually require in case of accidental breakage and for future replacement should a tile become cracked. You must remember that tiles, even the same color and made by the same manufacturer, are made according to dye lot and shade. Make sure all of your tiles are the same shade and dye lot number.

185

There are many special trim shapes in glazed ceramics for outside and inside corners, tub enclosures, tile wainscot borders, and even countertop and windowsill edge pieces. Take a rough sketch of your room along with you to your dealer for help in finding these special shapes. These are generally sold by the linear foot.

Lath and Plaster

Lath-and-plaster interior wall finishing has dropped in popularity in recent years, especially with the do-it-yourselfer. Plaster is much more difficult to apply than dry-wall and, because it is a wet material, it requires drying time before other work can be started. However, if you plan to have plastering professionally done, the cost of lathing and plastering may be estimated by the square yard, by the square foot, or, for some classes of work, by the linear foot. The square-yard method is the most popular. For example, if a lath and plaster job for a 12 × 20-foot room with an 8-foot ceiling is to be estimated, it would be figured as follows:

For walls = (12 feet + 20 feet) × 8 feet × 2   = 512 square feet
For ceiling = (12 feet × 20 feet)   = 240 square feet
Total lath and plaster needed   = 752 square feet

To find the square yards needed:

$$752 \div 9 = 83.6 \text{ square yards}$$

Within the plastering trade, the policy used to determine the area covered varies considerably. Some contractors do not deduct the areas of openings such as doors and windows when determining the area for cost purposes. Some contractors deduct one-half of the areas of all openings larger than a specified dimension, such as 20 square feet, but make no deductions for smaller areas. Still other contractors deduct the areas of all openings, regardless of size, to give the net area of the surface covered. When specifying a cost per unit area, the method of arriving at the total area used for payment purposes should be clearly stated. If in our example, no deductions for openings were made and the plastering contractor stated his price at $26 a square yard (including labor), the total cost of the job would be:

$$83.6 \times 26 = \$2,173.60$$

When payment is made by the linear foot, it is also necessary to state clearly the basis on which the number of units will be determined.

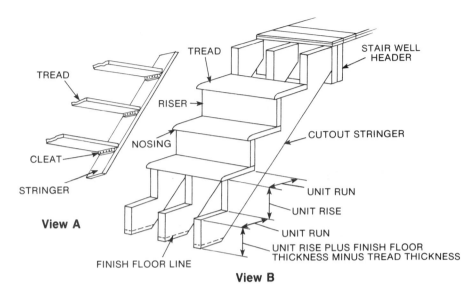

TREAD

TREAD

RISER →

NOSING

CLEAT

STRINGER

View A

TREAD

STAIR WELL
HEADER

CUTOUT STRINGER

UNIT RUN

UNIT RISE

UNIT RUN

UNIT RISE PLUS FINISH FLOOR
THICKNESS MINUS TREAD THICKNESS

FINISH FLOOR LINE

View B

FIG. 3-4

STAIR CONSTRUCTION

There are many different kinds of stairs, but all have two main parts in common: the treads people walk on and the stringers (also called strings, horses, and carriages) that support the treads. A very simple type of stairway, consisting only of stringers and treads, is shown in **Figure 3-4, view A.** Treads of the type shown here are called plank treads, and this simple type of stairway is called a cleat stairway, because cleats attached to the stringers support the treads.

A more finished type of stairway has the treads mounted on two or more sawtooth-edged stringers, and includes risers, as shown in **Figure 3-4, view B.** The stringers shown here are cut out of solid pieces of dimension lumber (usually 2-by-12), and are therefore called cutout or sawed stringers.

The first step in stairway layout is to determine the unit rise and unit run, shown in **Figure 3-4, view B.** The customary permissible unit rise for stairs is about 7 inches, but for a given stairway the exact unit rise is calculated on the basis of the total rise of the stairway.

The total rise is the vertical distance between the lower finish floor level and the upper finish floor level. This distance may be shown in the elevations; however, since the actual vertical distance as constructed may vary slightly from what it should have been, the distance should be measured.

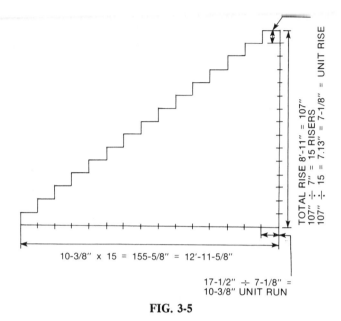

10-3/8" x 15 = 155-5/8" = 12'-11-5/8"

17-1/2" ÷ 7-1/8" =
10-3/8" UNIT RUN

TOTAL RISE 8'-11" = 107"
107" ÷ 7" = 15 RISERS
107" ÷ 15 = 7.13" = 7-1/8" = UNIT RISE

FIG. 3-5

At the time the stairs are to be laid out in new construction, the subflooring is laid, but the finish flooring usually is not. If both the lower and the upper floor are to be covered with finish flooring of the same thickness, the measured vertical distance from lower subfloor surface to the upper subfloor surface will be the same as the eventual distance between the finish floor surfaces and therefore equal to the total rise of the stairway. However, if you are measuring up from a finish floor (such as a concrete basement floor), then you must add to the measured distance the thickness of the upper finish flooring to get the total rise of the stairway. If the upper and lower finish floors will be of different thicknesses, then you must add the difference in thickness to the measured distance between subfloor surfaces to get the total rise of the stairway. Use a straight piece of lumber plumbed in the stair opening with a spirit level, or a plumb bob and cord, to measure the vertical distance.

Assume that a total rise measures 8 feet 11 inches, as shown in **Figure 3-5.** Knowing this, determine the unit rise as follows. First, convert the total rise to inches. In this case it comes to 107 inches. Next, divide the total rise by the average permissible unit rise, which is 7 inches. The result, disregarding any fraction, is the number of risers the stairway will have. In this case it is 107/7, or 15. Now divide the total rise by the number of risers, in this case, 107/15, which comes to 7.13 inches, or rounded off to the nearest $1/16$ inch, 7 $1/8$ inches. This, then, is the unit rise.

The unit run is calculated on the basis of the unit rise, and a general architects' rule that the sum of the unit run and unit rise should be $17\frac{1}{2}$ inches.

188

If the unit rise is 7 $\frac{1}{8}$ inches, the unit run is 17 $\frac{1}{2}$ inches minus 7 $\frac{1}{8}$ inches, or 10 $\frac{3}{8}$ inches.

You can now calculate the total run of the stairway. The total run is obviously equal to the product of the unit run times the total number of treads in the stairway. However, the total number of treads depends upon the manner in which the upper end of the stairway is anchored to the header.

In **Figure 3-6** three methods of anchoring the upper end of a stairway are shown. In **Figure 3-6, view A,** there is a complete tread at the top of the stairway. This means that the number of complete treads will be the same as the number of risers. For the stairway shown in **Figure 3-5,** there are 15 risers and 15 complete treads. Therefore, the total run of the stairway will be the product of the unit run times 15: $10\frac{3}{8} \times 15 = 155\frac{5}{8}$ inches, or 12 feet 11$\frac{5}{8}$ inches, as shown.

In **Figure 3-6, view B,** there is only part of a tread at the top of the stairway. If this method were used for the stairway shown in **Figure 3-5,** the number of complete treads would be 1 less than the number of risers, or 14. The total run of the stairway would be $14 \times 10\frac{3}{8}$ inches plus the run of the partial tread at the top. If this run were 7 inches, then the total run would be $14 \times 10\frac{3}{8} + 7 = 152\frac{1}{4}$ inches, or 12 feet 8$\frac{1}{4}$ inches.

In **Figure 3-6, view C,** there is no tread at all at the top of the stairway; the upper finish flooring serves as the top tread. In this case the total number of complete treads is again 14, but since there is no additional partial tread, the total run of the stairway is $14 \times 10\frac{3}{8} = 145\frac{1}{4}$ inches, or 12 feet 1$\frac{1}{4}$ inches.

When you have calculated the total run of the stairway, drop a plumb bob from the stairwell head to the floor below and measure off the total run from the plumb bob. This locates the anchoring point for the lower end of the stairway.

Cutout stringers for main stairways are usually made from 2-by-12 stock. First determine about how long a piece of stock you will need. Let us assume that you are to use the method of upper-end anchorage shown in the **Figure 3-6, view A,** to lay out a stringer for the stairway shown in **Figure 3-5.** This stairway has a total rise of 8 feet 11 inches and a total run of 12 feet 11$\frac{5}{8}$ inches. The stringer must be long enough to form the hypotenuse of a triangle with

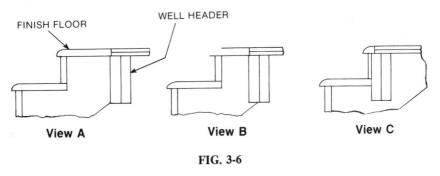

FINISH FLOOR

WELL HEADER

View A　　　　**View B**　　　　**View C**

FIG. 3-6

189

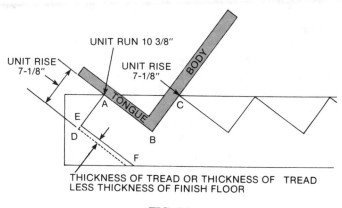

UNIT RUN 10 3/8"

UNIT RISE 7-1/8"

UNIT RISE 7-1/8"

THICKNESS OF TREAD OR THICKNESS OF TREAD
LESS THICKNESS OF FINISH FLOOR

FIG. 3-7

sides of those two lengths. For an approximate length estimate, call the sides 9 and 13 feet long. The length of the hypotenuse, then, will equal the square root of $9^2 + 13^2$, or about 15.8 feet, or about 15 feet 9½ inches.

Figure 3-7 shows the layout at the lower end of the stringer. Set the framing square to the unit run on the tongue and the unit rise on the body, and draw the line AB. This line represents the bottom tread. Then draw AD perpendicular to AB, as long as a unit rise. This line represents the bottom riser in the stairway. Now, you have probably noticed that, up to this point, the thickness of a tread in the stairway has been ignored. This thickness is about to be accounted for by making an allowance in the height of this first riser, a process which is called *dropping the stringer.*

As you can see in **Figure 3-4,** the unit rise is measured from the top of one tread to the top of the next for all risers except the bottom one. For this one, the unit rise is measured from the finish floor surface to the surface of the first tread. If line AD were cut to the unit rise, the actual rise of the first step would be the sum of the unit rise plus the thickness of a tread. Therefore, the length of AD is shortened by the thickness of a tread, as shown in **Figure 3-7,** or by the thickness of a tread less the thickness of the finish flooring. The first is done if the stringer will rest on a finish floor, such as a concrete basement floor. The second is done if the stringer will rest on subflooring.

When you have shortened line AD to AE, as shown, draw EF parallel to AB. This line represents the bottom horizontal anchor edge of the stringer. Then proceed to lay off the remaining risers and treads to the unit rise and unit run, until you have laid off 15 risers and 15 treads. **Figure 3-8** shows the layout at the upper end of the stringer. The line AB represents the top, that is, the 15th, tread. BC, drawn perpendicular to AB, represents the upper vertical anchor edge of the stringer, which will butt against the stairwell header.

We have been dealing with a common straight-flight stairway, one that

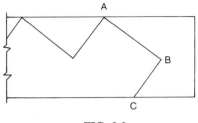

FIG. 3-8

follows the same direction throughout. When floor space is not extensive enough to permit construction of a straight-flight stairway, a change stairway is installed, one that changes direction one or more times. The most common types of these are 90-degree change and 180-degree change. These are usually *platform* stairways, that is, successive straight-flight lengths, connecting platforms at which the direction changes 90 degrees, or doubles back 180 degrees. Such a stairway is laid out simply as a succession of straight-flight stairways.

The stairs in a structure are broadly divided into principal stairs and service stairs. Service stairs are porch, basement, and attic stairs. Some of these may be simple cleat stairways; others may be open-riser stairways. An open-riser stairway has treads anchored on cutout stringers or stair-block stringers, but no risers. The lower ends of the stringers on porch, basement, and other stairs anchored on concrete are fastened with a kickplate like the one shown in **Figure 3-9.**

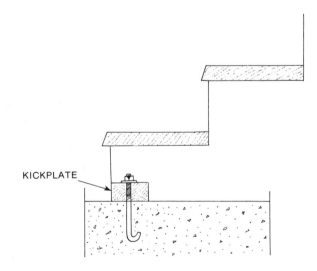

FIG. 3-9

191

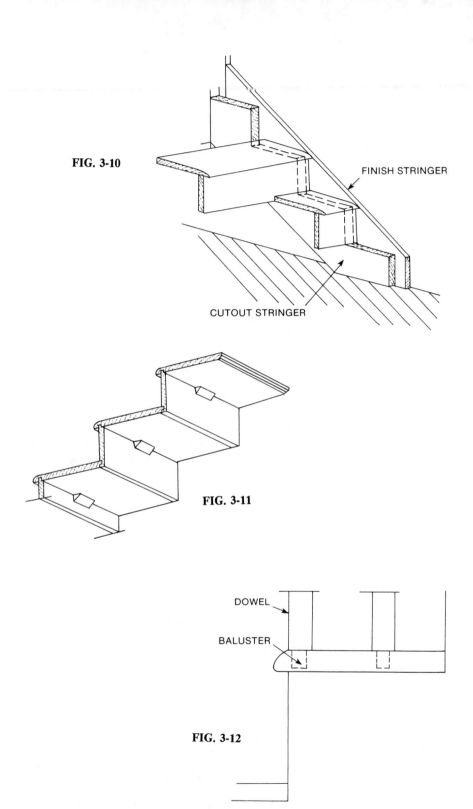

FIG. 3-10

FINISH STRINGER

CUTOUT STRINGER

FIG. 3-11

DOWEL

BALUSTER

FIG. 3-12

A principal stairway is usually more finished in appearance. Rough cutout stringers are concealed by finish stringers like the one shown in **Figure 3-10.** Treads and risers are often rabbet-joined, as shown in **Figure 3-11.** To prevent squeaking, glue triangular blocks into the joints, as shown in the figure.

The vertical members which support a stairway handrail are called *balusters.* **Figure 3-12** shows a method of joining balusters to treads. For this method, dowels shaped on the lower ends of the balusters are glued into holes bored in the treads.

Stringers should be toenailed to stairwell headers with 10d nails, three to each side of the stringer. Those that face against trimmer joists should be nailed to the joist with at least three 16d nails apiece. At the bottom, a stringer should be toenailed with 10d nails, four to each side, driven into the subflooring and if possible into a joist below. Treads and risers should be nailed to stringers with 6d, 8d, or 10d finish nails, depending on the thickness of the stock.

FINISH FLOORING

The term "finish flooring" refers, of course, to the material used as the final wearing surface that is applied to a floor. In its simplest form it might be paint over a concrete floor slab. A more sophisticated treatment might come from the wide selection of wood materials used for flooring. Hardwoods and softwoods are available as strip flooring in a variety of widths and thicknesses and as random-width planks and block flooring. Linoleum, asphalt, rubber, cork, vinyl, and other materials in tile or sheet forms can also be used. Tile flooring is also available in particleboard, which is manufactured by combining small wood particles with resin under extremely high pressure. Ceramic tile and carpeting are used in many areas in ways not thought practical a few years ago.

In fact, numerous flooring materials now available may be used over a variety of floor systems. Each has a property that adapts it to a particular usage. Of the practical properties, perhaps durability and maintenance ease are the most important. However, initial cost, comfort, and appearance must also be considered. Specific service requirements may call for special properties, such as resistance to hard wear or comfort.

Wood Flooring

Softwood finish flooring costs less than most hardwood species and is often used to good advantage in bedroom and closet areas where traffic is light. It might also be selected to fit the interior decor. It is less dense than the hardwoods, less wear-resistant, and shows surface abrasions more readily. Softwoods most commonly used for flooring are southern pine, Douglas fir, redwood, and western hemlock. Softwood flooring has tongue-and-groove edges

193

TABLE 3-5:
GRADES OF STRIP FLOORING

Species	Grain orientation	Size		Grades		
		Thickness	Exposed width	First	Second	Third
Softwoods						
Douglas fir ⎱	Edge	25/32	2 3/8, 5 3/16	B and better	C	D
Hemlock ⎰	Flat	25/32	2 3/8, 5 3/16	C and better	D	—
Southern pine	Edge and flat	5/16, 1 5/16	1 3/4, 5 7/16	B and better	C and better	D and No. 2 common
Hardwoods						
Oak	Edge	25/32	1 1/2, 3 1/4	Clear	Select	—
	Flat	3/8	1 1/2, 2 ⎱	Clear	Select	No. 1 common
		1/2	1 1/2, 2 ⎰			
Beech ⎰	Edge	25/32	1 1/2, 3 1/4 ⎱	First	Second	—
Birch	Flat	3/8	1 1/2, 2			
Maple		1/2	1 1/2, 2 ⎰	First	Second	—
Pecan* ⎰						

*Special grades are available in which uniformity of color is a requirement.

and may be hollow-backed or grooved. Some types are also end-matched. Vertical-grain flooring generally has better wearing qualities than flat-grain flooring under hard usage.

Hardwoods most commonly used for flooring are red and white oak, beech, birch, maple, and pecan. Manufacturers supply both prefinished and unfinished flooring.

Table 3-5 lists woods used in strip flooring, their grades, and other properties. Yard lumber, the softwood found in retail lumberyards, and used for general utility purposes, is divided into six grades, from strongest and most even to least: A, B, C, No. 1 common, No. 2 common, No. 3 common. Oak is available in five grades: clear, sap clear, select, No. 1 common, No. 2 common. Beech, birch, and maple come in three grades: first, second, and third.

Most wood-strip finish flooring is side-matched (tongue-and-groove on the edges), and some is end-matched (tongue-and-groove on the ends) as well.

Wood subfloors are covered with building paper or with a layer of heavy felt before wood-strip finish flooring is applied. If the specifications call for furring strips between the subflooring and the finish flooring, the strips are nailed on top of the paper or felt. Furring strips are laid at right angles to the line of the finish flooring; they are usually spaced 12 or 16 inches apart.

To determine the board feet of flooring needed to cover a given space, first find the area in square feet. Since most flooring is now $25/32$ inch, which is considered nominal 1 inch, this result is the number of board feet in the finished room. Where there are bay windows or other projections, allowance should be made for additional flooring. Also fitting, handling, cracking, and other exigencies create a certain amount of waste, which must be allowed for. The National Oak Flooring Manufacturers' Association, for instance, recommends that the percentages shown in Table 3-6 of floor area be added to cover waste from fitting. An additional 3 to 5 percent should be added to cover damage in handling and cutting. To calculate the amount of oak flooring

TABLE 3-6:
WASTAGE ALLOWANCES FOR
WOOD-STRIP FLOORING

Size of strip (in.)	Waste allowance (percent)
$25/32 \times 1\,1/2$	50
$25/32 \times 2\,1/4$	33
$25/32 \times 3\,1/4$	25
$3/8 \times 1\,1/2$	33 1/3
$3/8 \times 2$	25
$1/2 \times 1\,1/2$	33 1/3
$1/2 \times 2$	25

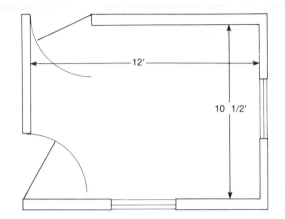

FIG. 3-13

$^{25}/_{32} \times 2^{1}/_{4}$ inches to order for the floor of a bedroom 10 feet 6 inches $\times$ 12 feet, shown in **Figure 3-13**, proceed as follows:

Calculate the number of board feet required to cover the floor.	10 ft. $^{1}/_{2}$ in. $\times$ 12 ft. = 126 b.f.n.
Add the percentages, $33^{1}/_{2}$ for waste and 5 for damage.	$33^{1}/_{2}$ percent + 5 percent = $38^{1}/_{2}$ percent
Find this percent of the number of board feet.	$126 \times 0.385 = 49$
Add this to the board feet in the floor.	$126 + 49 = 175$ board feet of $^{25}/_{32}$ by $2^{1}/_{4}$ inch flooring

If this flooring sells for $990.00 per thousand board feet, the total cost would be:

$$.175 \times \$990 = \$173.25$$

To this material cost, you must add that of nails, felt or paper, or furring (if used).

For a quick reference aid in estimating flooring needed, use **tables 3-7** and **3-7A.**

To use **Table 3-7** for a room $12 \times 11^{1}/_{2}$ feet, to be floored with strips $^{25}/_{32} \times 2^{1}/_{4}$ inches, calculate the area, 126 square feet, and look under the second column:

100	139
20	28
6	8
126 square feet	175 board feet needed

TABLE 3-7:
ESTIMATING FLOORING REQUIREMENTS

Figures below show the number of board feet of various sizes of flooring required to cover square footage of floor space, as shown in the left most column.

Square feet of floor space	Tile sizes						
	25/32 × 3 1/4	25/32 × 2 1/4	25/32 × 1 1/2	1/2 × 2	1/2 × 1 1/2	3/8 × 2	3/8 × 1 1/2
10	13	14	16	13	14	13	14
20	26	28	31	26	28	26	28
30	39	42	47	39	42	39	42
40	52	56	62	52	56	52	56
50	65	70	78	65	70	65	70
60	78	83	93	78	83	78	83
70	91	97	109	91	97	91	97
80	104	111	124	104	111	104	111
90	117	125	140	117	125	117	125
100	129	139	155	130	139	130	139
200	258	277	310	260	277	260	277
300	387	415	465	390	415	390	415
400	516	553	620	520	553	520	553
500	645	692	775	650	692	650	692
600	774	830	930	780	830	780	830
700	903	969	1085	910	969	910	969
800	1032	1107	1240	1040	1107	1040	1107
900	1161	1245	1395	1170	1245	1170	1245
1000	1290	1383	1550	1300	1383	1300	1383

TABLE 3-7A:
ADDITIONAL FLOOR ESTIMATING DATA

	Tile sizes						
	25/32 × 3 1/4	25/32 × 2 1/4	25/32 × 1 1/2	1/2 × 2	1/2 × 1 1/2	3/8 × 2	3/8 × 1 1/2
Called	1 × 4	1 × 3	1 × 2 1/4	1 × 2 1/2	1 × 2	1 × 2 1/2	1 × 2
Lbs. per 1,000 board feet	2300	2100	2000	1350	1300	1000	1000
Size of nails used	8d	8d	8d	5d	5d	4d	4d
Nail spacing	10 to 12 inches on center			8 to 10 inches on center		6 to 8 inches on center	
No. pieces per bundle	8	12	12	18	18	24	24
To obtain board feet from bundle multiply by	2 2/3	3	2 1/4	3 3/4	3	5	4

Resilient Flooring

Flooring surfaces made of elastic, or resilient, materials come in tiles and sheets. They are frequently used because they are inexpensive, durable, easy to install and maintain, and varied in design. They are available in solid colors, patterns, and convincing imitations of wood, brick, slate, and marble. They are usually cemented in place. (See **Table 3-8.**)

Tiles

Made of vinyl, asbestos fibers, and other components, resilient tiles are exceptionally durable and easy to keep clean. Available in 9- or 12-inch squares, they lend themselves to a variety of customizing effects, since tiles of different colors and styles may be easily combined. In addition, most tile floors are ideal for do-it-yourself installation.

Asphalt tile, the first resilient tile developed, is the least expensive and can be installed at any grade level. It offers good durability, but compared to other types of resilient floors, it ranks low in resistance to grease and soil. For this reason, it is not recommended for kitchens. Most asphalt tiles are $\frac{1}{8}$ inch thick.

Vinyl-asbestos tile is the most popular of all resilient tiles. It is inexpensive and can be installed anywhere: above, on, or below grade. Vinyl-asbestos tiles have exceptional durability and are easy to clean. They do not require waxing; they can be given a low sheen by buffing after a floor is mopped. These tiles are available $\frac{1}{16}$, $\frac{3}{32}$, and $\frac{1}{8}$ inch thick.

Solid (or homogeneous) vinyl tiles that have a backing are exceptionally durable. Their surface is smooth and nonporous, which makes upkeep easy and economical. You can use them on any grade level, and solid vinyl is available in many colors and patterns and thicknesses from .080-inch gauge (thin) to $\frac{1}{16}$ and $\frac{1}{8}$ inch.

Rubber tile, one of the most resilient of all flooring materials, offers a great deal of comfort underfoot. Wear and soil resistance and upkeep maintenance are good. Today's rubber tile can be used in all areas of your home, on walls as well as floors, but perhaps because it is relatively expensive, it has never become popular.

Cork, possibly the quietest of all floorings, is available pure or combined with vinyl to increase durability and ease in cleaning.

Table 3-9 will aid you in figuring the number of tiles to complete an installation job. For instance, if you are working with a floor area which is 280 square feet (a 14-by-20-foot family room), and you want to use 9-by-9-inch tiles, the table indicates 356 tiles for 200 square feet and 143 tiles for 80 square feet, a total number of 499 tiles.

When ordering tiles, it is most important to consider the waste factors. In our example, the allowance for waste is 7 percent of the total number of tiles, or an extra 35 tiles. This would make a grand total of 534 tiles. Since tiles are usually boxed 80 to a carton, this would mean that we need over $6\frac{3}{4}$ cartons.

TABLE 3-8:
GUIDE TO RESILIENT FLOORING

Material	Backing required	How installed	Where to install	Ease of installation	Ease of maintenance	Durability	Sound absorption
Tiles							
Asphalt	None	Adhesive	Anywhere	Fair	Difficult	Fair	Very poor
Vinyl-asbestos	None	Adhesive	Anywhere	Easy	Very easy	Excellent	Poor
Vinyl	None	Adhesive	Anywhere	Easy	Easy	Good-excellent	Fair
Rubber	None	Adhesive	Anywhere	Fair	Easy	Good	Good
Cork	None	Adhesive	On or above grade	Fair	Fair (with vinyl, good)	Good	Excellent
Sheets							
Inlaid vinyl	Felt	Adhesive	Above grade	Fair	Easy	Good	Fair
	Foam and felt	Adhesive	Above grade	Difficult	Easy	Good	Good
Printed vinyl							
Asbestos	Adhesive	Anywhere	Very difficult	Easy	Excellent	Fair	
Foam	Adhesive	Anywhere	Very difficult	Easy	Excellent	Good	
Felt	Loose-lay	Above grade	Easy	Fair	Poor	Poor	
Felt	Adhesive	Above grade	Fair	Easy	Fair	Poor	
Foam and felt	Loose-lay	Above grade	Easy	Easy	Fair	Good	
Foam and asbestos	Adhesive or loose-lay	Anywhere	Fair-easy	Easy	Good	Good	
Foam	Loose-lay	Anywhere	Easy	Easy	Good	Good	

TABLE 3-9:
COMPUTING NUMBER OF TILES NEEDED

Square feet	Number of tiles needed (inches)			Square feet	Number of tiles needed (inches)		
	9 × 9	12 × 12	9 × 18		9 × 9	12 × 12	9 × 18
1	2	1	1	60	107	60	54
2	4	2	2	70	125	70	63
3	6	3	3	80	143	80	72
4	8	4	4	90	160	90	80
5	9	5	5	100	178	100	90
6	11	6	6	200	356	200	178
7	13	7	7	300	534	300	267
8	15	8	8	400	712	400	356
9	16	9	8	500	890	500	445
10	18	10	9	600	1,068	600	534
20	36	20	18	700	1,246	700	623
30	54	30	27	800	1,424	800	712
40	72	40	36	900	1,602	900	801
50	89	50	45	1,000	1,780	1,000	890

Allowance for waste

1–50 square feet	14 percent
50–100 square feet	10 percent
100–200 square feet	8 percent
200–300 square feet	7 percent
300–1,000 square feet	5 percent
Over 1,000 square feet	3 percent

Even if the dealer is willing to split a carton, it would be wise to take the seven full cartons to assure an adequate supply of tiles from the same lot and also to allow for replacement if more are ever needed.

Sheet Flooring

The principal advantage of sheet flooring is seamlessness. Since it is installed in rolls up to 12 feet wide, there are few seams in the finished floor. The result is a beautiful wall-to-wall sweep of color and design, a perfect setting for room furnishings. Some sheet floors can also be customized by combining two or more colors or styles. Sheet vinyls are comfortable underfoot and resist grease and alkalis. With special backing they can be used below, on, or above grade. Resistance to wear is generally very good. However, the installation of standard sheet vinyl flooring with adhesive is not generally recommended for an amateur. It takes a definite skill to cut and fit it in place. This flooring comes in widths of over 6 feet and is rather heavy and awkward to handle. It is also fairly difficult to cut with an ordinary linoleum knife. Remember that if you make a wrong cut on a tile, not much is lost, but on sheet material, a bad cut can ruin considerable yardage. Flexible, lightweight cushioned vinyl flooring, on the other hand, is easy to cut and easy to lay. Most cushioned vinyls come 6, 9, and 12 feet wide, which makes it possible to fit a room with a minimum of seams and waste. They generally are priced in square yards.

All resilient flooring requires a good underbase. It is wise, if there is any doubt in your mind regarding the condition of the old flooring, to install an underlayment. Also, in new work, resilient floors should not be installed directly over a board or plank subfloor. An underlayment grade of a wood-based panel such as plywood, particleboard, or hardboard is widely used for suspended floor applications.

Plywood or particleboard 4 × 8-foot panels, in thicknesses from $\frac{3}{8}$ to $\frac{3}{4}$ inch, are generally used in new construction. Sheets of untempered hardboard, plywood, or particleboard, 4 × 4-foot or larger, $\frac{1}{4}$ or $\frac{3}{8}$ inch thick, are used in remodeling work because of the floor thicknesses involved. The underlayment grade of particleboard is a standard product and is available from many producers. Manufacturer's instructions should be followed in the care and use of the product. The cost of the underlayment and the special fasteners needed to hold it in place (if used) must be added to the total cost of the job.

Ceramic Tile

There are three types of ceramic tiles in common use today: quarry tiles, ceramic mosaics, and glazed tiles.

Glazed tiles for flooring are usually a little thinner than glazed wall tiles, but are made in various sizes, shapes, designs, and colors. Some are so evenly glazed that they form a monochromatic surface. Others have a shade variation within each tile and from tile to tile. They come bright-glazed or matte-glazed. There are also extra-duty glazed floor tiles suitable for heavy-traffic areas.

Ceramic mosaics are available in 1×1-inch and 2×2-inch squares, and come with or without a glaze. In addition to the standard units, they may be found in a large assortment of colorful shapes. Mosaics are usually sold mounted in 1×1-foot and 1×2-foot sheets for easy installation.

Quarry tiles, which are also made from natural ceramic materials, are available in a variety of colors; the most common are shades of red, chocolate, and buff. They come in shapes ranging from squares to Spanish forms.

Because of the various shapes of ceramic tiles, it is difficult to set a specific formula for determining the amount of tiles needed or the cost. However, most tiles are sold by the square foot.

Carpeting

Carpeting many areas of a home, from living room to kitchen and bath, is becoming more popular as new carpeting materials are developed. The cost, however, may be considerably higher than a finish wood floor, and the life of the carpeting is much shorter than that of the wood floor. Many wise home remodelers install wood floors over areas they expect to carpet. The resale value of the home is then retained even if the carpeting is removed. However, the advantage of carpeting in sound absorption and resistance to impact should be considered. If carpeting is to be used, subfloor can consist of $\frac{5}{8}$-inch (minimum) tongue-and-groove plywood (over 16-inch joist spacing). The top face of the plywood should be C-plugged grade or better. Mastic adhesives are also being used to advantage in applying plywood to floor joists. Plywood, particleboard, or other underlayments are also used for a carpet base when installed over a subfloor.

While a great deal of carpeting is sold on an installed basis, more and more installation is being done by the homeowner. Carpeting is available in two forms: tiles and roll carpeting. The former, usually in 12×12-inch squares, comes already backed with padding. There are also self-adhesive carpet tiles as well as those that require no adhesive, but are laid by placing two strips of double-faced tape at right angles across the room, attaching tiles both ways, then just laying the other tiles in place. Their nonskid rubber backing holds them in place.

Roll carpeting can be laid in two ways: with adhesive, or by using pressure-sensitive double-faced tape or tackless stripping. When laying roll carpeting with adhesive, the same technique is followed as when installing resilient sheet material with cement. The tackless stripping, available at most carpet dealers, consists of a 4-foot wooden strip with numerous fine spikes or points projecting at a 60-degree angle. The strips are nailed around the perimeter of the room, end to end, $\frac{1}{4}$ inch from the wall molding, with the spikes facing toward the wall. The spikes grip the backing of the carpet to hold it in place. The double-faced tape, available in several types, performs in much the same manner as the tackless stripping. For most carpet materials it holds just as well and is much easier to work with. Either the tape, tackless strips, or adhesive must be added to the cost of the job. The carpeting itself is usually sold by the square yard and in the same widths as resilient sheet material. In fact, the math of figuring the amount of material needed and how to determine its cost is also the same as for resilient sheet material.

One of the quickest ways to improve a staircase is to install carpeting. Stairways can be covered either with fitted carpeting or with strip carpeting. The former requires the services of an experienced carpet installer, but strip carpeting, often called runners, can be installed by the average do-it-yourselfer.

Runners for stairway use come in standard widths of 18, $22\frac{1}{2}$, 27, and 36 inches and are sold by the linear yard. To find the amount of carpeting needed, measure in inches the depth of one tread and the height of one riser; add the two measurements together and multiply by the number of stairs; to this figure, add the length of any landings and divide the resulting amount by 36 to determine the number of linear yards.

INTERIOR MILLWORK

Interior millwork include such items as baseboards, picture molding, chair rails, cornices, panel strips, window and door frames, windows and doors, casings, trim, fireplace mantels, built-in bookcases, wood cabinets, etc.

The cost of these items varies considerably with the kind and grade of materials and the grade of work required. The most dependable method of estimating the cost of interior finish and millwork is to list the quantity and cost of each item separately together with the quantity and cost of the labor required to install each item. Finish material, such as molding, baseboards, chair rails, and strip paneling, may be priced by the 100 linear feet, while window and door frames, sashes, doors, cabinets, etc. usually are priced by the unit.

Doors

Rough openings for interior doors are usually framed out to be 3 inches more than the door height and $2\frac{1}{2}$ inches more than the door width. This provides for the frame and its plumbing and leveling in the opening. Interior doorframes are made up of two side jambs and a head jamb and include stop moldings upon which the door closes. The most common of these jambs is the one-piece type. Jambs may be obtained in standard $5\frac{1}{4}$-inch widths for plaster walls and $4\frac{5}{8}$-inch widths for walls with $\frac{1}{2}$-inch dry-wall finish. The two- and three-piece adjustable jambs are also standard types. Their principal advantage is in being adaptable to a variety of wall thicknesses. Some manufacturers produce interior doorframes with the door fitted and prehung, ready for installing. Application of the casing (trim) completes the job. When used with two- or three-piece jambs, casings can even be installed at the factory.

Common minimum widths for single interior doors are 2 feet 6 inches for bedrooms and other habitable rooms, 2 feet 4 inches for bathrooms, and 2 feet for small closets and linen closets. These widths can be varied a great deal, and sliding doors, folding doors, and similar types often used for wardrobes may be 6 feet or wider.

Standard interior and exterior door heights for first floors are 6 feet 8 inches. On upper floors, 6 feet 2 inches or 6 feet 4 inches may be used. There are many types and styles of doors in a wide range of prices, which will have to be determined locally for each type of door used. It must be remembered that the cost of trim and hardware (nails, lock, and hinges) must be added to the cost.

Casings are nailed to both the jamb and the framing studs or header, about $\frac{3}{16}$ inch from the face of the jamb (**Figure 3-14, views A and B**). Finish or

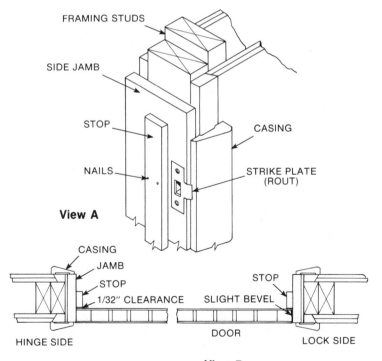

FIG. 3-14

205

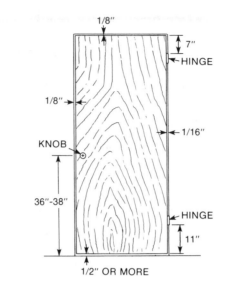

FIG. 3-15

casing nails in 6d or 7d sizes, depending on the thickness of the casing, are used to nail into the stud. Finishing nails 4d or 5d or $1\frac{1}{2}$-inch brads are used to fasten the thinner edge of the casing to the jamb. With hardwoods it is usually advisable to drill before nailing to prevent splitting. Nails in the casing are located in pairs and spaced about 16 inches apart along the full height of the opening and at the head jamb.

Interior doors are normally hung with two $3\frac{1}{2}$-inch loose-pin butt hinges. The door is fitted into the opening with the clearances shown in **Figure 3-15.** The clearance and location of hinges, lock set, and doorknob may vary somewhat, but all must closely conform to good millwork standards. The edge of the lock stile should be beveled slightly to permit the door to clear the jamb when swung open. If the door is to swing across heavy carpeting, the bottom clearance may be increased.

Molding and Trim

Here is a rundown of the more popular types of interior trim **(Figure 3-16).**
1. Baseboards protect the bottom of walls from wear and tear and conceal irregularities at the wall-floor joints. Quarter-round or base shoe moldings may be used to complete the trim.
2. Casing is used to trim doors, windows, and other openings. It may also be used for chair rails, cabinet trim, and other decorative purposes.

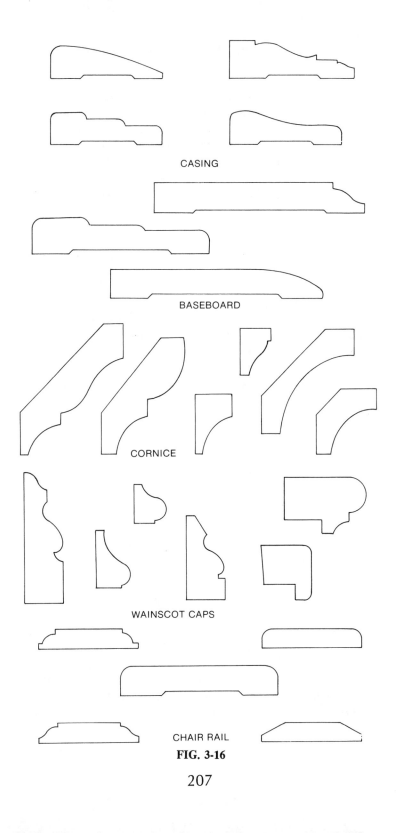

CASING

BASEBOARD

CORNICE

WAINSCOT CAPS

CHAIR RAIL

FIG. 3-16

207

3. Cornices, whether of the crown or cove type, give a rich appearance wherever two planes, such as wall and ceiling, meet. They are also used for trimming exposed beams and, singly or in combination with other moldings, in decorative mantels and frames.
4. Wainscot caps are applied to the top of wainscoting. Some patterns have a wrap-around lip to conceal craftsmanship defects. Others may be used to cap decorative baseboards.
5. Chair rail protects the wall in areas subject to chair-back damage, such as the playroom and dining room. It is installed at a height appropriate to the furniture style.

There are also many other moldings—quarter-rounds, half-rounds, stops, screen moldings, balusters, and picture moldings—that may be employed to add beauty to a room. Actually the variety of moldings seems endless, as a look at the molding board of your lumber dealer will suggest. While there are vinyl-coated, plastic, and metal moldings, most are made of wood. Wood moldings provide one of the least expensive ways to decorate a home.

Molding and trim are priced by the linear foot and require 2 to 4 pounds of nails per 100 linear feet. About 10 percent should be allowed for waste. For example, finishing nails cost 20 cents a pound and if a room needs 154 linear feet of baseboard molding that sells for 42 cents a linear foot, the total cost would be:

$$154 \times .10 = 15.4 \text{ or } 16 \text{ feet for waste}$$

$$154 + 16 = 170 \text{ feet total amount needed}$$

$$170 \times .42 = \$71.40 \text{ cost of trim}$$

$$3 \text{ pounds of nails} \times .20 = \$0.60$$

Total cost of material for job: $72

Windows

Although the price of windows varies with size, type, and material, they are generally sold at unit prices, with necessary trim sold separately. The casings around window frames on the interior of the house customarily have the same pattern as those used around the interior door frames. Other trim that is used for a double-hung window frame includes sash stops, stool, and apron (**Figure 3-17**). Alternatively, the entire opening around the window can be enclosed with casing. The stool is then a filler member between the bottom sash rail and the bottom casing.

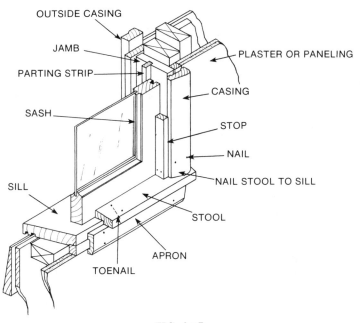

OUTSIDE CASING
JAMB
PARTING STRIP
SASH
SILL
PLASTER OR PANELING
CASING
STOP
NAIL
NAIL STOOL TO SILL
STOOL
APRON
TOENAIL

FIG. 3-17

It is common practice to furnish a wood sash with glass already installed by the manufacturer. Steel and aluminum sashes may be furnished with the glass installed for use in residences, but when such sashes are furnished for industrial and commercial buildings, the glass is usually installed after the sashes are set in the walls, usually just prior to completing a building, in order to reduce the danger of breakage.

An estimate covering the cost of furnishing glass should include a detailed list of the quantity for each size, kind, and grade of glass required and for each the cost of the glass, putty, and glazier paints.

There are many kinds and grades of glass. Glass used for glazing purposes is called window glass, and may be divided into sheet glass and plate glass. Sheet glass is manufactured in several grades: AA, A, and B, with AA that of highest quality. The thickness of ordinary window glass is classified single-strength or double-strength (see **Table 3-10** on page 210).

Many kinds of figured sheet glass are available, with various patterns or figures rolled or otherwise produced on them.

Plate glass used for glazing purposes is available in two grades: second silvering and glazing quality.

TABLE 3-10:
SHEET GLASS THICKNESSES AND WEIGHTS

Designation	Thickness (in.)		Average weight per sq. ft.	
	Min.	*Max.*	*Oz.*	*Lb.*
Single-strength	0.085	0.100	18.5	1.16
Double-strength	0.115	0.133	24.5	1.53
³⁄₁₆ in.	0.182	0.205	39.0	2.44
⁷⁄₃₂ in.	0.205	0.230	45.5	2.85
¼ in.	0.240	0.255	52.0	3.25
³⁄₈ in.	0.312	0.437	78.0	4.87
½ in.	0.438	0.556	104.0	6.50

Window glass is designated by size and grade, such as 20 × 36-inch B double-strength. The first number represents the width, and the second number the height of the sheet. Glass is sold by the square foot in sheets whose dimensions vary in steps of 2 inches. Fractional dimensions are figured for the next standard dimensions. Thus a sheet whose actual size is 17⅝ × 14⅝ inches is classified for cost purposes as 18 by 16 inches. Costs and certain operations related to glass are frequently based on the united inches of a sheet of glass, which is the sum of the width and height of a sheet.

PAINTING

One of the easiest and certainly one of the most effective ways to improve or alter the appearance of your home is by painting it.

Exterior Painting

When choosing among the great number of different types of paint, first consider the type of surface you are painting. Is it wood, metal, or masonry? Some paints can be used on all three; others on two. The condition of the surface is also important. Old chalky surfaces, for example, are not generally sound bases for water-base paints. Next consider any special requirements. For example, using nonchalking paint may be advisable where chalk rundown would discolor adjacent brick or stone surfaces. If mildew is a problem in your area, you may need to use mildew-resistant paint. Lead-free paints may be used in areas where sulfur fumes stain paints containing lead pigments. Color is a third consideration, but it is mostly a matter of personal preference. Some colors are more durable than others. Your paint dealer can help you with decisions on color durability and combinations.

"House paint" is the commercial term for exterior paints of many different formulations. It is the most widely used type of paint. Formulations are available for use on all surfaces and for all special requirements such as chalk or mildew resistance. White is the most popular color.

Exterior paint comes in both oil-base and latex (water-base) types. The vehicle of oil-base paint consists usually of linseed oil plus turpentine or mineral spirits as the thinner. Latex paint contains water as the vehicle thinner; its vehicle consists of fine particles of resin emulsified, or held in suspension, in water.

Another type of water-base paint has a vehicle consisting of a soluble linseed oil dissolved in water. This paint has the properties of both oil-base and water-base paints.

The advantages of latex paints include easy application, fast drying, good color retention, and resistance to alkalis and blistering. Also, they can be applied in humid weather and to damp surfaces. Brush and tool cleanup is simpler because it can be done with water.

Use **Table 3-11** as a guide in selecting exterior paint.

To figure the amount of paint you need for flat surfaces, simply divide the surface area by the coverage estimate on the paint can label; that is, to figure the siding area below the roof line add the length of your house to the width and multiply by twice the height. For pitched roofs and gables, multiply the height of each peak from the roof base by half the width of the area and add the area of each gable to the below-roof-line siding area.

Do not subtract for windows, unless they are very large, since the paint you save on the area occupied by windows is normally eaten up by what you need for board edges, eaves, soffits, etc. Roof dormers typically take 100 square feet of paint. If your house has an overhang no greater than a foot or so, ignore it. Larger overhangs should be computed on the basis of eave line distance times overhang.

When you have the total square footage, divide it by the number of square feet per gallon coverage given on the label of the paint. Square footage figures are not so much boasts about how far the paint will stretch as warnings not to stretch too far. Second coats generally require less paint. However, remember that these are average estimates of coverage **(Table 3-12)**. Some surfaces are more absorbent than others.

Three coats of house paint are recommended for new wood surfaces, one primer and two finish coats. (Two-coat systems are sometimes used and give long service when properly designed and properly applied.) On old surfaces in good condition, one top coat may be sufficient.

On bare surfaces or surfaces with little paint left on them, it is best to apply a primer and at least one top coat. A primer does two things: it penetrates a

TABLE 3-11:
WHICH OUTDOOR PAINTS TO USE WHERE

	House paint (oil alkyd)	Cement powder paint	Exterior clear finish	Aluminum paint	Wood stain	Roof coating	Trim paint	Porch and deck paint	Primer or undercoater	Metal primer	House paint (latex)	Water-repellent preservative
Masonry												
Asbestos cement	X								X		X	
Brick	X	X		X					X		X	X
Cement and cinder block	X	X		X								
Concrete/ masonry porches and floors								X	X		X	
Coal-tar-felt roof						X						
Stucco	X	X		X					X		X	
Metal												
Aluminum windows	X			X			X			X	X	

Surface						
Steel windows	X			X	X	X
Metal roof	X*				X	X*
Metal siding	X*			X*	X	X*
Copper surfaces		X				
Galvanized surfaces	X*			X*	X	X*
Iron surfaces	X*			X*	X	X*
Wood						
Clapboard	X*			X		X*
Natural wood siding and trim		X		X		
Shutters and other trim	X*			X	X	X*
Wood frame windows	X*			X	X	X*
Wood porch floor			X			
Wood shingle roof						X

X*indicates that a primer sealer, or fill coat, may be necessary before the finishing coat (unless the surface has been previously finished).

TABLE 3-12:
EXTERIOR PAINT COVERAGE, SQUARE FEET PER GALLON

Surface and paint type	First coat	Second coat	Third coat
Wood siding:			
Exterior house paint	420	520	620
Trim:			
Exterior trim paint	850	900	972
Porch floors and steps:			
Porch and deck paint	378	540	576
Asbestos wall shingles:			
Exterior house paint	180	400	
Shingle siding:			
Exterior house paint	342	423	
Shingle stain	150	225	
Shingle roof:			
Exterior oil paint	150	250	
Shingle stain	120	200	
Brick (exterior):			
Exterior oil paint	200	400	
Cement water paint	100	150	
Cement floors and steps (exterior):			
Porch and deck paint	450	600	600
Color stain and finish	510	480	
Medium texture stucco			
Exterior oil or latex paint	153	360	360
Cement water paint	99	135	

porous surface and grips tightly, and it makes a firm base for the second or finish coat, which may not be able to penetrate as well as the prime coat. The paint you buy bears a label on which recommendations for a primer coat are made. Apply the primer coat after you clean and repair the surface, but before you putty cracks or other defects.

Allow the primer coat to dry according to the manufacturer's label instructions. Allow longer drying time in humid weather. Apply the finish coats as soon as the primer has dried sufficiently. (If you must wait a month or more, wash the surface thoroughly before applying the top coats.) Allow about 48 hours' drying time between oil-base finish coats. Two coats of latex paint may be applied in one day.

The total number of gallons of paint required for an exterior house painting job may be found by the following formula:

$$\text{Gallons} = \frac{\text{area to be painted}}{\text{coverage}} \times \text{number of coats}$$

This means that the number of gallons required is the number of square feet to be painted divided by the number of square feet which one gallon will cover in one coat, and that this result is multiplied by the number of coats.

Trim paint is hard to figure in the above manner, since computation of square feet on the irregular shapes and surfaces of trim is just about impossible. However, a gallon of trim paint will take care of the average house. Even if 3 quarts would do it, there is little economy over buying a gallon, and you can always use the leftover paint for touching up. On the other hand, if your best guess is that a gallon will not quite do it, buy a gallon and a quart, and make a deal with the paint store to return the quart if you don't need it.

Floor paint, for porches, terraces, patios, and the like are simple enough to figure on a pure square foot basis. For odds and ends such as black wrought-iron railings and carriage lamps, your guess is as good as anyone's. Remember that a little left over, stored away on a shelf in the garage, is excellent insurance against damage that should be touched up.

Interior Painting

Interior paints include three broad categories: (1) flat paints that dry with no gloss and are most frequently used on walls and ceilings; (2) gloss finishes, usually used in kitchens, bathrooms, and on woodwork, that are available in various lusters from a low satin finish to a very high gloss; and (3) the primers, sealers, and undercoats that are used as bases. All are available in different grades or qualities, and many in both solvent-thinned (mineral spirits, turpentine, or benzine) or water-thinned (latex) forms.

Flat Paints

Latex interior paints are generally used for areas where there is little need for periodic washing and scrubbing, for example, living rooms, dining rooms, bedrooms, and closets. Flat latex paints are used for interior walls and ceilings since they cover well, are easy to apply, dry quickly, are almost odorless, and can be quickly and easily removed from applicators. Latex paints may be applied directly over semigloss and gloss enamel if the surface is first roughened with sandpaper or liquid sandpaper.

Flat alkyd paints are often preferred for wood, wallboard, and metal surfaces, since they are more resistant to damage. In addition, they can be applied in thicker films to produce a more uniform appearance. They wash better than interior latex paints and are nearly odorless.

Gloss Finishes

Enamels, including latex enamels, are usually preferred for kitchen, bathroom, laundry room, and similar work areas because they withstand intensive cleaning and wear. They form especially hard films, ranging from flat to full-gloss finishes. Fast-drying polyurethane enamels and clear varnishes provide excellent hard finishes for wood floors. Other enamels and clear finishes may be too soft and slow-drying or too hard and brittle. Polyurethane and epoxy enamels are also excellent for concrete floors. For a smooth finish, rough concrete should be properly primed with an alkali-resistant primer to fill the pores. When these enamels are used, adequate ventilation is essential for protection from flammable vapors.

Paint for Textured Walls

For walls that are rough or have patched plaster or uneven wallboard seams, a textured finish may be used. A heavy coat of a special paint, thicker than ordinary paint, is applied to the wall surface. The desired texture is added while the paint is still wet by the use of a brush, sponge, or a paint roller. Some skill is needed to obtain a good effect.

Finishes for Wood

Synthetic varnishes form durable and attractive finishes for interior wood surfaces such as wood paneling, trim, floors, and unpainted furniture. They seal the wood and form tough, transparent films that withstand frequent scrubbing and hard use, and are available in flat, semigloss or satin, and gloss finishes. Most varnishes are easily scratched, and the marks are difficult to conceal without redoing the entire surface. A good paste wax applied over the finished varnish, especially on wood furniture, provides some protection against scratches. Polyurethane and epoxy varnishes are notable for durability and high resistance to stains, abrasions, acids and alkalis, solvents, strong cleaners, fuels, alcohol, and chemicals.

Shellac and lacquer finishes are similar to those of most varnishes and are easy to repair or recoat. They are applied easily, dry fast, and are also useful

216

as sealers and clear finishes under some varnishes for wood surfaces. A first coat should be thinned as recommended on the container. After it is applied the surface should be sanded very lightly and then finished with one or more undiluted coats. Two coats will give a fair sheen, and three a high gloss.

Liquid and paste waxes are used on interior surfaces. They provide a soft, lustrous finish to wood and are particularly effective on furniture and floors. Waxes containing solvents should not be used on asphalt tile; wax emulsions are recommended for this purpose. Waxes should be applied to smooth surfaces with a soft cloth and rubbed with the grain. Brushes should be used to apply liquid waxes to raw-textured wood. Wax finishes can be washed with a mild household detergent, followed by rinsing with a clean, damp cloth. A wax finish is not desirable if a different type of finish may be used later, for wax is difficult to remove.

Unless you are an experienced painter, shop for a salesperson or paint store owner before you shop for paint. Find one who is willing and able to help you match the paint to the job. Read labels and company leaflets carefully. They are usually well written, accurate, and helpful. **Table 3-13**, on page 218, provides additional paint information.

To determine the amount of paint needed, measure the wall area to be covered.

Since windows and some doors do not require paint, deduct their area. If the door is to be painted the same color as the walls, do not deduct the door area.

Be sure to buy enough paint to complete the job, especially if you are having colors mixed. The second mixing may not match exactly. If the paint you choose is not available in the exact tint you want, have the dealer do the mixing even though it may add to the cost. Careful mixing is essential to the finished product, for a paint that is not well mixed may leave an uneven, spotty appearance. Whether you use more than one coat will depend on the type and color of paint you are using, the condition of the walls, and the color you are covering.

Besides paint and applicator (brushes, roller, or spray gun), other materials you might need include: extra pans or cans for stirring the paint, old cloths to wipe up spills and drops of paint, masking tape to cover window glass and other surfaces to prevent smearing them with paint, a stepladder or sturdy table to stand on for reaching high areas, newspapers or drop cloths to cover the floor, and cleaning materials for brushes.

Table 3-14 gives the amounts of time in which a painter does various interior jobs with a brush or roller. In each case, the figure given represents the labor required per 100 square feet of surface area, per 100 linear feet of trim, or per opening for windows and doors. A do-it-yourself painter with fair experience will probably take about twice as long to do a good job.

TABLE 3-13:
WHICH INTERIOR PAINTS TO USE WHERE

Surface	Aluminum paint	Casein	Cement-base paint	Emulsion paint (including latex)	Enamel	Flat paint	Floor paint or enamel	Floor varnish	Interior varnish	Metal primer	Rubber-base paint (not latex)	Sealer or undercoater	Semigloss paint	Shellac	Stain	Wax (emulsion)	Wax (liquid or paste)	Wood sealer
Floors																		
Asphalt tile																	X*	
Concrete																X*	X*	
Linoleum							X							X		X	X	
Vinyl and rubber							X	X								X	X	
Wood							X*	X*									X	
Masonry																		
Old	X	X	X	X	X*	X*					X	X	X*					
New			X	X	X*	X*					X	X	X*					
Metal																		
Heating ducts	X				X*	X*				X	X		X*					
Radiators	X				X*	X*				X	X		X*					
Stairs																		
Treads							X	X						X	X			
Risers					X*	X*			X	X		X*		X	X			
Walls and ceilings																		
Kitchen and bathroom				X	X*						X	X	X*					
Plaster		X		X		X*					X	X	X*					
Wallboard		X		X		X*					X	X	X*					
Wood paneling				X*		X*			X									
Wood trim				X*	X*	X*			X		X	X	X*	X	X		X	X
Windows																		
Aluminum	X				X*	X*				X	X		X*					
Steel	X				X*	X*				X	X		X*					
Wood sill				X*					X			X			X			

X*indicates that a primer or sealer may be necessary before the finishing coat, unless the surface has been previously finished.

TABLE 3-14:
PAINTING TIMES FOR A PROFESSIONAL PAINTER

Operation	Unit	Hours per unit
Plaster and wallboard size or seal	100 sq. ft.	0.40–0.50
Applying oil-based paint	100 sq. ft.	0.30–0.40
Applying latex paint	100 sq. ft.	0.20–0.30
Trim, mold, base, chair rail		
Sanding	100 lin. ft.	0.80–1.00
Varnishing	100 lin. ft.	0.50–0.75
Enameling	100 lin. ft.	0.50–0.75
Flat painting	100 lin. ft.	0.50–0.75
Staining	100 lin. ft.	0.40–0.60
Painting doors and windows	Each	0.50–0.75
Floors		
Sanding with power sander	100 sq. ft.	0.75–1.00
Filling and wiping	100 sq. ft.	0.50–0.60
Shellacking	100 sq. ft.	0.25–0.30
Varnishing	100 sq. ft.	0.40–0.50
Waxing	100 sq. ft.	0.40–0.50
Polishing with power polisher	100 sq. ft.	0.30–0.40

WALLCOVERINGS

Wallcoverings (of which wallpaper is still the most common) are the most versatile of all home improvement devices. They can make a room appear cozy or formal, restful or active, gay or dignified. By careful selection of colors and patterns in a wallcover, a room can be made to appear smaller or more spacious than it actually is. The ceiling can be made to appear higher or lower according to the needs of the room, and wallpaper can turn a dark gloomy room into a pleasant gay one. Certain types of wallcover seem to give more character and atmosphere to a room than painted walls do.

Wallpapers, or wallcoverings as they are now called, are available in almost any design you can think of and in various types and qualities, ranging in cost from $1.50 to $50 for a roll. The math of estimating the amount of wallcovering required for a job is based on the *roll,* the standard unit of measurement in the wallcovering industry.

Each roll of wallcovering contains approximately 36 square feet of material, regardless of varying width and lengths. Rolls are usually packaged in 2-roll bolts. However, when you hang the material, you will always have a certain amount of waste from trimming and cutting the strips to size, so you will actually obtain 30 square feet of usable material out of each roll. Border strips are usually sold by the linear yard.

To figure how many rolls you will need for a given room, first measure area to be covered. Then deduct the areas of doors and windows. Deduct 1 roll for every two ordinary-sized doors or windows. Now, divide this figure by 30.

To estimate the number of rolls of ceiling covering needed, multiply the length of the room by its width and divide by 30.

If a border strip is to be used, an estimate of the amount can be made by finding the perimeter of the room in yards. An extra yard is generally ordered for trimming and matching.

In addition to wallcovering material, however, you will need the following material and equipment for doing a good job of paperhanging: a ladder to reach the ceiling; a large flat surface or table; a large pail for paste; a brush or paint roller for applying paste; a smoothing brush to smooth the paper on the wall (a fiber brush about 10 inches wide or a clean clothes brush will do); a rotary beater or similar device to mix the paste; a pair of large sharp shears; a trimming knife or razor blade to trim the wallpaper; newspapers to cover the table while applying paste; wallpaper paste, unless you are using prepasted wallpaper; a yardstick or T-square for measuring straight edges; and a plumb line. If the walls need repairing, you may need patching plaster to fill the holes and cracks; a putty knife, paperhanger's size; a scraper; and sandpaper.

Kits containing tools needed for hanging wallcoverings are available at wallcovering stores, often on a rental basis.

For example, to cover a room 12 $\times$ 14 feet in area and 9 feet high, with baseboard and moldings equal, together, to 1 foot, and two doors and two windows, you would need 12 single rolls for the walls and 6 rolls for the ceiling. If the paper costs $9 for a roll, the paper would cost $162.

In addition, you purchase a wallpaper tool kit for $6, 5 pounds of paste at 30 cents per pound, 2 quarts of wall sizing at $3 per quart, and rent a wallpapering table for $4. The rest of the tools for installation are at hand. The cost of equipment needed would be

Wallpaper tool kit	$6.00
5 pounds paste @ $0.30	1.50
2 quarts sizing @ $3.00	6.00
Table rental	4.00
Total	$17.50

The total cost for wallpapering the room would then be

Material cost ($162) + equipment cost ($17.50) = $179.50

MATH IN THE SHOP

Math is in constant use in the shop. In fact, all shop measurement and mechanics are based on math.

MEASUREMENT AND MEASURING TOOLS

Most of the measurement work discussed thus far in the book can be accomplished with the basic measurement tools covered in this chapter.

Figure 4–1 shows some of the types of rules and tapes available today. Of all basic measuring tools, the simplest and most common is the steel rule. This rule is usually 6 or 12 inches in length, although other lengths are available.

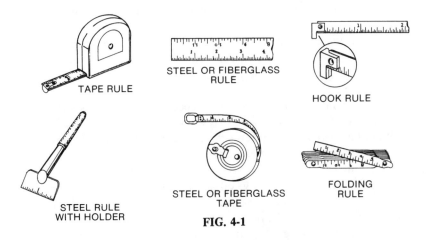

TAPE RULE

STEEL OR FIBERGLASS RULE

HOOK RULE

STEEL RULE WITH HOLDER

STEEL OR FIBERGLASS TAPE

FOLDING RULE

FIG. 4-1

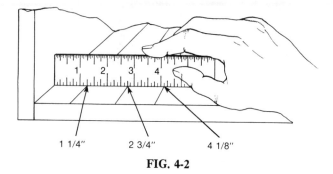

FIG. 4-2

Steel rules may be flexible or nonflexible, but the thinner the rule, the easier it is to measure accurately, because the division marks are closer to the work.

Generally a rule has four sets of graduations, one on each edge of each side. The longest lines represent the inch marks. On one edge, each inch is divided into 8 equal spaces; so each space represents ⅛ inch. The other edge of this side is divided into sixteenths. The ¼-inch and ½-inch marks are commonly made longer than the smaller division marks to facilitate counting, but the graduations are not, as a rule, numbered individually, as they are sufficiently far apart to be counted without difficulty. The opposite side is similarly divided into 32 and 64 spaces per inch, and it is common practice to number every fourth division for easier reading.

There are many variations of the common rule. Sometimes the graduations are on one side only, sometimes a set of graduations is added across one end for measuring in narrow spaces, and sometimes only the first inch is divided into sixty-fourths, with the remaining inches divided into thirty-seconds and sixteenths.

A metal or wood folding rule may be used. Folding rules are usually 2 to 6 feet long. They cannot be relied on for extremely accurate measurements because a certain amount of play develops at the joints after they have been used for a while.

Steel tapes come in lengths from 6 to about 300 feet. The shorter lengths are frequently made with a curved cross section so that they are flexible enough to roll up, but remain rigid when extended. Long, flat tapes require support over their full length when measuring, or else the natural sag will cause an error in reading.

The flexible-rigid tapes usually coil into metal cases. A hook at the free end hooks over the object being measured so one man can handle it without assistance. On some models, the outside of the case can be used as one end of the tape when measuring inside dimensions.

To take a measurement with a common rule, hold the rule with its edge on the surface of the object being measured. This will eliminate parallax and other errors which might result because of the thickness of the rule. Read the measurement at the graduation that coincides with the distance to be measured, and state it as being so many inches and fractions of an inch (**Figure 4-2**). Always reduce fractions to their lowest terms; for example, ⅝ inch would be called ¾ inch. (To reduce a fraction, find the largest whole number that will divide into both the top and the bottom number —numerator and denominator — evenly. In this case, 2 divides into both the 6 and the 8 for a reduced fraction of ¾.) A hook or eye at the end of a tape or rule is normally part of the first measured inch.

The Micrometer

One of the most important instruments for *precise* measuring is the micrometer (mike). It is an essential tool for anyone working with machinery or in a machine shop. **Figure 4-3** shows an outside micrometer caliper with the various parts clearly indicated. Micrometers are used to measure distances to the nearest thousandth of an inch. The measurement is usually expressed or written as a decimal, so to use the micrometer you must understand the decimal system.

The sleeve and thimble scales of the micrometer caliper are shown enlarged in **Figure 4-4**. To understand these scales, you need to know that the threaded section on the spindle, which revolves, has 40 threads per inch. Therefore, every time the thimble completes a revolution, the spindle advances or recedes $\frac{1}{40}$ inch (0.025 inch).

Notice that the horizontal line on the sleeve is divided into 40 equal parts per inch. Every fourth graduation is numbered 1, 2, 3, 4, etc., representing

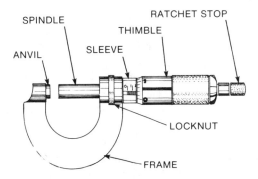

FIG. 4-3

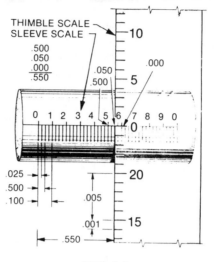

FIG. 4-4

0.100 inch, 0.200 inch, etc. When you turn the thimble so that its edge is over the first sleeve line past the 0 on the thimble scale, the spindle has opened 0.025 inch. If you turn the spindle to the second mark, it has moved 0.025 plus 0.025 inch, or 0.050 inch. You use the scale on the thimble to complete your reading when the edge of the thimble stops between graduated lines. This scale is divided into 25 equal parts, each part representing a twenty-fifth of a turn. And a twenty-fifth of 0.025 inch is 0.001 inch. As you can see, every fifth line on the thimble scale is marked 5, 10, 15, etc. The thimble scale, therefore, permits you to take very accurate readings to the thousandth of an inch, and, since you can estimate between the divisions on the thimble scale, fairly accurate readings to the ten-thousandth of an inch are possible.

The closeup in **Figure 4-5** will help you understand how to take a complete micrometer reading. Count the units on the thimble scale and add them to the reading on the sleeve scale. The reading in the figure shows a sleeve reading of 0.250 (the thimble having stopped slightly more than halfway between 2 and 3 on the sleeve) with the 10th line on the thimble scale coinciding with the horizontal sleeve line. Number 10 on this scale means that the spindle has moved away from the anvil an additional 10×0.001 or 0.010 inch. And this amount to the 0.250 sleeve reading, and you get a total distance of 0.260 inch.

Read each of the micrometer settings in **Figure 4-6** so that you can be sure of yourself when you begin to use this tool on the job. The correct readings are given following the figure so that you can check yourself.

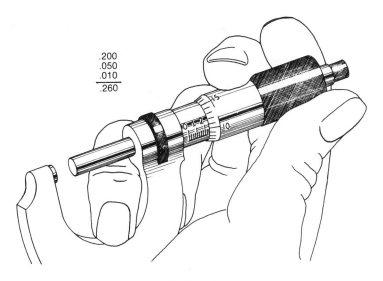

.200
.050
.010
—————
.260

FIG. 4-5

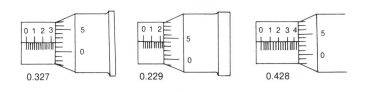

0.327

0.229

0.428

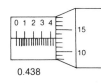

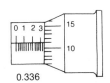

0.438

0.137

0.336

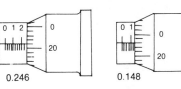
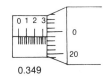

0.246

0.148

0.349

FIG. 4-6

225

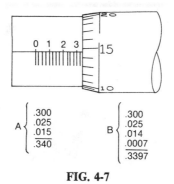

$$
A \begin{cases} .300 \\ .025 \\ .015 \\ \overline{.340} \end{cases} \qquad B \begin{cases} .300 \\ .025 \\ .014 \\ .0007 \\ \overline{.3397} \end{cases}
$$

FIG. 4-7

Figure 4-7 shows a reading in which the horizontal line falls between two graduations on the thimble scale and is closer to the 15 graduation than it is to the 14. To read this to *three* decimal places, refer to the figure's calculation A. To read it to *four* decimal places, estimate the number of tenths of the distance between thimble-scale graduations the horizontal line has fallen. Each tenth of this distance equals one ten-thousandth (0.0001) of an inch. Add the ten-thousandths to the reading as shown in calculation B.

Reading a Vernier Micrometer

If you want to make exceptionally precise dimensions, it is better to use a micrometer that is accurate to a ten-thousandth of an inch. You can obtain this degree of accuracy by using a vernier scale in addition to the micrometer. This scale, shown in **Figure 4-8,** furnishes the fine readings between the lines

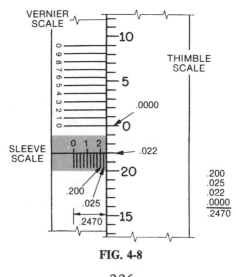

FIG. 4-8

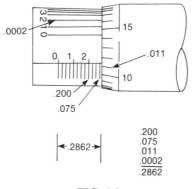

FIG. 4-9

on the thimble rather than making you estimate. The 10 spaces on the vernier are equivalent to 9 spaces on the thimble. Therefore, each unit on the vernier scale is equal to 0.0009 inch and the difference between the sizes of the units on each scale is 0.0001 inch.

When a line on the thimble scale does not coincide with the horizontal sleeve line, you can determine the additional space beyond the readable thimble mark by finding which vernier mark coincides with a line on the thimble scale. Add this number, as that many ten-thousandths of an inch, to the original reading. In **Figure 4-9** you can see how the second line on the vernier scale coincides with a line on the thimble scale.

This means that the 0.011 mark on the thimble scale has been advanced an additional 0.0002 inch beyond the horizontal sleeve line. When you add this to the other readings, the reading will be 0.200 + 0.075 + 0.011 + 0.0002 or 0.2862 inch, as shown.

The Vernier Caliper

As shown in **Figure 4-10**, the vernier caliper consists of an L-shaped member with a scale engraved on the long shank. A sliding member is free to move on

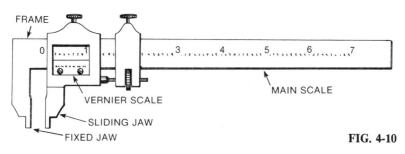

FIG. 4-10

the bar and carries a jaw that matches the arm of the L. The vernier scale is engraved on a small plate attached to the sliding member.

Perhaps the most distinct advantage of the vernier caliper is its ability to provide very accurate measurements over a large range. It can be used for both internal and external surfaces. Pocket models usually measure from zero to 3 inches, but sizes are available all the way to 4 feet. In using the vernier caliper, you must be able to measure with a slide caliper and read a vernier scale.

Principles of the Vernier Scale

It would be possible to etch graduations a thousandth of an inch (0.001 inch) apart on a steel rule or sliding caliper as shown in **Figure 4-11.** This enlarged illustration shows two graduated scales. The top scale has divisions which are 0.025 inch apart. The small sliding lower scale has 25 0.001-inch graduations that can divide any of the main scale divisions of 0.025 inch into 25 parts. When the first graduation marked 0 on this small scale aligns with a graduation on the main scale, the last, or 25th, will also align with a graduation on the main scale as shown. Consequently, the small 0.00 graduations are not significant in this position. But when the zero graduation does not align with a graduation on the main scale, you can readily determine how many thousandths the zero missed the 0.025-inch graduation by counting the misaligned graduation at either end of the small scale. When the zero or index line on the sliding scale does not quite reach the graduation, the amount of misalignment must be subtracted. But when it passes the 0.025 graduation from which the reading is made, it must be added. This illustrates the simple arrangement to increase the accuracy of a common scale. Unfortunately, the 0.001 inch graduations are not too legible and so the system is not practical. A vernier arrangement overcomes this problem.

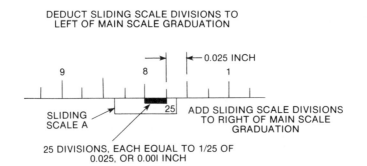

FIG. 4-11

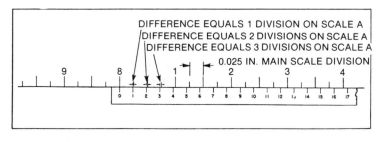

FIG. 4-12

The main difference between the vernier scale and the arrangement shown in **Figure 4-11** is the spacing of the 25 divisions. Instead of 25 graduations crowded within the space of one main scale division, the vernier graduations are arranged at intervals exactly 0.001 inch less than the main scale graduations, as shown in **Figure 4-12.** This arrangement results in an accumulation of misalignments starting with the first vernier graduation past the zero so that each may be marked as shown with a number representing the space in thousandths to the next upper scale graduation. For example, if the 0 index line was moved past the 8-inch graduation until the vernier graduation number 5 aligned with the next main scale graduation, the exact reading would be 8 inches plus 0.005 or 8.005 inches.

Reading a Vernier Caliper

Figure 4-13 shows a bar 1 inch long divided by graduations into 40 parts so that each graduation indicates one-fortieth of an inch (0.025 inch). Every fourth graduation is numbered; each number indicates tenths of an inch (4 × 0.025 inch). The vernier, which slides along the bar, is graduated into 25 divisions which together are as long as 24 divisions on the bar. Each division of the vernier is 0.001 inch smaller than each division on the bar. Verniers that are calibrated as explained above are known as English-measure verniers. The metric-measure vernier is read the same way, except that the units of measurement are millimeters.

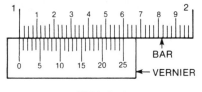

FIG. 4-13

Figure 4-14, view A, illustrates the English-measure vernier caliper. **View B** shows an enlarged view of the vernier section. As you can see in this figure, when the zero on the vernier coincides with the 1-inch mark, no other lines coincide until the twenty-fifth mark on the vernier.

To read the caliper in **view C,** write down in a column the number of inches (1.000 inch), of tenths of an inch (0.400 inch), and of thousandths of an inch that the zero mark on the vernier is from the zero mark on the rule. Because the zero mark on the vernier is a little past a 0.025-inch mark, write down the 0.025 inch and then note the highest number on the vernier where a line on the vernier coincides with one on the rule. In this case it is at the 0.011-inch line on the vernier, so you also write the 0.011 inch in the column, which will then look like this:

$$
\begin{array}{r}
1.000 \text{ inch} \\
.400 \text{ inch} \\
.025 \text{ inch} \\
\underline{.011 \text{ inch}} \\
1.436 \text{ inches}
\end{array}
$$

The reading on the caliper shown in **view C** is 1.436 inches and was obtained by adding four separate "readings." After a little practice you will be able to make these calculations mentally.

Now try to read the settings of the two verniers shown in **views D** and **E.** Follow the above procedure. You should read 2.350 inches on D and 2.368 inches on E.

To read a metric-measure vernier, note the number of millimeters, and the 0.25 millimeter if the setting permits, that the zero on the vernier has moved from the zero on the scale. Then add the number of hundredths of a millimeter indicated by the line on the vernier that coincides with a line on the scale.

For example, **Figure 4-15, view A,** shows the zero graduation on the vernier coinciding with a 0.5-millimeter graduation on the scale resulting in a 38.50-millimeter reading. The reading in **Figure 4-15, view B,** indicates that 0.08 millimeter should be added to the scale reading and results in 38.00 + 0.50 + 0.08 = 38.58 millimeters.

If a vernier caliper is calibrated in either English measure or in metric measure, usually one side will be calibrated to take outside measurements and the other to take inside measurements directly. The vernier plate for inside measurements is set to compensate for the thickness of the measuring points of the tools. But if a vernier caliper is calibrated for both English and metric measure, one of the scales will appear on one side and one on the other. Then it will be necessary, when taking inside measurements over the measuring

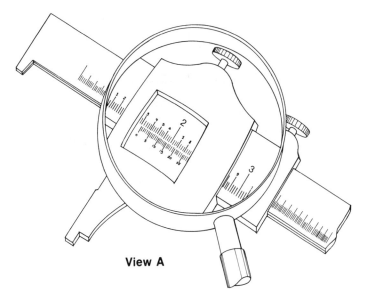

View A

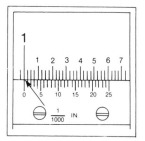

View B

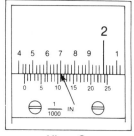

View C

View D

View E

FIG. 4-14

231

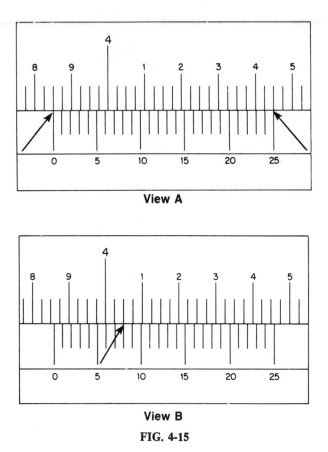

View A

View B

FIG. 4-15

points, to add certain amounts to allow for their thickness. For example, **Table 4-1** shows the amounts to be added for various sizes of vernier calipers.

TABLE 4-1:
MEASURING POINT ALLOWANCES

Size of caliper	English measure	Metric measure
6″ or 150 mm	Add 0.250″	Add 6.35 mm
12″ or 300 mm	.300″	7.62 mm
24″ or 600 mm	.300″	7.62 mm
36″ or 600 mm	.500″	12.70 mm

Gauges

There is a wide array of gauges that can be used in a shop. Two of the most used are the screw thread gauge and the wire gauge.

Screw Thread Gauge

Thread gauges (screw-pitch gauges) are used to determine the pitch and number of threads per inch of threaded fasteners **(Figure 4-16)**. They consist of thin leaves whose edges are toothed to correspond to standard thread sections.

To measure the unknown pitch of a thread, compare it with standards of the screw pitch gauge. Hold a gauge leaf to the thread being measured **(Figure 4-17),** substituting various sizes until you find an exact fit. Look at the fit toward a source of light for best results.

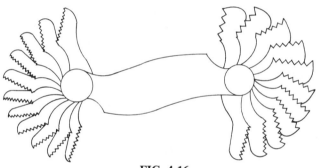

FIG. 4-16

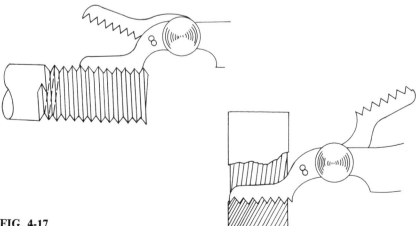

FIG. 4-17

The number of threads per inch is indicated by the numerical value on the blade that fits the unknown pitch of threads. Using this value as a basis, you can select correct sizes of nuts, bolts, tap cutters, and die cutters.

The screw thread gauge is based on simple decimal fraction mathematics. For example, if the screw thread gauge indicates a screw has a pitch of $\frac{1}{20}$, the number of threads per inch is:

$$1 \div \frac{1}{20} = 1 \times \frac{20}{1} = 20 \text{ threads per inch}$$

On the other hand, if a screw has 40 threads per inch, the pitch of such a screw would be:

$$1 \div 40 = 1 \times \frac{1}{40} = \frac{1}{40} \text{ screw pitch}$$

Wire Gauges

The wire gauge, shown in **Figure 4-18,** is used for measuring the diameters of wires or the thicknesses of sheet metal. This gauge is circular, with cutouts in the outer perimeter. Each cutout gauges a different size from No. 0 to No. 36. The larger the gauge number, the smaller the diameter or thickness.

Gauges similar to the one shown in **Figure 4-18** are available for measuring a variety of wires and sheet metals. The names of some common standard wire gauges and their uses are given in the column headings of **Table 4-2.** The body of this table contains gauge numbers and their corresponding equivalents in decimal fractions of an inch.

FIG. 4-18

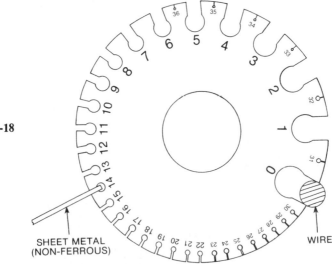

SHEET METAL
(NON-FERROUS)

WIRE

234

TABLE 4-2:
COMPARISON OF SHEET-METAL AND WIRE GAUGES

Dimensions are expressed in approximate decimals of an inch.

Gauge	AWG B&S (non-ferrous)	Birmingham or Stubs BWG	Steel wire gauge	British Imperial NBS SWG	United States Standard US
0000000	—	—	0.4900	0.500	0.5000
000000	0.5800	—	0.4615	0.464	0.4688
00000	0.5165	0.500	0.4305	0.432	0.4375
0000	0.4600	0.454	0.3938	0.400	0.4063
000	0.4096	0.425	0.3625	0.372	0.3750
00	0.3648	0.380	0.3310	0.348	0.3438
0	0.3249	0.340	0.3065	0.324	0.3215
1	0.2893	0.300	0.2830	0.300	0.2813
2	0.2576	0.284	0.2625	0.276	0.2656
3	0.2294	0.259	0.2437	0.252	0.2500
4	0.2043	0.238	0.2253	0.232	0.2344
5	0.1819	0.220	0.2070	0.212	0.2188
6	0.1620	0.203	0.1920	0.192	0.2031
7	0.1443	0.180	0.1770	0.176	0.1875
8	0.1285	0.165	0.1620	0.160	0.1719
9	0.1144	0.148	0.1483	0.144	0.1563
10	0.1019	0.134	0.1350	0.128	0.1406
11	0.0907	0.120	0.1205	0.116	0.1250
12	0.0808	0.109	0.1055	0.104	0.1094
13	0.0720	0.095	0.0915	0.092	0.0938
14	0.0641	0.083	0.0800	0.080	0.0781
15	0.0570	0.072	0.0720	0.072	0.0703
16	0.0508	0.065	0.0625	0.064	0.0625
17	0.0453	0.058	0.0540	0.056	0.0563
18	0.0403	0.049	0.0475	0.048	0.0500
19	0.0359	0.042	0.0410	0.040	0.0438
20	0.0320	0.035	0.0348	0.036	0.0375
21	0.0285	0.032	0.0318	0.032	0.0344
22	0.0254	0.028	0.0286	0.028	0.0313
23	0.0226	0.025	0.0258	0.024	0.0281
24	0.0201	0.022	0.0230	0.022	0.0250
25	0.0179	0.020	0.0204	0.020	0.0219
26	0.0159	0.018	0.0181	0.018	0.0188
27	0.0142	0.016	0.0173	0.0164	0.0172
28	0.0126	0.014	0.0162	0.0148	0.0156

Wire diameters may also be expressed in mils as well as in gauge numbers. One mil equals one thousandth of an inch. Each decimal equivalent in **Table 4-2** can be converted to mils by multiplying by 1,000. For example, the underlined decimal in the table is equivalent to .0641 × 1000 or 64 mils.

To use **Table 4-2,** select from the five gauges listed in the table the one that applies to the sheet of metal or wire you want to gauge. For instance, column 2 (AWG and B&S) is used for the non-ferrous sheet metal and wire shown in **Figure 4-18**. Notice that each of the five gauges has its own decimal equivalent for a particular gauge number.

To measure wire size, apply the gauge to the wire as shown in **Figure 4-18.** Do not force the wire into the slot. Find a slot that refuses to pass the wire without forcing. Then try the next larger slot until you find one that allows the wire to pass. This is the correct size. Remember, your measurements are taken at the slot portion of the cutout rather than the inner portion of the gauge. Now that you have the gauge number, turn your gauge over and read the decimal equivalent for that number, which is the same as given in **Table 4-2.**

To measure the gauge of a piece of metal, first remove any burr from the place where you intend to apply the gauge. Then select the appropriate gauge for the metal to be measured.

After selecting the right gauge, apply the gauge to the wire, or to the edge of the sheet as shown in **Figure 4-18.** The number opposite the slot that fits the wire or sheet is its gauge number. The decimal equivalent is stamped on the opposite face of the gauge.

MECHANICS

Mechanics is a science that treats the action of forces and their effect upon bodies. A *force* is defined as any cause which tends to produce or modify motion. It is measured in pounds, usually. Force has three characteristics— direction, place of application, and magnitude.

The most familiar force is the pull of the earth, which we call gravity. The earth pulls, or attracts, baseballs, footballs, stones, and all other bodies. It attracts everything. The earth pull on a body, or the attraction of the earth for the body, we call the weight of the body. When you put more and more paint cans onto a shelf, you must pull up with greater and greater force to support it, and you know that its weight is increasing.

Work is the product of force and distance. That is, work = force × distance moved. It is measured in foot-pounds or in inch-pounds. In other words, one foot-pound (ft.-lb.) is the work done when a force of 1 pound acts through 1 foot. Thus, if you lift a 1-pound tool 1 foot, you do 1 foot-pound of work. To lift a tool weighing ½ pound 2 feet, you must do the same amount of work. Here's how to calculate how much work is done when an automobile weighing 3,000 pounds is lifted 20 feet in an elevator:

work (W) = force × distance = 3000 × 20 = 60,000 foot-pounds

Power is the amount of work done in a given time. It is the product of force and distance divided by time, and is expressed in foot-pounds per minute or foot-pounds per second. The element of time is always included. Power should not be given the same meaning as force, although some people carelessly refer to an applied force as power. For instance, the power of a locomotive depends upon the pull it exerts on the train and how fast it goes. A freight engine pulling a 100-car train 10 miles per hour may be less powerful than a passenger engine pulling 20 cars 50 miles per hour.

Velocity is the rate of motion. It is distance divided by time, and is expressed in feet per minute or feet per second. Velocity does not include force or weight.

Friction is the opposite of velocity. Place a wooden block on its broad side and drag it over a table top. Then place it on its narrow side. The force required to drag it will be about the same as before. Usually sliding friction does not depend upon how big the rubbing surfaces are. However, this is not always true. Friction does depend on area if the rubbing cuts into the surface. On soft snow you find it harder to drag a sled with narrow runners than a sled with wide runners. The narrow runners cut into the snow. On soft ground it pays to use large tires on your automobile, but on a hard-surfaced street they are not needed. Tractors must have wide tires, or "tracks," to prevent their cutting deep furrows in the ground.

Graphical Representation of Forces

A force may be represented graphically by a straight line, the length being proportional to the magnitude. That is, the line is drawn to some scale. One end of the line represents the point of application, and an arrow head at the other end represents the direction. **Figure 4-19** represents a force that is acting along AB in a direction from left to right.

To find a single force which produces the same effect as two or more forces is to find the *resultant.* The operation is called the *composition of forces.*

A   B

FIG. 4-19

237

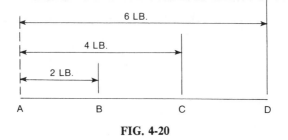

FIG. 4-20

To find two or more forces which combined are equivalent to a given or resultant force is to find the components. The operation is called the *resolution of forces.* In **Figure 4-19** let us assume that A is the point of application of a force that is exerted as a push. But if point B were the point of application, force would have to be exerted as a pull. If the line is 5 units long and if each unit represents 4 pounds, the line AB represents a pushing force of 20 pounds applied at A.

Remember that two or more forces may act together on a body. If the two forces are in the same direction, the resultant is equal to their sum. For example, in **Figure 4-20,** two forces AB equal to 2 pounds and AC equal to 4 pounds are both applied at point A. The resultant force (**AD**) would be: 2 + 4 = 6 pounds.

If the two forces act in opposite directions, the resultant force is their difference, and the resultant direction would be the same as that of the greater of the two. For instance, if two forces—AB equals 4 pounds and AC equals 8 pounds—are both applied at A, the resultant in the direction AC would be: 8 − 4 = 4 pounds.

Parallelogram of Forces

When two forces acting at a point can be represented in direction and magnitude by the adjacent sides of a parallelogram, the resultant will be represented in direction and magnitude by the diagonal of the parallelogram **(Figure 4-21).** AB and AC are the forces and AR the resultant. In **Figure 4-22,** force AB is 6 pounds while force AC is 8 pounds. Using the geometrical formula for a right triangle that the square of the hypotenuse is equal to the sum of the squares of the other sides, the resultant AR is found:

$$AR^2 = (AB)^2 + (AC)^2$$

$$AR^2 = (6)^2 + (8)^2 = 36 + 64$$

$$AR^2 = 100$$

$$AR = 10$$

238

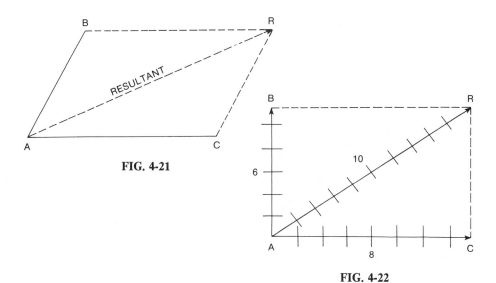

FIG. 4-21

FIG. 4-22

Parallel Forces

When two forces are parallel and act in the same direction, but not from the same point, their resultant is parallel to both, and is equal to their sum **(Figure 4-23, view A).** The resultant is located between the forces at a point that divides the line joining the points of application inversely as the magnitudes.

$$CD : AB = AE : EC$$

If the forces act in opposite directions, the resultant is parallel to both, but is located outside of them on the line produced by joining the points of application **(Figure 4-23, view B).** It is nearer the greater force and takes the same direction as the greater force, but in intensity it is equal to the difference between the components. The point of application of the resultant is:

$$AB : CD = CE : AE$$

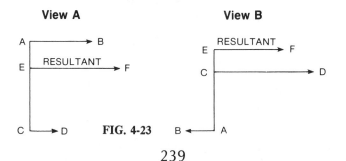

FIG. 4-23

239

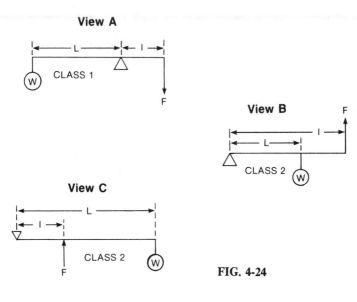

FIG. 4-24

Levers

Moments of forces are important factors in machines. These are defined as the force multiplied by the perpendicular distance from the fixed point to the direction of the force. The fixed point is called the center of moments, and the perpendicular distance is called the lever arm of the force. Moment of force is measured in foot-pounds or inch-pounds.

A lever is an inflexible rod, which may move about a fixed point called the fulcrum. The lever arms are the portions between the weights or forces and the fulcrum. To solve all problems relating to the lever, remember that the moments are the weights or forces multiplied by the distances from the fulcrum; that is, by the lever arms. As the lever is considered in balance, the product of the weight and length of weight arm is equal to the product of the power and length of power arm.

When the fulcrum is between the weight and the force **(Figure 4-24, view A)** and both weight and force act in the same direction:

$$W \times L = F \times 1 \text{ or } W : F = 1 : L$$

$$W = \frac{F \times 1}{L} \qquad L = \frac{F \times 1}{W}$$

$$F = \frac{W \times L}{1} \qquad 1 = \frac{W \times L}{F}$$

When the weight or load is between the fulcrum and the point at which the force is applied **(Figure 4-24, view B)**, the same principles apply; in fact, the same formulas are used.

In the third form of lever, the force is applied at a point between the fulcrum and the weight **(Figure 4-24, view C)**. The same formulas are used.

Mechanical advantage of any device is the number of times the resistance force is greater than effort force. In finding the mechanical advantage of a lever, measure the lever arm of each force. The resistance arm of the lever is the shortest distance from the fulcrum to the resistance force. The effort arm is the shortest distance from the fulcrum to the effort force. To get the mechanical advantage of the lever, divide its effort arm by its resistance arm.

Suppose that you use a bar to pry up a rock weighing 200 pounds. If the effort arm of the bar is 10 feet and the resistance arm 2 feet, what effort force must you exert if there is little friction?

$$200 \text{ pounds} = \text{resistance force } (f_R)$$

$$2 \text{ feet} = \text{resistance arm } (1_R)$$

$$10 \text{ feet} = \text{effort arm } (1_E)$$

Find the effort force (f_E).

$$\text{M.A.} = \frac{1_E}{1_R} \; ; \; \text{M.A.} = \frac{10 \text{ feet}}{2 \text{ feet}} \; ; \; \text{M.A.} = 5$$

$$\text{M.A.} = \frac{f_R}{f_E} \; ; \; 5 = \frac{200 \text{ pounds}}{f_E} \; ; \; 5f_E = 200 \text{ pounds}; \; f_E = 40 \text{ pounds.}$$

If the weight of the lever itself is to be considered, the moment of force (F $\times$ 1) remains the same, but there are then several moments of weight. The additional moments of weight are found by multiplying the weight of the lever arm by the distance of its center of gravity from the fulcrum. In a lever of the first class there will be two moments of weight because of the weight of the lever; one will act with the moment of force and the other will act with the moment of weight. With levers of the second and third class **(Figure 4-24)**, the additional moment of weight will act with the original moment of weight and therefore is added to it.

Often the moment of a force is called the torque of that force.

Suppose that you pull on the rim of the steering wheel of your car with a force of 8 pounds and suppose that the lever arm, or shortest distance from the fulcrum 0 to the force, is 1 foot. Then the moment of your force about 0 is 8 pound-feet.

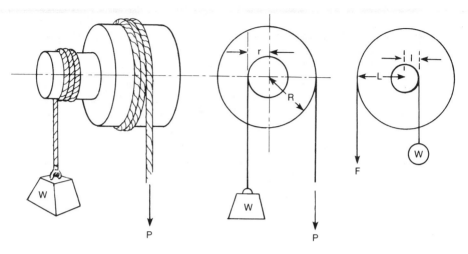

FIG. 4-25

The Windlass

The windlass shown in **Figure 4-25** is another form of lever. With it power and resistance may act through greater distances; the radius of the outer wheel or drum (L) is the lever arm of the power while the axle of the wheel or drum (1) is the lever arm of the resistance. The moment of force and the moment of weight are the means for finding the force required to lift a weight by a rope wound on the drum of a windlass.

$$F \times L = W \times 1$$

$$F = \frac{W \times 1}{L}$$

Suppose you wish to raise 1 ton with a windlass that has a periphery drum diameter of 32 inches and the drum on which the lifting rope is wound is 4 inches in diameter. What lifting force would be required?

$$F = \frac{W \times 1}{L} = \frac{2000 \times 2}{16} = \frac{4000}{16} = 250 \text{ pounds of force}$$

The mechanical advantage of a windlass equals the length of the crank divided by the radius of the axle. Suppose the crank on a bicycle is 7 inches long, and the radius of the sprocket wheel is 3.5 inches. If you exert a force of 80 pounds on the pedal, what force will act on the sprocket chain? To do this, we must find the mechanical advantage of the crank.

$$\text{M.A.} = \frac{\text{radius of circle}}{\text{radius of axle}} = \frac{7}{3.5} = 2$$

Then substitute in the formula:

$$\text{M.A.} = \frac{\text{force resistance}}{\text{effort resistance}} \text{ or } 2 = \frac{80}{f_E} \text{ or } 2f_E = 80$$

or 40 pounds of force on the sprocket

The Inclined Plane

The inclined plane is a sloping surface. It is one of the most useful of all simple machines. You can pull a 150-pound roller up an inclined plane, onto a platform, more easily than you can lift the roller vertically. When you roll it up the slope, your effort force acts through a distance greater than the height of the platform.

To lift the 150-pound roller up onto a platform 5 feet high, you must do 750 foot-pounds of work. By the law of work you must do the same amount to pull the roller 15 feet up the plane.

$$750 \text{ foot-pounds} = 15 \text{ feet} \times f_E$$

$$f_E = 50 \text{ pounds (effort force)}$$

For the inclined plane, neglecting friction:

$$\text{mechanical advantage} = \frac{\text{effort distance}}{\text{resistance distance}} = \frac{\text{length of plane}}{\text{height of plane}}$$

ROPES AND THEIR HANDLING LOADS

Most popular ropes (lines) are man-made synthetics—nylon, Dacron, polyethylene, and multifilament and monofilament polypropylene. Manila hemp, sisal, and braided cotton ropes are still on the market, but are not as common as previously.

All synthetics are virtually impervious to weather, rot, and mildew, although some polyethylene and polypropylene will break down under prolonged exposure to sun. To various degrees, they are resistant to abrasion, acids, and caustics. With the exception of Dacron, all synthetics are lighter than Manila hemp. Without exception, all of the synthetics are stronger than Manila for equivalent diameters.

Safe Working Load

To hoist a load of a given size, you should set up a hoisting device with a safe working load which is equal to or greater than the load to be hoisted. In order to do this, you must be able to calculate the following:

- the safe working load of a single rope of given size
- the safe working load of a given purchase which contains a rope of given size
- the minimum size of the rope and the minimum size of hooks or shackles required in a given type of purchase to hoist a given load

The best sources of information on the safe working load of a single rope are the manufacturer's tables, and these should always be used when available. Remember, however, that the values given in the manufacturer's tables apply only to new rope, and that they must be reduced as the rope deteriorates with use.

In the absence of tables there are certain rules of thumb for staying well within the margin of safety for any rope. In applying these rules, you *add* 30 percent to the value obtained from the formula if the rope is brand-new and in A-1 condition. If the rope has had a considerable amount of careful use but does not show any signs of deterioration, you use the value obtained from the formula. If the rope is nearing the stage where it requires replacement, you *subtract* 30 percent from the value obtained from the formula.

Where C means the circumference of (distance around) the rope in inches, a formula for finding the safe working load (SWL) for manila line in pounds is:

$$\text{SWL in pounds} = C^2 \times 150$$

Remember that the new synthetics are stronger than manila; thus their safe working load is greater.

Wire Rope

Wire rope is made of steel or iron wires laid together to form strands. Strands are laid together to form a rope, either wound about each other or wound together about a central core **(Figure 4-26, view A)**. Rope type—that is, the number of strands, number of wires per strand, type of material, and nature of the core—is usually selected based on the anticipated requirements.

244

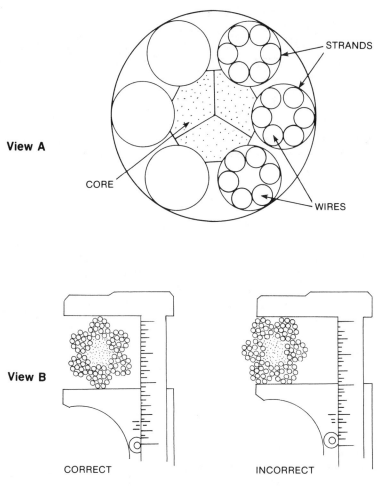

View A

STRANDS

CORE

WIRES

View B

CORRECT

INCORRECT

FIG. 4-26

Wire rope is designated as to size by its diameter in inches. The true diameter of a wire rope is considered to be the diameter of a circle which will just enclose all of its strands. The correct, as well as incorrect, method of measuring wire rope is illustrated in **Figure 4-26, view B.** Note, in particular, that the right way is to measure from the top on one strand to the top of the strand directly opposite it. The wrong way, as you will note, is to measure across two strands side by side. Use calipers to take the measurement; if calipers are not available, use an adjustable open-end wrench.

To ensure an accurate measurement of the diameter of a wire rope, always measure the rope at three places at least 5 feet apart. Use the average of the three measurements as the diameter of the rope.

The term "safe working load," as used in reference to wire rope, means the load that can be applied and still obtain most efficient service and also prolong the life of the rope. There are a number of rule-of-thumb formulas that you can use to compute the strength of a wire rope. The one recommended by most experts is as follows:

$$SWL \text{ (in tons)} = D^2 \times 4$$

In this formula, D represents the diameter of the rope in inches. Suppose you want to find the SWL of a 2-inch wire rope. Using the formula above, your figures would be:

$$SWL = (2)^2 \times 4$$

$$SWL = 4 \times 4 = 16$$

The answer is 16, meaning that the wire rope has an SWL of 16 tons.

Remember, any formula for determining SWL is only a rule of thumb. In computing the SWL of old rope, worn wire rope, or rope which is otherwise in poor condition, you should reduce the SWL as much as 50 percent, depending on the condition.

BLOCK AND TACKLE

A block consists of one or more sheaves fitted in a wood block or metal housing supported by a hook **(Figure 4-27)**. A tackle is an assembly of blocks and lines used to gain a mechanical advantage in lifting or pulling.

In a tackle assembly, the line is reeved over the sheaves of blocks. There are two types of tackle systems: simple and compound. A simple tackle system is an assembly of blocks in which a single line is used **(Figure 4-28)**. A compound tackle system is an assembly of blocks in which more than one line is used.

The function of the block or blocks in a tackle assembly is to change the direction of pull, to provide mechanical advantage, or to do both. The blocks are constructed for use with fiber line or with wire rope. Wire-rope blocks are heavily constructed and have a large sheave containing a deep groove. Fiber-line blocks are generally not as heavily constructed as wire-rope blocks and have smaller sheaves with shallower wide grooves. Wire rope requires a large sheave to prevent sharp bending. Since fiber line of equal thickness as wire rope has greater flexibility and pliability, it does not require as large a sheave.

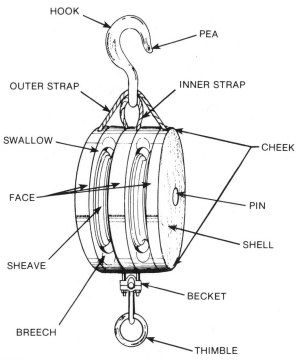

FIG. 4-27

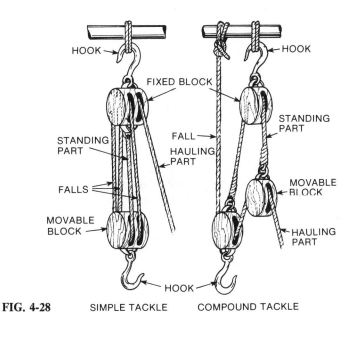

FIG. 4-28   SIMPLE TACKLE   COMPOUND TACKLE

247

Blocks fitted with one, two, three, or four sheaves are often referred to as single, double, triple, and quadruple blocks. Blocks are fitted with a varying number of attachments, depending upon their use. Some of the most commonly used fittings are hooks, thimbles, and beckets **(Figure 4-27)**.

The size of fiber-line blocks is designated by the length in inches of the shell or cheek. The size of standard wire-rope blocks is controlled by the diameter of the rope. With nonstandard and special-purpose wire-rope blocks, the size is determined by measuring the diameter of one of its sheaves in inches.

Take care in selecting the proper size of line or wire for the block to be used. If a fiber line is reeved onto a tackle whose sheaves are below a certain minimum diameter, the line will become distorted and will wear badly in a very short time. A wire rope too large for a sheave will tend to be pinched and to damage the sheave. The wire will be damaged also because of too tight a radius of bend. A wire rope too small for a sheave lacks the necessary bearing surface, thus placing the strain on only a few strands and shortening the life of the wire.

With fiber line, the length of the block used should be about three times the circumference of the line. However, an inch or so either way doesn't matter too much. For example, a 3-inch line may be reeved onto an 8-inch block with no ill effects. As a rule you are more likely to know the block size than you are the sheave diameter. However, the sheave diameter should be about twice the size of the circumference of the line used.

Manufacturers of wire rope issue tables that give the proper sheave diameters to be used with the various types and sizes of their product. In the absence of these, a rough rule of thumb is that the sheave diameter should be about 20 times the diameter of the wire rope. Remember that with wire rope it is diameter rather than circumference, and that this rule refers to the diameter of the sheave rather than the size of the block, as with fiber line.

Mechanical Advantage

The mechanical advantage of a tackle is the relationship between the load being lifted and the force required to lift that load. In other words, if a load of 10 pounds requires 10 pounds of force to lift it, the mechanical advantage is 1. However, if a load of 50 pounds requires only 10 pounds to lift it, then you have a mechanical advantage of 5 to 1; 5 units of weight are lifted for each unit of power applied.

The force required to lift the weight is equal to the weight divided by the number of lines that are shortened:

$$F = \frac{W}{N}$$

248

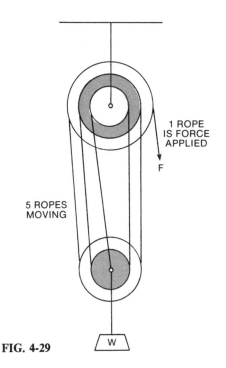

1 ROPE
IS FORCE
APPLIED

F

5 ROPES
MOVING

W

FIG. 4-29

Assume there are 5 moving lines on the moving block (**Figure 4-29**). The sixth line is considered separately as the unknown force needed. The weight is 300 pounds. To calculate force needed, use this formula:

$$F = \frac{300}{5} = 60 \text{ pounds}$$

The velocity with which the weight is raised is equal to the velocity of the force divided by the number of lines shortened.

$$\text{velocity} = \frac{\text{velocity of F}}{\text{N of ropes}}$$

Tackles are designated according to (1) the number of sheaves in the blocks that are used to make the tackle, such as single whip or twofold purchase; or (2) the purpose for which the tackle is used, such as yard tackles or stay tackles. In this section, we will discuss some of the different types of tackle in common use, namely, single whip, runner (not illustrated), gun tackle, single luff, twofold purchase, double luff, and threefold purchase. Before proceeding, we should explain that the purpose of the arrows in the figures is to indicate the sequence and direction in which the standing line is led in reeving.

249

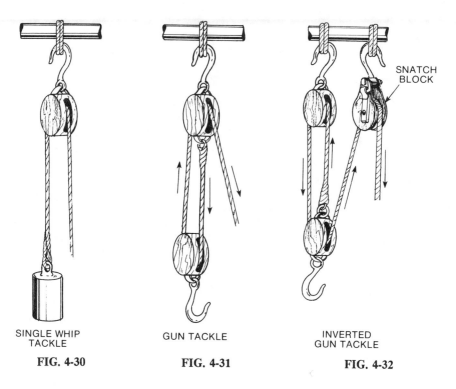

SINGLE WHIP
TACKLE

FIG. 4-30

GUN TACKLE

FIG. 4-31

INVERTED
GUN TACKLE

FIG. 4-32

The easiest way to determine the mechanical advantage of a tackle is by counting the number of lines or ropes (falls) at the moving block. If there are two lines, the mechanical advantage is two times the power applied (disregarding friction). A single-whip tackle (**Figure 4-30**) has no mechanical advantage. It merely changes the direction of force. A gun tackle (**Figure 4-31**) has a mechanical advantage of 2. Therefore, to lift a 200-pound load with a gun tackle would require 100 pounds of power, disregarding friction.

By inverting any tackle, you can gain 1 more mechanical advantage because the number of lines at the movable block is increased. By inverting a gun tackle (**Figure 4-32**) you can gain a mechanical advantage of 3. When a tackle is inverted, the direction of pull usually becomes impractical unless you add a snatch block, which changes the direction of the pull, but does not increase the mechanical advantage because it does not increase the number of lines at the moving block.

To ascertain the amount of force required to lift a given load by means of a tackle, determine the weight of the load to be lifted and divide that by the mechanical advantage.

Example: If it is necessary to lift a 600-pound load by means of a single luff tackle (**Figure 4-33**), first determine the mechanical advantage gained by using

250

this type of tackle. Do this by counting the lines at the movable block. Three lines indicate a mechanical advantage of 3. Therefore, by dividing the weight to be lifted, 600 pounds, by the mechanical advantage in this tackle, 3, we find that a theoretical 200 pounds of force is required to lift a weight of 600 pounds using a single luff tackle.

Accounting for friction, some of the force applied to a tackle is always lost through friction. Friction will develop in a tackle as the lines rub against each other, or against the shell of a block. Friction also is caused by the passing of the line over the sheaves, and by the rubbing of the pin against the sheaves. So to determine the force required to lift a given load, you must add an adequate allowance for friction loss to the weight being lifted. Roughly 10 percent of the load must be allowed for each sheave in the tackle.

For example, suppose you want to lift a load of 500 pounds with a twofold purchase (**Figure 4-33**). Simply take 10 percent of the 500 pounds, which is 50 pounds; that multiplied by 4 (the number of sheaves) gives you 200 pounds, which is the amount friction added to the load. The total load of 700 pounds is divided by 4, which is the mechanical advantage of a twofold purchase. The answer, 175 pounds, is the force required to lift the load.

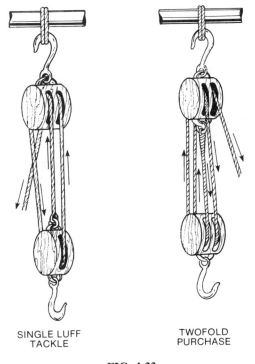

SINGLE LUFF
TACKLE

TWOFOLD
PURCHASE

FIG. 4-33

251

From earlier examples, you know that the force applied at the hauling line of a tackle is multiplied as many times as there are lines on the movable block. You also know that friction adds roughly 10 percent to the weight to be lifted for every sheave in the system. For example, if you are lifting a weight of 100 pounds with a tackle containing five sheaves, you must add 10 percent times 5, or 50 percent, of 100 pounds to the weight in your calculations. In other words, you figure that this tackle is going to lift 150 instead of 100 pounds.

Disregarding friction, the safe working load of a tackle would be equal to the safe working load of the line or wire rope used, multiplied by the number of lines on the movable block. To make the necessary allowance for the friction, multiply this result by 10, and then divide what you get by 10 plus the number of sheaves in the system.

For example, let us say you have a threefold purchase **(Figure 4-34)**, with a mechanical advantage 6, reeved with a line whose safe working load is 2 tons. Disregarding friction, 6 times 2, or 12 tons, would be the safe working load of this setup. To make the necessary allowance for friction, however, you first multiply 12 by 10, which gives you 120. This you divide by 10 plus 6 (number of sheaves in a threefold purchase), or 16. The answer is 7½ tons, safe working load. Mechanical advantage of other tackle and purchase arrangement are as follows: Gun tackle is 2; single luff tackle is 3; twofold purchase is 4; and double luff tackle is 5.

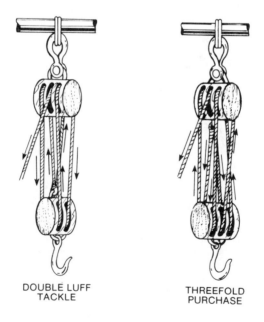

DOUBLE LUFF
TACKLE

THREEFOLD
PURCHASE

FIG. 4-34

252

Lifting a Given Weight

To find the size of fiber line required to lift a given load, use this formula:

$$C \text{ (in inches)} = \sqrt{15 \times P \text{ (tons)}}$$

C in the formula is the circumference, in inches, of the line that is safe to use. The number 15 is the conversion factor. P is the weight of the given load, expressed in tons. The radical sign, or symbol, over 15 × P indicates that you are to find the square root of that product. For instance, let us figure what size fiber line you would need to hoist a 5-ton load.

$$C = \sqrt{15 \times 5}, \text{ or } \sqrt{75}$$

The square root of 75 is approximately 8.6. Therefore, a fiber line $8\frac{1}{2}$ inches in circumference will do the job.

The formula for finding the size of wire rope to lift a given load is:

$$C \text{ (in inches)} = \sqrt{2.5 \times P \text{ (tons)}}$$

Work this formula in the way explained above for fiber line. One point you must consider is that these formulas call for the circumference of the wire. We otherwise talk about wire rope in terms of its diameter, so remember that circumference is a little over 3 times the diameter. (You can determine circumference more accurately by using the usual geometry formula, $C = \pi D$, Circumference = 3.1416 × Diameter).

Size of Line to Use in a Tackle

To find the size of line to use in a tackle for a given load, add to the weight to be hoisted one-tenth (or 10 percent) of its value for every sheave in the system. Divide the result you get by the number of lines at the movable block, and use this result as P in the previously given formulas:

$$C = \sqrt{15 \times P} \text{ (for fiber line)}$$

$$C = \sqrt{2.5 \times P} \text{ (for wire rope)}$$

For example, let's say you are trying to find the size of fiber line to reeve in a threefold (**Figure 4-34**) purchase to lift 1 ton. There are six sheaves in a threefold purchase, so you add $\frac{1}{10} \times 6$, or $\frac{6}{10}$, to the 1 ton. This gives you a theoretical weight to be lifted of 1.6 tons.

Divide 1.6 tons by 6 (number of lines on the movable block in a threefold purchase), and you get about 0.266 tons. Using this as P in the formula $C = \sqrt{15 \times P}$, you get:

$$C = \sqrt{15 \times .2666}, \text{ or } \sqrt{4}$$

The square root of 4 is 2, so it will take about a 2-inch line in this purchase to hoist 1 ton safely.

PULLEYS AND BELTS

A simple way to transmit force, either at the same speed or at a different speed, is to place a pulley on the driving shaft and another on the driven shaft and pass an endless belt over them. It is evident that the linear speed of the pulleys is the same; that is, one revolution of the driving pulley pulls the belt through a distance equal to its circumference, and a point on the periphery of the driven pulley will be pulled through this distance whether or not the periphery is equal to the circumference of the driving pulley.

Surface or Peripheral Speed of a Pulley

The surface or peripheral speed of a pulley (or wheel) is the number of feet a point on the rim of the pulley (or wheel) moves in 1 minute. This is stated in feet per minute (fpm), relating to either speed or the rate of feed of a machine.

The feet per minute speed of a pulley is equal to the circumference of the pulley (C) multiplied by the number of revolutions (rpm) the pulley makes in one minute, or

$$\text{fpm} = \text{C} \times \text{rpm}$$

Since the circumference is equal to π times the diameter, $\text{C} = \pi\,\text{D}$, thus

$$\text{fpm} = \pi\,\text{D} \times \text{rpm}$$

When the diameter is given in inches, to obtain the fpm, divide this result by 12:

$$\text{fpm} = \frac{\pi\,\text{D} \times \text{rpm}}{12} = \frac{3.14 \times \text{D} \times \text{rpm}}{12} = .2618 \times \text{D} \times \text{rpm}$$

For instance, to find the peripheral speed of a 36-inch pulley revolving at 450 rpm, you would proceed as follows:

$$\text{fpm} = .2618 \times 36 \times 450 = 4241.2 \text{ feet per minute}$$

Table 4-3 gives the typical recommended surface feet per minute for the various types of grinding wheels. If a 6-inch-diameter grinding wheel being used for knife sharpening has peripheral speed of 4,000 feet per minute, rpm of the wheel would be equal to:

$$\text{rpm} = \frac{\text{spm}}{.2618 \times \text{D}} = \frac{4000}{.2618 \times 6} = \frac{4000}{1.57} = 2547.7$$

A typical manufacturer's rating chart of grinding wheel speeds in rpm is given in Table 4-4.

TABLE 4-3:
GRINDING WHEEL SPEED

Type	Surface feet per minute
Chisel grinding	5,000 to 6,000
Cutlery wheels	4,000 to 5,000
Cut-off wheels	6,000 to 8,000
Cut-off wheels (rubber, shellac, resinoid)	9,000 to 16,000
Cylindrical grinding	5,500 to 6,500
General grinding	5,000 to 6,500
Hemming cylinders	2,100 to 5,000
Internal grinding	2,000 to 6,000
Knife grinding	3,500 to 4,500
Snagging, off-hand grinding (vitrified wheels)	5,000 to 6,000
Snagging (rubber and resinoid wheels)	7,000 to 9,500
Surface grinding	4,000 to 6,000
Tool and cutter grinding	4,500 to 6,000
Wet tool grinding	5,000 to 6,000

TABLE 4-4:
GRINDING WHEEL SPEEDS IN RPM

Diameter of wheel	RPM for stated surface feet per minute (SFPM)							
	4000 sfpm	4500 sfpm	5000 sfpm	5500 sfpm	6000 sfpm	6500 sfpm	7000 sfpm	7500 sfpm
1	15,279	17,189	19,098	21,008	22,918	24,828	26,737	28,647
2	7,639	8,594	9,549	10,504	11,459	12,414	13,368	14,328
3	5,093	5,729	6,366	7,003	7,639	8,276	8,913	9,549
4	3,820	4,297	4,775	5,252	5,729	6,207	6,685	7,162
5	3,056	3,438	3,820	4,202	4,584	4,966	5,348	5,730
6	2,546	2,865	3,183	3,501	3,820	4,138	4,456	4,775
7	2,183	2,455	2,728	3,001	3,274	3,547	3,820	4,092
8	1,910	2,148	2,387	2,626	2,885	3,103	3,342	3,580
10	1,528	1,719	1,910	2,101	2,292	2,483	2,674	2,865

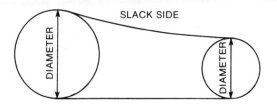

FIG. 4-35

Two Pulleys Joined by a Belt

When two pulleys are joined by a belt, the one in which the power or motion originates is called the *driver* pulley, while the one to which the power or motion is transmitted is called the *driven* pulley **(Figure 4-35)**. To change the rotative speeds of the driven shaft it is only necessary to make its pulley diameter different from the diameter of the driver pulley.

The revolutions are inversely proportional to the circumferences and, therefore, to the diameters. The smaller pulley runs at the higher rotative speed.

$$D = \text{diameter of driver}$$

$$d = \text{diameter of driven}$$

$$\text{rpm of driven : rpm of driver} = D : d$$

$$\text{rpm of driven} \times d = \text{rpm of driver} \times D$$

Thus the product of revolutions (rpm) and diameter of one pulley is equal to the product of the revolutions and diameter of the other pulley.

From

$$\text{rpm of driven} \times d = \text{rpm of driver} \times D$$

we have

$$d = \frac{\text{rpm of driver} \times D}{\text{rpm of driven}}$$

and

$$D = \frac{\text{rpm of driven} \times d}{\text{rpm of driver}}$$

To find the diameter of the driven pulley, multiply the revolutions of the driver by its diameter and divide by the revolutions of the driven. For example, the driving shaft makes 150 revolutions per minute and the driving pulley is 12 inches in diameter. If the driven shaft is to make 600 revolutions, what diameter pulley should you select?

$$d = \frac{150 \times 12}{600} = 3 \text{ inches}$$

Here's another problem: The driving shaft makes 200 revolutions and the driven shaft is to make 150 revolutions per minute. With a driven pulley of 24 inches diameter, what size driver pulley should be used?

$$D = \frac{150 \times 24}{200} = 18 \text{ inches}$$

To find speeds when sizes of pulleys are known:

$$\text{rpm of driver} \times D = \text{rpm of driven} \times d$$

$$\text{rpm of driver} = \frac{\text{rpm of driven} \times d}{D}$$

$$\text{rpm of driven} = \frac{\text{rpm of driver} \times D}{d}$$

For instance, the driver pulley is 16 inches in diameter and the driven is 18 inches in diameter. When the driver runs at 270 revolutions per minute, what will be the speed of the driven pulley?

$$\text{rpm of driven} = \frac{\text{rpm or driver} \times D}{d}$$

$$= \frac{270 \times 16}{18} = 240$$

Suppose two pulleys, one of 14 inches diameter and the other of 18 inches diameter, are available. The driven shaft is to run at 120 revolutions per minute. If the 14-inch pulley is placed on the driven shaft, what should be the speed of the driver?

$$\text{rpm of driver} = \frac{\text{rpm of driven} \times d}{D}$$

$$= \frac{120 \times 14}{18} = 93\frac{1}{3}$$

Formulas for Pulley Diameters and
Revolutions

When three factors are known, the fourth can be found by using one of the following formulas:

$$\text{diameter of driver} = \frac{\text{diameter of driven} \times \text{rpm of driven}}{\text{rpm of driver}}$$

$$\text{diameter of driven} = \frac{\text{diameter of driver} \times \text{rpm of driver}}{\text{rpm of driven}}$$

$$\text{rpm of driver} = \frac{\text{diameter of driven} \times \text{rpm of driven}}{\text{diameter of driver}}$$

$$\text{rpm of driven} = \frac{\text{diameter of driver} \times \text{rpm of driver}}{\text{diameter of driven}}$$

The same principles apply to more complex belting. Suppose two pulleys are mounted on the same shaft. We then have a combination that resembles a gear option. This arrangement is often desirable when it is not practical to get the speed reduction with one belt; that is, when the larger pulley would have to be very large as compared with the smaller.

In **Figure 4-36** the high rotative speed of pulley A (on a motor shaft for example) is reduced to a much lower figure at pulley D. Rpm of A × diameter of A = rpm of B × diameter of B, and rpm of C × diameter of C = rpm of D × diameter of D. But pulleys B and C are on the same shaft and have the same rotative speed: rpm of B = rpm of C.

Combining these equations, we may express the relation as follows: The speed of the first driver multiplied by the diameters of all the drivers is equal

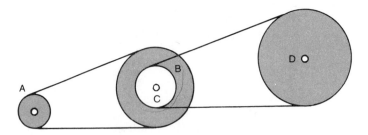

FIG. 4-36

258

to the speed of the last driven pulley multiplied by the diameters of all driven pulleys. Or

$$\text{rpm of A} \times \text{diameter of A} \times \text{diameter of C} =$$

$$\text{rpm of D} \times \text{diameter of B} \times \text{diameter of D}$$

If five of the above quantities are known the sixth is easy to find. For example, let's assume pulley A runs at 1,200 rpm, and is 4 inches in diameter. Pulley B is 12 inches in diameter, C is 5 inches, and D is 16 inches. What is the speed of D?

$$1200 \times 4 \times 5 = \text{rpm of D} \times 12 \times 16$$

$$24,000 = \text{rpm of D} \times 192$$

$$\text{rpm of D} = \frac{24,000}{192}$$

$$= 125$$

In the preceding example we have found the rotative speed of D without finding the rotative speed of B, but we had given the diameters of B and C. Suppose we had given the speed of D, but do not know what pulleys to use in place of B and C.

$$\frac{\text{rpm of first driver}}{\text{rpm of last driven}} = \frac{\text{product of diameters of all drivens}}{\text{product of diameters of all drivers}}$$

or $$\frac{\text{rpm of A}}{\text{rpm of D}} = \frac{\text{diameter of B} \times \text{diameter of D}}{\text{diameter of A} \times \text{diameter of C}}$$

The two unknown quantities are diameter of B and diameter of C, but the ratio can be found. Using the data in the above example we have this:

$$\frac{1200}{125} = \frac{16 \times \text{diameter of B}}{\text{diameter of C} \times 4}$$

$$\frac{\text{diameter of B}}{\text{diameter of C}} = \frac{4}{16} \times \frac{1200}{125}$$

$$= \frac{12}{5}$$

259

Length of Belts

Belts wear out and must be replaced. With an open belt arrangement, pass a tape, preferably a steel tape, around the pulleys. This will give the length direct, if it is a single belt; but if a double belt is to be used, add to the measurement twice the thickness of the belt. The length of small belts may be obtained by passing the belt around the pulleys and straining with hand pull.

New belts stretch and become slack after a short time, and the slack should be taken up. With long belts, you can anticipate stretching by cutting the belt 1 inch shorter for every 10 feet. To find the correct length of the belt when opened add the diameters of pulleys in inches and multiply the sum by 1.57 (approximately half the value of π), then add to this product twice the distance between centers in inches.

Formula for length of open belt:

$$L = 3.14 (R + r) + 2D + \frac{(R - r)^2}{D}$$

$$R = \text{radius of large pulley, inches}$$

$$r = \text{radius of small pulley, inches}$$

$$D = \text{distance between centers of shaft, inches}$$

$$L = \text{length of belt, inches}$$

Formula for length of crossed belt:

$$L = 3.14(R + r) + 2D + \frac{(R + r)^2}{D}$$

The ratio of the diameters is 12 : 5, and any pulleys having diameters in this ratio will give the desired speeds. The pulleys may be 12 and 5 inches, 18 and $7\frac{1}{2}$, or 24 and 10.

In **Figure 4-37,** the shaft of the 3-inch pulley D is to make 900 revolutions.

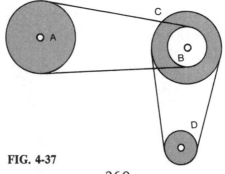

FIG. 4-37

260

What pulleys must be placed at B and C if A is 14 inches in diameter and makes 150 revolutions? The available pulleys have these diameters—8, 9, 10½, 11, 12, 13½ inches.

The formula to use is:

$$\frac{\text{rpm of first driver}}{\text{rpm of last driven}} = \frac{\text{product of diameters of all drivens}}{\text{product of diameters of all drivers}}$$

$$\frac{150}{900} = \frac{\text{diameter of B} \times 3}{14 \times \text{diameter of C}}$$

$$\frac{1}{6} = \frac{3}{14} \times \frac{\text{diameter of B}}{\text{diameter of C}}$$

$$\frac{\text{diameter of B}}{\text{diameter of C}} = \frac{1}{6} \times \frac{14}{3}$$

$$= \frac{14}{18} = \frac{7}{9}$$

Then multiply the ratio 7 : 9 by any number that will make 7 and 9 equal to the diameters of pulleys on hand. Multiplying by 1½ gives 10½ and 13½.

To prove that the calculation is correct, place these values in this expression: The speed of the first driver (150) multiplied by the diameters of all drivers (14) and (13½) is equal to the speed of the last driven (900) multiplied by the diameters of all driven pulleys (10½) and (3). The letters have the same values as above.

Let's now see how to figure belt lengths. For example, two pulleys are 11 feet apart and are 24 and 16 inches in diameter. What is the length of belt, open and crossed?

$$L = 3.14 \times (12+8) + (2 \times 132) + \frac{(12-8)^2}{132}$$

$$= 62.8 + 264 + \frac{16}{132}$$

$$= 326.8 + .12$$

$$= 326.92 \text{ inches, open belt}$$

$$L = 3.14 \times (12+8) + (2 \times 132) + \frac{(12 + 8)^2}{132}$$

$$= 62.8 + 264 + \frac{400}{132}$$

$$= 326.8 + 3.03$$

$$= 329.83 \text{ inches, crossed belt}$$

GEARS

Belts over pulleys and plain rolling cylinders cannot be depended upon to give a constant velocity ratio—there is always some loss of speed due to slip. But when two gears are in mesh, a point on the pitch circle of one moves at the same linear velocity as a point of the pitch circle of the other, and the number of revolutions for these two gears is always at a constant ratio.

Two gears in mesh must have the same pitch. That is, the distance from the center of a tooth to the center of the next tooth, measured along the pitch circle, must be the same for both gears. Therefore, two gears of the same pitch, but of different diameters, must have an unequal number of teeth. The space occupied by a tooth and the space between two teeth is the same in both gears if they have the same pitch. This fact shows immediately that the linear velocity of the pitch circles must be equal and the rotative speeds can be found in the same way as with belts. The pitch diameter or the number of teeth is substituted for the pulley diameter, for the numbers of teeth are proportional to the pitch diameters in the same way that the peripheries of pulleys are proportional to the diameters.

A gear having twice as many teeth as the gear meshing with it will make but one-half as many revolutions in a given time. Or, the speeds (rotative) vary inversely as the number of teeth; the gear with the smaller number of teeth, and thus smaller diameter, runs at the higher speed.

As in belts and pulleys, one gear of a pair is the driver and the other the driven or follower. The number of revolutions of the driver multiplied by the number of teeth on the driver is equal to the number of revolutions of the follower multiplied by the number of teeth on the follower.

If T = number of teeth on the driver and t = number of teeth on the follower, then rpm of driver × T = rpm of follower × t, or:

$$T = \frac{\text{rpm of follower} \times t}{\text{rpm of driver}}$$

$$t = \frac{\text{rpm of driver} \times T}{\text{rpm of follower}}$$

To find the number of teeth on the driver (T), multiply the revolutions of the follower by its number of teeth and divide the product by the revolutions of the driver. For example, the follower has 64 teeth and makes 30 revolutions per minute. The driver makes 80 revolutions per minute. How many teeth has the driver?

$$T = \frac{30 \times 64}{80} = 24$$

Let us consider a situation in which the driver makes 160 revolutions per minute and has 40 teeth. The follower makes 100 revolutions. How many teeth has the follower?

$$t = \frac{160 \times 40}{100} = 64$$

$$\text{rpm of driver} = \frac{\text{rpm of follower} \times t}{T}$$

$$\text{rpm of follower} = \frac{\text{rpm of driver} \times T}{t}$$

Suppose the follower has 90 teeth and makes 110 revolutions per minute. If the driver has 44 teeth, how many revolutions per minute?

$$\text{rpm of driver} = \frac{110 \times 90}{44} = 225$$

Another similar example occurs when the driver has 63 teeth and makes 800 revolutions per minute. If the follower has 42 teeth, what will be its speed?

$$\text{rpm of follower} = \frac{800 \times 63}{42} = 1200$$

Formulas for Speed of Gears

When three factors are known, the fourth can be found by using one of the following formulas:

$$\text{rpm of driver} = \frac{\text{rpm of follower} \times \text{teeth on follower}}{\text{teeth on driver}}$$

$$\text{rpm of follower} = \frac{\text{rpm of driver} \times \text{teeth on driver}}{\text{teeth on follower}}$$

$$\text{teeth on driver} = \frac{\text{rpm of follower} \times \text{teeth on follower}}{\text{rpm of driver}}$$

$$\text{teeth on follower} = \frac{\text{rpm of driver} \times \text{teeth on driver}}{\text{rpm of follower}}$$

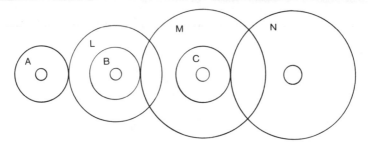

FIG. 4-38

As in the case of pulleys, great speed changes are made by trains of gears in place of a pair. Examples are found in hoists, clocks, lathes, etc. Each pair in the train has its driver and follower, and if the shafts are parallel, it is usual to get the speed change by keying two gears of unequal size on every shaft, except the first and last.

The velocity ratio of the first to the last is found as follows: The product of the number of teeth on all the drivers divided by the product of the number of teeth on all the followers is the velocity ratio.

Suppose the train has three drivers **(Figure 4-38)**, A, B, and C, and three followers, L, M, N. A has 14 teeth and drives L having 70 teeth. Pinion B on same shaft with L has 13 teeth and drives M having 104 teeth. Pinion C has 15 teeth, and is on the same shaft with M; C drives N having 75 teeth. What is the velocity of A to N?

$$\text{velocity ratio} = \frac{\text{teeth on A} \times \text{teeth on B} \times \text{teeth on C}}{\text{teeth on L} \times \text{teeth on M} \times \text{teeth on N}}$$

$$= \frac{14 \times 13 \times 15}{70 \times 104 \times 75} \; \; 2730$$

$$= \frac{1}{200}$$

Knowing the velocity ratio of the train, it is easy to find the speed of N if the speed of A is known. If A runs at 1,800 revolutions per minute, N will make only 9 revolutions, since $1,800 \div 200 = 9$.

When the speed of the first driver or the last follower is also known, the speed may be figured from the following: Multiply the revolutions per minute of the first driver by the continued product of the number of teeth on all drivers, and divide by the continued product of the teeth on all followers. The quotient will be the revolutions per minute of the last follower.

PUTTING SHOP MATH TO WORK

It is important to understand the math concepts involving force, power, energy and mechanics. But, to achieve results in the shop, you must also be able to put these concepts and math to work for you.

Power

Earlier in this chapter, we stated that power is the amount of work done in a given time. After James Watt invented the reciprocating steam engine, he found it was difficult to sell the engine unless its power could be compared with that of a horse. Consequently, he performed a series of experiments to determine the power of the average English draft horse.

In his experiments, he had a number of horses, one at a time, pull a 165-pound coal bucket up a mine shaft. He allowed 1 minute for each trial and found that the average horse covered 200 feet in that time. Watt called this new measurement *horsepower* and saw that it was a means by which mechanical power could be measured. He determined the average horsepower as follows:

$$P \text{ (work)} = F \text{ (force)} \times D \text{ (distance)}$$

$$P = F \times D$$

$$= 165 \text{ pounds} \times 200 \text{ feet}$$

$$= 33,000 \text{ foot-pounds}$$

Since *power* is equal to work divided by time:

$$P = \frac{\text{work}}{\text{time}} = \frac{33,000 \text{ foot-pounds}}{60 \text{ seconds}}$$

$$= 550 \text{ foot-pounds per second}$$

This formula can be used to find the rate of doing work. For instance, if a man exerts a force of 80 pounds in pushing a loaded dolly 95 feet in 1 minute, the amount of power exerted in foot-pounds is:

$$P = \frac{W}{t} = \frac{80 \times 95}{60} = 126.7 \text{ foot-pounds per second}$$

It is important to remember that *work* is expressed in foot-pounds, but *power* is expressed in foot-pounds per minute, or per second. Power includes the *rate*

265

at which work is done. Suppose a piece of machinery weighing 1,825 pounds is raised from a truck to the second story of a factory building 28 feet above the ground in 9 minutes from a bed of a truck 42 inches above the ground. The rate of work in foot-pounds per minute is:

$$d = 28 - 3\frac{1}{2} = 24\frac{1}{2} \text{ feet} \quad t = 9 \text{ minutes}$$

$$f = 1825 \text{ pounds}$$

$$p = \frac{24.5 \times 1825}{9} = \frac{44712.5}{9} = 4968 \text{ foot-pounds per minute}$$

Power is usually expressed in horsepower (hp). It is the power that is equal to 33,000 foot-pounds of work in one minute. (That is, 550 foot-pounds per second $\times$ 60 = 33,000 foot-pounds per minute.) For example, to find the horsepower of a motor that raises a maximum load of 2.5 tons 15 feet in 1 minute, proceed as follows:

$$hp = \frac{\text{foot-pounds per minute}}{33000} = \frac{3000 \times 15 \times 1}{33000} = 1.36 \text{ hp}$$

Machine Efficiency

The efficiency of a machine is the ratio of the energy given out (output) to the energy taken in (input) by the machine and is usually stated in a percentage. That is, the formula for efficiency is:

$$E \text{ (efficiency)} = \frac{O \text{ (output)}}{I \text{ (input)}} \times 100$$

Suppose an inclined plane leading to a storage room is 20 feet long and 5 feet high. If an effort of 80 pounds is needed to pull a load of 300 pounds up the incline, what is the efficiency of the machine?

$$\text{work output} = f_o \times d_o = 300 \times 5 = 1500$$

$$\text{work input} = f_i \times d_i = 80 \times 20 = 1600$$

$$\text{efficiency} = \frac{1500}{1600} = 0.937 = 93.7\%$$

Brake Horsepower

To find the actual power that is transmitted to a pulley or a shaft, a device known as a *Prony brake* is employed. There are several designs on the market,

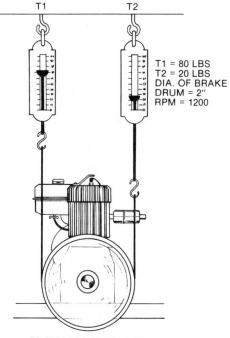

T1

T2

T1 = 80 LBS
T2 = 20 LBS
DIA. OF BRAKE
DRUM = 2"
RPM = 1200

PRONY BRAKE TEST OF
GASOLINE ENGINE

FIG. 4-39

but the type shown in **Figure 4-39** is used for Prony brake tests of gasoline engines. To find brake horsepower (bhp), use the formula:

$$bhp = \frac{2 \, D \text{ of the brake drum} \times \text{rpm} \times (T_2 - T_1)}{33000}$$

If in **Figure 4-39,** scale T_1 reads 80 pounds and T_2 reads 20 pounds, the diameter of the brake drum is 2 inches, and the shaft rpm is 1,200. The brake horsepower is:

$$bhp = \frac{2 \times 3.14 \times 2 \times 1200 \times 60}{33000} = 27.4 \text{ bhp}$$

S.A.E. Horsepower

The horsepower of automobiles is calculated according to a formula developed by the Society of Automotive Engineers (S.A.E.). This formula is used

267

by some states in determining license fee or tax to be paid on autos. The S.A.E. horsepower rating of an automobile engine is obtained as follows:

$$hp = \frac{D^2N}{2.5}$$

D = bore in inches

N = number of cylinders

For example, to find the rated S.A.E. horsepower for a 6-cylinder engine having a bore of 3 inches, proceed as follows:

$$hp = \frac{D^2N}{2.5} = \frac{(3)^2 \times 6}{2.5} = \frac{9 \times 6}{2.5} = 21.6 \text{ hp}$$

Indicated Horsepower

Another measure of the power developed in the cylinder engine is indicated horsepower (ihp). It is found with this formula:

$$ihp = \frac{PLAN}{33,000}$$

P = mean effective pressure on the piston in

pounds per square inch

L = length of the stroke in feet

A = area of the piston in square inches

(A − .754d²)

N = number of strokes per minute

Suppose we have the following data: Pressure on piston is 35 pounds per square inch; the length of the stroke is 24 inches; the diameter of the piston is 14 inches; and the rpm is 185. The ihp of this engine is found:

$$ihp = \frac{35 \times 2 \times 0.754 \times 196 \times 185}{33000} = \frac{1913802.8}{33000} = 58 \text{ ihp}$$

For complete information on electrical power, see Chapter 5.

Cutting Speed

A good machinist must fully understand cutting speed. Too fast a cutting speed will result in premature tool failure; too slow a cutting speed will greatly increase machining times and make the part expensive to produce. Good finish,

TABLE 4-5:
**CUTTING SPEEDS IN FPM FOR VARIOUS MATERIALS USING
HIGH-SPEED STEEL CUTTING TOOLS**

	Lathe	Drill press	Milling machine
Aluminum	150–400	300	400–1000
Brass	150–700	200	300–700
Bronze	80–150	100	70–90
Cast iron	40–90	60	80–100
Machine steel	100–200	80	80–100
Malleable iron	70–120	90	60–80
Nickel steel	85–110	70	50–70
Stainless steel	100–150	50	80–120
Tool steel	70–130	60	30–50

good sizes, and good production rates require the use of proper cutting speeds.

Cutting speed is the peripheral speed of the work passing the cutting tool or the rotating cutter passing the surface of the work. Theoretically, in a lathe the cutting speed would be the length of the chip produced in one minute and is usually expressed in feet per minute.

Cutting speed is relatively constant for a given material (**Table 4-5**) using the same cutting-tool material, but the rpm of the machine will vary as the diameter of the work or tool varies. Calculating the approximate rpm is accomplished by using this formula:

$$\text{rpm} = \frac{\text{CS} \times 4}{\text{D}}$$

rpm = revolutions per minute

CS = cutting speed in feet per minute

D = diameter of the rotating work or the rotating cutter

If the material is 2 inches in diameter and the cutting speed is 100 feet per minute, rpm can be determined by applying the formula:

$$\text{rpm} = \frac{100 \times 4}{2} = 200 \text{ rpm}$$

Cutting Speeds for Drills

The cutting speed of a drill is the distance in feet traveled in 1 minute by the outer corners (point A in **Figure 4-40**) of the cutting edges of the drill. If

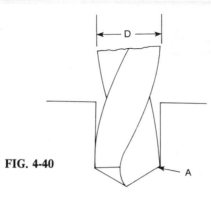

FIG. 4-40

D is the diameter of the drill and N is the number of revolutions it makes per minute, the cutting speed (CS) in feet per minute is:

$$CS = \frac{\pi \times D \times N}{12}$$

For example, to find the cutting speed in feet per minute (fpm) when using a $\frac{7}{8}$-inch high-speed drill at a speed of 250 rpm to cut carbon steel, proceed as follows:

$$CS = \frac{3.14 \times .8125 \times 250}{12} = \frac{637.8}{12} = 53.2 \text{ fpm}$$

To find the safe drilling speed for any of the following metals, just multiply the number of rpm in **Table 4-6** by the number given after the metals listed below. For example, to find the safe drilling speed for aluminum under home-workshop conditions and using a $\frac{1}{4}$-inch high-speed drill:

$$760 \text{ rpm} \times 2.5 = 1,900 \text{ rpm}$$

Die castings (zinc base)	3.5
Aluminum	2.5
Brass and bronze	2.0
Cast iron, soft	1.15
Malleable iron	0.85
Cast iron, hard	0.80
Tool steel	0.60
Stainless steel, hard	0.30
Chilled cast iron	0.20
Manganese steel	0.15

TABLE 4-6:
SAFE DRILLING SPEEDS FOR MILD STEEL IN ROTATIONS PER MINUTE

Drill size (in inches)	Industrial use (with machine feed and copious lubrication)		Home-shop use (with hand feed and intermittent or no lubrication)	
	Carbon	High-speed	Carbon	High-speed
1/16	1,830	6,110	920	3,060
3/32	1,220	4,075	610	2,050
1/8	920	3,060	460	1,530
3/16	610	2,040	310	1,020
1/4	460	1,530	230	760
3/18	370	1,220	180	610
3/8	310	1,020	150	510
1/2	230	764	115	380

The formula $CS = \frac{\pi \times D \times N}{12}$ can also be used to determine the cutting speed of a milling machine cutter as well as the surface speed of a grinder. For instance, if a $2\frac{3}{4}$-inch angular milling machine cutter is cutting cast iron revolving at 125 rpm, what is its cutting speed?

$$CS = \frac{3.14 \times 2.75 \times 125}{12} = \frac{1079.3}{12} = 89.9 \text{ fpm}$$

Cutting Speeds for Woodworking Tools

The cutting speed of belt-driven woodworking tools such as table saws, jointers, and band saws can be determined by the following formula:

$$CS = \frac{\pi \times CD \times rpm \times D}{d \times 12}$$

CS = cutting speed in fpm

CD = diameter of cutter

rpm = revolutions per minute of the motor

D = diameter of the driving pulley

d = diameter of the driven pulley

271

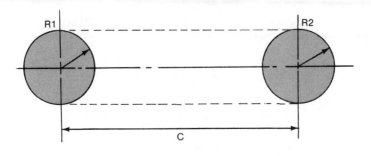

FIG. 4-41

Suppose we wish to find the cutting speed of a 6-inch jointer cutter attached to a 6-inch pulley driven by a motor that makes 2,800 rpm and holds a 10-inch pulley.

$$CS = \frac{3.14 \times 6 \times 2800 \times 10}{6 \times 12} = \frac{527520}{72} = 7,326.7 \text{ fpm}$$

Incidentally, if your band-saw blade breaks and you do not know the proper length, the following suggestions and formula may be used:

1. Adjust wheels to correct position: not at the outer extreme because some takeup will be needed to tension the band; also, not at the shortest point because some allowance must be made for rewelding where necessary.
2. Having adjusted the wheels at about halfway in the takeup range, measure center distance C in inches.
3. Find the radius of each wheel (R1, R2) in inches **(Figure 4-41).**
4. Use the formula:

$$(R1 \times 3.1416) + (R2 \times 3.1416) + (2 \times C) = \text{band length}$$

Screws, Bolts, and Nuts

Screws, bolts, and nuts play an important part in most shops. Let us take a look at math that goes into their making.

Screw Threads

For ordinary machine screws, bolts, studs, etc., screw threads are made with special tools called threading dies. These are screwed upon the bolt, screw, or stud to be threaded by rotating either the work or the die. Threading dies are used both by hand and in power-driven machines.

272

A screw thread is known as a *right-hand* thread when the screw, bolt, or nut has to be turned in a clockwise direction in order to engage or tighten. This is the more common of the two threads. When the thread runs counterclockwise it is a *left-hand* thread. When the thread is on the outside surface it is called an *external* thread, and when it is on the inside, in a nut, for example, it is an *internal* thread. The part of the surface that lies between the two sides of adjacent threads is known as the *root* (**Figure 4-42**).

While most screws are cut with a single continuous groove and are hence known as *single-thread* screws, threads can be made with two, three, or four grooves, and the screws are then designated as *multiple-thread.*

Pitch in a thread is a measurement of the distance from any given point on the thread, such as the top, to the corresponding point on the next thread. Pitch is the reciprocal of the number of threads per inch; for example, if there are 7 screw threads per inch, the pitch equals 1 divided by 7, of ¹⁄₇-inch pitch, sometimes abbreviated in shop practice to 7 pitch, and written 7P. Pitch may be expressed in fractions of an inch. A ¹⁄₈-inch pitch, for example, refers to a screw with threads ¹⁄₈ inch apart from center to center.

Lead (pronounced *leed*) is the term used to represent the distance a screw advances when given a single turn. In a single-thread screw, the lead is equal to the pitch. In a multiple-thread screw, the lead is the number of threads times the pitch.

Figures 4-42 to **4-44** show the pitch of the three most common screw thread types: Sharp V-thread; American National Form thread [both National Coarse (NC) and National Fine (NF)]; and Acme square thread. The following math formulas can be used to obtain the basic information on each type.

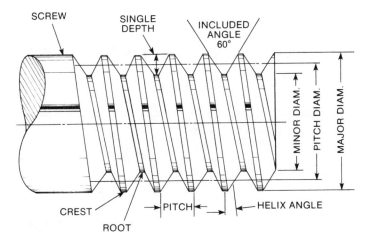

SHARP V THREAD   **FIG. 4-42**

273

SHARP V-THREAD

See **Figure 4-42**.

$$H = .866p \text{ and } H = \frac{.866}{n} \text{ and } p = \frac{1}{n}$$

H = depth

p = pitch

n = number of threads per inch

The minor diameter of a thread is the major diameter minus double the thread depth. Thus, to find pitch, the depth, and the minor diameter of $\frac{3}{4}$ -inch-12 Sharp V-thread, proceed as follows:

$$p = \frac{1}{n} = \frac{1}{12} = 0.083 \text{ inch}$$

$$d = \frac{.866}{12} = .072 \text{ inch}$$

major diameter =	.750 inch
double depth = 2 × .072 =	.144 inch
minor diameter =	.606 inch

AMERICAN NATIONAL FORM THREAD

See **Figure 4-43**.

$$H = .649p \text{ and } h = \frac{.6495}{n}$$

$$F = .125p \text{ and } F = \frac{p}{8}$$

F = width of flats

For example, to find the pitch, depth, minor diameter, and the width of flats of a $\frac{3}{8}$-inch-24 NF thread, proceed as follows:

$$p = \frac{1}{24} = 0.042 \text{ inch}$$

$$d = \frac{.6495}{24} = 0.027 \text{ inch}$$

Minor diameter = .875 inch − .054 inch = 0.821 inch

$$f = \frac{.042}{8} = 0.005 \text{ inch}$$

274

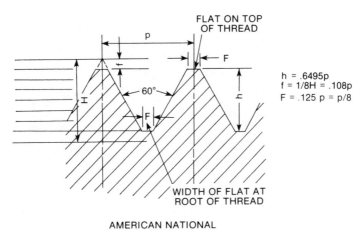

h = .6495p
f = 1/8H = .108p
F = .125 p = p/8

FLAT ON TOP
OF THREAD

WIDTH OF FLAT AT
ROOT OF THREAD

FIG. 4-43

AMERICAN NATIONAL
FORM THREAD

ACME THREAD

See **Figure 4-44.**

$$h = \frac{p}{2} + .010$$

$$F_t = .3707 \times p$$

$$F_b = .3707 \times p - .0052$$

$$F_t = \text{width of top flat}$$

$$F_b = \text{width of bottom flat}$$

To find the pitch, depth, the width of the top flat, the width of the bottom flat, and the root (minor) diameter of $\frac{7}{8}$-inch-8 Acme thread, use the following procedure:

$$p = \frac{1}{8} = .125 \text{ inch}$$

$$h = \frac{.125}{2} + .01 = 0.0725 \text{ inch}$$

$$F_t = 0.3707 \times 0.125 = 0.0463 \text{ inch}$$

$$F_b = 0.3707 \times 0.125 - .0052 = 0.0411 \text{ inch}$$

$$\text{root diameter} = 0.875 - 0.145 = 0.73 \text{ inch}$$

275

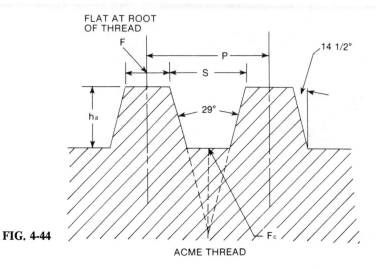

FLAT AT ROOT
OF THREAD

FIG. 4-44

ACME THREAD

Tap Drills

Thread depth over 75 percent does not appreciably increase thread strength. As thread depth approaches 100 percent, driving torque must be increased and may reach a point where the tap breaks. For the majority of tapping jobs, standard-size tap drills listed here should be adequate. They are for thread depths ranging from 60 to 75 percent. To figure the proper tap drill size to make a tap hole for, say, an American Standard $\frac{3}{4}$-inch-10 NC thread, proceed as follows:

$$p = \frac{1}{N} = \frac{1}{10} = 0.1 \text{ inch}$$

$$h = 0.6495 \times p = 0.6495 \times 0.1 = 0.06495 \text{ inch}$$

Then use the formula:

$$T_H = M_D - (0.75 \times d_d)$$

T_H = tapped-hole size

M_D = major diameter

d_d = double depth of the thread

Substitute the values in the example:

$$T_H = 0.75 - (.75 \times 0.1299)$$

$$T_H = 0.75 - 0.0974 = 0.6526$$

276

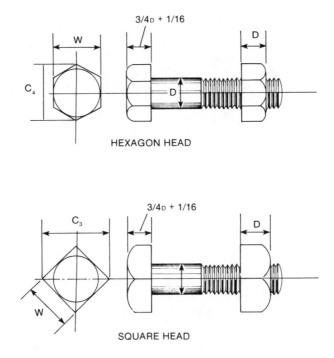

3/4D + 1/16

W

D

C₄

D

HEXAGON HEAD

3/4D + 1/16

C₃

D

W

SQUARE HEAD

FIG. 4-45

To find the nearest drill size, multiply the decimal part by 64 and take the next largest whole number, or in this case:

$$0.6526 \times 64 = 41.766, \text{ or } 42$$

The nearest commercial tap drill is $^{42}\!/_{64}$ or $^{21}\!/_{32}$ inches.

Bolts and Nut Heads

Figure 4-45 shows a square-head and hexagon-head bolt with their corresponding nuts. The dimensions of the heads of the bolts, and of the nuts to go with the bolts, are expressed in terms of the diameter (D) of the bolt, as follows:

1. Distance across the flats for both, $W = 1.5D + 0.125$
2. Distance across the corners for hexagon-head bolts, $C_H = 1.15W$
3. Distance across the corners for square-head bolts, $C_S = 1.414W$
4. The thickness of head in both cases $= \frac{3}{4}D + \frac{1}{16}$
5. The thickness of the nut in both cases $= D$, the diameter of the shank

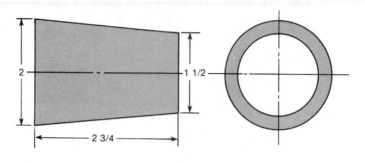

FIG. 4-46

Tapers and How They Are Cut

A taper on a piece of round work is the difference between the diameter of the large end and that of the small end. For the piece of stock shown in **Figure 4-46,** the large end is 2 inches in diameter, and the small end is $1\frac{1}{2}$ inches in diameter; thus the taper is $\frac{1}{2}$ inch $(2 - 1\frac{1}{2} = \frac{1}{2})$.

To find the taper per inch, divide the taper by the number of inches from end to end. Thus, in our example, the taper per inch would be 0.25 inch $(\frac{0.5}{2})$. Another way of stating the taper inch formula is:

$$\text{T per inch} = \frac{\text{T total}}{\text{L of taper}} \text{ or } \frac{\text{D large} - \text{d small}}{\text{L of taper}}$$

$$\text{T per foot} = \frac{\text{D large} - \text{d small}}{\text{L of taper}} \times 12$$

Taper Turning

To turn a taper it is necessary to use a lathe provided with a taper attachment or to adjust the tailstock of the engine lathe sufficiently off center to give the required diameter change. Since all taper attachments are graduated for direct reading, they are easily set for the required taper. Adjustment of the tailstock of an engine lathe is not so simple as the taper attachment. In setting the taper attachment, the axial distance the center points are set apart is not important, while this distance is imperative in setting over the tailstock of the lathe.

To turn a taper by the tail offset method **(Figure 4-47),** a procedure such as the following is generally undertaken.

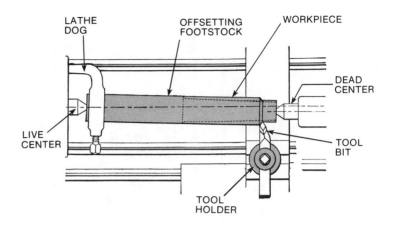

LATHE DOG   OFFSETTING FOOTSTOCK   WORKPIECE

DEAD CENTER

LIVE CENTER

TOOL BIT

TOOL HOLDER

FIG. 4-47

1. Calculate the amount of taper per inch.
2. Calculate the amount of tailstock offset by means of the following formula:

$$\text{offset} = \frac{\text{taper/inch} \times \text{total length of workpiece}}{2}$$

EXAMPLE: #3 Morse Taper equals .6024 inch taper per foot (**Table 4-7**, pages 280–281), piece 6 inches long:

$$\frac{.6024}{12} = .0502 \text{ inch taper per inch}$$

$$\text{offset} = \frac{.0502 \times 6}{2} = .1506 \text{ inch}$$

3. To offset the tailstock we must loosen the tailstock clamp and loosen the screw of the tailstock base that is opposite the direction we desire to offset the tailstock. Move the tailstock toward the operator a total of $\frac{5}{32}$ inch (.156 inch), which is approximately the correct offset. A steel rule is used for this measurement.
4. Tighten the tailstock clamp.
5. Take a trial cut over the workpiece until the tapered area is approximately $2\frac{1}{2}$ inches long and has a good finish.
6. Remove the piece from the machine and check taper per inch.
7. To correct for error in taper per inch, multiply the amount of error per inch by $\frac{1}{2}$ length of the workpiece.

279

TABLE 4-7:
MORSE TAPER SHANKS

	General dimensions		Shank				Tongue				Keyway				
Number of taper	Diameter of plug at small end	Diameter at end of socket	Whole length of shank	Shank depth	Depth of hole	Standard plug depth	Thickness of tongue	Length of tongue	Rad. of mill for tongue	Diameter of tongue	Width of keyway	Length of keyway	End of socket to keyway	Taper per foot	Number of key
	D	A	B	S	H	P	t	T	R	d	W	L	K		
0	.252	.35	2 11/32	2 7/32	2 1/32	2	5/32	1/4	5/32	.235	11/64	9/16	1 15/16	.6246	0
1	.369	.47	2 9/16	2 7/16	2 5/32	2 1/8	13/64	3/8	3/16	.343	0.218	3/4	2 1/16	.5986	1
2	.572	.70	3 1/8	2 15/16	2 39/64	2 9/16	1/4	7/16	1/4	17/32	0.266	7/8	2 1/2	.5994	2
3	.778	.93	3 7/8	3 11/16	3 1/4	3 3/16	5/16	9/16	9/32	23/32	0.328	13/16	3 1/16	.6024	3
4	1.020	1.23	4 7/8	4 5/8	4 1/8	4 1/16	15/32	5/8	5/16	31/32	0.484	1 1/4	3 7/8	.6233	4
5	1.475	1.74	6 1/8	5 7/8	5 1/4	5 3/16	5/8	3/4	3/8	1 13/32	0.656	1 1/2	4 15/16	.6315	5
6	2.116	2.49	8 9/16	8 1/4	7 21/64	7 1/4	3/4	1 1/8	1/2	2	0.781	1 3/4	7	.6257	6
7	2.750	3.27	11 5/8	11 1/4	10 5/64	10	1 1/8	1 3/8	3/4	2 5/8	1.156	2 5/8	9 1/2	.6240	7

Courtesy: Starrett

TABLE 4-7 (Cont.)

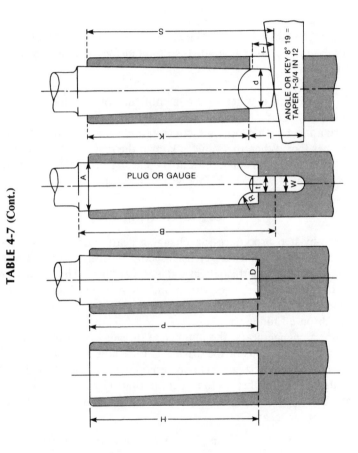

ANGLE OR KEY 8° 19' =
TAPER 1-3/4 IN 12

PLUG OR GAUGE

EXAMPLE: Desired taper per inch = .050 inch; length of work = 6 inches; taper per inch after trial cut = .047 inch.

.050

.047
———
.003 inch error per inch

.003 × ½ L = .003 × 3 = .009 inch correction of the tailstock position. In this case more taper is needed, so the tailstock is moved toward the operator .009 inch.

8. Continue with another trial cut until the correct taper per inch is obtained.

To turn a taper with a taper attachment, it is necessary only to compute the taper per foot. When this value is known the scale on the taper attachment is then set for this amount and the cutting procedure given by the manufacturer of attachment is followed to the letter.

Lathe Gearing

The step-by-step procedures on changing gears for various screw-cutting and other lathe operations are given in books on metal lathes. There is one formula that is purely mathematical and is covered here. That is, the continued product of the speed of the first driver and the number of teeth on all drivers is equal to the speed of the last follower multiplied by the continued product of the teeth on all followers.

In figuring change gears, the number of threads per inch to be cut corresponds to the revolutions of the driver, and the number of turns on the lead screw to move the carriage 1 inch corresponds to the speed of the follower.

Then the number of threads to be cut multiplied by the teeth on the spindle stud equals the number of threads on the lead screw multiplied by the teeth on the lead-screw gear. Or:

$$\frac{\text{threads to be cut}}{\text{threads on lead screw}} = \frac{\text{teeth on lead-screw gear}}{\text{teeth on spindle stud}}$$

Suppose there are 6 threads on the lead screw and 40 teeth on the lead screw gear—how many threads will be cut if a 24-tooth gear is placed on the spindle stud?

$$\frac{\text{threads to be cut}}{6} = \frac{40}{24}$$

$$\text{threads to be cut} = \frac{40}{24} \times 6 = 10$$

The above assumes that the lathe is geared 1 : 1; that is, the lathe screw constant is equal to the number of threads per inch on the lead screw. If the lathe is not so geared, the lathe screw constant should be used in place of the threads per inch on the lead screw.

The foregoing example shows how the figuring can be done when the gears are on the spindle stud and lead screw; but the problem is usually one of finding out what gears to use. Suppose 7 threads are to be cut, and there are 5 threads per inch on the lead screw. What gears are to be used?

$$\frac{\text{threads to be cut}}{\text{threads on lead screw}} = \frac{\text{teeth on lead screw gear}}{\text{teeth on stud gear}}$$

$$\frac{7}{5} = \frac{\text{teeth on lead screw gear}}{\text{teeth on stud gear}}$$

The ratio of the gears is as 7 : 5.

By multiplying both 7 and 5 by any number, such as 6, we get:

$$\frac{42}{30} = \frac{\text{teeth on lead screw gear}}{\text{teeth on stud gear}}$$

Using the formula as above may aid in disposing of that troublesome question "Which gear goes on the stud?" In some cases it may seem easier to assume one gear and go through the calculation to find the other, there being then one unknown quantity and three known quantities.

Stresses

There are three principal types of stresses:

Tension, produced when a force, applied externally, tends to pull the material apart.
Compression, produced when a force, applied externally, tends to crush or push the material together.
Shear, produced when a force, applied externally, acts in such a way to cut through the material.

Stress is generally expressed in pounds per square inch. In the following formula for unit stress, P represents the total external force in pounds that is exerted on an object, A the area of the cross section of the object, and S the unit stress in pounds per square inch.

$$P = A \times S$$

283

For example, if a steel tie rod 2 inches in diameter is subjected to a load of 36,000 pounds, what is the unit stress within the rod?

$$P = (\pi r^2) \times S = (3.14 \times 1^2) \times 36000$$

$$= 3.14 \times 36000 = 113,040 \text{ pounds}$$

Elastic Limit

With all materials, there is a relationship between the amount of extension or compression of that material and the load or force producing that extension or compression. This relation is called *modulus of elasticity* and is defined as the load per unit of section divided by the extension per unit of length. That is, the modulus of elasticity (E) is found by dividing the stress per inch by the elongation (e) in one inch caused by this stress (P), or:

$$E = \frac{P}{e}$$

For example, if the elongation of 0.025 inch is produced in a bar 20 inches long by a load 36,000 pounds per square inch of cross-section of a bar, the modulus of elasticity would be:

$$E = \frac{36,000 \times 20}{.025} = 28,800,000$$

TABLE 4-8:
AVERAGE ULTIMATE STRENGTHS OF SOME METALS, IN POUNDS PER SQUARE INCH

Metal	Tension	Compression	Shear
Aluminum, cast	15,000	12,000	12,000
Aluminum, half hard sheet	19,000	60,000	19,000
Brass, cast	30,000	30,000	36,000
Copper, cast	24,000	40,000	25,000
Copper, rolled	37,000	60,000	28,000
Iron, cast	22,000	90,000	25,000
Iron, cast (2 percent nickel)	50,000	150,000	50,000
Lead	3,000		4,000
Steel, casting	70,000	65,000	60,000
Steel, boiler plate	70,000	70,000	60,000
Steel (mild)	70,000	65,000	55,000
Steel (soft)	60,000	60,000	45,000
Tin, sheet	5,000	6,500	5,000

The approximate moduli of elasticity for various materials are:

Brass, cast	9,170,000	Iron, cast	12,000,000
Copper	15,000,000	Steel	28,000,000
Lead	1,000,000	Tin, cast	4,600,000

There comes a point, known as the elastic limit, where the unit stress becomes so great that deformation will occur. That is, when the stress is less than the elastic limit, the object will return to its original form; when the unit stress is greater than the elastic limit, the object does not return to its original form. The point at which this change takes place is called the yield point.

As the load on the material increases beyond its elastic limit, the material extends rapidly until finally the load breaks or crushes it. The ultimate strength (Table 4-8) is the highest unit stress that the material will bear, and it is from two to four times a material's elastic limits. In some materials it is much greater in compression than in tension.

BASIC ELECTRICAL
CALCULATIONS

When a load, such as a light bulb, is connected to a battery, the flow of current always travels from negative to positive terminals. Because it is flowing in only one direction and is flowing at an unfluctuating and steady rate, it is called regular direct current. We'll describe later how other types of current are produced. The flow of regular direct current can be compared with the flow of water produced by a centrifugal pump. In fact, the factors that affect the movement of water in a piped system can also be applied to the movement of electrons in an electric circuit. They are *pressure, quantity, rate of flow,* and *resistance.*

Pressure is the force that moves water through pipes. It is also the force that moves electrons through conductors. Just as the pump produces water pressure, the battery produces electric pressure. Quantity is in one case the amount of water moved by the pump, and in the other it is the amount of electrons moved by the battery.

Rate of flow is the speed or the strength of flow of water through the pipes and of electrons through the conductors. Resistance is the opposition produced by the pipes and fittings to the flow of water as well as the opposition produced by the conductors to the flow of electrons. Just as the pump must produce a sufficient pressure to overcome the resistance in order to move a unit quantity of water through a pipe, so must the battery produce a sufficient pressure to move a unit quantity of electrons through a conductor.

While the terms *electromotive force,* or *voltage,* and *potential difference* are closely related and are often used interchangeably, there are technical differences among them. In brief, *emf,* or *voltage,* is the pressure produced throughout an electric circuit, while *potential difference* indicates the ratio of electron potency or concentration between the electrodes of a battery or between certain components of other current-producing devices.

286

Just as units of measure have been established to measure the quantity of liquids, so have units been established to measure the quantity of electricity. When we deal with large quantities of water, we use the term *gallon*. A gallon is 4 quarts, or 8 pints, or 128 ounces. While the electron can be considered to be a quantity of electricity, it is too small to be used as a standard measure. A larger unit, comprising 6.3 billion billion of electrons, is called a *coulomb* (C) and is the standard electrical unit of quantity measure. The unit is named for Charles Coulomb, a French physicist, who made investigations into magnetism and electricity. Although the coulomb is a definite quantity of electrons which can be measured in a laboratory, it is of little concern to us from a practical standpoint.

Coulombs alone can no more measure the strength of an electric current than the gallon alone can measure the strength of a waterfall. Both must be considered in their relation to time. If we say that Niagara Falls spills 5 million gallons of water, it means very little unless the time required for this amount of spill is also given. If it takes a year to spill this amount, it would not be much of a waterfall. However, if it is known that it takes only an hour, from this its strength can be determined. The rate of flow of electrons is measured in *amperes*.

The last, but very important, factor in our understanding of electricity is the resistance to the flow of electrons encountered in a conductor. Most metals have a low resistance and are considered good conductors, because the molecules are loosely hung together and have many free electrons. Or in other words, the attraction between the electrons and the protons (or nucleus) is weak, and the electrons can be readily pushed out. Copper is one of these metals, and is widely used for conducting electricity. All matter, including copper, presents a certain amount of resistance to the flow of current by attempting to retain its own electrons. In any circuit, the resistance of the conductor must be overcome by the force of the current. If the force is great or the resistance is small, strong current flows. On the other hand, if the force is small or the resistance is great, only a small amount of current will flow.

Just as the *volt* is a unit of measure for electromotive force and the *ampere* is a unit of measure for the rate of flow of electric current, so is the *ohm* (Ω) the unit of measure for the resistance of a conductor to the flow of electrons.

DC CIRCUITS

An electric circuit is a path or a group of interconnected paths capable of carrying electric currents. Before an electric current can do useful work, it must be passed through an electrically operated device. The device is referred to as the load. This load device is connected to a power source, which may be a battery or a generator, in such a way that the current leaves the power source, passes through the load which it operates (or in which it does useful work), and returns to the power source.

A simple electric circuit is illustrated in **Figure 5-1.** Current flows from the negative terminal of the generator or battery, via the top wire, through the switch and the load, and back via the bottom wire to the positive terminal of the generator or battery. The current continues to flow in this manner as long as the connections are intact and the generator or battery is able to maintain the necessary electromotive force (emf), or voltage. As previously stated, the emf is the electric pressure that drives the current through the circuit. The wires leading to and from the load (resistor) form a conducting path for the current, or flow of electrons. If the path is broken at any point, the current will stop flowing in the entire circuit. The circuit is then said to be open. If the path is not broken at any point, the circuit is said to be closed. The switch placed in the top wire lead is simply a device for opening and closing the circuit at will.

A circuit is any route in which the current must travel from the power source to the load and back to the power source. It may be a single path or it may be a group of interconnected paths. But since we have established that electric circuits are the electron carriers of an electric system, and since they can be quite complex, it is important that several fundamental facts be thoroughly understood. However, no matter how complex any particular

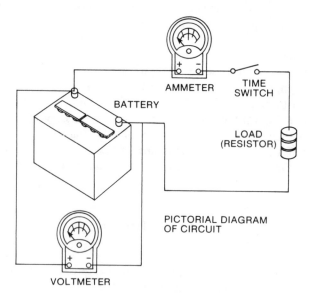

FIG. 5-1

288

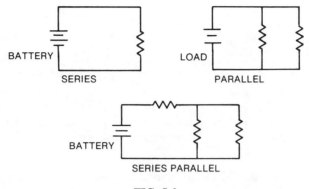

FIG. 5-2

circuit becomes, it is one of three general types. The three types of circuits are the *series,* the *parallel,* and the *series-parallel* (**Figure 5-2**).

The series is a one-path circuit that can be recognized in two ways. It will never have more than one conductor connected to one terminal, and there will be only one path from source to load and back to source.

In a parallel circuit there are two or more paths between the terminals of the source of current.

A series-parallel circuit, as the name implies, is a combination of both.

Every electric load is designed to have a specific resistance and to operate at a certain voltage. The resistance controls the amount of current at the rated voltage.

Ohm's Law

Ohm's law states that the current in an electric circuit is directly proportional to the applied voltage and inversely proportional to the circuit resistance. Ohm's law may be expressed as an equation:

$$I = \frac{E}{R}$$

I = current (flow), in amperes

E = voltage (pressure), in volts

R = resistance of the load, in ohms

If any two of the quantities in an equation are known, the third may be easily found. For example, the schematic diagram in **Figure 5-3** shows a circuit

289

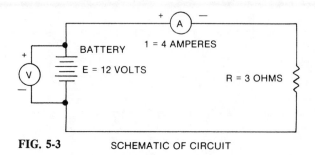

FIG. 5-3   SCHEMATIC OF CIRCUIT

containing a resistance of 3 Ω and a source voltage of 12 V. How much current flows in the circuit?

$$I = \frac{E}{R}$$

$$I = \frac{12}{3}$$

$$I = 4 \text{ A}$$

To observe the effect of source voltage on circuit current, the above problem is computed below using double the previous source voltage.

$$I = \frac{E}{R}$$

$$I = \frac{24}{3}$$

$$I = 8 \text{ A}$$

Notice that as the source voltage doubles, the circuit current also doubles. That is, circuit current is directly proportional to applied voltage and will change by the same factor that the voltage changes. To verify the statement that current is inversely proportional to resistance, assume the resistor in the schematic diagram **(Figure 5-3)** to have a value of 6 Ω.

$$I = \frac{E}{R}$$

$$I = \frac{12}{6}$$

$$I = 2 \text{ A}$$

Comparing this current of 2 A for the 6-Ω resistor to the 4 A of current obtained with the 3-Ω resistor shows that doubling the resistance will reduce the current to one-half the original value. Circuit current is inversely proportional to the circuit resistance.

In many circuit applications current is known and either the voltage or the resistance will be the unknown quantity. To solve a problem in which current and resistance are known, the basic formula for Ohm's law must be transposed to solve for E as follows:

$$I = \frac{E}{R}$$

Multiply both sides of the equation by R:

$$IR = \frac{E}{\cancel{R}} \cancel{R}$$

$$IR = E$$

$$E = IR$$

To transpose the basic formula when resistance is unknown:

$$I = \frac{E}{R}$$

Multiply both sides of the equation by R:

$$IR = \frac{E}{\cancel{R}} \cancel{R}$$

$$IR = E$$

Divide both sides of the equation by I:

$$\frac{\cancel{I}R}{\cancel{I}} = \frac{E}{I}$$

$$R = \frac{E}{I}$$

Rise or Fall of Potential Voltage Drops

It is important to understand what is meant by a rise of voltage, a fall of voltage, and a voltage drop. In **Figure 5-4, view A,** the battery voltage, or

291

potential difference between the battery terminals, is 200 V, as indicated by voltmeter V_1. By Ohm's law, the current through resistor A-B is

$$I = E/R = 200/100 = 2 \text{ A}$$

Also by Ohm's law, the voltage across the resistor is:

$$E = IR = 2 \times 100 = 200 \text{ V}$$

This voltage is, of course, the same as the battery voltage, for it is assumed that the resistance of the connecting leads is negligible.

The negative terminal of the battery in **Figure 5-4, view A,** is being used as the reference or zero point for measuring the potentials of all other points in the circuit. Thus, point A is the point of highest potential (200 V) and is positive with respect to the point of lowest potential (zero) at B. In **Figure 5-4, view B,** the 100-Ω resistor of **Figure 5-4, view A,** is replaced by four 25-Ω resistors R_1, R_2, R_3, and R_4, which are connected between points A-B, B-C, C-D, and D-E, respectively. Measurements with voltmeters (V_1, V_2, V_3, and V_4) show that the potentials of E, D, C, B, and A (taken in this order) are 0, 50, 100, 150, and 200 V positive. This shows that there is an increase or rise

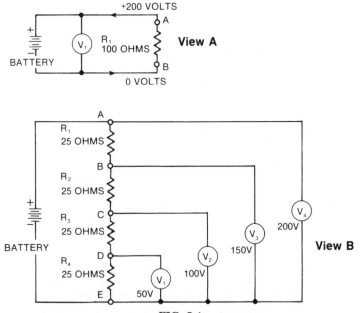

FIG. 5-4

292

of voltage from E toward A. If the resistance is distributed uniformly along the length E-A, the voltage rise will also be uniform. This is indicated by the fact that the rise across each section in **Figure 5-4, view B,** is 50 V.

Suppose that, in **Figure 5-4, view B,** the potential at A is first measured and that the potential at B is then measured. Obviously, the potential at B is lower than the potential at A, and we say that there is a fall or drop of potential from A to B. Apparently, whether there is a potential rise or fall between two points depends entirely on our point of view. For example, in **Figure 5-4, view B,** it is equally correct to say that there is a voltage rise from B to A as it is to say there is a voltage fall from A to B.

In practical work, as previously mentioned, our interest usually is centered on voltages and currents in operating circuits. A voltmeter always indicates the potential difference between the two points to which it is connected. Thus, if a voltmeter is successively connected across A-B, B-C, C-D, and D-E, it will in each instance show a potential difference of 50 V. The voltage across a portion of a circuit is called the voltage drop across that portion of the circuit. Consider points D-E. The resistance between these points is 25 Ω and the current is 2 A. From Ohm's law, E = IR and, in this instance,

$$E_{\text{C-D}} = 2 \times 25 = 50 \text{ V}$$

Similarly considering points C-E, the resistance is 25 Ω (C-D) plus 25 Ω (D-E), or 50 Ω, and the current is 2 A. Then,

$$E_{\text{C-E}} = 2 \times 50 = 100 \text{ V}$$

Voltage drops are also called IR drops. The meaning of "IR drop" is apparent when it is remembered that the voltage drop E across a resistance is calculated from the Ohm's law formula, E = IR.

In practical work the term "voltage drop" is usually used to indicate the potential difference required to produce the current through the two points being considered. As explained previously, the sum of the voltage drops around the entire circuit is equal to the emf. When the entire circuit is not considered, the sum of the voltage drops in the external circuit will equal the potential difference between the terminals of the source with the external circuit connected. Thus,

$$E_{R_1} + E_{R_2} + E_{R_3} + E_{R_4} = E_{\text{battery}}$$

and

$$50 + 50 + 50 + 50 = 200 \text{ V}$$

Series DC Circuits

As previously mentioned, an electric circuit is a complete path through which electrons can flow from the negative terminal of the voltage source, through the connecting wires or conductors, through the load or loads, and back to the positive terminal of the voltage source. A circuit is thus made up of a voltage source, the necessary connecting conductors, and the effective load.

If the circuit is arranged so that the electrons have only one possible path, the circuit is called a series circuit. Therefore, a series circuit is defined as a circuit that contains only one path for current flow.

Resistance in Series Circuits

As shown in **Figure 5-4,** a 100-Ω resistor **(view A)** can be replaced by four 25-Ω resistors in series **(view B)**. Similarly, a 10-Ω resistor and two 20-Ω resistors in series can be replaced by a single 50-Ω resistor. This illustrates a law for resistances in series: The total resistance is the sum of the individual resistances. In **Figure 5-4, view B,** the four resistances R_1, R_2, R_3, and R_4 are in series. If R_T represents the total resistance from A to E, then

$$R_T = R_1 + R_2 + R_3 + R_4$$

If R_T is the total resistance and E is the applied (in this instance) battery voltage, the current I can be determined from Ohm's law:

$$I = \frac{E}{R_T}$$

Current in Series Circuits

In **Figure 5-5,** current flow is from the negative terminal of the battery through ammeter A, resistance R_1, ammeter A_1, resistance R_2, ammeter A_2, resistance R_3, ammeter A_3, and through the battery from the positive to the negative terminal. Obviously, there is but one path for the current, and so the same current must be indicated by ammeters A, A_1, A_2, and A_3. This illustrates a law for series circuits: In a series circuit the current is everywhere the same; or, the same current flows in each part of the circuit. Thus, in the schematic,

$$I = I_1 = I_2 = I_3$$

Voltage in Series Circuits

Energy is expended in the resistance of an electric circuit; that is, in a resistance electric energy is converted to heat energy. In **Figure 5-6,** a 24-V battery is connected to three resistances in series: R_1 of 3 Ω, R_2 of 6 Ω, and

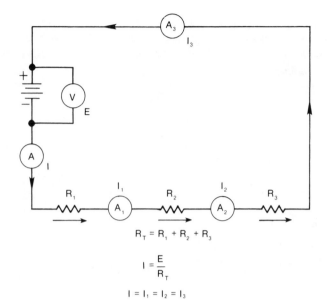

FIG. 5-5

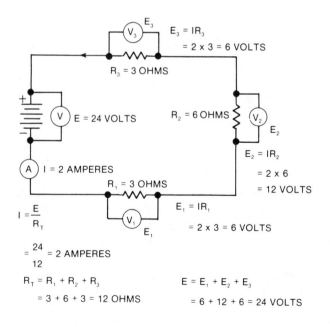

FIG. 5-6

R_3 of 3 Ω. The voltage required to produce the current in each of these resistances is called the voltage drop across each resistor. These voltage drops may also be calculated from Ohm's law. The total resistance R_T is the sum of the individual resistances:

$$R_T = R_1 + R_2 + R_3 = 12$$

E is given as 24 V; therefore,

$$I = \frac{E}{R_T} = \frac{24}{12} = 2 \text{ A}$$

Applying Ohm's law to each part of the circuit:

$$E_1 = R_1 \times I = 3 \times 2 = 6 \text{ V (across } R_1)$$
$$E_2 = R_2 \times I = 6 \times 2 = 12 \text{ V (across } R_2)$$
$$E_3 = R_3 \times I = 3 \times 2 = 6 \text{ V (across } R_3)$$

On adding the individual drops, we find that their sum is equal to the battery voltage:

$$E = E_1 + E_2 + E_3$$
$$E = 6 + 12 + 6 = 24 \text{ V}$$

This illustrates a law for series circuits: In a series circuit, the sum of the individual voltage drops is equal to the applied voltage.

A common example of this law is a string of Christmas-tree lights of the series type. The rated voltage of each bulb is approximately 19 V. When the bulbs are connected in a series of eight, the combined voltage totals approximately that of the source of 120 V.

Parallel DC Circuits

As already mentioned, a parallel circuit is defined as one having more than one current path connected to a common voltage source. Parallel circuits, therefore, must contain two or more load resistances which are not connected in series. A comparison of a basic series and parallel circuits is shown in **Figure 5-7.**

In the parallel circuit **(Figure 5-7, view B)**, if we start at the voltage source and trace counterclockwise around the circuit, we can identify two complete and separate paths in which current can flow. One path is traced from the source through resistance R_1 and back to the source; the other is from the source through resistance R_2 and back to the source.

296

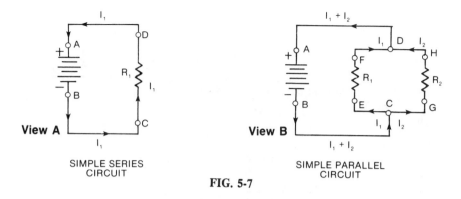

FIG. 5-7

SIMPLE SERIES
CIRCUIT

SIMPLE PARALLEL
CIRCUIT

Voltage in Parallel Circuits

You have seen that the source voltage in a series circuit divides proportionately across each resistor in the circuit. In a parallel circuit, the same voltage is present across all the resistors of a parallel group. This voltage is equal to the applied voltage. For example, **Figure 5-8, view A,** is the schematic diagram of a circuit in which the negative terminal of a 6-V battery is connected to point B, the positive terminal is connected to point A, and resistors R_1, R_2, and R_3 are connected in parallel between points A and B. Since A and B are directly connected to the battery terminals, the potential difference between A and B is 6 V. Each resistor is also connected between points A and B, and the same voltage is applied to each resistor. Thus, voltmeters V_1, V_2, and V_3 indicate the same voltage. This illustrates how voltages react in a parallel circuit; in a parallel circuit, the same voltage is applied to each branch. Thus E, E_1, E_2, and E_3 are the same voltage.

Current in Parallel Circuits

As we know, current in a circuit is inversely proportional to the circuit resistance. This fact, obtained from Ohm's law, establishes the relationship upon which the following discussion is developed. A single current flows in a series circuit. The value of this current is determined in part by the total resistance of the circuit. However, the source current in a parallel circuit divides among the available paths in relation to the value of the resistors in the circuit. Ohm's law remains unchanged. For a given voltage, current varies inversely with resistance.

If **Figure 5-8, view A,** is rearranged so that only R_1 is in the circuit **(Figure 5-8, view B),** we have a simple series circuit consisting of the 6-V battery and R_1. From Ohm's law the current I_1 through R_1 is

$$I_1 = \frac{E}{R} = \frac{6}{3} = 2 \text{ A}$$

This current is indicated by ammeters A and A_1. When the 2-Ω resistor R_2 is placed in parallel with R_1 **(Figure 5-8, view C),** the same voltage is applied

297

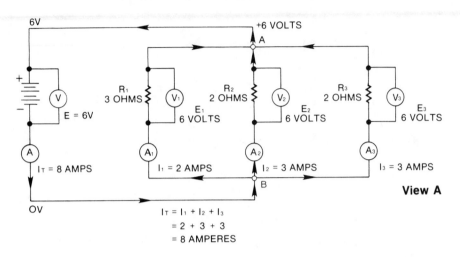

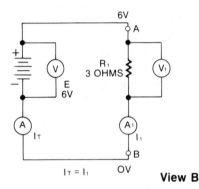

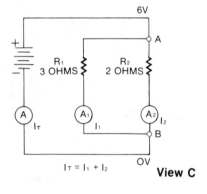

View A

$I_T = I_1 + I_2 + I_3$
$= 2 + 3 + 3$
$= 8$ AMPERES

$I_T = I_1$ 0V   **View B**

$I_T = I_1 + I_2$ **View C**

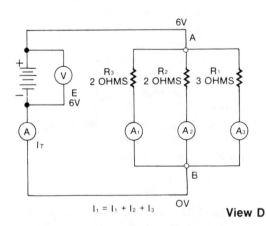

FIG. 5-8

$I_1 = I_1 + I_2 + I_3$ 0V   **View D**

to both resistors. (This assumes that the battery voltage remains constant at 6 V.) The current I_2 through R_2 is

$$I_2 = \frac{E}{R} = \frac{6}{2} = 3 \text{ A}$$

This 3-A current is indicated on ammeter A_2. The current I_T from the battery is the sum of the two currents, $I_1 + I_2$, or

$$I_T = 2 + 3 = 5 \text{ A}$$

When the 2-Ω resistor R_3 is connected in parallel with R_1 and R_2, as shown in **Figure 5-8, view D,** the same 6 V applied to R_3 is

$$I_3 = \frac{E}{R} = \frac{6}{2} = 3 \text{ A}$$

This 3-A current is indicated by ammeter A_3. The total current from the battery is thus increased by 3 A and now is

$$I_T = I_1 + I_2 + I_3 = 2 + 3 + 3 = 8 \text{ A}$$

This 8-A current is indicated on ammeter A. From these results, a rule for current in parallel circuits may be stated: The total current in a parallel circuit is equal to the sum of the currents in the individual branches. Note that the current from the negative terminal of the battery divides to follow three paths from point B **(Figure 5-8, view A),** recombines at point A, and returns to the positive terminal of the battery. The current that returns to the battery flows through the battery and is exactly equal to the current that leaves the battery. The current through any branch may be computed from Ohm's law, $I = E/R$, and depends on the amount of resistance in the branch.

Resistance in Parallel Circuits

The total or effective resistance of the circuit **(Figure 5-8, view A)** may be computed from the Ohm's law formula $R = E/I$. Since the applied voltage E is 6 V and the total current I_T is 8 A,

$$R_T = \frac{E}{I_T} = \frac{6}{8} = 0.75 \ \Omega,$$

where R_T is the effective resistance of the three resistors R_1, R_2, and R_3 in parallel; I_T is the total current from the battery. Note that the effective resistance of R_1, R_2, and R_3 is only 0.75 Ω, considerably less than the resistance of any one of the resistances. The rule for resistances in parallel may be stated as follows:

The effective resistance of a parallel circuit may be determined by dividing the applied voltage by the total current; it is always less than the resistance of the lowest resistance in the circuit.

As can be seen, the Ohm's law formula $R = E/I$ is satisfactory for finding the effective resistance when the voltage E and the total current I_T are known. However, it is often necessary to determine R when neither the voltage nor the current is known.

The simplest parallel arrangement consists of equal resistances in parallel. To obtain the effective resistance of such a combination, it is necessary only to divide the resistance of one resistor by the number of resistances. Thus, in

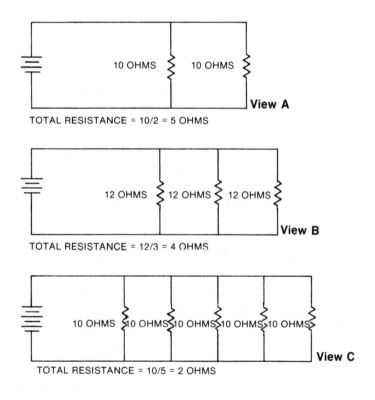

FIG. 5-9

300

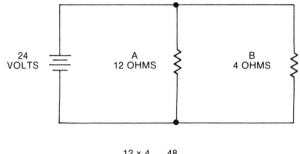

$$\text{TOTAL RESISTANCE} = \frac{12 \times 4}{12 + 4} = \frac{48}{16} = 3 \text{ OHMS}$$

FIG. 5-10

Figure 5-9, view A, two 10-Ω resistors are connected in parallel, and the effective resistance is 10 divided by 2, or 5 Ω. With three 12-Ω resistors in parallel **(Figure 5-9, view B),** the effective resistance is $^{12}/_{3}$, or 4 Ω. With five 10-Ω resistors in parallel **(Figure 5-9, view C),** the effective resistance is $^{10}/_{5}$, or 2 Ω. This method for determining the effective resistance is called the *like method* because all the resistances must be equal.

In **Figure 5-10,** two unequal resistances, A of 12 Ω and B of 4 Ω, are connected in parallel across a 24-V battery. Obviously, the rule for like resistances cannot be applied. Since the same voltage is applied to each branch, the current through any branch is a function of the resistance in that branch. In this example, the current through resistor A is

$$I_A = \frac{E}{R_A} = \frac{24}{12} = 2 \text{ A}$$

The current through resistor B is

$$I_B = \frac{E}{R_B} = \frac{24}{4} = 6 \text{ A}$$

The total current I_T is

$$I_T = I_A + I_B = 2 + 6 = 8 \text{ A}$$

The effective resistance of the circuit can be determined from the Ohm's law formula R = E/I.

$$R_T = \frac{E}{I_T} = \frac{24}{8} = 3 \text{ }\Omega$$

When the applied voltage is not known, assume any convenient voltage. For example, assume that a voltage of 6 V is applied to the parallel resistors A and

B. The current through R will be

$$I_A = \frac{E}{R_A} = \frac{6}{12} = 0.5 \text{ A}$$

The current through R_B will be

$$I_B = \frac{E}{R_B} = \frac{6}{4} = 1.5 \text{ A}$$

The total current I_T will be

$$I_T = I_A = 0.5 + 1.5 = 2 \text{ A}$$

The effective resistance can now be calculated:

$$R = \frac{E}{I_T} = \frac{6}{2} = 3 \text{ } \Omega$$

When only two parallel resistances are involved, another method, called the *product over the sum (product/sum) method,* may be the simplest to use. The rule for this method may be stated as follows: The effective resistance of two resistances in parallel is equal to their product divided by their sum. Applying this rule to the circuit just described,

$$R = \frac{\text{product}}{\text{sum}} = \frac{12 \times 4}{12 + 4} = \frac{48}{16} = 3 \text{ } \Omega$$

Notice that this result agrees with that obtained when an applied (or assumed) voltage is divided by the total current. But only resistance values are used here. (This method can, of course, be applied to equal resistances.)

The product/sum method may be used to solve problems involving more than two resistances in parallel. To do this, first determine the effective resistance of any two of the parallel resistors, then combine the result of this calculation with any one of the remaining resistances. Continue the process of combining the calculated resistance with one of the remaining resistances until all the resistances have been included in the calculations. For example, **Figure 5-11** shows a circuit with three unequal resistances connected in parallel. The problem is to find the effective resistance. In other words, what is the resistance of a single resistor which offers the same opposition to current as the parallel combination? Apply the product/sum rule to resistors B and C, and call the resultant resistance R_D.

$$R_D = \frac{\text{product}}{\text{sum}} = \frac{B \times C}{B + C}$$

$$R_D = \frac{6 \times 3}{6 + 3} = \frac{18}{9} = 2 \text{ } \Omega$$

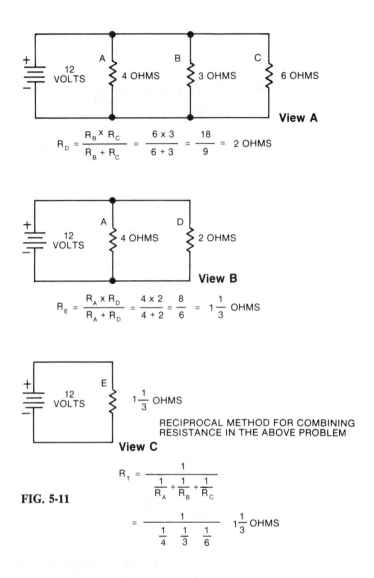

FIG. 5-11

Since R_D is the effective resistance of B and C in parallel, R_D may now be substituted for B and C, as indicated in the schematic drawing. Applying the product/sum method to A and D, and calling the result R_E,

$$R_E = \frac{4 \times 2}{4 + 2} = \frac{8}{6} = 1\frac{1}{3}\ \Omega$$

A single resistance R_E of $1\frac{1}{3}$ can be substituted for A, B, and C (**Figure 5-11, view A**) as shown in **Figure 5-11, view C**, that is, the effective resistance of A, B, and C in parallel is $1\frac{1}{3}\ \Omega$.

303

The product/sum method can be used only for two resistances at a time. If a circuit contains three or more resistances, the product/sum method of solution becomes long and tedious. The reciprocal method may be more conveniently used to determine the effective resistance of a number of parallel resistances. Stated as a rule:

The effective resistance of parallel resistances is equal to the reciprocal of the sum of the reciprocals of the individual resistances.

The reciprocal of a number is 1 divided by the number. Thus, the reciprocal of 2 is $\frac{1}{2}$ and the reciprocal of $\frac{1}{2}$ is 2; the reciprocal of 5 is $\frac{1}{5}$ and the reciprocal of $\frac{1}{5}$ is 5; and so on. The reciprocal method is stated by the following formula:

$$R_T = \frac{1}{1/R_A + 1/R_B + 1/R_C}$$

R_T is the effective resistance and R_A, R_B, R_C, and so on are the parallel resistances. Substituting the values of A, B, and C (**Figure 5-11, view C**) in the formula:

$$R = \frac{1}{\frac{1}{4} + \frac{1}{3} + \frac{1}{6}}$$

$$R = \frac{1}{\frac{3}{12} + \frac{4}{12} + \frac{2}{12}} = \frac{1}{\frac{9}{12}} \text{ (adding fractions)}$$

$$R = 1 \times \frac{12}{9} = 1\frac{1}{3} \ \Omega \text{ (dividing 1 by } \frac{9}{12})$$

This result is the same as that obtained by using the product/sum method. You should be familiar with all these methods for determining the effective resistance of resistances in parallel. If necessary, one method may be used to prove results obtained with another. Remember, too, that the effective resistance is always lower than the resistance of the lowest individual resistance in the circuit.

Series-Parallel DC Circuits

Many circuits are neither simple series nor simple parallel, but a combination of both. While this may seem to present a fairly complex situation, it can be readily analyzed by distinguishing one type from the other and applying the correct laws for each type. For example, **Figure 5-12, view A,** is a schematic of a simple series-parallel circuit. This circuit is solved by applying the rules

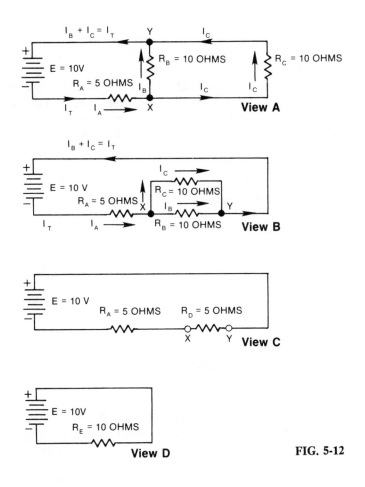

FIG. 5-12

for simple series and simple parallel circuits. In such circuits we are concerned with:

1. The applied or source voltage and the voltage drops across each part of the circuit
2. The total current from the source and the current in each part of the circuit
3. The effective resistance and the resistance of each part of the circuit

In **Figure 5-12, view A,** a 10-V battery is connected to a 5-Ω resistor, R_A, in series with two parallel resistors, R_B and R_C; **Figure 5-12, view A,** is redrawn in **Figure 5-12, view B,** to show clearly that R_A is in series with the parallel resistances R_B and R_C, and that there are two current paths between point X

305

and point Y. The current (I_T) from the battery goes through R_A to point X. At point X the current divides, part (I_B) going through R_B and the remainder (I_C) going through R_C. At Y these two currents reunite ($I_B + I_C = I_T$) and go to the positive terminal and through the battery to the negative terminal.

The battery voltage and the resistance of each resistor is given **(Figure 5-12, view A)**, and it is necessary to determine the currents I_T, I_A, I_B, and I_C, the voltage drops E_A, E_B, and E_C, and the effective resistance R_E. Here are the steps to find these:

1. Since all the individual resistances are known, the first step is to determine the effective resistance of the circuit. R_B and R_C are like resistances, and their effective resistance (R_D) is found by the like method:

$$R_D = \frac{10}{2} = 5 \ \Omega$$

2. This effective resistance R_D is in series with R_A, as shown in **Figure 5-12, view C**. The effective resistance R_E of R_A and R_D in series is found by adding the individual resistors:

$$R_E = R_A + R_D = 5 + 5 = 10 \ \Omega$$

3. R_E is the effective resistance of the circuit; that is, as far as the battery is concerned, the circuit of **Figure 5-12, view D**, is the equivalent of that shown in **Figure 5-12, view A**. Therefore, the current from the battery is

$$I_T = \frac{E}{R_E} = \frac{10}{10} = 1 \ A$$

4. Referring to **Figure 5-12, view A**, we see that I_T must go through R_A; that is, $I_A = I_T$. Since we now know the current through R_A, we find the voltage drop E_A from Ohm's law formula $E = IR$:

$$E_A = I_A \times R_A = 1 \times 5 = 5 \ V$$

5. The voltage drop across points X and Y can be found in either of two ways.
   a. The battery voltage E is equal to the sum of the voltage drop E_A across R_A plus the voltage drop E_{XY} across X and Y; that is, $E = E_A + E_{XY}$. Therefore,

$$E_{XY} = E - E_A = 10 - 5 = 5 \ V$$

306

b. Since R_B and R_C are equal (10 Ω each), the 1-A current I_T divides equally between them, so that

$$I_B = I_C = \frac{I_T}{2} = \frac{1}{2} \text{ A}$$

Then,

$$E_{XY} = I_B \times R_B = I_C \times R_C = 0.5 \times 10 = 5V$$

This agrees with the rule that the same voltage is across each branch of a parallel circuit.

6. In this circuit we determined the branch currents, I_B and I_C, by dividing I_T by 2. Usually, however, the current in each branch must be determined by dividing the voltage across the branch by the resistance in the branch. Thus:

$$I_B = \frac{E_{XY}}{R_B} = \frac{5}{10} = 0.5 \text{ A}$$

$$I_C = \frac{E_{XY}}{R_C} = \frac{5}{10} = 0.5 \text{ A}$$

When series and parallel circuits are combined, it becomes harder to determine the amount of current flowing in the various branches. In other words, Ohm's law is not always sufficient for determining currents in complicated circuits. The reason is that Ohm's law is a special case of much more general relations. Methods of treating complicated circuits are based on Kirchhoff's laws. These laws are simple, but the methods of applying them are difficult. For instance, Kirchhoff's current law states that the current flowing toward a point in a circuit must equal the current flowing away from that point. Now, if the point divides into two or more paths, note what must occur: The current flowing toward the point must equal the sum of all the lesser currents flowing away from that point. If the two were not equal, some current would remain with no place to go—this is obviously impossible.

The circuit in **Figure 5-13** illustrates Kirchhoff's current law. Note that 4 A of current flow toward point A, with 2 A flowing away through the two 5-Ω resistors and 2 A through the 10-Ω resistor. Thus, there are 4 A flowing toward point A and 4 A flowing away from point A.

When a circuit contains both series and parallel branches, the solution is much more involved. **Figure 5-14** illustrates such a circuit. Suppose we want to find the amount of current flowing through R_2. We might think that battery B_2, with a higher voltage than battery B_1, would overpower B_1 and force current through the left-hand circuit. This, however, is not true. The circuit is actually considered as two circuits linked together by the same resistor, R_2.

307

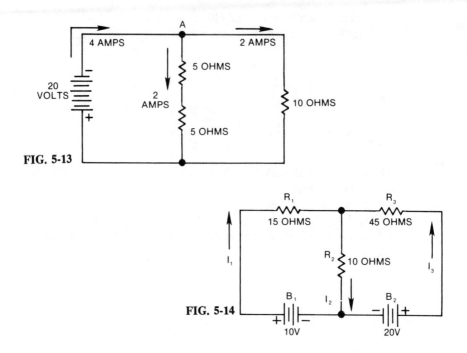

FIG. 5-13

FIG. 5-14

The current through R_2 is made up of two currents, one through R_1 from B_1, and the other through R_3 from B_2.

The formula for Kirchhoff's current law for **Figure 5-15** is

$$I_2 = I_1 + I_3 \qquad\qquad \textbf{Equation 5.1}$$

where

$$I_1 = \text{current in amperes through } R_1$$
$$I_3 = \text{current in amperes through } R_3$$
$$I_2 = \text{current in amperes through } R_2$$

Kirchhoff's voltage law states that

$$VB_1 = R_1I_1 + R_2I_2 = 15I_1 + 10I_2$$

or

$$10 = 15I_1 + 10I_2 \qquad\qquad \textbf{Equation 5.2}$$

308

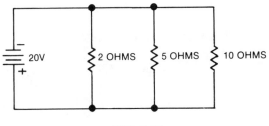

FIG. 5-15

where

$$VB_1 = \text{voltage of battery } B_1$$
$$R_1 = \text{resistance in ohms of } R_1$$
$$I_1 = \text{current in amperes through } R_1$$
$$R_2 = \text{resistance in ohms of } R_2$$
$$I_2 = \text{current in amperes through } R_2$$

The right-hand circuit is considered in a similar manner:

$$VB_2 = R_2I_2 + R_3I_3 = 10I_2 + 45I_3 \qquad \textbf{Equation 5.3}$$

or

$$20 = 10I_2 + 45I_3$$

where

$$VB_2 = \text{voltage of battery } B_2$$
$$R_2 = \text{resistance in ohms of } R_2$$
$$I_2 = \text{current in amperes through } R_2$$
$$R_3 = \text{resistance in ohms of } R_3$$
$$I_3 = \text{current in amperes through } R_3$$

There are now three equations and three unknowns. To solve for the unknowns, we subtract I_3 from both sides of Equation 5.1:

$$I_1 = I_2 - I_3$$

309

Substitute this value of I_1 into Equation 5.2:

$$10 = 15(I_2 - I_3) + 10I_2$$

$$10 = 15I_2 - 15I_3 + 10I_2$$

$$10 = 25I_2 - 15I_3 \qquad \textbf{Equation 5.4}$$

Multiply both sides of Equation 5.4 by 3:

$$30 = 75I_2 - 45I_3 \qquad \textbf{Equation 5.5}$$

Add Equation 5.3 and Equation 5.5:

$$20 = 10I_2 + 45I_3$$

$$\underline{30 = 75I_2 - 45I_3}$$

$$50 = 85I_2 + 0$$

or

$$I_2 = \frac{50}{85}$$

$$I_2 = 0.5882 \text{ A}$$

Substitute this value of I_2 into Equation 5.3:

$$20 = 10(0.5882) + 45I_3$$

$$20 = 5.882 + 45I_3$$

$$45I_3 = 20 - 5.882$$

$$I_3 = \frac{14.188}{45}$$

$$I_3 = 0.3153 \text{ A}$$

From Equation 5.1:

$$I_1 = I_2 - I_3$$

$$I_1 = 0.5882 - 0.3138$$

$$I_1 = 0.2744 \text{ A}$$

310

Therefore,

$$I_1 = 0.2744 \text{ A}$$

$$I_2 = 0.5882 \text{ A}$$

$$I_3 = 0.3153 \text{ A}$$

Power or Watt's Law

Electrical power is measured in much the same manner as mechanical power, discussed in the preceding chapter. An electric motor can be substituted for a horse. If the motor did the same amount of work as the horse in the same amount of time, it would be rated as a 1-horsepower motor. The electrical energy input of a 1-horsepower electric motor is always equal to 746. This figure represents the pressure difference in volts multiplied by the current in amperes. Although the term *volt-amperes* is often referred to, the unit *watt* was coined in honor of the man who first defined horsepower. The power (watts) in a dc circuit is equal to the current (I) multiplied by the voltage (E). The Watt's law formula is:

$$P = I \times E$$

There are three common forms of the Watt's law formula:

1. Power in watts is equal to the current multiplied by the voltage:

$$P = I \times E$$

2. Current in amperes is equal to the power in watts divided by voltage:

$$I = \frac{P}{E}$$

3. Voltage is equal to the power in watts divided by the current in amperes:

$$E = \frac{P}{I}$$

Let us see how much power is required to heat an electric iron **(Figure 5–16)** operating on 120 volts and drawing 6 amperes. Using Watt's law:

$$P = I \times E = 6 \times 20 = 720 \text{ watts}$$

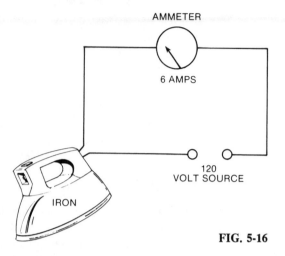

FIG. 5-16

Referring to **Figure 5–17, view A,** we can find the voltage required to light a 150-watt lamp that normally draws 1.5 amperes, using the formula:

$$E = \frac{W}{I} = \frac{150}{1.5} = 100 \text{ volts}$$

How much current will be drawn if the same 150-watt lamp is operated on 120 volts, as shown in **Figure 5–17, view B?** The Watt's formula is:

$$I = \frac{W}{E} = \frac{150}{120} = 1.25 \text{ amperes}$$

In the Watt's law formula $P = I \times E$, power in watts cannot be found unless both the current and the voltage are known. Therefore, if we know the resistance and current but do not know the voltage, we must perform two steps. Here is a problem: How much power is consumed in a resistance of 10 ohms

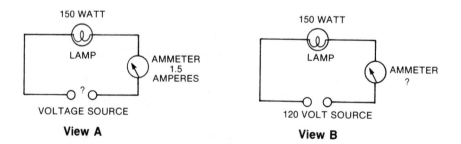

FIG. 5-17

when the current is 5 amperes? To use the Watt's law formula $P = I \times E$, we must find the voltage, using Ohm's law:

$$E = I \times R = 5 \times 10 = 50 \text{ volts}$$

Then find the power:

$$P = I \times E = 5 \times 50 = 250 \text{ watts}$$

Instead of having to use two formulas when the voltage is unknown, we can combine them by substituting $(I \times R)$ in the place of E:

$$P = I \times (I \times R) = I^2R = 5^2 \times 10 = 25 \times 10 = 250 \text{ watts}$$

This gives us the same answer, 250 watts.

The problem can be worked when the voltage and resistance are known but the current is unknown. Here is a problem: How much power is consumed when a resistance of 20 ohms is connected to a power source of 200 volts? To use the Watt's law formula, first find the current by using Ohm's law:

$$I = \frac{E}{R} = \frac{200}{20} = 10 \text{ amperes}$$

Then find the power:

$$P = I \times E = 10 \times 200 = 2000 \text{ watts}$$

Here again we must use two formulas. However, we can combine them by substituting E/R in place of I:

$$P = \frac{E}{R} \times E \text{ or } P = \frac{E^2}{R} = \frac{200^2}{20} = \frac{40,000}{20} = 2,000 \text{ watts}$$

This will give the same answer, 2,000 watts.

Now we have three formulas for finding the power in any circuit. They are:

$$P = I \times E$$

$$P = I^2R$$

$$P = \frac{E^2}{R}$$

There is a total of twelve formulas concerning Ohm's law and Watt's law.

313

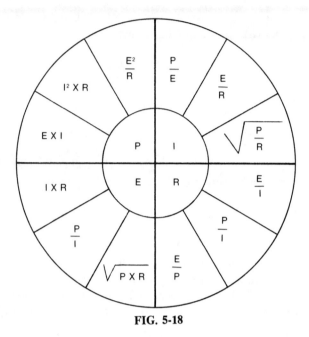

FIG. 5-18.

All twelve formulas can be conveniently arranged in the wheel shown in **Figure 5-18.**

The watt is a small unit of electrical power. When larger amounts of electrical power are measured, the unit of measurement is the kilowatt, which is 1,000 watts. A motor rated at 1 horsepower of mechanical power will use 746 watts, or 0.746 kilowatt, of electrical power.

Since power is the time rate of doing work, it follows that the greater the length of time the power is consumed, the greater will be the total amount of power consumed. Electric power is purchased commercially in watt-hours (watts × hours) or kilowatt-hours (watts × hours ÷ 1,000). A 100-W lamp requires 100 W of power for proper operation and consumes 100 Wh of power in 1 h, 200 Wh in 2 h, etc. In terms of kWh, the lamp uses 100/1000 = 0.1 kWh of power in 1 h; in 10 h, the lamp uses 10 times as much, or 1 kWh of power.

EXAMPLE   1: A kWh meter reads 0.09 kW in 10 h. What is the average rate of consumption?

$$0.09 \text{ kW} = 90 \text{ W}$$

$$\frac{90}{10} = 9 \text{ Wh}$$

314

EXAMPLE 2: If a 2-hp motor is connected to the power line and operated for 10 h continuously, what will be the power consumed in kWh?

$$746 \text{ W} = 1 \text{ hp}$$

$$1,492 \text{ W} = 1.492 \text{ kW}$$

$$1.492 \text{ kW} \times 10 \text{ h} = 14.92 \text{ kWh}$$

How to Figure Your Electric Bill

There are two types of electric meters: the clock type (**Figures 5-19** and **5-20**) and the digital (**Figure 5-21**). With the clock-type meter, the first, third, and fifth dials read clockwise. The second and fourth turn in the opposite or counterclockwise direction. If a dial rests between numbers, the utility company's meter reader will record the highest of the two digits. The "clock-face" or dial in the center (**Figure 5-19, view A**) is an example: the "hand" or indicator is between 4 and 5, so the reading is 5.

Suppose the illustrated clocks were your readings (2-6-5-9-4) when your meter was read by the utility company last month. It will appear on your bill as *prior reading.* Now suppose that today is the day that your meter is read for this month, and the faces on the clock are as shown in **Figure 5–19, view**

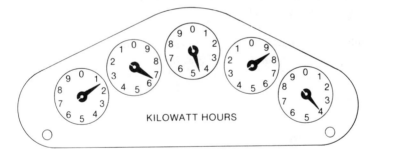

FIG. 5-19

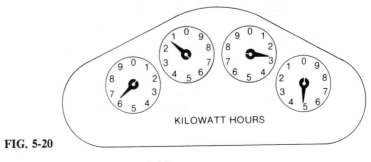

FIG. 5-20

315

B. This, then (2-7-7-9-4), will be the *current reading,* and will be stated as such on your electric bill.

To compute your bill, simply subtract the prior reading from the current reading:

Current: 2-7-7-9-4
Prior: 2-6-5-9-4
              1-2-0-0

That means you have used 1,200 kilowatt-hours for the month, and your bill in dollars and cents will be 1,200 multiplied by your current rate. If you do not know the existing rate in your area, refer to a recent bill, or call the utility company. In some older homes, you may have four-clock or four-dial kilowatt-hour meters **(Figure 5-20).** On this type meter, the hand on the right usually turns in the clockwise direction; the next one turns counterclockwise; the third clockwise; and the one on the left counterclockwise. The reading on **Figure 5-20** is 6-1-3-5, or 6,135 kilowatt-hours.

Most digital-type meters have a "fixed" zero at the end; only the first four numbers move to record consumption. For example, if last month's reading looked like **Figure 5-21, view A,** and this month's looks like **Figure 5-21, view B,** then subtract 2-6-5-9-0 from 2-7-7-9-0, and you get 1,200. That is the kilowatt-hours consumed. Again, multiply kilowatt-hours used by your current rate to compute your bill. For instance, if the cost of one kilowatt-hour is 3½ cents, your bill would be:

number of kilowatt-hours $\times$ cost per one kilowatt-hour =
1,200 Kh $\times$ \$0.035 = \$42

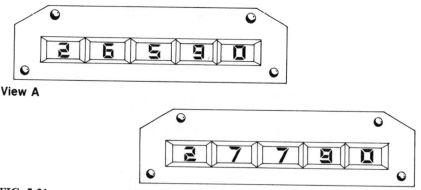

View A

FIG. 5-21   **View B**

In some states a service rate or energy charge—based on the kilowatt-hours used—is added to your electric bill. If your statement includes a 1 mil ($\frac{1}{10}$ of a cent) per kilowatt-hour service rate, for example, an additional charge of $1.20 would be added to your bill:

$$1,200 \times \$0.001 = \$1.20$$

Electrical Unit Prefixes

The simple units of electrical measure—volts, amperes, ohms, and watts—are rather clumsy when very large or very small quantities are involved. Therefore, a system of electrical unit prefixes is used to indicate large and small quantities. They are *kilo-* (k), *milli-* (m), *mega-* (M), and *micro-* (μ). For example, as mentioned earlier in this chapter, a generator that delivers 1,000 watts is called a 1 kW generator. Instead of saying the flow of current is one-thousandth ($\frac{1}{1000}$) of a volt, we say it is 1 mV. If we are testing insulation, we might say it has a resistance of 1 M Ω instead of 1 million ohms. The term *farad* (F) is used as a unit of measure for electric capacity; but the farad is very large, and so the capacity of capacitors is given in μF, or so many millionths of a farad.

AC CIRCUITS

An alternating current (ac) continually changes in potential—going from zero to maximum voltage and back to zero. In addition, ac periodically reverses its direction—from positive to negative. This is in contrast to a direct current (dc), which maintains a steady potential and flows in one direction only.

Figure 5-22 shows how the voltage of an ac generator changes. At point A the voltage is zero. Immediately afterward it has a small, positive value. This value increases until it is maximum at B. A moment later the voltage, still positive, continues to drop steadily until it reaches zero again at C. Below C the voltage becomes negative. Therefore, the voltage is shown below the zero line from C to E. Notice that the polarity does not reverse at B or D—these merely are the points of maximum positive or negative potential. The points of polarity reversal are at A, C, and E.

The complete series of voltage values, represented by the curve from A to E, represents 1 complete cycle. When the curve is continued, the cycle is repeated. The time necessary to complete 1 full cycle is called a period.

The number of cycles generated in 1 second determines the frequency of the ac voltage. The electricity supplied to most homes is 60 hertz, which means the voltage goes through 60 complete cycles—from zero to positive to zero to negative to zero—in 1 second.

317

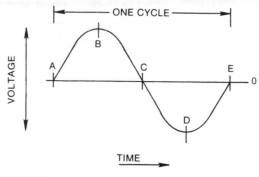

FIG. 5-22

Advantages of AC

Alternating current can be transmitted more economically over long distances than dc. This is one of the great advantages of ac. It is easily transformed to higher or lower voltages. This is a very desirable characteristic for radio and television circuit applications. Many types of motors are designed for ac operation. Some ac motors operate without brushes, eliminating a common source of wear and motor maintenance problems. Although ac differs from dc in many ways, practically all the basic principles of electricity that apply to dc also apply to ac.

General Theory

When a conductor moves in a magnetic field, a voltage is induced in the conductor. This voltage depends upon (1) the strength of the field (number of lines of force), (2) how fast or slow the conductor is moved across the lines of force, and (3) the direction the conductor moves with respect to the field.

Most electrical generators generate an electromotive force by the rotary movement of a conductor within a magnetic field. This principle is illustrated in **Figure 5-23**. The conductor moves through a circular path between the north and south poles of a magnet, cutting across magnetic lines of force as it moves. The position of the conductor is illustrated for each 30 degrees that the generator armature rotates. The magnetic lines of force are not shown. However, we may assume that they extend from one pole to the other and that they form a magnetic field of uniform strength between the poles. The direction of rotation of the conductor is shown as counterclockwise, thus following the mathematical rule for the generation of angles. The same result occurs when the conductor is rotated in a clockwise direction.

At position 1 **(Figure 5-23)** the conductor is cutting the fewest number of lines of force per second; therefore, the induced voltage is very small. This

318

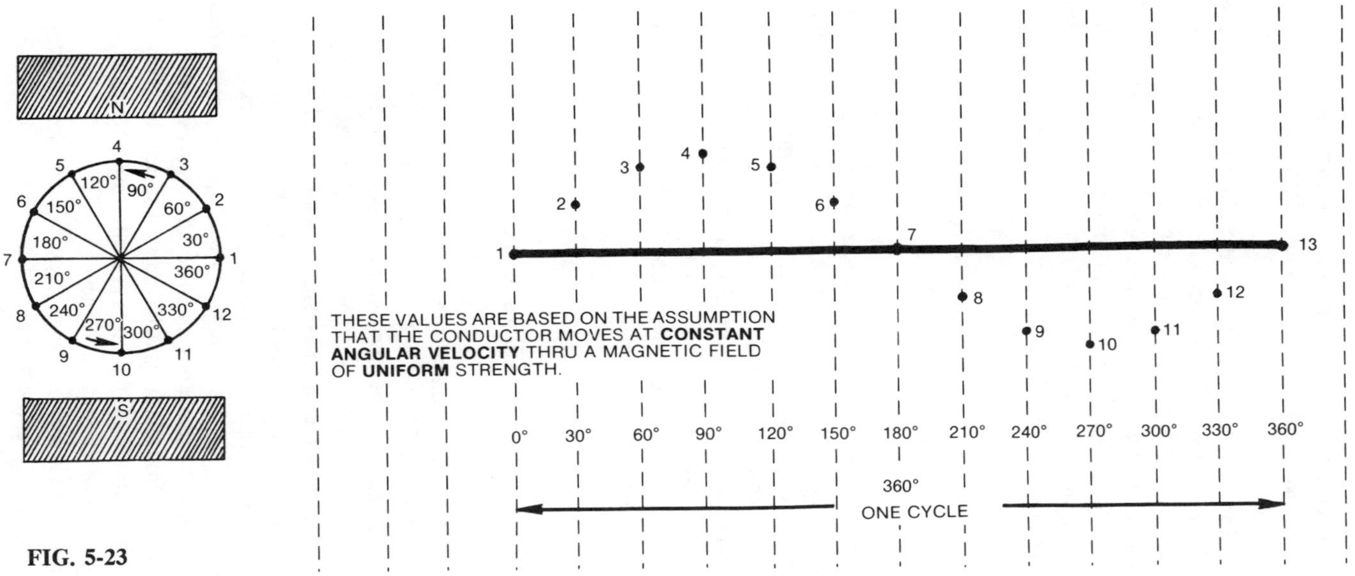
N
S
4
5
3
6
2
7
1
8
12
9
11
10
120°
90°
150°
60°
180°
30°
210°
360°
240°
330°
270°
300°
1
2
3
4
5
6
7
8
9
10
11
12
13
THESE VALUES ARE BASED ON THE ASSUMPTION THAT THE CONDUCTOR MOVES AT **CONSTANT ANGULAR VELOCITY** THRU A MAGNETIC FIELD OF **UNIFORM** STRENGTH.
0°
30°
60°
90°
120°
150°
180°
210°
240°
270°
300°
330°
360°
360°
ONE CYCLE

FIG. 5-23

voltage is plotted at point 1 on the graph at the right. At position 2, more magnetic lines of force are cut each second. At position 3, still more lines of force are cut. The corresponding voltages are plotted at points 2 and 3 on the graph.

At position 4, the conductor is moving at right angles to the magnetic field and thus cuts the most lines of force per second. This corresponds to point 4 on the graph, the point where the greatest voltage is shown. The voltage decreases at points 5 and 6, until it reaches zero again at point 7. From points 7 through 12, the conductor is moving through the magnetic lines of force in the opposite direction. As a result, the polarity of the voltage is reversed. This reversed polarity is shown on the graph by the points below the center line of the graph.

Development of a Sine Curve

The manner in which an induced voltage varies from point to point, as a conductor rotates, is shown by the graph in **Figure 5–23.** Points have been plotted for each 30 degrees of rotation. If other points are also plotted, they will lie on a curve known as a sine wave **(Figure 5–24).** This curve is called a sine wave because the amplitude (height) of any point on the curve is the sine of the angle through which the conductor has moved to that point. The graph is plotted horizontally in fractions of a second instead of in degrees of rotation. The frequency of rotation is 60 hertz.

Values of AC

A peak voltage is the maximum voltage during a complete cycle. It is represented in **Figures 5-23** and **5-24** by points 4 and 10. The highest value reached by the voltage may be positive or negative (E or $-E$).

THE RMS VALUE. The effective (rms) value of an ac voltage is that value which will produce the same effect as a numerically equal value of a dc voltage. The effective value of 1 ac ampere is an ac value that will produce the same heating effect as 1 dc ampere. If we take all possible values of I for half a cycle and square them, then find the average of these squares and extract the square root, the result would be the route-mean-square (rms) value. If we figured the rms value, we would find that it is 0.707 times the peak value of the sine wave. Most electrical instruments and meters are calibrated in rms units. This allows a direct comparison of ac and dc values.

The average voltage is merely the average value of the sine wave during half a cycle. Geometrically, it is the height of a rectangle with the same area as the space between the sine wave and its base line for half a cycle.

320

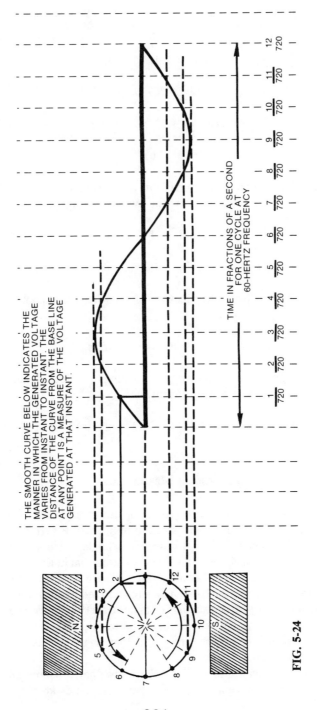

THE SMOOTH CURVE BELOW INDICATES THE MANNER IN WHICH THE GENERATED VOLTAGE VARIES FROM INSTANT TO INSTANT. THE DISTANCE OF THE CURVE FROM THE BASE LINE AT ANY POINT IS A MEASURE OF THE VOLTAGE GENERATED AT THAT INSTANT.

TIME IN FRACTIONS OF A SECOND FOR ONE CYCLE AT 60-HERTZ FREQUENCY

$\frac{1}{720}$ $\frac{2}{720}$ $\frac{3}{720}$ $\frac{4}{720}$ $\frac{5}{720}$ $\frac{6}{720}$ $\frac{7}{720}$ $\frac{8}{720}$ $\frac{9}{720}$ $\frac{10}{720}$ $\frac{11}{720}$ $\frac{12}{720}$

FIG. 5-24

321

The relationships between the ac values we have been discussing are as follows:

$$peak = 1.414 \times rms$$

$$rms = 0.707 \times peak$$

$$peak = 1.57 \times average$$

$$average = 0.637 \times peak$$

EXAMPLE 1:   What is the maximum voltage in an ac circuit when the rms voltage is 120 volts? What is the average voltage in this circuit?

$$120 \times 1.414 = 170 \text{ volts (peak)}$$

$$170 \times 0.637 = 108 \text{ volts (average)}$$

EXAMPLE 2:   What is the effective voltage when the maximum voltage is 311 volts?

$$311 \times 0.707 = 220 \text{ volts}$$

EXAMPLE 3:   An ac ammeter reads 15 amperes (effective value). What is the maximum value of the current?

$$15 \times 1.414 = 21.21 \text{ amperes}$$

Radian Measurement

It is quite common to measure generating angles and their corresponding portions of sine waves in radians instead of in degrees. **Figure 5-24** illustrates the meaning of the term *radian*. A radian is an angle which, if placed with its vertex at the center of a circle, will subtend an arc equal in length to the radius of the circle. Picture a clock. Let us say that the arc between the one and the three is as long as the minute hand. The angle formed by the minute hand and the hour hand at 1:15 is the radian. Or, assume that the circle in **Figure 5-25** is made of string. If we cut out the string between points A and B, and pull it until it is straight, and if the string is as long as the radius OA, the angle AOB will be a radian.

How many radians are in a circle? We know that the circumference of a circle equals 2 π r. Since an angle of 1 radian subtends an arc equal to the

322

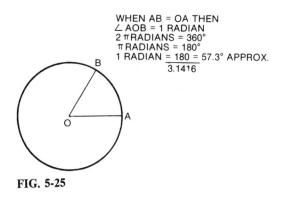

WHEN AB = OA THEN
∠ AOB = 1 RADIAN
2 π RADIANS = 360°
π RADIANS = 180°
1 RADIAN = $\frac{180}{3.1416}$ = 57.3° APPROX.

FIG. 5-25

radius, there must be 2 π radians in a circle. The values of a sine waveform are often shown in radians instead of in degrees or seconds. For example, in **Figure 5-23,** point 1 on the graph could be labeled "0 radians," point 4 is "$\frac{\pi}{2}$ radians," point 7 is "π radians," etc. The term *radians* is usually omitted, and the points are simply marked π, $\frac{\pi}{2}$, $\frac{3}{4}$ π, etc. Whenever the symbol appears in this manner, the unit is understood to be the radian. For example, the following degrees of rotation are expressed in radians:

$$45° = \frac{\pi}{4} \qquad 180° = \pi \qquad 360° = 2\pi$$

$$90° = \frac{\pi}{2} \qquad 225° = \frac{5\pi}{4} \qquad 540° = 3\pi$$

Inductive Reactance

We have seen in the previous section how a conductor passing through a magnetic field will have a voltage induced in it. Anytime a conductor cuts through magnetic lines of flux, voltage will be induced. To cut the lines of flux, either the conductor can be moved through the magnetic field or the magnetic field can be moved through the conductor.

When a circuit will produce 100,000,000 magnetic linkages for each ampere of electron flow, it has an inductance of 1 *henry.* In a circuit that has an inductance of 1 henry, electron flow changing at the rate of 1 ampere per second will produce a self-induced potential difference of 1 volt in the circuit.

In a dc circuit, the rate of current flow does not change periodically. Therefore, the only opposition to current flow is the resistance of the conductors. In either a pulsating dc circuit or an ac circuit, however, other kinds of opposition may appear in the form of opposing voltages. These voltages, often referred to as *counter emf* or *back emf,* may be responsible for most of the opposition to the electron flow.

323

This opposition to a changing current can be compared to the resistance of a resistor in a dc circuit. In an inductive circuit this resistance is called inductive reactance. Its symbol is X_L, and its value is expressed in ohms.

The relation between inductance (L) and inductive reactance (X_L) is given by the equation:

$$X_L = 2 \pi fL$$

$$X_L = \text{inductive reactance in ohms}$$

$$f = \text{frequency in hertz}$$

$$L = \text{inductance in henrys}$$

EXAMPLE: An alternating current having a frequency of 60 hertz is passed through a coil whose inductance is 0.6 henry. What is the reactance?

$$X_L = 2 \pi fL = 2 \times 3.1416 \times 60 \times 0.6 = 226.2 \text{ ohms}$$

Since the quantity of reactance is of the same nature as a resistance, the Ohm's law expression $E = IR$ may be used to obtain the volts necessary to overcome a reactance:

$$E = 2 \pi fLI$$

Thus, to find the number of volts necessary to force a current of 2 amperes with a frequency of 60 hertz through a coil whose inductance is 0.6 henry, proceed as follows:

$$E = 2\pi fIL = 2 \times 3.1416 \times 60 \times 2 \times 0.6 = 452.4 \text{ volts}$$

Capacitive Reactance

When a capacitor is connected to a source of dc voltage, a rush of current enters the capacitor and charges it. If a higher voltage is then applied, the charge already in the capacitor tends to oppose the additional charge. From this we can see that capacitance opposes the flow of current, just as inductance does. The opposition of a capacitor to the flow of current is called its *capacitive reactance,* and depends upon the capacitance of the capacitor and the frequency of the voltage applied. The symbol for capacitive reactance is X_C. Its

324

value is given in ohms and can be computed from the following formula:

$$X_C = \frac{1}{2\,fC}$$

X_C = capacitive reactance in ohms

f = frequency in hertz

C = capacitance in farads

EXAMPLE: In a circuit containing a capacitor of 50 microfarads, what is the reactance when a current is supplied at a frequency of 100 hertz?

$$50 \text{ microfarads} = 50 \times \frac{1}{1,000,000} = .00005 \text{ farad}$$

$$X_C = \frac{1}{2\pi fC} = \frac{1}{2 \times 3.1416 \times 100 \times .00005} = 31.8 \text{ ohms}$$

Impedance

Impedance is the total opposition to current flow. In all circuits this opposition includes resistance. In ac circuits and in pulsating dc circuits in which the current is constantly changing in value, this opposition also includes the inductive reactance and capacitive reactance. The symbol for impedance is Z, and its value is given in ohms. The value of the impedance Z (in ohms) of a circuit may consist of the resistance R (in ohms) only, the inductive reactance X_L (in ohms) only, the capacitive reactance X_C (in ohms) only, or any combination of these opposition effects. The formulas for determining Z in terms of R, X_L, and X_C are shown in **Figures 5-26, 5-27, and 5-28.**

$$I = \frac{E}{Z}$$

Ohm's law for ac: $Z = \frac{E}{I}$

$$E = I \times Z$$

I = current in amperes

E = voltage in volts

Z = impedance in ohms

325

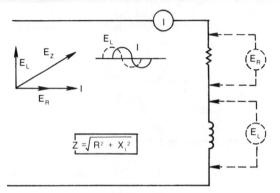

$$Z = \sqrt{R^2 + X_L{}^2}$$

FIG. 5-26

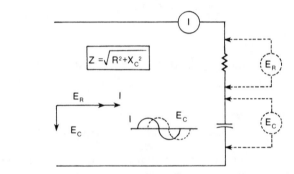

$$Z = \sqrt{R^2 + X_C{}^2}$$

FIG. 5-27

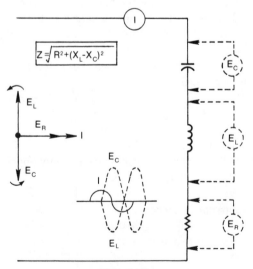

$$Z = \sqrt{R^2 + (X_L - X_C)^2}$$

FIG. 5-28

Note that the only difference between this formula and the one for current, voltage, and resistance is that impedance (the total opposition) has been substituted for resistance, which is only one of three forms of opposition that may be present in a circuit.

If the sum of E_R and E_L in **Figure 5-26** is compared with the applied line voltage, we will find that the sum $(E_R + E_L)$ is greater than the applied voltage. The reason is that voltages E_R and E_L do not reach their maximum values at the same instant. As shown by the curves and vector diagrams in **Figure 5-24,** these voltages are actually "out of phase" with each other by one-quarter of a cycle or 90 electrical degrees. It is due to this phase difference that the total opposition in the ac circuit cannot be added, but must be combined by means of the equations shown previously.

EXAMPLE: If an alternating current having a frequency of 60 hertz is impressed on a coil whose inductance is 0.05 henry and whose resistance is 6 ohms, what is the impedance?

$$Z = \sqrt{R^2 + X_L^2} = \sqrt{6^2 + (2\pi\,[6.2832] \times 60 \times 0.05)^2}$$

$$= \sqrt{391} = 19.8 \text{ ohms}$$

The conditions in **Figure 5-27** are similar to those in **Figure 5-26** except that the voltage E_C lags voltage E_R by the same amount that E_L leads E_R in **Figure 5-26.** The voltage across a resistor is always "in phase" with the current flowing through it. The voltage (E_L) in an inductive circuit leads the current flow by 90 degrees. In a capacitive circuit, however, the voltage (E_C) lags the current flow by 90 degrees. The term "out of phase" indicates that the voltages of E_C and E_L do not pass through corresponding values at the same instant, as is true in a circuit with resistance only.

In **Figure 5-28** the phase relationships are shown for R, L, and C in a series circuit. Voltage E_R and current I are always in phase with each other. E_L leads E_R by 90 degrees, whereas E_C lags E_R by 90 degrees. From the illustration you can also see that E_L and E_C are out of phase by 180 degrees. Also, if the values of E_L and E_C are equal, the two will cancel each other. Thus, the only opposition to current flow remaining in the circuit is from R.

Figures 5-26, 5-27, and **5-28** show the formulas for finding the total impedance (Z) of a circuit containing both resistance and inductive or capacitive reactance. Not shown is a circuit with capacitive and inductive reactance only. However, the formula in **Figure 5-28** is still used because there will always be some resistance in a circuit, even though there is no resistor. The value of R would probably be so small that it would not be used.

327

EXAMPLE: A current has a frequency of 100 hertz. It passes through a circuit of 4 ohms resistance, of 0.15 henry inductance, and of 22 microfarads capacity. The impedance is:

$$R = 4 \text{ ohms}$$

$$X_L = 2\pi fL = 2 \times 3.1416 \times 100 \times 0.15 = 94.3 \text{ ohms}$$

$$X_C = \frac{1}{2\pi fC} = \frac{1}{2 \times 3.1416 \times 100 \times .000022} = 72.3 \text{ ohms}$$

$$Z = \sqrt{R^2 + (X_L - X_C)^2} = \sqrt{4^2 + (94.3 - 72.4)^2} = \sqrt{496} = 22.3 \text{ ohms}$$

AC POWER

Alternating current flows in a circuit when an alternating voltage is applied. If the circuit contains resistance only, the current (I) passes through zero and maximum at the same instant as the voltage (E). The current and the voltage then are in step, or in phase. The voltage and current are normally in phase in a resistive circuit only. For a resistive ac circuit, Ohm's law is the same as for dc: $E = I \times R$. In an ac circuit containing resistance only, the power (in watts) at any instant is equal to the resistance times the square of the instantaneous current ($P = R \times I_i^2$). The average power during an ac cycle is the average of the instantaneous power values. The square root of the average of all I_i^2 terms is I_{rms}; the average power equals $R \times I_{rms}^2$ ($P_{av} \times I_{rms}^2$).

Since the introduction of fluorescent lights and the mass production of motor-powered refrigeration systems and appliances, the term *power factor* has come into fairly common use. Before entering into this discussion we should not confuse the power factor with the efficiency of an electrical device.

Efficiency

All appliances and motors lose some power; otherwise they would be 100 percent efficient, a situation never encountered in practice. The most common loss of electric power is the power which is dissipated in the form of heat when current flows through a resistance. This power loss is sometimes called the I^2R loss or copper loss, and is always present when current is flowing. The heat is usually dissipated into the air and lost, but it may be utilized, as in the case of the electric oven, toaster, soldering iron, or filament of a light bulb. The power loss may be calculated by the following formulas:

$$P = I^2R \quad \text{or} \quad P = \frac{E^2}{R}$$

Electric motors have losses due both to friction and to resistance of the windings. Therefore, the mechanical output of any power-consuming device divided by the input and multiplied by 100 will give its power efficiency in percent:

$$\% \text{ efficiency} = \frac{\text{output}}{\text{input}} \times 100$$

EXAMPLE 1: If a 1-hp motor draws 6 A of current at 220 V, what is the efficiency of the motor?

$$\text{efficiency} = \frac{\text{output}}{\text{input}} \times 100$$

$$= \frac{746}{220 \times 6} \text{ W} \times 100$$

$$= \frac{74,600}{1,320} = 56.52\%$$

EXAMPLE 2: A certain tube when operating in a circuit draws 20 mA of current at 150 V. How much power is used?

$$20 \text{ mA} = 0.02\text{A}$$

$$P = E \times I$$

$$P = 150 \times 0.02 = 3\text{W}$$

EXAMPLE 3: If 45 kW is supplied to a motor and its output is found to be 50 hp, what is the efficiency of the motor?

$$45 \text{ kW} = 45,000 \text{ W} = \text{input}$$

$$50 \text{ hp} = 50 \times 746 = 37,300 \text{ W} = \text{output}$$

$$\text{efficiency} = \frac{\text{output}}{\text{input}} \times 100$$

$$= \frac{37,300}{45,000} \times 100 = 83\%$$

POWER FACTOR. A complete coverage of the subject of power factor is beyond the scope of this book. For our purpose, it may be defined as the number of watts indicated by a watt meter, divided by the apparent watts, the latter being the watts as measured by a voltmeter and ammeter. The power factor may be expressed as being equal to:

$$\frac{\text{true power}}{\text{apparent power}} = \frac{\text{true watts}}{\text{apparent watts}} = \frac{\text{true watts}}{\text{volts} \times \text{amperes}}$$

The power factor is that quantity by which the apparent watts must be multiplied in order to give the true power. That is,

$$\text{true power} = \text{apparent watts} \times \text{power factor}$$

Numerically, the power factor is equal to the cosine of the angle of phase difference between current and pressure. That is,

$$\text{power factor} = \cos \phi$$

EXAMPLE 1: If in an ac circuit the voltmeter and ammeter readings are 120 volts and 15 amperes and the angle of lag is 45°, what is the apparent power and true power?

The apparent power is simply the product of the voltage and current readings, or

$$\text{apparent power} = 120 \times 15 = 1{,}800 \text{ watts}$$

The true power is the product of the apparent power multiplied by the cosine of the angle of lag. Cos 45° = .707, hence

$$\text{true power} = 1{,}800 \times 0.707 = 1{,}272.6 \text{ watts}$$

EXAMPLE 2: A circuit having a resistance of 3 ohms, and a resultant reactance of 4 ohms, is connected to a 120-volt ac line. What are: (a) the impedance; (b) the current; (c) the apparent power; (d) the angle of lag; (e) the power factor; and (f) the true power?

$$\text{(a)} \quad Z = \sqrt{R_T^2 + X_T^2} = \sqrt{3^2 + 4^2} = 5 \text{ ohms}$$

$$\text{(b)} \quad I = \frac{E}{Z} = \frac{120}{5} = 24 \text{ amperes}$$

$$\text{(c)} \quad \text{apparent power} = E \times I = 120 \times 24 = 2{,}880 \text{ watts}$$

$$\text{(d)} \quad \text{angle of lag } (\tan \phi = \frac{X_T}{R_T} = \frac{4}{3} = 1.33$$

330

From Table of Natural Tangents (Chapter 11) $\phi = 53°$

(e)   power factor $= \cos 53 = 0.602$ (Chapter 11)

(f)   true power $=$ apparent power $\times$ power factor $=$
     $2,880 \times 0.602 = 1,733.8$ watts

Transformers

A transformer is an electrical device which changes, by electromagnetic induction, the values of both alternating voltage and current.

There are many types of transformers, some large and some small. Some of the common types are the doorbell transformer, the power transformer which hangs on a power pole and furnishes homes with electricity, and the transformers that power television sets, radios, and children's toys such as electric trains.

A common type of transformer construction consists of two separate windings of insulated wire wound around an iron core. One winding is known as the primary winding and the other as the secondary winding. The primary winding of a transformer receives energy from an ac voltage source. Changing magnetic lines of flux are set up by the changing current flowing through the primary. The changing current in the primary winding causes an electromagnetic field to build up and collapse. This field cuts through the secondary coil winding and induces a voltage in the secondary. In this way the electrical energy is transferred from the primary to the secondary by induction. Notice that the frequency of the electromagnetic waves does not change as the power is transferred from the primary to the secondary windings.

Theory of Transformer Operation

Since a transformer operates on the principle of induction, caused by changing currents flowing through the windings, it will not operate if pure dc is applied to the primary coil. When dc of a fluctuating nature is applied, the ac component causes a transfer of energy from the primary to the secondary. The current in the primary coil of a transformer must be interrupted or must be varied. That is the reason transformers are generally used with alternating current.

Since the current in the primary coil in a transformer is a constantly changing value, it follows that the magnetic flux in the core is also constantly changing. The magnetic flux and its polarity are dependent upon the current flowing in the primary coil. As the direction of the current in the primary coil changes, the direction of the magnetic flux also changes.

It should be remembered that the polarity of the voltage induced in the secondary coil of the transformer depends upon the direction the magnetic field is moving. The magnetic field builds up to a maximum and falls to zero;

331

then it reverses and builds up to a maximum in the opposite direction and again falls to zero. The voltage in the secondary coil will build up, then fall off and reverse, just as the voltage in the primary coil does. The polarity of the voltage induced in the secondary coil will be opposite to the direction of the current in the primary coil if the primary coil and the secondary coil are wound in the same direction.

The strength of a magnetic field produced in a coil will be directly proportional to its ampere turns. Thus 1 ampere of current will produce a certain number of lines of force in 1 turn of a coil. Either 2 amperes in 1 turn of a coil or 1 ampere in 2 turns of a coil will produce twice as many lines of force. You can see that the voltage induced in the secondary coil will depend upon the number of ampere turns of the primary coil and upon the number of turns in the secondary winding. This can be expressed by the equation:

$$\frac{E_P(\text{primary volts})}{E_S(\text{secondary volts})} = \frac{N_P(\text{primary turns})}{N_S(\text{secondary turns})}$$

A given number of ampere turns for the primary winding will cause a certain voltage to be induced in each turn of the secondary coil. Two turns of the secondary winding will induce twice that amount; 3 turns, three times that amount, etc. This results from the fact that all the turns of the secondary coil are in series with each other. The total voltage is equal to the sum of all the individual voltages. A transformer having the same number of turns of the primary and secondary windings will have a voltage induced in the secondary winding equal to the voltage applied to the primary winding.

Figure 5-29 represents a transformer that has 100 turns on the primary coil and 100 turns on the secondary coil. When 100 volts ac is applied across the primary coil of the transformer, 100 volts ac will appear across the terminals of the secondary coil.

If, instead of having 100 turns in the secondary coil, as shown in **Figure 5-29,** the transformer had 1,000 turns, as in **Figure 5-30,** we would have 1,000 volts

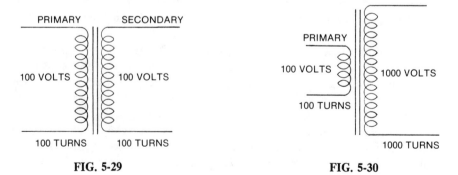

PRIMARY   SECONDARY

100 VOLTS   100 VOLTS

100 TURNS   100 TURNS

FIG. 5-29

PRIMARY

100 VOLTS   1000 VOLTS

100 TURNS

1000 TURNS

FIG. 5-30

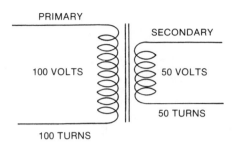

PRIMARY

SECONDARY

100 VOLTS

50 VOLTS

50 TURNS

100 TURNS

FIG. 5-31

across the secondary coil. A comparison of the number of turns in the primary coil with the number of turns in the secondary coil is called the *turns ratio.*

We can obtain lower voltages than those applied to the primary coil of a transformer by using fewer turns on the secondary coil than on the primary coil. **Figure 5-31** shows how we can transform 100 volts in the primary winding to 50 volts in the secondary winding by using 50 turns on the secondary winding and 100 turns on the primary winding.

Since it is so easy to increase or decrease voltage merely by altering the turns ratio of a transformer, one might assume that power might be increased or decreased. This assumption, of course, is not valid, since it violates the law of conservation of energy. It is impossible to get as much power out of a transformer as is put into it, because no device can be made to operate at 100 percent efficiency. There is always some loss. However, if we assume a transformer to be operating at an efficiency of 100 percent, the amount of transformed energy from the transformer is neither increased nor decreased. Only the ratio of the values of voltages and currents is changed.

Figure 5-32 illustrates the relationship between the power input and the power output, together with the relationship between the turns ratio and the voltage-to-current ratio of a transformer.

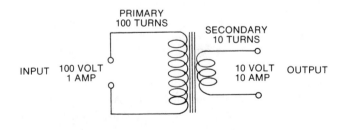

PRIMARY
100 TURNS

SECONDARY
10 TURNS

INPUT 100 VOLT
1 AMP

10 VOLT
10 AMP OUTPUT

TURNS RATIO = 10 TO 1
INPUT = 100V x 1 AMP (P = E x I) = 100 WATTS
OUTPUT = 10V x 10 AMP = 100 WATTS

FIG. 5-32

333

The current in the secondary coil always changes by the inverse of the ratio by which the voltage changes. If the voltage is doubled, the current is halved. If the voltage is raised to 10 times its original value by the transformer, the current in the secondary coil will be reduced to one-tenth the value of the current in the primary coil.

This means that the voltage in the primary winding is multiplied by the turns ratio to find the voltage in the secondary winding. To find the current in the secondary coil, divide the current in the primary coil by the turns ratio.

Motors

The ac motors are available in single-phase, two-phase, and three-phase. For the latter, a special three-phase service entrance is necessary. Three-phase current is furnished by the power company and is usually required when the motor load is in excess of 5 hp. A three-phase motor does not require any special electric components. It has strong starting torque, high operating efficiency, and a lower initial cost than a single-phase motor of comparable size. The three-phase motor has three individual windings, each with its own phase voltage impressed across it. Therefore, the currents will start at different times in each winding when the voltages are first impressed across them. The timing sequence causes a very strong starting torque. Each winding might be visualized as the thumb and first two fingers of your hand spread evenly around the rotor, providing a powerful magnetic hold to grasp the rotor and start turning it.

The formulas in **Table 5-1** are for computing current, power, and horsepower with different types of common power-distribution systems.

HOUSE WIRING

The term *house wiring,* as used here, means all the built-in wiring and accessories for all types of building having 120-V and/or 240-V service.

There is no mystery to house wiring. When it is properly installed such things as lights, motors, heaters, and other electrical appliances can operate on the electricity (electric power) furnished by it. Today, electric power generally is furnished by a commercial power company (the source). The power company is responsible for making the electric power available (conducting it) to the purchaser. This is accomplished by means of main power lines, which serve many customers, and by individual service lines, which connect each customer with the main power lines.

A customer receives electric power from the end of the service line (usually, the company wires terminate at least 10 feet above the ground level on the

TABLE 5-1:
FORMULAS FOR COMPUTING CURRENT, POWER, AND HORSEPOWER OF MOTORS

Required	Direct current	Alternating current		
		Single-phase	Two-phase, four-wire	Three-phase
Current when horsepower is known	$\dfrac{hp \times 746}{E \times eff}$	$\dfrac{hp \times 746}{E \times eff \times PF}$	$\dfrac{hp \times 746}{2 \times E \times eff \times PF}$	$\dfrac{hp \times 746}{1.73 \times E \times eff \times PF}$
Current when kilowatts are known	$\dfrac{kW \times 1{,}000}{E}$	$\dfrac{kW \times 1{,}000}{E \times PF}$	$\dfrac{kW \times 1{,}000}{2 \times E \times PF}$	$\dfrac{kW \times 1{,}000}{1.73 \times E \times PF}$
Current when kVA is known		$\dfrac{kVA \times 1{,}000}{E}$	$\dfrac{kVA \times 1{,}000}{2 \times E}$	$\dfrac{kVA \times 1{,}000}{1.73 \times E}$
Power in kilowatts	$\dfrac{I \times E}{1{,}000}$	$\dfrac{I \times E \times PF}{1{,}000}$	$\dfrac{2 \times I \times E \times PF}{1{,}000}$	$\dfrac{1.73 \times I \times E \times PF}{1{,}000}$
Power in kVA		$\dfrac{I \times E}{1{,}000}$	$\dfrac{2 \times I \times E}{1{,}000}$	$\dfrac{1.73 \times I \times E}{1{,}000}$
Horsepower output of a motor	$\dfrac{I \times E \times eff}{746}$	$\dfrac{I \times E \times eff \times PF}{746}$	$\dfrac{2 \times I \times E \times eff \times PF}{746}$	$\dfrac{1.73 \times I \times E \times eff \times PF}{746}$

I = current, in amperes
PF = power factor
E = potential, in volts
kW = power in kilowatts
eff = efficiency (expressed as a decimal)
kVA = power in kilovoltamperes
hp = horsepower

outside of the building), and it is the customer's responsibility to be sure that it is safely conducted throughout the home to wherever needed. House wiring accomplishes this. Adequate house wiring will provide for all of your present and future electric power requirements. But, unfortunately, many homes are inadequately wired.

If the house is 15 or more years old, it probably has "outgrown" its wiring. When it was built, the wiring was probably sufficient for the basic electrical needs of the time. But, as more electrical devices have been developed and introduced, newer standards of electrical living have become commonplace. **Table 5-2** lists typical major appliances and the current they consume.

Estimating Wiring Materials and Costs

The cost of wiring a building will be affected by the type, size, and arrangement of the building and the materials used in constructing the building. Wiring for a frame building may be attached to the framing members or run through holes drilled in the members. Wiring for a building constructed of masonry may be placed in conduit attached to or concealed within the walls. Wiring for concrete structures is placed in conduit installed in the concrete, which will require the installation of the conduit prior to placing the concrete.

The best method of preparing a dependable estimate is to prepare an accurate material takeoff which lists the items separately by type, size, quantity, quality, and cost. When working from plans, it is good practice to indicate on the plans, using a colored pencil, each item as it is transferred to the material list. This procedure will reduce the risk of omitting items or counting them more than once. The application of appropriate costs for materials and labor to these items will give a dependable estimate.

When preparing a detailed estimate covering the cost of wiring a project, it is good practice to start with the first item required to bring electric service to the project. The listing should proceed from the first item to and including the last ones, which may be the fixtures. The following list may be used as a guide:

1. Service wires, if required
2. Meter box
3. Entrance switch box and fuses
4. Wire circuits
   a. Conduit
   b. Wires
5. Junction boxes
6. Outlets for:
   a. Switches, single-pole, double-pole, three-way
   b. Plugs, wall and floor
   c. Fixtures
7. Bell systems, with transformers
8. Sundry supplies, such as solder, tape, torch, wire, nuts, etc.

336

TABLE 5-2:
ELECTRICAL CONSUMPTION OF HOUSEHOLD APPLIANCES

Appliances	Power (watts)	Current required (amps) at 12v	at 120v	Time used (hrs. per mo.)	Total kWh per mo.
Air conditioner (window)	1,566	130	13.7	74	116.
Blanket, electric	177	14.5	1.5	73	13.
Blender	350	29.2	3.0	1.5	0.5
Broiler	1,436	120.	12.5	6	8.5
Clothes dryer, electric	4,856		42.0	18	86.
Clothes dryer, gas	325	27.	2.8	18	6.0
Coffee pot	894	75.	7.8	10	9.
Dishwasher	1,200	100.	10.4	25	30.
Drill (¼ in. elec.)	250	20.8	2.2	2	.5
Fan (attic)	370	30.8	3.2	65	24.
Freezer (15 cu. ft.)	340	28.4	3.0	290	100.
Freezer, frostless (15 cu. ft.)	440	36.6	3.8	330	145.
Frying pan	1,196	99.6	10.4	12	15.
Garbage disposal	445	36.	3.9	6	3.
Heat, electric baseboard, average-size home	10,000		87.	160	1600.
Iron	1,088	90.5	9.5	11	12.
Light bulb, 75-watt	75	6.25	.65	120	9.
Light bulb, 40-watt	40	3.3	.35	120	4.8
Light bulb, 25-watt	25	2.1	.22	120	3.
Oil burner, ⅛ hp	250	20.8	2.2	64	16.
Range	12,200		106.0	8	98.
Record player, tube	150	12.5	1.3	50	7.5
Record player, solid-state	60	5.0	.52	50	3.
Refrigerator-freezer (14 cu. ft.)	326	27.2	2.8	290	95.
Refrigerator-freezer, frostless (14 cu. ft.)	615	51.3	5.35	250	152.
Skill saw	1,000	83.5	8.7	6	6.
Sunlamp	279	23.2	2.4	5.4	1.5
Television, b&w	237	19.8	2.1	110	25.
Television, color	332	27.6	2.9	125	42.
Toaster	1,146	95.5	10.0	2.6	3.
Typewriter	30	2.5	.26	15	.45
Vacuum cleaner	630	52.5	5.5	6.4	4.
Washing machine, auto	512	42.5	4.5	17.6	9.
Washing machine, wringer	275	23.	2.4	15	4.
Water heater	4,474		39.	89	400.
Water pump	460	38.3	4.0	44.	20.

Here is a typical method:

Quantity	Unit	Description	Unit cost	Cost
250	ft.	No. 14 BX wire	.15	37.50
2	ea.	3-way switches	2.00	4.00
1	ea.	D.P. switch	1.50	1.50
4	ea.	3"-deep outlet boxes	.60	2.40
3	ea.	Single switch boxes	.80	2.40
12	ea.	BX connectors	.18	2.16
			Total	$49.96

Wire Types and Sizes

Basically, there are three types of approved interior wiring in general use for modern residential and farm applications. They are (1) flexible armored cable, usually called BX, a trade name; (2) nonmetallic cable or Romex, also a trade name, and plastic-covered cable; (3) thin-wall conduit, also called EMT.

Although it would seem that the subject of wires would be a relatively simple one, it actually involves many factors, including math. For instance, the three major factors that affect the current-carrying capacity of a conductor are the amperage, the wire size, and the wire temperature. The higher the amperage, the smaller the wire, and the higher the wire temperature, the lower will be the wire's safe current-carrying capacity. In other words, if the wiring is to be maintained at a safe temperature, it must be large enough to carry more than the rated amperage of the connected load. Also, if the wiring is exposed to relatively high temperatures, its size should be increased accordingly.

Wires for electric circuits are identified by number. The larger the number, the smaller the diameter of the wire. The wires used for wiring homes and average-size business establishments range in numbers from No. 000 to No. 14. Wires larger than No. 000 are especially for industrial applications, where exceptionally high voltages and current are required. Wires smaller than No. 14 are used for many applications such as low-voltage control circuits, doorbells, solenoid coils, etc.

Table 5-3 lists the wires from size No. 000 to size No. 14 and their maximum current-carrying capacity in amperes. It should be noted that some of the ratings depend on the type of wire insulation. Local codes determine which type is acceptable for a particular locality. In most instances, types RH and RHW are acceptable for indoor wiring. The wiring sizes mentioned in the following discussion pertain to RH and RHW types.

338

TABLE 5-3:
WIRING-SIZE DATA (ENCLOSED WIRES)

Wire size	Maximum ampere rating	
	Types R, RW, RU, T, and TW	Types RH and RHW
14	15	15
12	20	20
10	30	30
8	40	45
6	55	65
4	70	85
3	80	100
2	95	115
1	110	130
0	125	150
00	145	175
000	165	200

R	= code rubber	TW	=	moisture-resistant thermoplastic
RW	= moisture-resistant rubber	RH	=	heat-resistant rubber
RU	= latex rubber	RHW	=	moisture- and heat-resistant rubber
T	= thermoplastic			

The diameters of electric wires are usually in mils. A mil is $\frac{1}{1000}$ inch (0.001 inch). It takes 1,000 wires each 1 mil in diameter to equal 1 inch. A circular mil is the area enclosed by a circle that is 1 mil in diameter.

The area of a circle in circular mils (CM) is obtained by squaring the diameter (in mils) of the circle. For example, if a wire is 100 mils in diameter, what is its area in circular mils?

$$A = D^2 = 100 \times 100 = 10,000 \text{ CM}$$

Specific resistance is the resistance of a piece of material 1 foot long and with a cross-sectional area of 1 circular mil. A piece this size is known as a mil foot or circular mil foot. A piece of copper 1 foot long and with a cross-sectional area of 1 circular mil has a resistance of 10.4 ohms. Therefore, copper has a specific resistance of 10.4. The specific resistances for several common metals are listed as follows:

Silver	9.8 ohms
Iron	63.4 ohms
German silver	128.3 ohms
Copper	10.4 ohms
Aluminum	17.2 ohms

339

Obviously, resistance varies directly with the kind of material. A formula for finding the resistance of a conductor should include temperature, length, area, and material. However, ordinary temperature changes have such a small effect that they can be ignored. The following formula is used:

$$R = \frac{KL}{A}$$

R = resistance of the conductor in ohms

K = specific resistance of the material

L = length of the conductor

A = cross-sectional area (diameter²) of the conductor

EXAMPLE 1: What is the resistance of copper cable having a diameter of 0.229 inch and a length of 2,500 feet?

$$R = \frac{KL}{A} = \frac{10.4 \times 2500}{(229)^2} = 0.495 \text{ ohms}$$

If aluminum wire was substituted for the copper in the preceding illustration, the resistance would be:

$$R = \frac{KL}{A} = \frac{17.2 \times 2500}{(229)^2} = 0.819 \text{ ohms}$$

EXAMPLE 2: What is the length of 40.3-mils-diameter iron wire that would have a resistance of 26 ohms?

$$L = \frac{R \times A}{K} = \frac{26 \times (40.3)^2}{63.4} = 666.03 \text{ feet}$$

Gauge is a term used frequently for describing the size of wire. **Table 5-4** gives the gauge number and the important as well as interesting data about copper wire. For instance, note that as the gauge number increases the size of the wire decreases.

Also notice the very interesting fact that if you first select a certain size wire such as No. 1 with area of 83,694 circular mils and resistance 0.125 ohm, then select another wire three sizes smaller, gauge No. 4, this second size has an area half as large as the other, 41,742 circular mils, and resistance twice as large as the resistance of the other, 0.25 ohm.

The wire resistance formula can be used to find the size of wire required. That is, substituting the values of Ohm's law ($R = \frac{E}{I}$) in the formula, we have:

$$d^2 = \frac{L \times K}{\frac{E}{I}} = \frac{L \times K \times I}{E}$$

TABLE 5-4:
STANDARD ANNEALED COPPER AT A TEMPERATURE OF 25° CENTIGRADE (77° FAHRENHEIT)

American wire gauge

Gauge no.	Diam. in mils d	Area Cir. mils d²	Weight Lbs. per 1,000 ft.	Weight Lbs. per ohm	Length Ft. per lb.	Length Ft. per ohm	Resistance Ohms per 1,000 ft.	Resistance Ohms per lb.
0000	460.0	211660.	640.5	12810.	1.561	20010.	0.04998	0.00007805
000	409.6	167800.	507.9	8057.	1.968	15870.	.06303	.0001217
00	364.8	133100.	402.8	5067.	2.482	12580.	.07947	.0001935
0	324.9	105500.	319.5	3187.	3.130	9979.	.1002	.0003138
1	289.3	83690.	253.3	2004.	3.947	7913.	.1264	.0004990
2	257.6	66370.	200.9	1260.	4.977	6276.	.1594	.0007934
3	229.4	52640.	159.3	792.7	6.276	4977.	.2009	.001262
4	204.3	41740.	126.4	498.6	7.914	3947.	.2534	.002006
5	181.9	33100.	100.1	313.5	9.980	3130.	.3195	.003189
6	162.0	26250.	79.46	197.2	12.58	2482.	.4029	.005071
7	144.3	20820.	63.02	124.0	15.87	1968.	.5080	.008064
8	128.5	16510.	49.98	77.99	20.01	1561.	.6406	.01282
9	114.4	13090.	39.63	49.05	25.23	1238.	.8078	.02039
10	101.9	10380.	31.43	30.85	31.82	981.8	1.019	.03242
11	90.74	8234.	24.92	19.40	40.12	778.5	1.284	.05155
12	80.81	6530.	19.77	12.20	50.59	617.4	1.620	.08196
13	71.96	5178.	15.68	7.673	63.80	489.6	2.042	.1303
14	64.08	4107.	12.43	4.826	80.44	388.3	2.576	.2072
15	57.07	3257.	9.858	3.035	101.4	307.9	3.248	.3295
16	50.82	2583.	7.818	1.909	127.9	244.2	4.095	.5239
17	45.26	2048.	6.200	1.200	161.3	193.7	5.164	.8330
18	40.30	1624.	4.917	0.7549	203.4	153.6	6.512	1.325
19	35.89	1288.	3.899	.4748	256.5	121.8	8.210	2.106
20	31.96	1022.	3.092	.2986	323.4	96.59	10.35	3.349

For example, if a copper power line of 1,000 feet is needed to operate a motor requiring 20 amperes and with a voltage drop of not greater than 15 volts, the wire size should be:

$$d^2 = \frac{L \times K \times I}{E} = \frac{1000 \times 2 \times 10.4 \times 20}{15} = 27{,}733.3 \text{ circular mils}$$

Referring to **Table 5-4,** the wire size next larger than this area would be Gauge 5, and this should be the wire used.

To simplify wire calculations, charts such as the one shown in **Table 5-5** are given in electricians' handbooks.

To use such a typical table, it is necessary to know the load requirement in amperes. The ampere load is located in the first column of the proper system voltage table. On this line going horizontally to the right, the required circuit length is found, and at the top of the latter column the proper wire size is found. For example, to find the wire size needed for a 120-volt, three-wire lighting circuit 40 feet long and carrying a balanced lighting load of 12 amperes, it can be seen by reading across **Table 5-5** that 40 feet does not appear. The next higher value, 50, is therefore selected. The top of this column indicates that No. 12 wire is the proper size to employ.

Calculating Wire Sizes and Needs for Single Family Homes

The requirements of the National Electrical Code (which is distributed by the National Fire Protection Association) govern the entire operation of planning and installation of wiring systems. They give specifications for wire sizes and circuit loading in terms of the power requirements of the lights and appliances to be installed. For instance, the sizes of feeder wires to supply both light and power loads are determined on a basis of the type of building they are to serve and the floor areas. The minimum watts per unit area and demand factors for single-family dwellings, for example, are: 3 watts per square foot, plus 1,500 watts for appliances. Areas of 3,000 or fewer square feet demand 100 percent; for the next 117,000 square feet, 35 percent. No demand will be applied in connection with appliance loads.

The average do-it-yourselfer is concerned more with the branch circuits of the dwelling. A branch circuit is defined by the National Electrical Code as the part of a wiring system beyond the final fuse box protecting the circuit. Branch circuits carry electric current to appliance outlets, light fixtures, and switches.

The code recognizes four branch circuits with ratings of 15, 20, 30, and 50 A. The 50-A branch circuit is recommended for ranges and water heaters only. The 30-A branch circuit is usually used for appliances or lights in nonresidential applications. The 20-A branch circuit (as well as the 30- and 50-A branches) can have only heavy-duty lampholders of the mogul or porcelain

TABLE 5-5:
AVERAGE LENGTHS FOR 3- AND 4-WIRE BALANCED 120 V LIGHTING LOADS WITH 1 PERCENT (1.2 VOLTS) DROP FROM SUPPLY CABINET TO FIRST OUTLET SUPPLYING PERMANENTLY CONNECTED CURRENT-CONSUMING APPLIANCE OR LIGHTING FIXTURE

All conductors grouped in same conduit.

Amperes (A),	Watts (W), with Conduit Conductor (C), Fills (F)					
Maximum overcurrent	Intermittent loads			Continuous loads		
	100% F	80% F	70% F	100% F	80% F	70% F
Circuit protection	2–3 C	4–6 C	7–9 C	2–3 C	4–6 C	7–9 C
15 A	15 A	12 A	10.5 A	12 A	9.6 A	8.4 A
	1725 W	1380 W	1207 W	1380 W	1104 W	966 W
20 A	20 A	16 A	14 A	16 A	12.8 A	11.2 A
	2300 W	1840 W	1610 W	1840 W	1472 W	1288 W

Loads and lengths in feet for 1 percent drop on 3- and 4-wire 120 V circuits

Ampere load	# 10 wire	# 12 wire	# 14 wire
1	946	596	374
2	474	298	188
3	316	198	124
4	236	148	94
5	190	120	76
6	158	100	62
7	136	86	54
8	118	74	46
9	106	66	42
10	94	60	38
11	86	54	34
12	78	50	32
13	72	46	28
14	68	42	26
15	64	40	24
16	60	38	
17	56	36	
18	52	34	
19	50	32	
20	48	30	
21	46		
22	44		
23	42		
24	40		
25	38		
26	36		
27	36		
28	34		
29	32		
30	32		

TABLE 5-6:
WIRE GAUGES FOR FEEDER AND BRANCH CIRCUITS*

Amperes	Continuous operation*		Noncontinuous operation*	
	Wire size—copper	Wire size—aluminum	Wire size—copper	Wire size—aluminum
15	14	12	14	12
20	12	10	12	10
25/30	10	8	10	8
35/40	8	6	8	6
45/50	6	4	6	4
60	4	4	4	4
70	4	3	4	3
80	3	2	3	3
90	2	1	3	2
100	1	0	2	1
110	0	00	1	0
125	0	000	1	00
150	00	0000	0	000
175	000		00	0000
200	0000		000	
225			0000	

*American Wire Gauge (AWG) sizes. Continuous loads are those expected to continue for 3 or more hours; noncontinuous loads are those where 67 percent or less of the load is expected to be continuous.

keyless type when used for lighting purposes. Also, the fixture wire to the lampholder must be no smaller than No. 14. The only branch circuit suitable for general lighting is the 15-A branch circuit. Any type of lampholder may be used on the 15-A branch circuit, and this type of circuit may be used for appliances as well as for lighting. **Table 5-6** lists the wire gauges for feeder and branch circuits.

The branch-circuit requirements for homes vary with local codes, but most are similar to those of the National Electrical Code. Under modern electrical practices, branch circuits are divided into the following three general classes, according to their use.

General-purpose circuits serve not only lights in all parts of the house, but also convenience outlets, except for those in the kitchen, laundry, and dining areas. These circuits usually require No. 14 wire, which cannot be fused at more than 15 A, to handle up to a maximum capacity of 1,750 W. For today's systems, it is recommended that the No. 12 wire be used as the minimum size, fused at 20 A to handle up to 2,300 W. Allow one of these circuits for each 500 square feet of floor area. Always divide outlets evenly among circuits on different floors to avoid complete darkness if a fuse blows.

Since the floor area referred to here means floor space intended for occupancy, the first step is to determine the number of square feet contained in the complete floor plan. For instance, in a 41-by-32 foot single-story home, the complete or occupied floor space would be 40 by 32 feet, or 1,312 square feet. The code recommends one branch circuit for each 500 square feet of occupied floor space. If the 1,312 square is divided by 500, we find that 2.62 circuits for general purposes are needed. Since this requirement exceeds the needs of two branch circuits, it will be necessary to provide three branch circuits to take care of general-purpose needs. The third circuit is thus a safety factor to prevent circuit overloading and will also provide for the basement lighting. Thus, calculations call for three branch circuits for general purposes.

Appliance circuits are circuits with outlets for appliances alone. Install convenience outlets, independent of lighting fixtures, in the kitchen, laundry, and dining areas to serve the refrigerator, the washing machine, and portable high-wattage appliances. Plan at least one circuit of this type, using No. 12 wire. If more than one heavy-duty appliance will be connected to the same circuit, the use of No. 10 wire is recommended. It is often most practical to install three appliance circuits—two for kitchen appliances and one for the laundry room or basement. To compute the power requirements of appliances, use the wattage given in **Table 5-2.**

Individual circuits are provided for major appliances. Wire size and types of fuses or circuit breakers needed for individual circuits serving one piece of major electrical equipment, such as a clothes dryer, range, water heater, electric space heater, or room air conditioner, will depend upon the amperage rating of these appliances. Wire type and sizes are given in **Table 5-3.**

Allowable Voltage Drop

Most appliances and equipment are designed to allow for a 10 percent total voltage drop. This means that the voltage at the equipment must be at least 90 percent of the equipment's rated voltage and no more than 110 percent. The National Electrical Code is followed for large installations having central power plants to determine the electrical installation requirements. The Code allows a maximum of 5 percent voltage drop from the generator to the most distant service entrance. Therefore, inside a building another 5 percent drop may be tolerated. This normally is divided into a 3 percent drop for branch circuits and a 2 percent drop for feeders or main. The above requirements are necessary for large complexes but, under field conditions, the engineer may be able to accept larger voltage drops in a system.

MATH FOR HEATING, COOLING, AND PLUMBING

While mathematics may not be able to provide actual how-to work skills to correct a heating, cooling, or plumbing problem, it can frequently tell you why a problem has occurred. Also, as explained in this chapter and Chapter 7, math can save you a great deal of money when you do a job in these fields.

ESTIMATING YOUR HEATING AND COOLING REQUIREMENTS

Throughout most of this country there are periods of cold and periods of heat, both of which create personal discomfort for people whose homes are not properly conditioned. Although being cold is more distressing, being hot and sticky can cause excessive fatigue and a "below-par" feeling. If your present heating and/or cooling system is not supplying adequate hot or cool air, the problem could be the size of the unit. Simple mathematical calculation can provide the answer. Also, if you are planning to install a new system, these same calculations will tell you what size unit to install.

Sizing a Heating System

If your heating system is to operate properly, the furnace and piping must be large enough to replace the natural loss of heat from your home. Each house must be surveyed individually, because variables of size, construction, and

TABLE 6-1 & 2:
RECOMMENDED OUTSIDE DESIGN CONDITIONS FOR LOCALITIES IN THE UNITED STATES

State	City	Winter (Heating), °F	Summer (Cooling) Dry Bulb, °F	Summer (Cooling) Wet Bulb, °F
Alabama	Birmingham	10	95	78
	Mobile	15	95	80
Alaska	Anchorage	−20	67	59
	Fairbanks	−50	75	73
Arizona	Flagstaff	−10	90	65
	Phoenix	25	105	76
	Yuma	30	110	78
Arkansas	Little Rock	5	95	78
California	Bakersfield	25	105	70
	El Centro	25	110	78
	Fresno	25	105	74
	Los Angeles	35	90	70
	San Diego	35	95	68
	San Francisco	35	85	65
Colorado	Denver	−10	95	64
	Pueblo	−20	95	65
Connecticut	Bridgeport	0	95	75
Delaware	Wilmington	0	95	78
District of Columbia	Washington	0	95	78
Florida	Jacksonville	25	95	78
	Miami	35	91	79
Georgia	Atlanta	10	95	76
	Savannah	20	95	78
Hawaii	Honolulu	62	84	73
Idaho	Boise	−10	95	65
Illinois	Chicago	−10	95	75
	Springfield	−10	98	77
Indiana	Indianapolis	−10	95	76
	Terre Haute	0	95	78
Iowa	Des Moines	−15	95	78
	Sioux City	−20	95	78
Kansas	Topeka	−10	100	78
Kentucky	Louisville	0	95	78
Louisiana	New Orleans	20	95	80
Maine	Augusta	−15	90	73
Maryland	Baltimore	0	95	78
Massachusetts	Boston	0	92	75
	Worcester	−5	93	75
Michigan	Detroit	−10	95	75
	Lansing	−10	95	75

(Continued)

347

State	City	Winter (Heating), °F	Summer (Cooling) Dry Bulb, °F	Summer (Cooling) Wet Bulb, °F
Minnesota	Duluth	−25	93	73
	Minneapolis	−20	95	75
Mississippi	Vicksburg	10	95	78
Missouri	Kansas City	−10	100	76
	St. Louis	0	95	78
Montana	Butte	−20		
	Miles City	−35		
Nebraska	Omaha	−10	95	78
Nevada	Reno	−5	95	65
New Hampshire	Concord	−15	90	73
New Jersey	Newark	0	95	75
New Mexico	Albuquerque	0	95	70
New York	Buffalo	−5	93	73
	New York	0	95	75
	Syracuse	−10	93	75
North Carolina	Asheville	0	93	75
	Raleigh	10	95	78
North Dakota	Bismarck	−30	95	73
Ohio	Akron	−5	95	75
	Dayton	0	95	78
	Toledo	−10	95	75
Oklahoma	Tulsa	0	101	77
Oregon	Portland	10	90	68
Pennsylvania	Philadelphia	0	95	78
	Pittsburgh	0	95	75
Puerto Rico	San Juan	68	87	79
Rhode Island	Providence	0	93	75
South Carolina	Charleston	15	95	78
South Dakota	Sioux Falls	−20	95	75
Tennessee	Nashville	0	95	78
Texas	Austin	20	100	78
	Dallas	0	100	78
	El Paso	10	100	69
	Houston	20	95	78
Utah	Salt Lake City	−10	95	65
Vermont	Burlington	−10	90	73
Virginia	Richmond	15	95	78
Washington	Seattle	15	85	65
	Spokane	−15	93	65
West Virginia	Charleston	0	95	75
	Wheeling	−5	95	75
Wisconsin	Milwaukee	−15	95	75
Wyoming	Cheyenne	−15	95	65

Source: Courtesy of Frigidaire Division, General Motors Corporation.

location make it different from any other house. Houses lose heat through exposed ceilings and floors, outer walls, windows, and doors. Heat is lost through each of these areas at a different rate because of sizes, types of materials, and use or absence of insulation or storm sashes. All factors are reduced to a common measurement of thermal energy, or heat, the Btu (British thermal unit). This makes it easy to match a proper-size furnace or boiler (outputs expressed in Btu per hour or Btuh) with the heat loss of any house (also expressed in Btuh).

Each geographical location has a design temperature for heating. This is *not* the lowest temperature recorded, but the lowest temperature reached during 97.5 percent of the time. It provides the only practical approach in designing heating systems. You will find the design temperature for your area in **Table 6-1 & 2.**

All the information needed for sizing your furnace or boiler can be entered on a work sheet such as that shown in **Figure 6-1.** Much of this information is found just by looking at the house from the outside: type of house and construction, number of windows and doors, use of storm sashes.

How to Use the Work Sheet

There is only one "cold" ceiling—the one immediately below the attic. "Cold" floors are over an open area, on a concrete slab, or over an unexcavated area. Measure the length and width of these surfaces. When you have the measurements and other information filled in, figure the areas by multiplying the length times the width, as indicated on the work sheet.

Gross area of exposed walls is the house perimeter (distance in feet around the outside) times ceiling height. For houses with more than one story, add the ceiling heights of all levels except the basement before multiplying by the perimeter.

Multiply each of these areas by its indicated construction factor, called a *multiplier,* to be found in the "multipliers" table on the work sheet. The answers will be in Btuh and will show the heat loss. Equipment is rated in Btuh, so if the total heat loss of the house is known, it is easy to pick a furnace or boiler of the proper size.

Determining the Heat Loss

The information and calculations entered on the work sheet in **Figure 6-1** pertain to the typical house in **Figure 6-2.** Our typical house has a single story and a full basement. Both the walls and the attic have insulation, but the doors and windows are not protected by storm sashes. The design temperature is −10° F.

HEATING ESTIMATE WORK SHEET

				DESIGN TEMPERATURE	
TYPE OF HOUSE	• ATTIC INSULATION	☒YES ☐NO	OUTSIDE	_− 10_	°F
_/_ STORY	• WALL INSULATION	☒YES ☐NO	INSIDE	_+ 70_	°F
	• STORM SASH	☒YES ☐NO	DIFFERENCE	_+ 80_	°F

TYPE OF EXPOSURE	GROSS AREA IN SQUARE FEET	X MULTIPLIER	= HEAT LOSS IN BTU'S
EXPOSED WALLS	PERIMETER X CEILING HT. = SQ. FT. _148_ x _8_ = _1184_	X _11_	_13,024_
GLASS NO. OF WINDOWS NO. OF DOORS TOTAL GLASS	_10_ x _15_ = _150_ _2_ x _20_ = _40_ _190_	X _130_	_24,700_
COLD CEILING	LENGTH X WIDTH = SQ. FT. _46_ x _28_ = _1288_	X _8_	_10,304_
COLD FLOOR		X _0_	_0_
TOTAL HEAT LOSS IN BTU'S NEEDED AT REGISTER OR RADIATOR ➤			_48,028_

MULTIPLIERS

TYPE OF CONSTRUCTION		MULTIPLIERS FOR 70° AT OUTSIDE DESIGN TEMPERATURE						
		-30	-20	-10	0	+10	+20	+30
WALLS	FRAME OR BRICK VENEER STANDARD WALL NO INSULATION WITH 2" OR MORE INSULATION	26 13	24 12	21 ⑪	18 9	15 8	13 6	10 5
WINDOWS DOORS	PLAIN SINGLE GLASS WITH STORM SASH	170 80	150 70	⑬⓪ 60	120 55	105 50	85 40	65 30
CEILINGS	ATTIC ABOVE—NO INSULATION ATTIC ABOVE—3-5/8" INSULATION	32 10	29 9	25 ⑧	22 7	19 6	15 5	12 4
FLOORS	OVER BASEMENT (with furnace) OVER ENCLOSED CRAWL SPACE—4" INSULATION OVER ENCLOSED CRAWL SPACE—NO INSULATION OVER UNENCLOSED CRAWL SPACE ON A 4" CONCRETE SLAB	0 5 14 28 10	0 5 13 25 9	⓪ 4 11 22 8	0 4 10 20 7	0 3 9 17 6	0 3 7 14 5	0 2 6 12 4

FIG. 6-1

Exposed Walls

In our example the perimeter is 46 feet + 28 feet + 46 feet + 28 feet, or a total of 148 feet, which is entered on the form. Now we multiply this number by the ceiling height (8 feet) to obtain a total wall area of 1184 square feet. Looking down the − 10° F column in the multiplier table, we find the number 11 for insulated walls. Multiplying these figures (1184 × 11) gives a wall heat loss of 13,024 Btuh.

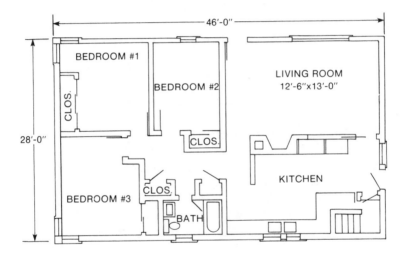

FIG. 6-2

Glass

The number of windows (10) multiplied by 15 gives 150 square feet for windows. Similarly, the number of doors (2) multiplied by 20 gives 40 square feet. Adding window area (150) and door area (40) gives a total glass area of 190 square feet. The multiplier for windows and doors without storm sashes at −10° F is 130. Multiplying these numbers (190 × 130) gives the heat loss of 24,700 Btuh.

Cold Ceiling

The cold ceiling area is the length of the house times its width (46 feet × 28 feet) a total of 1,288 square feet. The multiplier for an insulated ceiling at −10° F is 8. The heat loss of the ceiling then is (1,288 × 8) or 10,304 Btuh.

Cold Floor

Since the house has a full basement in which the furnace will be located, the multiplier is 0. Therefore, the area of the floor need not be considered (since anything multiplied by 0 is still 0); the heat loss through the floor is 0.

Total Heat Loss

This is just the sum of the individual heat losses (13,024 + 24,700 + 10,304 + 0), which gives a total of 48,028 Btuh. This is the total amount of heat (in Btuh) that will be needed in the house. To obtain this amount of heat, you would need a furnace with an output rating (at the registers) of 48,028 Btuh, or more.

Sizing a Cooling System

"Sizing" means simply the selection of cooling equipment that will have the right capacity (in Btu) to properly cool your home. If you are also planning a forced-air heating system and wish to include central air conditioning for summer use, your plans will already include the necessary ductwork, etc., for distribution of the heated (or cooled) air. The only additional equipment to be selected is the air-conditioning unit (which will be installed as part of your heating/cooling system). However, if you are planning only for a central air-conditioning system (without central heat), your cooling equipment must also include the necessary ductwork and registers.

Many people believe that comfort cooling calls for lowering the house temperature by 12 to 15° F below the outdoor temperature, and that's all. This is an error. Regardless of the outdoor temperature in summer, the indoor temperature should ideally be in the neighborhood of 75° F, and the relative humidity should be about 50 percent. If it is any hotter or more humid than this, the overwhelming majority of people will feel distinctly warm and uncomfortable, whether the outdoor temperature is 85° or 110° F. This fact has been proved conclusively by research conducted by the American Society of Heating, Refrigerating, and Air Conditioning Engineers. It is also borne out through surveys conducted among families with air conditioning. Thus, 75° F and 50 percent relative humidity is said to be the ideal air condition for virtually all air-conditioned spaces, including houses.

Home cooling systems should have enough capacity to provide this much cooling and dehumidifying at all times. This means that a larger cooling unit is needed for a house in Phoenix, where summer temperatures often climb to 105° F, than is needed for an identical house in Chicago, where outside temperatures seldom exceed 95° F. It also means that more capacity is needed in a humid area like New Orleans than in a drier area like Chicago, which has the same dry-bulb temperature. You may choose to set your thermostat higher than 75° F to save energy, but you should still size your unit to enable you to cool to 75° F if necessary.

As in heating, each geographical location also has a design temperature for cooling. This is not the highest temperature recorded; it is the recommended high (dry-bulb) temperature on which to base practical cooling requirements. You will find the design ("Summer DB") temperature for your area in **Table 6-1 and 6-2**. The same chart also lists wet-bulb ("Summer WB") temperatures, which are adjusted to indicate the prevailing humidity conditions. In any area where the WB temperature does not exceed 75° F, you do not have to worry about the humidity; but if it does exceed 75° F, you will have to increase your cooling unit's capacity for proper humidity control.

How to Calculate Cooling Requirements

An air-conditioning estimate work sheet is shown in **Figure 6-3**. When filling it out, remember that there is only one "ceiling," the one at the top of the space to be cooled. In the case of a whole house, this ceiling may be one with an attic above it or one without an attic. In the case of a first-floor apartment, do not include the ceiling if the floor above is cooled, but do count it if the floor above is not cooled and there is no insulation between. This same rule applies to the floor of a second-floor apartment; but in the case of a whole house the floor is counted only when there is an open crawl space (do not count it if it is over a basement or an enclosed crawl space or on a slab).

The gross area of exposed walls is the house perimeter times the above-ground wall height. Windows and doors are counted as for heating calculation, except that you count those on each side of the house (north, south, etc.) separately, and must also consider whether or not each window is normally shaded (by blinds, drawn draperies, etc.). People (house occupants, at two per bedroom) must also be counted, as shown on the work sheet.

Multiply each of the above by the proper "cooling factor" listed on the form. Add these together with the 1,500 Btu listed for your kitchen to arrive at a total (you can scratch this off if the kitchen is entirely separate from the area to be cooled). If your DB temperature (**Table 6-1 & 2**) does not exceed 95° F and your WB temperature does not exceed 75° F, this total is the cooling-unit

353

AIR CONDITIONING—ESTIMATE WORK SHEET				
DESIGN TEMPERATURES		DRY BULB _100_ °F INSIDE _75_ °F DIFFERENCE _25_ °F	*WET BULB _78_ °F	
COOLING ESTIMATE				
TYPE OF EXPOSURE		COOLING FACTORS	X AREA	B.T.U./hr.
PEOPLE—FIGURE 2 PEOPLE PER BEDROOM		400	X Number *5*	= *2000*
CEILING		*3*	X Lgth. X Width *28 X 25*	= *2100*
EXPOSED WALLS	GROSS AREA	*4*	Perim. X Ceil. Ht. X *106 X 16*	= *6784*
PARTITION— NEXT TO WARM ROOM	GROSS AREA	*6.5*	Lgth. X Ceil. Ht. X	=
FLOOR	(ONLY OVER WARM AREA)		Lgth. X Width X	=
KITCHEN INCLUDE IN TOTAL		⟶		*1,500*
GLASS WINDOWS AND DOORS			No. Windows X 15 or Area	
NORTH, OR COMPLETE SHADE		40	X =	
SOUTH, UNSHADED		65	X	=
SOUTH, VEN. BLINDS OR DRAPES		45	X	=
EAST AND WEST UNSHADED		117	X	=
EAST AND WEST VEN. BLINDS OR DRAPES		80	X	
WOOD DOORS		16	X No. Doors X 20 *2 X 20*	= *640*
TOTAL—Based on 20° Temperature Difference (Total Includes Moisture Removal Load)		▶		*23224*
YOUR DESIGN TEMPERATURE CORRECT FOR			X	*1.25*
15° = .75 25° = 1.25 30° = 1.50 35° = 1.75				*29030*
*CORRECTION FOR HIGH HUMIDITY AREAS If Wet Bulb Temp. is 78° Add 5% If Wet Bulb Temp is 80° Add 10%				*1451*
TOTAL ▶				*30 481*

FIG. 6-3

354

capacity (in Btuh) needed to maintain a 75 ° F inside temperature. However, if your DB temperature exceeds 95° F or if you want an inside temperature lower than 75° F, first figure the difference between your DB temperature and the desired inside temperature, then subtract 20 from this to learn how many more degrees of cooling you will need. Now add to the above total the amount indicated under "your design temperature correction for" on the work sheet (for instance, if you need 15° F more cooling, you must add on .75 times the above total; for 25° F more, add 1.25 times, etc.). Finally, if your WB temperature exceeds 75° F, you must add on still more (5 percent of the first total if it is 78° F; 10 percent if it is 80° F) to maintain an inside 50 percent relative humidity.

For a typical two-story house, look at **Figure 6-4** and note the following information and calculations that should be entered on the work sheet:

People

This three-bedroom home will normally house five people, which multiplied by 400 gives a cooling load of 5 $\times$ 400, or 2,000 Btuh.

Ceiling

The area is length of the house times width (28 feet $\times$ 25 feet) or 700 square feet. The ceiling cooling factor, for a dark-color roof and an attic space with between 2 inches and 4 inches of insulation is 3. The load then is 700 $\times$ 3, or 2,100 Btuh.

Exposed Walls

Total area of exposed walls is perimeter of house times ceiling height (of upper ceiling). This is 106 $\times$ 16 (2 stories) or 1,696 square feet. The cooling factor table shows frame walls with 2-inch insulation have a factor of 4. Multiplying 1,696 square feet by 4 gives a load of 6,784 Btuh.

Floor

Over basement—no factor required.

Windows

The house has 17 windows, either facing north or completely shaded by awnings. This means that each window will have a cooling factor of 40. First, multiply the 17 windows by 15 for glass area (17 $\times$ 15 = 255), then by 40 (255 $\times$ 40 = 10,200). This means that the cooling load for the total glass is 10,200 Btuh.

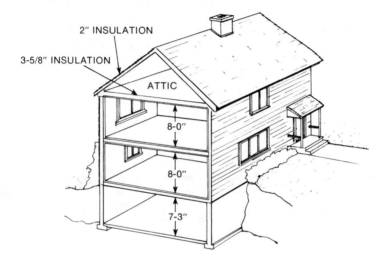

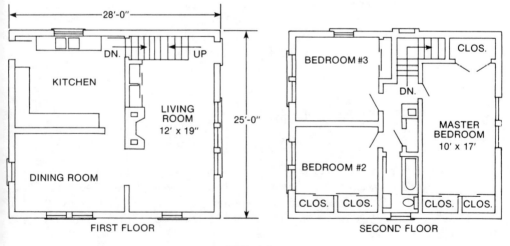

FIG. 6-4

356

FIG. 6-4 (Continued)

AIR CONDITIONING—ESTIMATE WORK SHEET				

TYPE OF HOUSE _two_ Story,
SIZE OF HOUSE _25'_ x _28'_
WINDOWS SHADED?   Awnings ☑   Venetian Blinds ☐   No ☐

Attic Insulated? _3½_ in.
Walls Insulated? _2_ in.

COOLING FACTORS		NATURAL VENTILATION		
CEILINGS		ATTIC VENT. FAN	DARK ROOF	LIGHT ROOF
WITH ATTIC SPACE	NO INSULATION	9	13	10
	2" INSULATION	3	6	5
	4" INSULATION	2	(3)	3
BUILT-UP ROOF NO ATTIC SPACE	NO INSULATION		23	18
	2" ROOF INSULATION		11	9
	3" ROOF INSULATION		8	7
CEILING UNDER WARM ROOM, NO INSULATION		4		
EXPOSED WALLS				
FRAME OR BRICK VENEER OR STUCCO	NO INSULATION	8		
	1" INSULATION OR ONE REFLECTIVE AIR SPACE	6		
	2" INSULATION OR TWO REFLECTIVE AIR SPACES	(4)		
	3-5/8" INSULATION OR THREE REFLECTIVE AIR SPACES	3		
8" BRICK OR BLOCK	PLAIN OR PLASTERED DIRECT	10		
	FURRED, LATH & PLASTER, NO INSULATION	6		
	FURRED, 1" INSULATION OR ONE REFLECTIVE AIR SPACE	4		
	FURRED 2" INSULATION OR TWO REFLECTIVE AIR SPACES	3		
	FURRED, 3-5/8" INSULATION OR THREE RELFECTIVE AIR SPACES	2		
	12" ADOBE WALL	5		
FLOOR				
	OVER WARM ROOM	5		
	OVER BASEMENT OR SLAB FLOOR OR CLOSED CRAWL SPACE	0		
	OVER OPEN CRAWL SPACE	7		

NOTE: MOST OF THE ABOVE FACTORS WERE DERIVED FROM MANUAL J PUBLISHED BY THE NATIONAL WARM AIR HEATING & AIR CONDITIONING ASS'N
SELECT FROM THESE FACTORS IN ESTIMATING COOLING LOAD AT RIGHT

Wood Doors

The two wood doors to the outside are multiplied by 20 for area (2 × 20 = 40), then by the indicated factor 16 (40 × 16 = 640) for a load of 640 Btuh.

Kitchen

A standard load of 1,500 Btuh is added for kitchen activities.

Total Cooling Load

Based on a 20° F difference, this is the total of the preceding individual loads. In this example, it is 2,000 + 2,100 + 6,784 + 10,200 + 640 + 1,500, or 23,224 Btuh.

Design Temperature Correction

An allowance must be made because the difference between the outside dry-bulb temperature (100° F) and the desired inside temperature (75° F) is greater than 20° F. The work sheet indicates that a difference of 25° F (100° F − 75° F) requires a correction factor of 1.25. The adjusted cooling load (23,224 × 1.25) then becomes 29,030 Btuh.

High-Humidity Correction

This area has a wet-bulb reading of 78° F. The work sheet indicates that under such conditions, 5 percent must be added to the cooling load: (29,030 × 0.05 = 1,451) (29,030 + 1,452 = 30,481). The final cooling load then becomes 30,841 Btuh.

The completed load forms indicate the major load sources. Thus these forms

TABLE 6-3:
INSTALLATIONS THAT REDUCE COOLING AND HEATING LOADS

Installation	Cooling	Heating
Double glass	80% of single glass	44% of single glass
Outside shading	28% of glass without shading	
Wall insulation 1″	80% of uninsulated wall	80% of uninsulated wall
Wall insulation 2″	40% of uninsulated wall	40% of uninsulated wall
Wall insulation 3″	30% of uninsulated wall	30% of uninsulated wall
Ceiling insulation 2″	26% of uninsulated ceiling	31% of uninsulated ceiling
Ceiling insulation 4″	18% of uninsulated ceiling	22% of uninsulated ceiling
Ceiling insulation 6″	15% of uninsulated ceiling	19% of uninsulated ceiling

should be studied carefully. Frequently, it is more economical to reduce the major loads than to install larger units. Reduced loads will also pay dividends in the form of lower operating costs. **Table 6-3** gives an approximate indication of the effect of reducing loads.

Light-colored shingles reduce the heat load of the roof by approximately 30 percent. Positive (forced) attic ventilation will also reduce the cooling load. An air change at least every 2 to 3 minutes is recommended. The necessary fan capacity can be estimated by the following formula:

$$cfm = \frac{L \times W \times H}{3 \text{ minutes}}$$

$$cfm = \text{cubic feet per minute}$$

$$L = \text{length of attic in feet}$$

$$W = \text{width of attic in feet}$$

$$H = \text{average height of attic in feet}$$

Figure 6-5 illustrates the approximate heating fuel savings that can be achieved by means of various installations. Similar savings will also be reflected in the operating costs of heating and/or cooling units. Other energy-saving tips are given in Chapter 7, where proper selection of room air conditioners is also discussed.

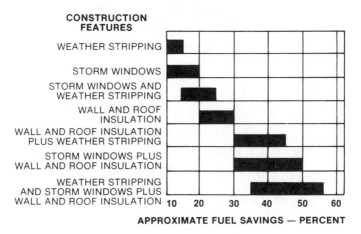

FIG. 6-5

359

Heating Degree-Days

One of the most practical of weather statistics is the heating degree-day. First devised some 50 years ago, the degree-day system has been in general use by the heating industry for more than 30 years.

Heating degree-days are the number of degrees the daily average temperature is below 65° F. Normally heating is not required in a building when the outdoor average daily temperature is 65° F. Heating degree-days are deter mined by subtracting the average daily temperatures below 65° F from the base 65° F. A day with an average temperature of 50° F has 15 degree-days (65 − 50 = 15), while one with an average temperature of 65° F or higher has none.

Several characteristics make the degree-day figures especially useful. They are cumulative. Thus the degree-day sum for a period of days represents the total heating load for that period. The relationship between degree-days and fuel consumption is linear, thus doubling the degree-days usually doubles the fuel consumption. Comparing normal seasonal degree-days in different locations gives a rough estimate of seasonal fuel consumption. For example, it would require roughly $4\frac{1}{2}$ times as much fuel to heat a building in Chicago, where the mean annual total degree-days are about 6,200, than to heat a similar building in New Orleans, where the annual total degree-days are around 1,400. (**Table 6-4** gives the normal total degree-days for various cities in the U.S.) Using degree-days has the advantage that the consumption ratios are fairly constant, i.e., the fuel consumed per 100 degree-days is about the same whether the 100 degree-days occur in only a few days or are spread over several days.

The rapid adoption of the degree-day system paralleled the spread of automatic fuel systems in the 1930s. Oil and gas are more costly to store than solid fuels, and this places a premium on the scheduling of deliveries and the precise evaluation of use rates and peak demands. Charts for your area are available from local offices of the United States Weather Bureau.

SOLAR HEATING

In the past few years a great deal has been written about solar heating, which has lead to three basic questions:

1. Is it suitable for my house?
2. Is it a worthwhile investment?
3. Can I afford it?

Here we'll try to help you answer the first two questions—with the help of math. Only you can answer the third.

TABLE 6-4:
HEATING DEGREE DAYS

Heating degree days indicate the number of degrees the daily average temperatures are below 65° F. The figure 65° is used because it is the average outdoor temperature below which most people feel the need for indoor heat. Degree days are computed like this: A day with an average temperature of 50° has 15 heating degree days (65 - 50 = 15). Days that average 65° or over have no heating degree days.

This table shows the monthly and annual totals by city. Note: There is a direct relation between heating degree days and fuel consumption that allows fairly accurate comparisons of heating energy needs. For example, it would take roughly seven times as much energy to heat a house in Duluth as it would for the same house in New Orleans (10,000 ÷ 1385 = 7). And the relation of heating degree days to energy needs is fairly constant, whether any 100 degree days occur over many or only a few calendar days. The fuel industry uses this system on a month-to-month basis to determine fuel rates and peak demands. Table source: *Climatic Atlas of the United States*

NORMAL TOTAL HEATING DEGREE DAYS (Base 65°)

STATE AND STATION	JUL	AUG	SEP	OCT	NOV	DEC	JAN	FEB	MAR	APR	MAY	JUN	ANNUAL
ALA. Birmingham	0	0	6	93	363	555	592	462	363	108	9	0	2551
Huntsville	0	0	12	127	426	663	694	557	434	138	19	0	3070
Mobile	0	0	0	22	213	357	415	300	211	42	0	0	1560
ALASKA Anchorage	245	291	516	930	1284	1572	1631	1316	1293	879	592	315	10864
Barrow	803	840	1035	1500	1971	2362	2517	2332	2468	1944	1445	957	20174
Fairbanks	171	332	642	1203	1833	2254	2359	1901	1739	1068	555	222	14279
Juneau	301	338	483	725	921	1135	1237	1070	1073	810	601	381	9075
Nome	481	496	693	1094	1455	1820	1879	1666	1770	1314	930	573	14171
ARIZ. Flagstaff	46	68	201	558	867	1073	1169	991	911	651	437	180	7152
Prescott	0	0	27	245	579	797	865	711	605	360	158	15	4362
Tucson	0	0	0	25	231	406	471	344	242	75	6	0	1800
ARK. Fort Smith	0	0	12	127	450	704	781	596	456	144	22	0	3292
Little Rock	0	0	9	127	465	716	756	577	434	126	9	0	3219
Texarkana	0	0	0	78	345	561	626	468	350	105	0	0	2533
CALIF. Eureka	270	257	258	329	414	499	546	470	505	438	372	285	4643
Fresno	0	0	0	78	339	558	586	406	319	150	56	0	2492
Mt. Shasta	25	34	123	406	696	902	983	784	738	525	347	159	5722
San Diego	6	0	15	37	123	251	313	249	202	123	84	36	1439
San Francisco	81	78	60	143	306	462	508	395	363	279	214	126	3015
COLO. Alamosa	65	99	279	639	1065	1420	1476	1162	1020	696	440	168	8529
Denver	6	9	117	428	819	1035	1132	938	887	558	288	66	6283
Pueblo	0	0	54	326	750	986	1085	871	772	429	174	15	5462
CONN. Bridgeport	0	0	66	307	615	986	1079	966	853	510	208	27	5617
Hartford	0	6	99	372	711	1119	1209	1061	899	495	177	24	6172
New Haven	0	12	87	347	648	1011	1097	991	871	543	245	45	5897
DEL. Wilmington	0	0	51	270	588	927	980	874	735	387	112	6	4930
FLA. Jacksonville	0	0	0	12	144	310	332	246	174	21	0	0	1239
Miami Beach	0	0	0	0	0	40	56	36	9	0	0	0	141
Tallahassee	0	0	0	28	198	360	375	286	202	36	0	0	1485
Tampa	0	0	0	0	60	171	202	148	102	0	0	0	683
GA Atlanta	0	0	18	127	414	626	639	529	437	168	25	0	2983
Columbus	0	0	0	87	333	543	552	434	338	96	0	0	2383
Savannah	0	0	0	47	246	437	437	353	254	45	0	0	1819
IDAHO Boise	0	0	132	415	792	1017	1113	854	722	438	245	81	5809
Idaho Falls 46W	16	34	270	623	1056	1370	1538	1249	1085	651	391	192	8475
ILL. Cairo	0	0	36	164	513	791	856	680	539	195	47	0	3821
Chicago	0	0	81	326	753	1113	1209	1044	890	480	211	48	6155
Springfield	0	0	72	291	696	1023	1135	935	769	354	136	18	5429
IND. Evansville	0	0	66	220	606	896	955	767	620	237	68	0	4435
Indianapolis	0	0	90	316	723	1051	1113	949	809	432	177	39	5699
South Bend	0	6	111	372	777	1125	1221	1070	933	525	239	60	6439
IOWA Des Moines	0	9	99	363	837	1231	1398	1165	967	489	211	39	6808
Dubuque	12	31	156	450	906	1287	1420	1204	1026	546	260	78	7376
KANS. Dodge City	0	0	33	251	666	939	1051	840	719	354	124	9	4986
Goodland	0	6	81	381	810	1073	1166	955	884	507	236	42	6141
KY. Covington	0	0	75	291	669	983	1035	893	756	390	149	24	5265
Louisville	0	0	54	248	609	890	930	818	682	315	105	9	4660
LA. Baton Rouge	0	0	0	31	216	369	409	294	208	33	0	0	1560
New Orleans	0	0	0	19	192	322	363	258	192	39	0	0	1385
Shreveport	0	0	0	47	297	477	552	426	304	81	0	0	2184
MAINE Caribou	78	115	336	682	1044	1535	1690	1470	1308	858	468	183	9767
Portland	12	53	195	508	807	1215	1339	1182	1042	675	372	111	7511
MD. Baltimore	0	0	48	264	585	905	936	820	679	327	90	0	4654
Frederick	0	0	66	307	624	955	995	876	741	384	127	12	5087
MASS. Blue Hill Obsy	0	22	108	381	690	1085	1178	1053	936	579	267	69	6368
Boston	0	9	60	316	603	983	1088	972	846	513	208	36	5634
Nantucket	12	22	93	332	573	896	992	941	896	621	384	129	5891
MICH. Detroit (City)	0	0	87	360	738	1088	1181	1058	936	522	220	42	6232

(Continued)

TABLE 6-4:
HEATING DEGREE DAYS (continued)

STATE AND STATION	JUL	AUG	SEP	OCT	NOV	DEC	JAN	FEB	MAR	APR	MAY	JUN	ANNUAL
Grand Rapids	9	28	135	434	804	1147	1259	1134	1011	579	279	75	6894
Marquette	59	81	240	527	936	1268	1411	1268	1187	771	468	177	8393
Sault Ste. Marie	96	105	279	580	951	1367	1525	1380	1277	810	477	201	9048
MINN. Duluth	71	109	330	632	1131	1581	1745	1518	1355	840	490	198	10000
International Falls	71	112	363	701	1236	1724	1919	1621	1414	828	443	174	10606
Minneapolis	22	31	189	505	1014	1454	1631	1380	1166	621	288	81	8382
Rochester	25	34	186	474	1005	1438	1593	1366	1150	630	301	93	8295
MISS. Jackson	0	0	0	65	315	502	546	414	310	87	0	0	2239
Vicksburg	0	0	0	53	279	462	512	384	282	69	0	0	2041
MO. Columbia	0	0	54	251	651	967	1076	874	716	324	121	12	5046
Kansas	0	0	39	220	612	905	1032	818	682	294	109	0	4711
St. Joseph	0	6	60	285	708	1039	1172	949	769	348	133	15	5484
Springfield	0	0	45	223	600	877	973	781	660	291	105	6	4561
MONT. Great Falls	28	53	258	543	921	1169	1349	1154	1063	642	384	186	7750
Havre	28	53	306	595	1065	1367	1584	1364	1181	657	338	162	8700
Missoula	34	74	303	651	1035	1287	1420	1120	970	621	391	219	8125
NEBR. Lincoln	0	6	75	301	726	1066	1237	1016	834	402	171	30	5864
Omaha	0	12	105	357	828	1175	1355	1126	939	465	208	42	6612
Valentine	9	12	165	493	942	1237	1395	1176	1045	579	288	84	7425
NEV. Ely	28	43	234	592	939	1184	1308	1075	977	672	456	225	7733
Las Vegas	0	0	0	78	387	617	688	487	335	111	6	0	2709
Reno	43	87	204	490	801	1026	1073	823	729	510	357	189	6332
N. H. Concord	6	50	177	505	822	1240	1358	1184	1032	636	298	75	7383
Mt. Wash. Obsy.	493	536	720	1057	1341	1742	1820	1663	1652	1260	930	603	13817
N. J. Atlantic City	0	0	39	251	549	880	936	848	741	420	133	15	4812
Trenton	0	0	57	264	576	924	989	885	753	399	121	12	4980
N. MEX. Albuquerque	0	0	12	229	642	868	930	703	595	288	81	0	4348
Silver City	0	0	6	183	525	729	791	605	518	261	87	0	3705
N. Y. Albany	0	19	138	440	777	1194	1311	1156	992	564	239	45	6875
Buffalo	19	37	141	440	777	1156	1256	1145	1039	645	329	78	7062
Central Park	0	0	30	233	540	902	986	885	760	408	118	9	4871
Syracuse	6	28	132	415	744	1153	1271	1140	1004	570	248	45	6756
N. C. Nasheville	0	0	48	245	555	775	784	683	592	273	87	0	4042
Cape Hatteras	0	0	0	78	273	521	580	518	440	177	25	0	2612
Raleigh	0	0	21	164	450	716	725	616	487	180	34	0	3393
Wilmington	0	0	0	74	291	521	546	462	357	96	0	0	2347
N. DAK. Bismarck	34	28	222	577	1083	1463	1708	1442	1203	645	329	117	8851
Devils Lake	40	53	273	642	1191	1634	1872	1579	1345	753	381	138	9901
Fargo	28	37	219	574	1107	1569	1789	1520	1260	690	332	99	9226
OHIO Akron	0	9	96	381	726	1070	1138	1016	871	489	202	39	6037
Cincinnati	0	0	54	248	612	921	970	837	701	336	118	9	4806
Cleveland	9	25	105	384	738	1088	1159	1047	918	552	260	66	6351
OKLA. Oklahoma City	0	0	15	164	498	766	868	664	527	189	34	0	3725
Tulsa	0	0	18	158	522	787	893	683	539	213	47	0	3860
OREG. Eugene	34	34	129	366	585	719	803	627	589	426	279	135	4726
Medford	0	0	78	372	678	871	918	697	642	432	242	78	5008
Portland	25	28	114	335	597	735	825	644	586	396	245	105	4635
PA. Erie	0	25	102	391	714	1063	1169	1081	973	585	288	60	6451
Philadelphia	0	0	60	291	621	964	1014	890	744	390	115	12	5101
Scranton	0	19	132	434	762	1104	1156	1028	893	498	195	33	6254
R. I. Block Is.	0	16	78	307	594	902	1020	955	877	612	344	99	5804
Providence	0	16	96	372	660	1023	1110	988	868	534	236	51	5954
S. C. Charleston	0	0	0	59	282	471	487	389	291	54	0	0	2033
Spartanburg	0	0	15	130	417	667	663	560	453	144	25	0	3074
S. DAK. Huron	9	12	165	508	1014	1432	1628	1355	1125	600	288	87	8223
Rapid City	22	12	165	481	897	1172	1333	1145	1051	615	326	126	7345
TENN. Bristol	0	0	51	236	573	828	828	700	598	261	68	0	4143
Chattanooga	0	0	18	143	468	698	722	577	453	150	25	0	3254
TEX. Amarillo	0	0	18	205	570	797	877	664	546	252	56	0	3985
Austin	0	0	0	31	225	388	468	325	223	51	0	0	1711
Corpus Christi	0	0	0	0	120	220	291	174	109	0	0	0	914
Fort Worth	0	0	0	65	324	536	614	448	319	99	0	0	2405
Houston	0	0	0	6	183	307	384	288	192	36	0	0	1396
UTAH Milford	0	0	99	443	867	1141	1252	988	822	519	279	87	6497
Wendover	0	0	48	372	822	1091	1178	902	729	408	177	51	5778
VT. Burlington	28	65	207	539	891	1349	1513	1333	1187	714	353	90	8269
VA. Cape Henry	0	0	0	112	360	645	694	633	536	246	53	0	3279
Lynchburg	0	0	51	223	540	822	849	731	605	267	78	0	4166
Norfolk	0	0	0	136	408	698	738	655	533	216	37	0	3421
WASH. Olympia	68	71	198	422	636	753	834	675	645	450	307	177	5236
Seattle	50	47	129	329	543	657	738	599	577	396	242	117	4424
Spokane	9	25	168	493	879	1082	1231	980	834	531	288	135	6655
Stampede Pass	273	291	393	701	1008	1178	1287	1075	1085	855	654	483	9283
W. VA. Charleston	0	0	63	254	591	865	880	770	648	300	96	9	4476
Elkins	9	25	135	400	729	992	1008	896	791	444	198	48	5675
Parkersburg	0	0	60	264	606	905	942	826	691	339	115	6	4754
WIS. Green Bay	28	50	174	484	924	1333	1494	1313	1141	654	335	99	8029
La Crosse	12	19	153	437	924	1339	1504	1277	1070	540	245	69	7589
Madison	25	40	174	474	930	1330	1473	1274	1113	618	310	102	7863
Milwaukee	43	47	174	471	876	1252	1376	1193	1054	642	372	135	7635
WYO. Cheyenne	19	31	210	543	924	1101	1228	1056	1011	672	381	102	7278
Lander	6	19	204	555	1020	1299	1417	1145	1017	654	381	153	7870
Sherian	25	31	219	539	948	1200	1355	1154	1054	642	366	150	7683

Types of Solar Systems

Understanding how a total solar energy system works is important in determining whether a unit can be used in your home. Actually there are four main end uses of a residential solar energy system: heating water for domestic use, heating a swimming pool, heating the home (space heating), and heating and cooling the home (space heating and cooling). Of course, there are various combinations of these end uses. A system could be used to heat the house during the winter and to heat the swimming pool in late spring or early fall when house heating is not needed. Or a unit could be designed to handle both heating the home and supplying the hot water.

There are two basic types of systems. An *active system* uses mechanical means such as pumps, valves, and so on for operating. A *passive system* uses natural forces such as gravity, convection, and nocturnal radiation to accomplish the same objective. Both types of systems have their advantages and disadvantages.

Passive systems are more economical to operate. Especially in hot, dry regions, solar energy for heating and cooling is economically competitive with conventional forms of energy. However, these systems are limited by seasonal conditions and architectural restraints. In areas with cold temperatures or high humidity they are subject to such problems as freezing or excessive humidity. They may not be able to provide uninterrupted comfort levels. In most cases, the requirements of a passive system dictate the overall design of the structure more than the requirements of active systems do. For instance, one type of passive cooling system requires a water pond on the roof with movable shutters. These cool the home by evaporation and nocturnal radiation. They are closed during the daytime to prevent reheating. This system is most effective in areas of low humidity and clear night skies.

Active Solar Systems

Active systems, properly designed, can work in almost any area. Initial costs for an active system are generally higher than those for a passive system, but costs may be more economical in terms of Btu delivered per dollar invested. Active systems are not as architecturally restrictive as passive systems. Some solar manufacturers utilize both passive and active techniques, combining some of the economic values of the passive system with some of the versatilities of the active method. These are called *hybrid systems.*

Within the system, there may be a vast array of components such as heat exchangers, relief valves and vents, controls, piping supports, and fans. These are very difficult for the average person to evaluate. However, all solar heating systems **(Figure 6-6)** consist of three basic parts: (1) collector, (2) storage system, and (3) distribution system.

363

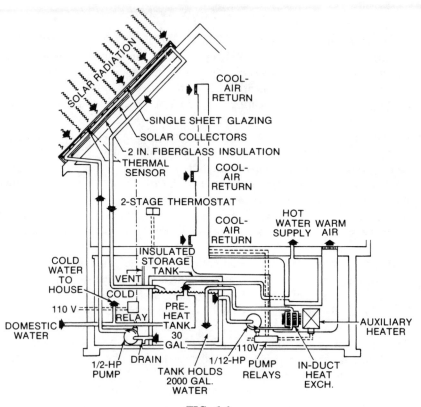

FIG. 6-6

The Collector

This is the key to any solar system. It picks up the widely scattered solar energy, transforms it into heat, and allows us to carry it away for use. There are many types of solar collectors, but by far the most common is the flat-plate type. This is essentially a flat black metal plate housed in an insulated box with one or more glass covers. The sun shines into the box through the covers and strikes the black plate. There the sun's heat is concentrated. The insulated box keeps the heat from escaping until it can be carried off for use.

The average collector is about 55 percent efficient. This means it captures about 55 percent of the solar energy striking it. However, when you buy a collector, you are not really interested in efficiency percentages. What is important is dollar efficiency. How many Btu will the collector produce for every

364

dollar it costs? A collector that is only 10 percent efficient yet costs just $2 a square foot is more economical than one that is 60 percent efficient but costs $20 a square foot.

All things considered, the amount of energy a given collector can produce is directly proportional to its area. Double the area of your collector array and you get twice as many Btu. In Washington, D.C., for example, the average daily solar radiation is about 357 langleys per day (**Figure 6-7**). A Langley is equal to 3.69 Btu per square foot. So Washington gets an average of 1,317 Btu per square foot every day. Thus a collector with an area of 1 square foot and an efficiency of 50 percent would gather about 659 Btu per day.

Obviously, 1 square foot of collector is not going to provide enough Btu to heat your home. Although there are many variables to take into consideration to determine the approximate area needs for a solar heating system, as a rough calculation, estimate 1 square foot of collector for every $2\frac{1}{2}$ to 4 square feet of house. If you have a well-built, 1,500-square-foot house in a cold, sunny climate, about 550 square feet of collector can supply two-thirds to three-fourths of the annual heat requirements. If the efficiencies of collectors increase in the future, the size of the collector necessary will decrease. By the way, most collectors available today cost at least $10 a square foot, so a 500-square-foot array would run at least $5,000.

AIR-TYPE COLLECTOR. We can blow air through the collector and over the heated plate. As the air passes through the collector, it picks up the heat. This type is for space heating.

LIQUID-TYPE COLLECTOR. The other way to pick up heat is to use a liquid such as water or a water/antifreeze mix. The liquid can trickle over the plate or run through pipes built into it. Either way, the liquid picks up the heat from the plate. A liquid system is best for heating domestic water supplies, and is shown schematically in **Figure 6-8.**

Speaking of hot water, the rule of thumb for the size of the collector is about 1 square foot for every gallon of hot water required every day. Not counting dishwashing and washing machines, the average family uses about 15 gallons of hot water per person. With a family of four, a typical collector area for a hot-water installation would be about 60 square feet. This would take care of 50 to 80 percent of the total hot-water needs, depending upon climate. A conventional system would supply the remainder. A system could be designed, of course, to handle nearly all hot-water needs, but it could cost several times as much.

FIG. 6-7: AVERAGE SOLAR RADIATION (LANGLEYS)

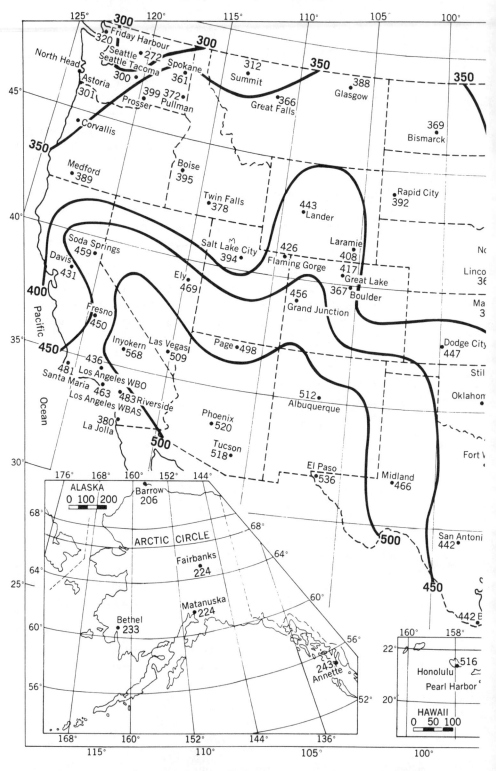

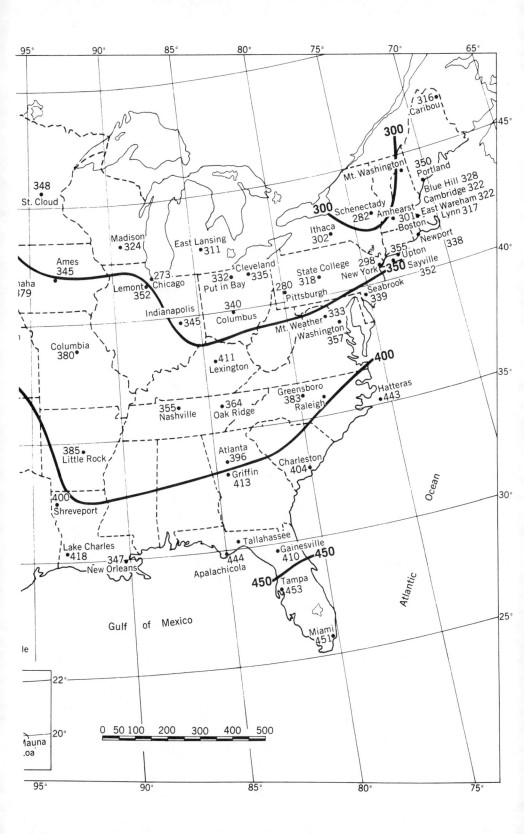

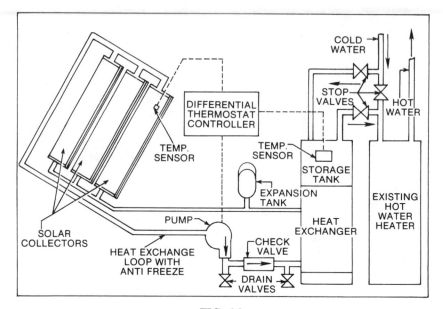

FIG. 6-8

Storage

Once the heat is picked up at the collectors, it is usually routed into storage, from which heat can be tapped during cloudy periods and at night. (Of course, the heat can also be routed past storage, directly to the home.) If the collectors are of the air type, heat is usually stored in a large bin full of rocks located in the basement. The hot air from the collectors is ducted into this bin, and the fist-size rocks pick up the heat and hold it. The air then returns to the collectors for reheating. This cycle goes on and on as long as the sun shines, with the rocks in storage becoming hotter and hotter and storing more and more energy. Figure on 50 to 60 pounds of rock for each square foot of collector. Volume of the storage area will be about ½ cubic foot per square foot of collector. For passive systems, triple these figures.

If the collectors are of the liquid type, energy is usually stored in a large tank of water. The liquid circulates through the collectors, picks up heat, then goes to the storage tank, then back to the collectors in an endless loop. With each pass through the collectors the temperature of the water rises. Soon the tank is full of hot water, and thermal energy.

The approximate volume needed for water storage is 1 to 2 gallons (0.13 to 0.25 cubic feet) for every square foot of collector. Liquid storage for a passive system will require about three times as much water.

Distribution System

This lets you extract heat from storage and use it to heat your home. If you have a hot-air collection system, you extract the heat simply by blowing house air through the bin of rocks. The air, warmed by the hot rocks, is ducted to the individual rooms of the house. If you have a hot-water storage system, you extract heat by running the hot water through a series of finned pipes in a heat exchanger. When air is blown over the fins, the air becomes heated and travels through ductwork to your home.

Another way to distribute heat involves a heat pump. Heat pumps are relatively expensive to buy, and they cost more to run than heat exchangers, but they can extract useful heat even from relatively cool storage tanks, which would be too cool to use to heat your home by any other method. This makes heat pumps useful for solar installations in areas only marginally suited to solar heating.

Backup Systems

In theory at least, a solar heating system can provide your home with 100 percent of its heating needs. Unfortunately, it cannot do so economically. Why not? Periodically each winter your home will probably be hit with several days of cloudy weather. This period, during which your system can collect no heat, might even last a week or more. A solar heating system designed to cope with a situation like this would require a tremendous amount of collector area and a huge storage tank or bin. This would make the system so expensive it could never pay for itself in saved fuel.

To solve this problem, solar heating systems are engineered to provide about 50 to 75 percent of your heating needs. The rest of your heat is provided by conventional means, such as gas, oil, coal or wood, or electricity. Doing this brings the cost of the solar system down. A system designed to provide 100 percent solar heat might cost 10 times as much while it would provide only 25 percent more *useful* heat than a solar system designed to provide 75 percent of your needs; much of the excess heat collected during sunny weather would simply be wasted.

Some solar designers have used alternate energy systems such as windpower and wood stoves for heat and power backup, thus eliminating the need for utility service. However, the user would have to be prepared to accept inconvenience and occasional discomfort.

Solar Heat and Your Home

Solar energy is not suitable for every house. You will have to know whether your house or lot can handle a large enough collector and storage system. The house should be oriented with the ridge of the roof running east and west. This lets you place your collectors on the sloping south face of the roof, for maximum exposure to the sun. Ideally, the south face of the roof should be sloped at an angle equal to your geographic latitude plus 10 degrees. The house should also be positioned on its site to take maximum advantage of shading and prevailing winds.

Since solar hardware is expensive, any home to be solar-heated should retain as much of the heat collected as long as feasible. This requires insulation to the maximum R-values as shown on the R-value **Table 7-3.** The home should also be well weatherstripped and caulked. All glass areas should be double- or triple-glazed. And the house should have a minimum amount of surface area in relation to volume.

Of course your home need not fit these requirements perfectly. Roof angles can be off by 30 degrees without great loss. If the collectors face up to 23 degrees east or west of due south, losses will amount to only about 5 percent. You can even put your collectors vertically on a fence or flat on their backs on a flat roof if desired. However, the closer to the ideal you can come, the cheaper and more effective the system will be. Do not be tempted to skimp in preparing your home for solar heat, especially in insulation, caulking, and weatherstripping. Experts say $1 spent on insulation is more effective than $2 spent on solar hardware. More tips on energy saving are given in the next chapter.

Solar Heat Systems as Investments

Is a solar heat system a good investment for you? How much will it save you? How long will it be until it pays for itself? The questions are simple, the answers are complex.

There are times when a solar system is not a smart purchase, when conventional systems are a better buy. You may find that initial costs are prohibitive, or that the time period to pay back your investment is too long for your needs, or that some of the unknowns about solar energy, such as solar rights and property appreciation or depreciation, are too risky.

One of the best ways to determine the applicability of solar energy is to undertake a life-cycle cost analysis. Simply put, this means comparing all the money spent on a system with all the money it can save. On the debit side for a solar system, you will have initial costs, anticipated annual maintenance costs, interest and principal payments on a loan (which may be pivotal), extra insurance, possible tax increases, and possible depreciation. On the plus side, you will have annual savings (as opposed to operating costs for a conventional system), possible extra appreciation for the house because of the solar system, possible tax breaks from the federal or state government, tax deductions for your interest payments, and energy inflation (this may also be pivotal). Some of these factors, such as taxes, are sometimes difficult to analyze, and you or your engineering consultant will have to determine from local, state, and federal authorities what the outlook is when it comes time to buy. Further, because some solar systems do not have a long history, annual maintenance costs may be hard to calculate. But again, a good engineering consultant will give you some estimate of how durable a system may be.

By comparing costs with savings you can find out how long you will need to recover your investment. Let us say you presently heat your home for $500 a year. You pay $7,500 for a solar system that is engineered to produce 75 percent of your needs. Thus the system will produce 75 percent of $500, or $375 worth of heat every year. Divide $375 into the cost of the system, and you get 20 years for the system to pay for itself. Is that a good deal? No. You could simply put your $7,500 in the bank, draw from it to pay for fuel, and come out ahead. But all this assumes the current price of fuel will remain constant for the next 20 years. It will not. It could double within a year or two of your installing solar heating. If that happens, payback time is cut to 10 years, and your investment makes much more sense.

Any life-cycle analysis of a solar system begins with an evaluation of the thermal energy requirements (in Btu) for the specific end use of your solar system. These requirements can then be balanced against the ability of your proposed solar system to provide the necessary heat. For this kind of work, yearly figures are of little value. Both the ability of a system to collect heat, and your needs for that heat, vary throughout the season. For that reason, you must determine your energy needs on a monthly basis.

With domestic hot water systems you will need to know how much hot water your family uses. If we take the rule of thumb that each person uses 15 gallons of hot water per day we can come up with a figure for the number of Btu required using this formula:

$$\text{Persons in family} \times 15 \text{ gallons} \times 8.3 \times \triangle T \times 30 = \text{Btu per month}$$

In this formula, 8.3 equals the number of pounds each gallon of water weighs, and $\triangle T$ is the number of degrees you will be raising the temperature of the water (difference between the temperature of the water before and after heating it). The number 30 is roughly the average number of days in a month.

EXAMPLE: Say that you have a family of four, that your cold water runs at around 50° F, and that you want to heat it up to 120° F (a 70° F rise). Your formula would look like this:

$$4 \times 15 \times 8.3 \times 70 \times 30 = 1,045,800 \text{ Btu per month}$$

To determine the heating needs of your home you will need records of your fuel use for one year in the past, plus the total number of degree days for that year. Let's say, for example, that during one heating season you burned a total of 1,200 gallons of oil and that the degree day total for that year was 4,000. Divide 4,000 degree days by 1,200 gallons and you'll see that for every 3.33 degree days you burn a gallon of oil.

Now that you know that, you can check **Table 6-3,** showing monthly degree days, and quickly compute the fuel you would use on average, each month of the year. Simply take the degree day total for any given month and divide it by 3.3 (if that is the figure you determined in the paragraph above) to find gallons of oil used per month.

The same method can be used for gas and coal heat, simply by computing fuel use in degree days per cubic foot of gas, or ton of coal. Electric heat poses a problem: It's a bit difficult to isolate the electricity used for heating from the rest of your electric bill. Still, you can get a rough estimate of the amount of electricity used for heating by subtracting the amount of electricity you use during a typical summer month, from the amount you use each month during the heating season. This system isn't perfect, but it's the best you can do unless you have your electric heat metered separately from the rest of your electricity.

At any rate, once you know how much oil, gas, coal, or electricity you use per month, you can easily convert those figures to Btu requirements. Simply multiply them by the figures given in **Table 6-5.** Note that this table assumes 75 percent efficiencies for gas, coal, and oil, and 100 percent efficiency for electric heat.

TABLE 6-5:
USEFUL BTU PER FUEL UNIT FOR FOSSIL FUELS AND ELECTRIC FURNACES IN GOOD REPAIR*

Fuel	Unit	Yield** (Btu)
No. 2 fuel oil	gallon	91,000
Liquefied petroleum gas	gallon	68,250
Natural gas	cubic foot	750
Electricity	kilowatt-hour	3,410
Coal	ton	18,750,000

*Good repair means yearly professional servicing, including thorough internal cleaning, lubrication of blowers and pumps, barometric adjustments of draft controls, etc. (electric furnaces excepted). All forced-air systems are assumed to have unobstructed ducts and filters.
**Yield is thermal energy (in Btu) delivered inside home. Allows for normal stack losses.

Shortcut Calculation of Solar Economies

Predicting future costs and benefits from a solar hot water system is at best an inexact science because there are so many uncertain variables. One big variable, of course, is the future costs of conventional energy. In different regions of the country, these costs have risen at widely differing rates. Another important variable is your own water usage. That usage may vary from year-to-year; and with a solar hot water system the more hot water you use, the more money you will save. That is, you'll save especially much if you use the system the way it should be used, when the sun is loading up your storage tank with solar Btu.

When you purchase a solar hot water system, you are paying for many years of energy all at once because these systems have negligible operating costs.

Any ethical solar dealer will tell you how many Btu your solar hot water system can deliver a year in your area. These estimates should be based on independent laboratory reports, which are required in a number of states. Be sure to ask for documentation for these estimates. Normally, though, a solar hot water system will deliver anywhere from 11 million to 15 million Btu a year, depending upon the efficiency of the system, the amount of sunshine available in your area, and how you use the system.

You can then compare the dealer's solar Btu estimates with equivalent energy costs for oil, gas, and electric heat by using **Table 6-6.** To use the table, you should determine your current costs for heating fuel—be it oil, gas, or electricity. For illustration purposes, let's say you are heating with electricity at \$.05 per kWh. First, locate \$.05 in the electricity column. Then move left horizontally to the solar column, and you can see that solar would save the equivalent of \$14.75 per million Btu. If your solar system is capable of delivering 13 million Btu a year, that means that your system has the potential of saving \$14.75 $\times$ 13 = \$191.75 in the first year compared to electric heating costs without solar. You can calculate oil and gas savings in the same manner, assuming as the table does, that gas and oil systems will operate at about 70 percent efficiency.

To project future energy savings, you can conservatively estimate that at a *minimum,* conventional energy costs will escalate at least 15 percent a year.

Take the projected annual rate of increase, multiply it by the present rate, add the results to present costs. This will give you the second-year projected rates. Continue this process until you have estimated costs for a ten year period. In this way you will have a ballpark estimate for long-range solar savings.

Note that **Table 6-6** is a short cut. Federal tax credits, maintenance costs, and interest costs for loans were not included. But if you use the table, and the calculations look appealing, you may want to explore possibilities with a few solar contractors.

TABLE 6-6:
EQUIVALENT ENERGY COSTS FOR COMPETING CONVENTIONAL FUELS

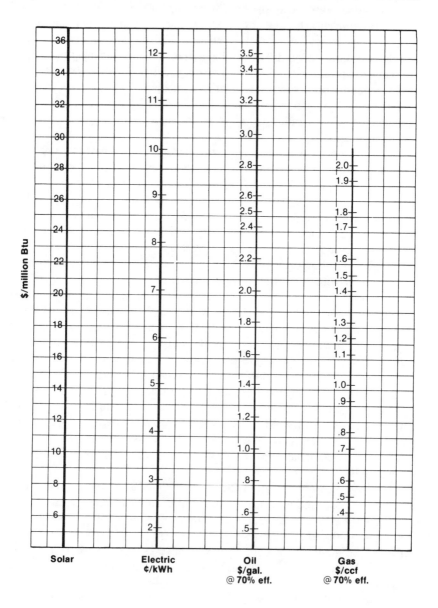

WOOD HEATING

In the past few years, wood has become a very popular fuel, and for good reason. It can cost less to heat your home with slash pine at $130 per cord than oil at $1.00 per gallon; or with red oak at $135 per cord than with liquefied petroleum gas (LPG) at $0.68 per gallon; or with black birch at an astronomical $325 per cord than with electricity at $0.08 per kilowatt-hour.

Calculating the Economics of Wood as Fuel*

What about your home? What about fuel prices in your area? The following tables and calculations might seem imposing at first glance, but your calculations based on them require only three operations—addition, multiplication, and division—to figure approximately how much you would save or lose by switching from your present fuel to wood. Here, step by step, is how.

STEP 1: Read the following descriptions and find what most nearly matches the wood-burner you will use (**Figure 6-9**). If you do not have specific plans for burning wood, try using the figures for airtight or high-efficiency stoves in the following tables. These types provide the best return on your fuel-wood dollars and will give you the greatest opportunity to make substantial savings over your present fossil fuel.

Simple fireplaces are ordinary metal or masonry units with standard grates.

High-efficiency fireplaces are equipped with efficiency-boosting devices such as internal ductwork or hollow grates through which air or water is circulated.

Box stoves are freestanding metal wood-burners that completely enclose a fire. All wood stoves, from expensive cast-iron kitchen ranges to low-cost sheet-steel cabin warmers, fall into this category unless they conform to one of the following two descriptions.

Airtight stoves feature tight-fitting draft controls and seams that either are welded shut or packed with a ceramic material. Stoves of this type burn wood very slowly and effectively.

High-efficiency stoves are those with built-in heat exchangers and scientifically designed internal flow patterns. Stoves such as these burn the

---

*This section originally appeared in slightly altered form in the February 1978 issue of *Popular Science* magazine under the title "Wood as Fuel." It is here reprinted with permission of its author, F. S. Langa, and *Popular Science.*

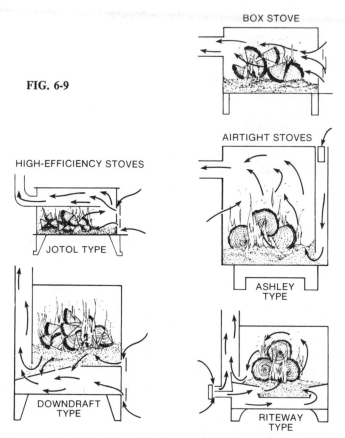

FIG. 6-9

wood from end to end and send the hot smoke through the heat exchanger in an efficient S-shaped pattern. Vortex stoves spiral the smoke to the flue; downdraft stoves burn their fuel upside down, drawing flammable gases given off by the heated wood through a bed of coals for complete combustion. All stoves of this type are expensive but, in terms of fuel economy, well worth the extra cost.

STEP 2:   Make a list of the woods you will be burning. If you do not know which woods are available in your area, you can easily find out by calling a wood dealer listed in newspaper ads or the Yellow Pages, calling your county forestry agent, asking a knowledgeable friend, or taking to the woods with a field guidebook for trees.

Wood is sold by the cord. If you can buy "straight" cords—that is, cords made up of only one wood species—simply note what that species is. But if, like most people, you can obtain only mixed cords, made up of a number of different woods, make a list of all the woods contained in a typical cord. The following is a typical way of listing an average cord.

376

Wood type	Percentage of cord
American beech	60
Paper birch	20
Red oak	10
Hop hornbeam	5
Miscellaneous	5

STEP 3: Use **Table 6-7** to find the net heat output of your combination of wood and wood-burner. (The table takes into account the gross fuel values of the 62 listed species and the efficiencies of the listed wood-burners.)

If you will be burning straight cords, simply find your fuel wood listed at left in the table and read across to the column headed by the type of wood-burner you will be using. The number listed at the intersection represents the amount of heat, in millions of Btu, that a cord of your wood will deliver when burned in the wood-burner of your choice.

For mixed cords, use the list you made in step 2 and the column in **Table 6-7,** page 378, indicating the type of wood-burner you will be using. Look up each wood on your list and jot down its Btu per cord. For example, if we use a high-efficiency stove, then, looking up each of the woods listed in step 2, we would write:

Wood type	Fraction of cord × Figs. from Table 6-7		Actual Btu (millions)
American beech	0.60	× 12.6	= 7.56
Paper birch	0.20	× 11.4	= 2.28
Red oak	0.10	× 12.6	= 1.26
Hop hornbeam	0.05	× 13.8	= 0.69
Miscellaneous	0.05	× 11.4	= 0.57
Total			= 12.36

Our typical mixed cord, burned in a high-efficiency stove, would deliver about 12.36 million Btu.

STEP 4: **Table 6-5** lists the four standard home-heating fuels and the thermal energy in Btu per gallon, cubic foot, or kilowatt-hour that these fuels produce when used in standard furnaces. Again, as in **Table 6-7,** furnace efficiencies are already taken into account. Write down the thermal energy in Btu per unit for the type of fuel you now use. This is the figure against which wood's heating ability will be compared. For in-

TABLE 6-7:
THERMAL ENERGY VALUES OF SPECIES OF WOOD IN VARIETIES OF STOVES (IN MILLIONS OF BTU PER CORD)

Wood dried 8 months	Simple fireplace	High-efficiency fireplace	Box stove	Airtight stove	High-efficiency stove
Apple, black birch, dogwood, hickory, hop hornbeam, live oak, locust, persimmon, shadbush, slash pine, yew	2.3	5.75	6.9	11.5	13.8
American beech, American hornbeam, black ash, black walnut, longleaf pine, red ash, red oak, rock elm, sugar maple, white ash, yellow birch, yellow pine	2.1	5.25	6.3	10.5	12.6
Cherry, holly pine, juniper, loblolly pine, nut pine, paper birch, shortleaf pine, spruce, tamarack, western larch	1.9	4.75	5.7	9.5	11.4
American elm, bald cypress, black gum, chestnut, Douglas fir, gray birch, magnolia, Norway pine, pitch pine, red maple, sycamore, white cedar	1.7	4.25	5.1	8.5	10.2
Alder, balsam fir, black spruce, black willow, butternut, catalpa, hemlock, ponderosa pine, Sitka spruce, tulip poplar	1.5	3.75	4.5	7.5	9.0
Aspen, balsam poplar, basswood, cottonwood, noble fir, sugar pine, white pine	1.3	3.25	3.9	6.5	7.8

stance, if your home has a liquefied-petroleum-gas (LPG) furnace, reading the row from **Table 6-5,** you would note 68,250 Btu per gallon.

STEP 5: Divide the figure you got in step 3 (Btu per cord) by the figure you just got from **Table 6-5** (Btu per fossil-fuel unit). Your answer (the quotient) tells you how much of your present fuel it would take to match the heat output of your combination of fuel wood and wood-burner; or, in other words, your wood's fossil-fuel equivalence:

$$\frac{\text{Figures from step 3}}{\text{Figures from step 4}} = \text{fossil-fuel equivalence}$$

In our example:

$$\frac{12,360,000}{68,250} = 181$$

This means that we would have to burn about 181 gallons of LPG to get the same amount of heat as that produced by one of our mixed cords burned in a high-efficiency stove. Or, to put it another way, each of our mixed cords would save or replace 181 gallons of LPG.

STEP 6: If wood burning is to be economical, then the fuel wood obviously must cost less than the fossil fuel it replaces. Take the figure you just found in step 5 and multiply it by the unit price you are now paying for that fuel (include all temporary surcharges, fuel adjustments, and so forth). Your answer tells you the maximum allowable price you can afford to pay for a cord of your wood; beat that price and you are on your way to saving money. For instance, if each of your mixed cords replaces 181 gallons of LPG, at a price of, say, $0.68 per gallon, it is worth

$$181 \text{ gallons} \times \$0.68 = \$123.08$$

Therefore, if you can buy a mixed cord equivalent to our typical one for less than $123.08, you will be saving money by burning wood over LPG. Of course, you have to consider the convenience of your present fuel against the complications of buying, stacking, stoking, and regularly visiting the woodpile. But, if your calculation shows it, you may find enough saving there to completely offset the purchase price of a wood stove and the extra work required to operate it.

Computing Cordage

A cord of wood is a pile 4 feet wide, 4 feet high, and 8 feet long (4 × 4 × 8) and so contains 128 cubic feet. (Actually, because of spaces between logs, only about 85 cubic feet of this is solid, usable fuel; the tables allow for this.) Thus, to find the contents of a pile of wood in cords, multiply the length, width, and height together, and divide by 128. For example, to find the number of cords in a pile 4 by 4 by 70 feet, proceed as follows:

$$4 \times 4 \times 70 = 1,120 \text{ cubic feet} \div 128 = 8.75 \text{ or } 8\frac{3}{4} \text{ cords}$$

379

Calculating the Efficiency of a Wood-Burner*

When you burn wood in your stove or fireplace, it gives off heat—a certain number of Btu. Some of those Btu warm your house; some go up the chimney with the flue gases and are lost. Efficiency is a measure of how much of the heat does useful work, compared with the total amount generated by the burning of the fuel. It is expressed as a percentage. An efficiency of 75 percent, for example, means that you are making use of 75 percent of the heat generated by the wood while the other 25 percent is going up the chimney.

In principle, measuring efficiency is simple. You measure the amount of fuel used and calculate how much heat it generates. Then you find out how much of this heat is being delivered to your home to warm it. With these numbers

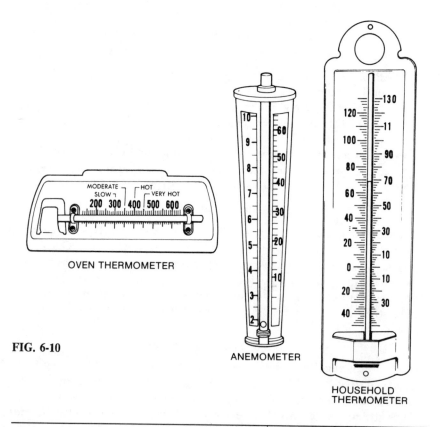

OVEN THERMOMETER

ANEMOMETER

HOUSEHOLD THERMOMETER

FIG. 6-10

---

*This section originally appeared in slightly altered form in the January 1979 issue of *Popular Science* magazine under the title "Woodburner Efficiency." It is here reprinted with permission of its author, James Trefil, and *Popular Science.*

TABLE 6-8:
THERMAL ENERGY CONTENT OF HARDWOODS*

Air-dried weight (lbs.) per cu. ft.	Per cord	Type of wood	Millions of Btu per cord
53	4,505	Shagbark and pignut hickory	31.535
52	4,420	Eastern hop hornbeam	30.940
51	4,335	Mockernut hickory, dogwood	30.345
49	4,165	American hornbeam	29.155
48	4,080	White oak, sweet birch, black locust	28.560
47	3,995	Chestnut (rock) oak, bitternut hickory	27.965
46	3,910	Red oak, Pacific madrone	27.370
45	3,825	American beech	26.775
44	3,740	Sugar maple	26.180
43	3,655	Black oak, southern red oak	25.585
42	3,570	White ash	24.995
40	3,400	Yellow birch, California white oak	23.800
39	3,315	California laurel	23.205
38	3,230	Red maple	22.610
37	3,145	Paper birch	22.015
36	3,060	Black cherry	21.420
34	2,890	American elm, sycamore	20.230
32	2,720	Sassafras	19,040
26	2,210	Tulip tree	15.470
25	2,125	Quaking aspen	14.875

*Figures are based on average weights published by the American Forestry Association.

you can easily calculate efficiency by dividing the heat content (in Btu) of the wood burned into the heat actually delivered to the house. In practice, it takes a few more steps than that, plus three instruments (**Figure 6-10**): oven thermometer, anemometer, and household thermometer. A bathroom scale can be used to weigh the wood.

Table 6-8 lists hardwoods by rates of thermal energy (in Btu) per cord.

Note the great range of weight given for the wood per cubic foot. A pound of any well-dried hardwood will have about the same heat content—6,900 Btu per pound—no matter what tree it comes from. Softwoods, because of the greater content of volatile chemicals, have a somewhat higher value—around 7,600 Btu per pound. But a pound of softwood takes up more space than a pound of hardwood, so you have to put more pine logs into a fire to get a given amount of heat than you would if you were burning oak. As a matter of convenience, as well as creosote reduction, you will probably want to use hardwood.

To find your system's total thermal energy input in Btu, multiply the total poundage of hardwood used by 6,900 and the total poundage of softwood used by 7,600.

Calculating Waste Heat

Measuring useful heat actually delivered to your home is difficult. It is easier to measure waste heat. Most waste heat goes up the flue that carries exhaust gases to the outside. The amount of heat lost depends on flue size, rate of flow, and temperature of the flue gas.

Begin by calculating the flue's cross-sectional area. If it is square or rectangular, multiply the two dimensions. If it is circular, the area is π times the square of the radius. For convenience, get the area in square feet. So if you measured the dimensions in inches, divide the final answer by 144.

To measure the velocity of the gas leaving the flue, you can use a hand-held anemometer (wind gauge). However, the problem with this gauge is that the air flow you want to measure is moving upward (coming out of the chimney) rather than parallel to the ground. Since the gauge depends partly on gravity, you cannot hold it perpendicular to the flow as you would in measuring a normal wind. To get around this, hold the gauge in the flue gases at an angle of 45°, with the top of the gauge tilted back away from the chimney opening. The airspeed figure you obtain will be in miles per hour. To convert it to feet per second, multiply it by 1.47. This will give your velocity (v) in feet per second.

You measure the temperature of the flue gas in the same way you measure any other temperature, with a thermometer. An ordinary glass mercury thermometer is good for most high-efficiency wood stoves. In fireplaces, where the gases are at higher temperatures, use an oven thermometer. Once you know the temperature, you can figure out how much waste heat is being carried out with each cubic foot of the gas from the equation:

$$q = C \, (T_{Fl} - T_{in})$$

q = heat energy (in Btu) of a cubic foot of gas

T_{Fl} = temperature as measured at the top of the flue

T_{in} = temperature inside your home
(the temperature at which the gas started its journey)

The quantity C is called the specific heat of the gas and represents the amount of energy (in Btu) needed to raise the temperature of 1 cubic foot of the gas 1° F. For the kinds of flue-gas temperatures you will encounter, C (in Btu per cubic foot) is given by:

$$C = (1.9 - 0.002T_{Fl}) \times 0.01$$

Finally, the total heat loss Q (in Btu per second) in a flue of cross-section area A through which gas is moving with velocity v is given by:

$$Q = Avq$$

Here is how all of this works in practice. For example, suppose you found that airspeed from a circulating-air fireplace was 11.6 feet per second and the flue had a temperature of 269° F. The inside room temperature was 65° F, and the flue area was 0.52 square feet. Then, the specific heat is given by:

$$C = (1.9 - 0.002 \ T_{Fl})(0.01) = [1.9 - (0.002)(269)] \ (0.01)$$

$$C = 0.0136 \text{ Btu per cubic foot}$$

So the heat loss per cubit foot was:

$$q = C \ (T_{Fl} - T_{in})$$

$$q = 0.0136 \times (269 - 65) = 2.77 \text{ Btu}$$

And the heat loss was:

$$Q = Avg$$

$$Q = (0.52)(11.6)(2.77) = 16.7 \text{ Btu per second}$$

If this flow persisted for 1 minute, the total heat lost would be

$$(16.7)(60) = 1,002 \text{ Btu per minute during that particular minute}$$

Losses by chimney conduction. There is one more source of heat loss sometimes: the amount the chimney heats up. Since part of the chimney is outside of the house, heat is lost through conduction in that outside portion. If only a short run of the chimney is exposed to the outside, this extra loss is not important, but for tall outdoor chimneys it can be significant.

383

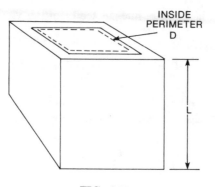

INSIDE
PERIMETER
D

L

FIG. 6-11

You can find how much heat is being lost through conduction by consulting **Figure 6-11.** Call the inside perimeter of the flue D and the length of exposed chimney L. Heat lost each hour through condition is:

$$Q = \frac{DL \ (T_{Fl} - T_{out})}{R}$$

T_{out} = outside air temperature

R = heat resistance of the chimney material

For masonry chimneys, R has a value of 0.25 for each inch of material between the flue and the outside, while for insulated metal chimneys it has a value of about 3 for each inch of asbestos.

An example of a heat-loss calculation for the fireplace mentioned above is as follows: The length D of the interior perimeter of the flue was 3 feet, and the chimney stood 4 feet above the roof. It had 4 inches of masonry in the walls, so the R was equal to 1. For the same flue temperature quoted above (269° F) on a day when the outside temperature was 50° F, the heat loss was:

$$Q = \frac{3 \times 4 \times 219}{1} = 2,628 \text{ Btu per hour}$$

Comparing this number with the amount of heat going up the stack shows that this particular source of heat loss is small but not negligible for this system. Depending on whether your chimney is located inside or outside of your house and how tall it is, you may find this source of heat loss important or insignificant.

Circulating-Air Fireplace vs. Airtight Stove

To see how all of this works in practice, let us compare two systems: a circulating-air fireplace and an airtight stove. The fireplace is equipped with a 16-foot masonry chimney, of which all but the top 4 feet is inside the house, while the stove has a 6-inch asbestos-insulated pipe running up to a 14-foot ceiling. In both cases, several hours' supply of well-dried wood is weighed and fed to the fire as needed, and flue temperatures and gas velocities are taken periodically to monitor heat loss. The results are as follows:

	Fireplace	Stove
Amount of wood (lbs.)	41.2	6.7
Type of wood	maple/locust	locust
Energy input (Btu)	284,000	46,000
Interval between measurements (min.)	30	60
Length of experiment (hr.)	3	4
Typical gas velocity (ft. per sec.)	8	3
Typical temperature (°F)	250	120
Total heat loss through flue (Btu)	190,000	11,200
Conduction loss (Btu)	7,700	—
Total useful heat (Btu)	86,000	34,800
Efficiency (percent)	30	75

For the fireplace, which has a fairly rapid response to the addition of wood, velocity and temperature readings, taken every half hour, get the total heat loss under the assumption that the same temperature and velocity will exist until the time of the next reading. For the stove the changes in the state of the fire occur more slowly, and hourly readings do the job. After all the readings are taken, the hourly heat losses are computed and then averaged out. For example, if at three different hours heat-loss measurements are 1,100, 1,000, and 1,150 Btu per minutes, the average, 1,083 Btu per minutes, is used in the calculations.

When you are finished, the efficiency you calculate is the efficiency of the entire heating system, not just that of the stove or fireplace by itself. For example, a lot of the heat delivered by the fireplace comes from heat conducted through the interior masonry. Had this heat been lost (for example, by having the entire 16-foot chimney outside), the efficiency of the system would have been substantially lower. Since 4 feet of exposed chimney lost 7,700 Btu during the trial, you can estimate this reduction in efficiency by assuming the loss from a 16-foot chimney to be $4 \times 7,700 = 30,800$ Btu. In this case the efficiency would have been 22 percent instead of 30 percent.

The method just described is an adaptation and simplification of an engineering technique known as the "stack-loss method." Like most simplifications, it tends to gloss over some potentially important points. We have described how you can measure the heat content of flue gases, but there are other ways energy can be carried up the chimney. The most important of these is by unburned or incompletely burned chemicals that can be present in the smoke of a wood fire. These chemicals represent a loss of potential heat energy. However, without getting the kind of complicated chemical-analysis test equipment used by professional engineers there is not much you can do to estimate how much.

SOLVING VENTILATION PROBLEMS

Proper house ventilation is necessary the year round, as indicated by **Figure 6-12.** In the summer, for instance, heat often builds up in attic spaces to 135° F; it may even reach 160° F when the sun beats down on the roof. This heat soon penetrates through ceilings (even if insulated) into the living area below. Thus, if you and your house are to live comfortably together, you need a proper ventilation system. As mentioned earlier, proper ventilation will substantially reduce air-conditioning costs. The coefficient of heat gain at a dry-wall ceiling is 0.12 Btu per square foot per hour per degree of temperature difference. With a house of 2,000 square feet, an inside temperature of 75° F, and an attic temperature of 125° F, the heat gain is given by:

$$2{,}000 \text{ square feet} \times 0.12 \text{ Btu} \times 50° \text{ F} = 12{,}000 \text{ Btu}$$

This is the equivalent of 1 ton of cooling. Reducing cooling requirements by this amount with attic ventilation potentially can save about 25 percent of air-conditioning costs in a home this size. In houses without air conditioning, the living area will be kept at a more comfortable temperature level by ventilating the attic.

In winter, open attic vents let moisture vapor escape. This vapor comes from various household appliances, such as dishwashers, dryers, and humidifiers. As well, daily use of the shower and tub, and also cooking vapors, all contribute to excessive moisture within your home. When moisture-laden air from the living area rises to the attic, problems will result. Condensed moisture can soak insulation, impairing its efficiency. It can stain or crumble ceilings and blister exterior paint. Frozen and thawed, it can damage roof boards and shingles.

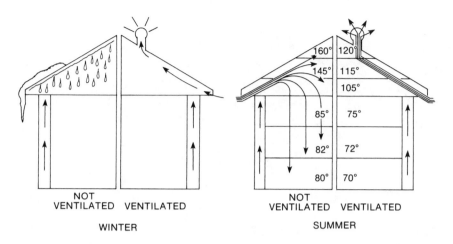

NOT
VENTILATED   VENTILATED

WINTER

NOT
VENTILATED   VENTILATED

SUMMER

FIG. 6-12

Ventilation Systems

There are two types of ventilation systems: natural (or static) ventilation and power ventilation **(Figure 6-13).** The system best suited for your house will depend on the type of roof construction and whether you are planning to ventilate an existing home or are constructing a new home.

An important aspect, common to both the natural and power ventilation systems, is the need for an intake ventilator for fresh air and an outlet ventilator for hot or moist air.

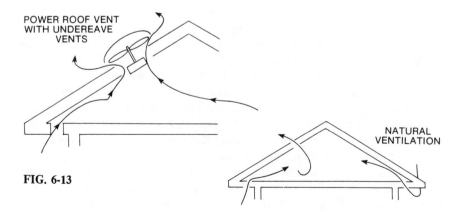

POWER ROOF VENT
WITH UNDEREAVE
VENTS

NATURAL
VENTILATION

FIG. 6-13

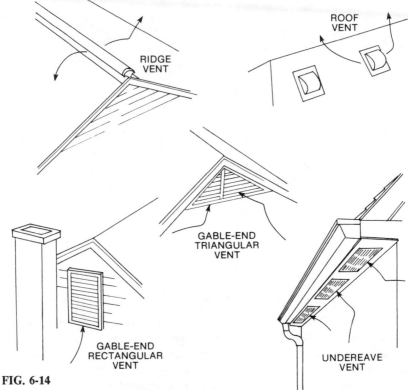

RIDGE
VENT

ROOF
VENT

GABLE-END
TRIANGULAR
VENT

GABLE-END
RECTANGULAR
VENT

UNDEREAVE
VENT

FIG. 6-14

Natural Ventilation Systems

These employ fixed or nonmechanical devices usually referred to as ventilators. These ventilators are installed in openings in an attic space and must be properly positioned to take advantage of the natural flow of air.

There are five basic types of attic ventilators **(Figure 6-14)**: ridge, roof, undereave, gable-end rectangular, and gable-end triangular. These do satisfactory jobs with most roof designs. Also they blend with any style of architecture.

Ridge ventilators with undereave strip ventilators are regarded as the best natural ventilation system. Ridge vents are designed to provide a continuous opening along the entire ridgeline of a pitched roof. These vents are formed to prevent rain and snow from entering the attic, but to allow a full flow of air to be ventilated from the attic. The intake ventilator, to complete this effective system, is the undereave strip vent. It is recommended that these intake vents be installed in the roof overhang on both sides of the house. Since the installation of ridge vents is a fairly big job, most homeowners select this system when building a new home, so the vents can be installed at the time the roof is being constructed.

Optional systems classified as natural ventilation are also available. Roof vents with undereave vents provide a good ventilation system for a hip-style roof, while gable-end roofs may be equipped with either a rectangular or triangular gable-end vent mounted in the high point of the gable. In all cases, intake undereave ventilators complete the system.

Power Ventilation Systems

These include mechanical devices to control the air change in an attic space. Power ventilators are usually equipped with automatic thermostats which activate the unit at a preselected temperature and shut the unit off when the attic temperature is sufficiently reduced. In this way, power ventilation provides positive air removal. It removes excess summer heat on hot days, and on cold days the optional humidistat will actuate the unit to remove excess winter moisture. Thus the power ventilator moves more air and with better control than methods that depend on the natural flow of air or on inconstant winds.

Power ventilators with undereave vents for intake provide an extremely effective attic venting system. This system is recommended for existing structures because of its ease of installation, although it is not limited to this application and is found in new-home construction as well. The power ventilator typically is placed on the rear slope of the roof, near the peak and centered, with air intakes at the eaves. It reaches all attic space efficiently. If a roof location is not practical or desirable, a power gable ventilator may be installed vertically on the gable sidewall.

A power ventilator automatically keeps homes cooler and reduces the high cost of air conditioning. Obviously, lifting such a summer heat load with a unit that uses only about the energy of a 75-watt light bulb (part-time) saves significant electrical energy, how much depending on various factors of individual housing and living characteristics. Direct field results conducted by the National Bureau of Standards indicate 10 to 30 percent reductions in air-conditioning load. When installing an air conditioner, initial savings resulting from the purchase of a smaller-capacity unit are often possible when an automatic power ventilation system exists. And some homeowners, especially in the North, require only the use of a power ventilator system for summer comfort.

How Much Ventilation is Needed?

Natural Venting

To determine how much vent area you will need with a natural system, you will need to know the floor area of your attic. This is easily obtained by multiplying width times length, in feet. If your attic is oddly shaped, break it

FIG. 6-15

down into a series of rectangles, find their areas, and then add them all together as shown in **Figure 6-15.**

If your attic insulation has a vapor barrier on the side facing the living space, the total free area of your venting should be equal to the floor area divided by 300. Free area is the clear or free opening of the ventilators through which air can move. Roughly half this area should be in the soffits if possible, and the rest in the gable or ridge of the roof.

If your attic has no vapor barrier, you will need twice as much free area or floor area divided by 150. Thus for an attic measuring 30 by 50 (1,500 square feet) you would need 10 square feet of vent area without a vapor barrier, and only 5 square feet with a vapor barrier.

Power Venting

If you plan to install a power ventilator or fan, its size will also depend on attic floor area. It should move enough air to complete 10 changes of attic air per hour. Fans are rated in cubic feet per minute, so you will need one with a CFM rating high enough to achieve that figure of 10 air changes per hour (ach).

Here's an easy way to figure your requirements in cfm:

1. Multiply length times width to find attic area.
2. Multiply the area by 0.7 to get cfm requirements for the fan. Note, however, that if you have a dark roof it will absorb more heat than a light one, and you will need to compensate. Do so by multiplying your cfm rating by 1.15.

   Warning: The cfm rating of a fan may be measured under static air pressure or at "free air delivery." If you are buying a fan rated at free air delivery, multiply its cfm rating by 0.75.

For example, if your attic is 40 × 50 feet, you would first multiply those dimensions to get 2,000 square feet. To get the fan cfm requirements, you then multiply the area (2,000) by 0.7. That gives 1,400 cfm. If the roof is dark, you multiply 1,400 cfm by 1.15 and come up with a 1,610 cfm.

This rule-of-thumb computation is easily verified by **Figure 6-16,** which computes the volume of air enclosed in an attic. Multiply this volume by 10 to get the total volume of air that must be moved to provide 10 changes per hour. Now, compare this number with the result of multiplying our example rating of 1,400 cfm by 60 minutes per hour.

Note that a powered vent can not work effectively if the attic does not have intake vents that allow fresh air to flow in and replace the air exhausted by the fan. Without them the fan will fail by working against a vacuum and will not be able to move its rated volume of air. These intake vents should be equal in free area to $\frac{1}{150}$ of attic floor area. For best results, however, the intake vents should be properly placed to allow air flow throughout the attic. If, for example, the fan is mounted on a gable, the intake vents should be at the opposite end of the attic, and in the soffits. If the fan is mounted near the peak of the roof, several small intakes spaced along both soffits would provide the best air flow pattern.

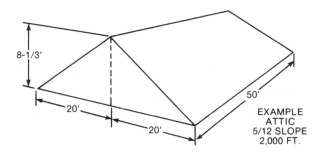

8-1/3'
20'
20'
50'
EXAMPLE
ATTIC
5/12 SLOPE
2,000 FT.

A
VOLUME OF ATTIC EQUALS (2) x (1/2) x (8-1/3) x (20) x (50)
EQUALS 8,330 CUBIC FEET
FOR 10 CHANGES OF ATTIC AIR PER HOUR, 10 TIMES 8,330 = 83,300 CU. FT./HR.

B
IF FAN CAPACITY IS 1,400 CUBIC FEET PER MINUTE
$\frac{1,400 \text{ cu. ft.}}{\text{min.}}$ X $\frac{60 \text{ min.}}{\text{hr.}}$ = $\frac{84,000 \text{ cu. ft.}}{\text{hr.}}$

A IS EQUAL TO B
THERE OUR RULE OF THUMB USING 0.7 IS JUSTIFIED

FIG. 6-16

TABLE 6-9:
RECOMMENDED ROOM VENTILATORS

Wall and ceiling fans	Recommended air changes per hr.	Formula (8-ft. ceiling)
Kitchen	15	Square feet of floor $\times$ 2 = cfm *Example:* 100 square feet $\times$ 2 = 200 cfm
Bathroom	8	Square feet of floor $\times$ 1.07 = cfm* *Example:* 55 square feet $\times$ 1.07 = 60 cfm (rounded)*
Recreation room, utility room, laundry room, basements, other rooms	6	Square feet of floor $\times$ 0.8 = cfm *Example:* 150 square feet $\times$ 0.8 = 120 cfm

*Formula for roof power vent.

Ventilating Fans for Other Rooms

Other rooms in a house can also use ventilating fans. **Tables 6-9** and **6-10** show how to figure cfm and the proper ventilation recommended by Home Ventilating Institute (HVI) and the U.S. Department of Housing and Urban Development/Federal Housing Administration (HUD/FHA).

Often it is better to select a fan with more than a minimum capacity and control it with a multispeed switch, such as a solid-state control. The fan will run very quietly during normal use at low or medium speeds but still have extra capacity when needed.

Crawl-Space Ventilation

At least two vents, opposite each other, should be provided in an unheated crawl space. Basic minimum opening size, with moisture seal (polyethylene sheeting 4 mil or thicker or 55-pound asphalt roll roofing, lapped at least 3 inches) on the ground: 1 square foot of vent for each 1,500 square feet of crawl space area. Basic minimum opening size without moisture seal: 1 square foot for each 150 square feet of area. Four vents, one on each of the four sides, are recommended. If crawl-space vents are protected by screening or rain louvers, the basic opening size should be increased as shown in **Table 6-11.**

TABLE 6-10:
MATCHING VENTILATION RATES TO ROOM AREAS FOR HVI*
STANDARD VENTILATION

Recom- mended cfm	Kitchen area (sq. ft.)	Laundry, family, or recreation room area (sq. ft.)	Bathroom cfm	sq. ft.
40	—	50	40	35
60	—	75	50	45
80	—	100	60	55
100	—	125	70	65
120	60	150	80	75
140	70	175	90	85
160	80	200	100	95
180	90	225	110	105
200	100	250		
250	125	310		
300	150	375		
350	175	435		
400	200	500		
450	225	560		
500	250	625		
550	275	685		

*Ceiling height is 8 feet.

TABLE 6-11:
CRAWL-SPACE VENTILATION

Type of covering	Size of opening
¼-inch hardware cloth	1 × net vent area
¼-inch hardware cloth and rain louvers	2 × net vent area
8-mesh screen	1¼ × net vent area
8-mesh screen and rain louvers	2¼ × net vent area
16-mesh screen	2 × net vent area
16-mesh screen and rain louvers	3 × net vent area

PLUMBING MATH

Math can be a great help when planning and installing plumbing. As shown in **Figure 6-17**, the total plumbing system includes all pipes, fixtures, and fittings used to convey water into and out of the home. It can be divided into three basic areas: (1) the water supply system; (2) the drainage system; and (3) the fixtures. The object of it all, of course, is to make water available where wanted in the home, and to get rid of water, plus wastes, that has served its purpose.

Water Supply System

In every plumbing system, there must be a source of water for the pipes to carry to the fixtures. This water supply system must be adequate to carry pure water for drinking, supply a sufficient quantity of water at any outlet in the system, at correct operating pressure, and furnish occupants with hot or cold water, as required.

In most incorporated areas the water source is a public or privately operated water "works" from which purified water is distributed through mains to which each user can be connected by arrangement with the proper authorities. However, if such a source is not available, you can install a private source of

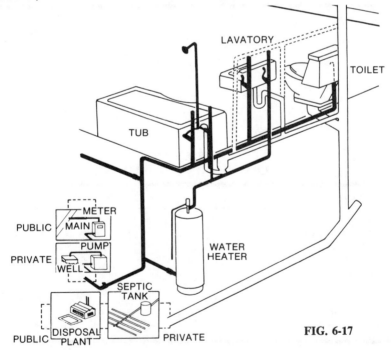

FIG. 6-17

TABLE 6-12:
APPROXIMATE WATER SUPPLY REQUIREMENTS

Home fixture	Requirement
Filling ordinary lavatory	2 gallons
Filling average bath tub	30 gallons
Flushing toilet	6 gallons
Taking shower bath	Up to 60 gallons
Running dishwashing machine	3 gallons per load
Operating automatic laundry machine	Up to 50 gallons per load
Backwashing domestic water softener	Up to 100 gallons

Yard fixtures	
½-inch hose with nozzle	200 gallons per hour
¾-inch hose with nozzle	300 gallons per hour
Lawn sprinkler	120 gallons per hour

your own. In the latter case, the most efficient source in rural areas is the drilled well. In most cases, this is a job for a professional well digger. Wells are expensive and require special equipment for drilling. Local experts will be able to provide the answers to your questions concerning locating the well and its necessary equipment.

If you have a good well (ample water), all that you need to obtain "city-type" water service is proper pumping equipment. When selecting a water system, here are the three factors that must be kept in mind:

A. WATER NEEDED. How much water in gallons per hour (gph) or gallons per minute (gpm) do you need? This will tell you what size pump to use. First you must determine the rate of flow, or capacity, which might be needed at peak periods. Each outlet that might be turned on and left on for a while requires at least 4 gallons per minute. Such outlets include shower stalls, lawn sprinklers, stock troughs, automatic washers. These are "continuous-use" outlets (Table 6-12).

In a one-bathroom house, enough water should be available for two continuous-use outlets to be in operation at the same time. This means we must have at least 8 gallons per minute, or gallons per hour (8 gal. × 60 minutes = 480 gph).

Another way of determining the amount of water necessary is to consider the number of fixtures. For example, suppose the number of fixtures in a typical one bathroom house were as follows: 1 bathtub and/or shower, 1 lavatory, 1 toilet, 2 sinks and/or laundry tubs, 1 automatic clothes washer, 1 automatic dishwasher, 1 garden hose outlet. For a total of 8.

395

Using the formula

$$gph = number\ of\ fixtures \times 60$$

The pump capacity should be ($8 \times 60 = 480$) at least 480 gph. It generally is wise to figure on one extra fixture when ordering a pump. Of course, be sure the well can provide the quantity of water needed; otherwise plan for an extra-large tank.

B. SHALLOW OR DEEP WELL? What is the total suction lift? To answer this question, proceed as follows:

1. Determine the vertical distance from the tank (basement floor or pump-house floor) to the pumping level of water in the well. If this vertical distance is more than 25 feet, use a deep-well pump and skip paragraphs 2 and 3 below. If vertical distance is less than 25 feet, a shallow-well pump can be used. Continue to paragraph 2.

2. Determine the friction loss in the suction pipe, using **Table 6-13.** The suction pipe is that pipe which conducts the water from the well into the suction opening of a shallow-well pump. To do this you need to know: (a) Capacity needed at peak periods; (b) overall length of suction pipe; and (c) size of pipe to be used. The larger the pipe, the lower the friction and the higher the final usable capacity. However, to keep the cost down, there is no need to use any pipe larger than is required. For example, if the capacity needed is about 480 gph, the overall length of suction pipe is 100 feet, and the pipe size is 1 inch, the resulting friction loss from **Table 6-13** would be 4.54 feet.

3. Determine total suction lift. Add vertical distance and friction loss obtained in paragraphs 1 and 2 above. Thus, if vertical distance is 17 feet and friction loss is 4.54 feet, total suction lift is 21.54 feet, or rounded off as 22 feet. We have now determined that we can use a shallow-well pump. We also know that the pump selected must be able to deliver 480 gallons per hour or more from a 22-foot total suction lift.

   We do not know the pressure at which the pump must deliver 480 gph. A pressure of 20 pounds per square inch for pressure-switch cut-in may or may not be adequate (**Tables 6-14** and **6-15**).

4. If the vertical distance from pump tank location to the pumping level of the water in the well, as determined in paragraph 1, is more than 25 feet, use a deep-well pump.

396

TABLE 6-13:
FRICTION LOSS TABLES FROM STANDARDS OF THE HYDRAULIC INSTITUTE

FRICTION OF WATER PER EACH 100 FEET OF NEW STEEL PIPE

Gal. per min.	Gal. per hr.	3/8" Pipe Ft.	Lbs.	1/2" Pipe Ft.	Lbs.	3/4" Pipe Ft.	Lbs.	1" Pipe Ft.	Lbs.	1 1/4" Pipe Ft.	Lbs.	1 1/2" Pipe Ft.	Lbs.	2" Pipe Ft.	Lbs.	2 1/2" Pipe Ft.	Lbs.	3" Pipe Ft.	Lbs.	4" Pipe Ft.	Lbs.
1	60	4.30	1.85	1.86	.80	0.26	0.11														
2	120	15.00	6.45	4.78	2.06	1.21	0.52	0.38	0.16												
3	180	31.80	13.67	10.00	4.30	2.50	1.08	0.77	0.33												
4	240	54.90	23.61	17.10	7.35	4.21	1.81	1.30	0.56	0.34	0.15										
5	300	83.50	35.91	25.80	11.09	6.32	2.72	1.93	0.83	0.51	0.22										
6	360			36.50	15.70	8.87	3.81	2.68	1.15	0.70	0.30	0.24	0.10								
7	420			48.70	20.94	11.80	5.07	3.56	1.53	0.93	0.40	0.33	0.14	0.10	0.04						
8	480			62.70	26.96	15.00	6.45	4.54	1.95	1.18	0.51	0.44	0.19	0.13	0.06						
9	540					18.80	8.08	5.65	2.43	1.46	0.63	0.56	0.24	0.17	0.07						
10	600					23.00	9.89	6.86	2.95	1.77	0.76	0.69	0.30	0.21	0.09	0.11	0.05	0.04	0.01		
12	720					32.60	14.02	9.62	4.14	2.48	1.07	0.83	0.36	0.25	0.11	0.15	0.06	0.05	0.02		
15	900					49.70	21.37	14.70	6.32	3.74	1.61	1.16	0.50	0.34	0.15	0.22	0.09	0.08	0.03		
20	1200					86.10	37.02	25.10	10.79	6.34	2.73	1.75	0.75	0.52	0.22	0.36	0.15	0.13	0.06		
25	1500							38.60	16.60	9.65	4.15	2.94	1.26	0.87	0.37	0.54	0.23	0.19	0.08		
30	1800							54.60	23.48	13.60	5.85	4.48	1.93	1.30	0.56	0.75	0.32	0.26	0.11		
35	2100							73.40	31.56	18.20	7.83	6.26	2.69	1.82	0.78	1.00	0.43	0.35	0.15		
40	2400							95.00	40.85	23.50	10.11	8.37	3.60	2.42	1.04	1.28	0.55	0.44	0.19		
45	2700									30.70	13.20	10.79	4.64	3.10	1.33	1.60	0.69	0.55	0.24		
50	3000									36.00	15.48	13.45	5.78	3.85	1.66	1.94	0.83	0.66	0.28	0.18	.08
70	4200									68.80	29.58	16.40	7.05	4.67	2.01	3.63	1.56	1.22	0.52	0.35	.15
100	6000											31.30	13.46	8.86	3.81	7.11	3.06	2.39	1.03	0.63	.27
150	9000											62.20	26.75	17.40	7.48	15.40	6.62	5.14	2.21	1.32	.57
200	12000													38.00	16.34	26.70	11.48	8.90	3.83	2.27	.98
250	15000													66.30	28.51	42.80	18.40	14.10	6.06	3.60	1.55
300	18000													90.70	39.00	58.50	25.15	19.20	8.26	4.89	2.10
350	21000															79.20	34.06	26.90	11.57	6.72	2.89

TABLE 6-14:
FEET HEAD OF WATER AND EQUIVALENT PRESSURES

To reduce head in feet to pressure in pounds, multiply by .434.

Feet head	Pounds per sq. in.	Feet head	Pounds per sq. in.	Feet head	Pounds per sq. in.	Feet head	Pounds per sq. in.
1	.43	30	12.99	140	60.63	300	129.93
2	.87	40	17.32	150	64.96	325	140.75
3	1.30	50	21.65	160	69.29	350	151.58
4	1.73	60	25.99	170	73.63	400	173.24
5	2.17	70	30.32	180	77.96	500	216.55
6	2.60	80	34.65	190	82.29	600	259.85
7	3.03	90	38.98	200	86.62	700	303.16
8	3.46	100	43.31	225	97.45	800	346.47
9	3.90	110	47.64	250	108.27	900	389.78
10	4.33	120	51.97	275	119.10	1000	433.09
20	8.66	130	56.30	. . .	. . . .	. . .	. . . .

Source: Gould's Pump Catalog

TABLE 6-15:
PRESSURE AND EQUIVALENT FEET HEAD OF WATER

To change pounds pressure to feet head, multiply by 2.3.

Pounds per sq. in.	Feet head	Pounds per sq. in.	Feet head	Pounds per sq. in.	Feet head	Pounds per sq. in.	Feet head
1	2.31	20	46.18	120	277.07	225	519.51
2	4.62	25	57.72	125	288.62	250	577.24
3	6.93	30	69.27	130	300.16	275	643.03
4	9.24	40	92.36	140	323.25	300	692.69
5	11.54	50	115.45	150	346.34	325	750.41
6	13.85	60	138.54	160	369.43	350	808.13
7	16.16	70	161.63	170	392.52	375	865.89
8	18.47	80	184.72	180	415.61	400	922.58
9	20.78	90	207.81	190	438.90	500	1154.48
10	23.09	100	230.90	200	461.78	1000	2309.00
15	34.63	110	253.98	. . .	. . . .	. . . .	. . . .

Source: Gould's Pump Catalog

C. DISCHARGE CONDITIONS. How much pressure must you have at the pump? How much do you get at the faucet? Water systems are normally set for the pump to cut in at 20-pounds per square inch (psi) tank pressure and to cut out when pressure builds up to 40 psi. When the unit is installed in the house or near the discharge outlets, no further considerations usually need to be weighed regarding discharge pressure. However, the following factors do affect discharge pressure (**Figure 6-17B**):

1. Service pressure required at the faucet or outlet.
2. Vertical distance between the pump and/or tank and the farthest and highest outlet. (Divide by 2.31 to change feet to pounds per square inch pressure.)
3. Friction loss in the discharge piping, obtained from the friction tables in the same manner as for suction piping, but using the "pounds" column.

The total of these three factors is the cut-in pressure at which the system should be set, normally about 20 psi. If any of these factors is unusually high, the pump must cut in at a higher tank pressure than 20 psi, and a pump must be selected that can pump the required capacity at the higher pressure. Suppose you need to supply water to a one-bathroom house, with the pump installed in the house, and the well about 80 feet away. Answer the three original questions A, B, and C:

a. Rate of flow of water needed: about 400 gph
b. 1. Vertical distance, pump to water: 12 feet; 2. Friction loss in overall length of pipe (80 feet horizontal and 20 feet vertical): 100 feet of 1-inch suction pipe 3.56 feet (based on a capacity of 420 gph); 3. Total suction lift: 15.56 feet
c. Discharge pressure conditions: normal (20–40 psi)

The number of fittings and valves also accounts for some friction loss in figuring a water system (**Table 6-16**, page 402). In most cases it need not be figured in at all. But when it does, in a case such as this, the loss in feet of head due to friction when pumping 100 gpm through 250 feet of 2½-inch steel pipe with four 90-degree elbows, one check valve, and one fully open gate valve, all fittings 2½-inch, results in the following:

Pipe	250.0 feet
90° elbows: 6.5 feet × 4	26.0 feet
Check valve	23.0 feet
Gate valve	1.4 feet
	Equivalent feet: 300.4

We use the formula

total friction loss = equivalent feet × loss per 100 feet

(Table 6-15)

300.4 equivalent feet × 7.11 feet loss per 100 feet =
21.35 feet friction loss

Referring to the manufacturer's catalogs, you would find the following two shallow-well pumps would meet the requirements **(Table 6-17,** page 403). At a 15-foot suction lift, and at 20 psi pressure, the $\frac{1}{3}$-hp balanced-flow pump will deliver 410 gallons per hour, which will meet the above requirements. Another pump that might fit this application is the $\frac{1}{3}$-hp jet pump. From its rating table in the catalog it will deliver 530 gallons per hour from a 15-foot total suction lift and at 20 psi discharge pressure. In most cases this would be considered the wiser selection.

Water Supply Problems

Most water supply problems can be found, with the help of math, by careful consideration and investigation of the following problems and their explanations:

1. PUMP CAPACITY TOO SMALL. There is not enough water. When the pump is running, it is delivering its rated capacity in gallons per hour into the tank. Water cannot be drawn from the tank at a greater rate. A rate of 4 gallons

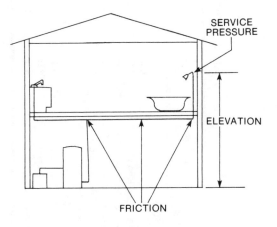

FIG. 6-17B

401

TABLE 6-16:
EQUIVALENT NUMBER OF FEET STRAIGHT PIPE FOR DIFFERENT FITTINGS

Fitting	½	¾	1	1¼	1½	2	2½	3	4	5
				Size of fitting (in.)						
90° elbow	1.5	2.0	2.7	3.5	4.3	5.5	6.5	8.0	1.0	14.0
45° elbow	0.8	1.0	1.3	1.7	2.0	2.5	3.0	3.8	5.0	6.3
Long sweep elbow	1.0	1.4	1.7	2.3	2.7	3.5	4.2	5.2	7.0	9.0
Close return bend	3.6	5.0	6.0	8.3	10.0	13.0	15.0	18.0	24.0	31.0
Tee straight run	1.0	1.4	1.7	2.3	2.7	3.5	4.2	5.2	7.0	9.0
Tee side inlet or outlet	3.3	4.5	5.7	7.6	9.0	12.0	14.0	17.0	22.0	27.0
Globe valve open	17.0	22.0	27.0	36.0	43.0	55.0	67.0	82.0	110.0	140.0
Angle valve open	8.0	11.0	14.0	18.0	22.0	27.0	33.0	41.0	53.0	70.0
Gate valve fully open	0.4	0.5	0.6	0.8	1.0	1.2	1.4	1.7	2.3	2.9
Gate valve half open	8.0	11.0	14.0	18.0	22.0	27.0	33.0	41.0	53.0	70.0
Check valve	4.0	6.0	8.0	12.0	14.0	19.0	23.0	32.0	43.0	58.0

TABLE 6-17:
PERFORMANCE RATINGS

Total suction lift (ft.)	Pump discharge pressure (gal/hr)			Max. shut-off
	20 psi	*30 psi*	*40 psi*	*(psi)*
with 1/3-hp balanced flow pump				
5	525	380		51
10	480	330		49
15	410	290		46
20	350	255		44
25	265	220		42
with 1/3-hp jet pump				
5	690	630	370	59
10	620	560	320	56
15	530	500	280	54
20	430	430	230	51
25	330	330	170	49

per minute, which is a rate of 240 gallons per hour, is the absolute minimum requirement for a shower. Much more is desirable. If other uses, such as kitchen sink, dishwasher, clothes washer, must be turned on at the same time the shower is in use, the pump must be capable of supplying the capacity requirements for all of those being used at the same time.

2. EXCESSIVE SUCTION LIFT. High suction lift can be causing a big reduction in capacity expected from a pump in a shallow well. In the problem illustrated in **Figure 6-18**, it is desirable to be able to use the shower (4 gpm), the kitchen sink or dishwasher (4 gpm), and the clothes washer (4 gpm) all at the same time. Pump capacity must be $3 \times 4 = 12$ gpm $= 720$ gph.

The total suction lift is given by vertical height, 10 feet, plus friction loss (based on 720 gph in 50 feet of ¾-inch pipe) 16.3 feet, for a total suction lift of 26.3 feet. The capacity in gallons per hour of the pump in **Table 6-18** will be considerably less than 700 gallons per hour if ¾-inch suction pipe is used because of the very high total suction lift it causes.

The same calculations for 1-inch suction pipe are vertical height, 10 feet, plus friction loss in 50 feet of 1-inch pipe for 720 gallons per hour, 4.81 feet, for a total suction lift of 14.81 feet.

The capacity of the pump rated above on a 15-foot lift at 20 psi pressure is 820 gallons per hour.

403

TABLE 6-10.
SHALLOW-WELL RATING TABLE

		Pump discharge pressure					
		20		30		40	
	Vertical height	*Max. capacity (gal./hr.)*	*Max. working pressure (lb./in.²)*	*Max. capacity (gal./hr.)*	*Max. working pressure (lb./in.²)*	*Max. capacity (gal./hr.)*	*Max. working pressure (lb./in.²)*
Max.	5 ft.	1,050	53	880	53	430	53
capacity	10 ft.	940	51	770	51	360	51
(gal.	15 ft.	820	49	660	49	290	49
per	20 ft.	690	47	570	47	240	47
hour)	25 ft.	520	45	490	45	180	45

3. EXCESSIVE DEPTH. Depth to water in a deep well can be too great for pump in use, causing the pump capacity to be much less than required. The capacity in gallons per hour required to deliver water at several outlets at the same time is larger than can be expected from most deep-well jet pumps for depths greater than about 40 feet. A submersible pump is less expensive to buy, to install, and to operate. However, a submersible pump should be selected that can deliver the required amount of water from the depth to the low-water level in the well, at the required pressure.

4. INSUFFICIENT DISCHARGE PRESSURE. This really means the pump capacity is not enough at higher pressures. The pressure at any faucet or shower in the problem illustrated will be the tank pressure minus the pressure losses between that faucet or shower and the tank. These losses are caused by:

a. Differences in height yield 1 psi for 2.3 feet (**Table 6-15**). A 23-foot difference in height between the tank and the shower causes a loss of 10 psi (**Tables 6-14** and **6-15**).

b. Friction loss in pipes. Actually, the pressure at the shower or faucet isn't important. Our real concern is to select the pump that can deliver the required rate of flow of water into the tank at a pressure that is high enough to overcome the pressure losses and maintain an adequate flow at one or more outlets. When we know the friction loss we add this to the pressure for height, then add another 5 or 10 psi to have adequate discharge at the shower, and select our pump to deliver its capacity at this total pressure.

404

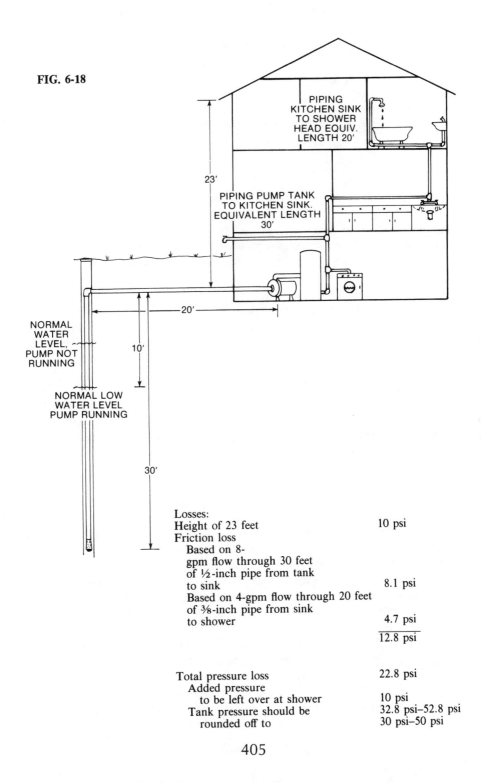

FIG. 6-18

PIPING
KITCHEN SINK
TO SHOWER
HEAD EQUIV.
LENGTH 20'

PIPING PUMP TANK
TO KITCHEN SINK.
EQUIVALENT LENGTH
30'

23'

20'

NORMAL
WATER
LEVEL,
PUMP NOT
RUNNING

10'

NORMAL LOW
WATER LEVEL
PUMP RUNNING

30'

Losses:
Height of 23 feet   10 psi
Friction loss
   Based on 8-
   gpm flow through 30 feet
   of ½-inch pipe from tank
   to sink   8.1 psi
   Based on 4-gpm flow through 20 feet
   of ⅜-inch pipe from sink
   to shower   4.7 psi
                                                            ‾‾‾‾‾‾‾
                                                            12.8 psi

Total pressure loss   22.8 psi
   Added pressure
      to be left over at shower   10 psi
   Tank pressure should be   32.8 psi–52.8 psi
      rounded off to   30 psi–50 psi

405

In the problem just described the pump selection should be as follows:

1. Capacity required: 700-plus gallons per hour
2. Shallow well: 15 feet total suction lift when 50 feet of 1-inch suction pipe used
3. Pressure required: 32.8 psi (set switch at 30–50, but be sure pump will make the 50 psi shutoff)

Pressure Tanks

The capacity of any centrifugal-type pump (jet pumps and submersible pumps) changes as the discharge pressure (tank pressure) changes. Maximum output occurs at low pressure. As tank pressure rises, pump capacity becomes less and less, until the maximum pressure the pump can develop is reached. At this pressure the pump is churning the water in the pump casing. No water is delivered from the pump. An ideal pump selection would be one with sufficient capacity at switch cut-in pressure to supply the peak demand. At a few pounds per square inch pressure below cut-out pressure, its capacity would be as little as 1 or 2 gallons per minute. Every time the pump would start it would continue running as long as any water was being used, whether the demand was the maximum or the minimum. Under these conditions short cycling would not be a factor and the tank size would not be important.

There are two conditions which call for larger tanks.

1. USAGE WITH PUMPS THAT HAVE VERY LITTLE REDUCTION IN CAPACITY AT HIGHER PRESSURE. Even at switch cut-out pressure the pump will deliver more water than might be drawn from one faucet. This will cause short cycling with a small tank.

For example, a submersible pump is to be installed at 140 feet, with pressure requirements at the tank of 30–50 psi and a capacity required of about 700 gallons per hour.

A $\frac{3}{4}$-hp submersible pump will deliver 710 gallons per hour from a 140-foot depth at 30 psi discharge pressure. This pump will deliver 570 gallons per hour at 50 psi. If a small delivery of 2 or 3 or 4 gallons per minute were in use at one faucet, the excess capacity from the pump would build up tank pressure and cause the pressure switch to stop the pump (Figure 6-19). If the water use of a few gallons per minute continued, the pump would start and stop at a frequency determined by tank size.

What is the minimum length of time the $\frac{3}{4}$-hp motor in the above example should be allowed to run? What size should the tank be? The average capacity of the pump in this example is $\frac{1}{2}(710 + 570) = 1,280 \div 2 = 640$ gph, or approximately 10 gpm. If the faucets were all turned off at the instant the pump started, the tank size would have to be 10 × 10, or 100 gallons, to permit the pump to run approximately 1 minute. (The draw-off from a tank operated at

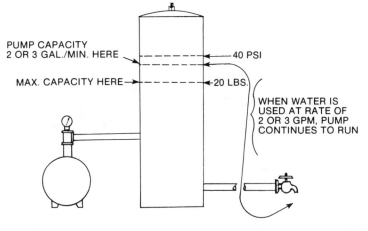

PUMP CAPACITY
2 OR 3 GAL./MIN. HERE —————————————— 40 PSI

MAX. CAPACITY HERE→ — — — — — —←20 LBS.

WHEN WATER IS
USED AT RATE OF
2 OR 3 GPM, PUMP
CONTINUES TO RUN

FIG. 6-19

30–50 psi is approximately 10 psi.) If a 42-gallon tank were used with no precharge, the minimum running time would be about 30 seconds.

2. WEAK WELLS AND LARGER TANKS. For example, a maximum well output of 6 gpm × 60 minutes × 24 hours = 8,640 gallons per day. Probably peak demand in a two-bath home is 10 gpm. Minimum time duration of peak load is about 20 minutes. Will 20–40 psi tank pressure be adequate?
    The quantity of water required during peak demand is

$$20 \text{ minutes} \times 10 \text{ gpm} = 200 \text{ gallons.}$$

Pump can produce

$$6 \text{ gpm (well output)} \times 20 \text{ minutes} = 120 \text{ gallons.}$$

Tank draw-off of

$$200 \text{ gallons} - 120 \text{ gallons} = 80 \text{ gallons is required.}$$

Draw-off at
$$20\text{--}40 \text{ psi} = \frac{1}{8} \text{ tank size.}$$
Tank size required is

$$8 \times 80 \text{ gal.} = 640 \text{ gallons with no precharge.}$$

With 15 psi precharge, 320 gallons will be adequate. A draw-off of 80 gallons will be available from the tank if the peak load always occurs when tank pressure is at 40 psi shut-off pressure.

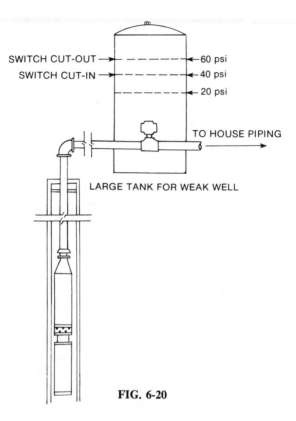

SWITCH CUT-OUT →----------←60 psi
SWITCH CUT-IN →----------←40 psi
----------← 20 psi

TO HOUSE PIPING →

LARGE TANK FOR WEAK WELL

FIG. 6-20

If other minor uses have lowered tank pressure so that it is less than 40 psi, there will be correspondingly less draw-off available **(Figure 6-20)**. If pressure switch is set at 40–60 psi, the 80 gallons required draw-off or even more will always be available.

Pumps should be selected for 360 gallons per hour from depth required and at 20 psi pressure. Pump must also be capable of developing something more than 60 psi pressure from depth at which it is to be installed.

Hot Water Heaters

Hot water is obtained by routing cold water through a water heater. This heater may be part of the central heating plant or a separate unit. When part of a central system, a separate hot water storage tank is generally provided to hold the heated water. On the other hand, when a separate heater is used, the water is stored within the unit.

A separate heater unit may be electric, oil, or gas, but all are automatically controlled by a preset thermostat. Each style of heater comes in a wide variety of sizes. All automatic heaters have the necessary internal piping already installed; the only additional connections required are the hot and cold water and fuel lines. Oil- or gas-fired water heaters also require flues to vent the products of combustion.

A new hot water heater might be necessary when you add new plumbing to your present system. Even if the present water heater is functioning properly (that is, if it is not scaled up or rusted out), there may not be sufficient hot water available for your family. Actually the size of the hot water storage tank needed in the house depends upon the number of persons in the family, the volume of hot water that may be needed during peak use periods (for instance, during laundering and bathing times), and the recovery rate of the heating unit. A good rule to follow when estimating the capacity of the tank required is 10 gallons per hour for each member of the family. For a family of four, for example, the hot water demand will be 40 gallons of hot water per hour. This does not mean that the system will operate continuously at that capacity, but that it must be capable of producing that amount of hot water to keep up with normal usage. If any unusual demands are anticipated, a larger capacity should be provided.

The recovery rate of water heaters varies with the type and capacity of the heating element. In standard conventional models, oil and gas heaters usually have higher recovery rates than electric heaters of similar size. For this reason, you would want a slightly larger capacity with an electric heater than with either oil or gas.

Math and Pipe Measurement

Water-supply piping is available in: (1) galvanized steel pipe; (2) brass pipe; (3) rigid copper tubing; (4) flexible copper tubing; (5) rigid plastic pipe; and (6) flexible plastic pipe.

Of these pipes, copper is most widely used today, although the plastic pipes are becoming more popular. Galvanized pipe is common in older homes, but the labor involved in cutting it and threading it to allow it to be screwed into fittings has limited its use in recent times.

As a general rule, when you are repairing an existing plumbing system, you should use the same type of pipe for the repairs as was used in the original system. If, however, the existing system is steel or threaded brass (very rare these days) you might consider using copper or plastic for your repairs since they are much easier to work with. Either of these materials may be connected to iron or brass by using special adapters.

There are three types of pipe used today for drainage: (1) cast iron and threaded steel; (2) plastic such a PVC and ABS; (3) copper. Whenever possible, use plastic for drainage. It is cheap and easy to use and can be adapted to other systems by using special fittings.

TABLE 6-19:
EXTRA LENGTH NEEDED IN PIPE FOR SCREWING INTO FITTINGS

Pipe size (in.)	Distance pipe is screwed into fitting (in.)	
	Standard fitting	*Drainage fitting*
½	½	
¾	½	
1	⅝	
1 ¼	⅝	⅝
1 ½	⅝	⅝
2	¾	⅝
3		⅞
4		1

Measuring Pipe

With galvanized steel pipe, lengths to be cut should be measured very carefully, as allowance must be made for the threads needed to engage the fittings. The easiest way to measure is to use the face-to-face method. First measure the exact distance from face to face of fittings **(Figure 6-21, view A)**. Next, refer to **Table 6-19** to determine the extra length necessary for screwing into the fittings. Remember that double this length is needed with two ends.

For example, if the face-to-face measurement is 5 feet and ¾-inch pipe is being used, **Table 6-19** shows that ½ inch is needed for engagement with the fitting at one end. If both ends are to be engaged with a fitting, then twice this, or 1 inch of extra length, is required. The total length of the pipe will be 5 feet 1 inch.

While the face-to-face method is the simplest way to measure for pipe lengths, it is not always the best method. It is fine for calculating the length

FIG. 6-21

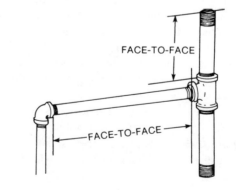

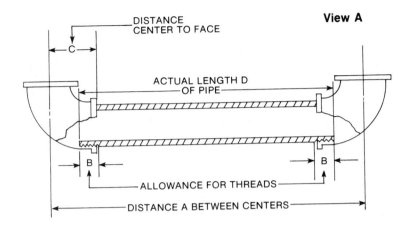

FIG. 6-22

CENTER-TO-FACE DIMENSIONS FOR COMMON PIPE SIZES

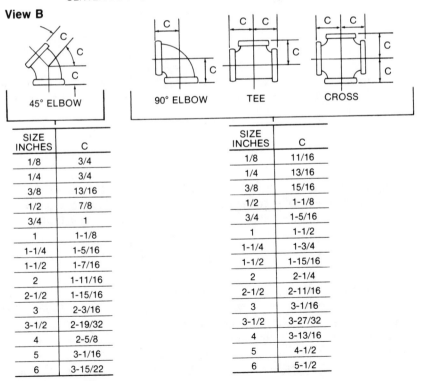

SIZE INCHES	C
1/8	3/4
1/4	3/4
3/8	13/16
1/2	7/8
3/4	1
1	1-1/8
1-1/4	1-5/16
1-1/2	1-7/16
2	1-11/16
2-1/2	1-15/16
3	2-3/16
3-1/2	2-19/32
4	2-5/8
5	3-1/16
6	3-15/22

SIZE INCHES	C
1/8	11/16
1/4	13/16
3/8	15/16
1/2	1-1/8
3/4	1-5/16
1	1-1/2
1-1/4	1-3/4
1-1/2	1-15/16
2	2-1/4
2-1/2	2-11/16
3	3-1/16
3-1/2	3-27/32
4	3-13/16
5	4-1/2
6	5-1/2

411

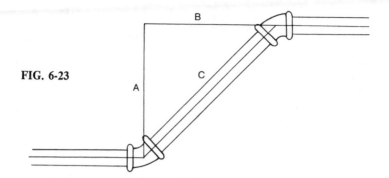

FIG. 6-23

of pipe needed to connect a pair of fittings that are already in place, for example. But if you have to lay out a whole new section of plumbing where no pipes went before, it is sometimes easier to use a different method. This is the center-to-center method.

When using the center-to-center method, you start by measuring the distance between the centers of the two fittings you plan to connect. From this measurement you must then subtract the "C" dimensions or center-to-face dimensions. Finally you add on the distance the pipe will thread into the fitting (as listed in **Table 6-19**).

Thus $$D = A + 2B \text{ minus } 2C$$

Center-to-face or "C" dimensions are given for common fittings in the table in **Figure 6-22, view B.** Also see **Figure 6-22.**

There are times when it is necessary to offset pipes when making connections. **Figure 6-23** shows how the length of pipe is calculated from the trigonometry of the triangle ABC:

$$AC = \sqrt{AB^2 + BC^2}$$

Suppose the distance between pipe lines E and F to be 20 inches (offset AB), what length of pipe D is required to connect with the 45-degree elbows A and C? When the 45-degree elbows are used, both offsets are equal; hence

$$AC = \sqrt{(20)^2 + (20)^2} = \sqrt{800} = 28.3 \text{ inches.}$$

Note that the value for the length of the pipe as just obtained does not allow for the projections of the elbows, which must be taken into account. This is shown in **Figure 6-24.** For the allowance of the elbows, see **Table 6-19.**

There are elbows of angles other than 45 degrees, such as $22\frac{1}{2}$, $11\frac{1}{4}$, etc., which the pipe fitter often encounters. For such, the distance between elbow centers can easily be found by use of the constants given in **Table 6-20.**

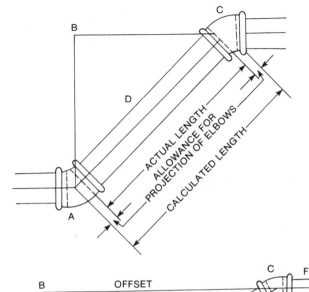

FIG. 6-24

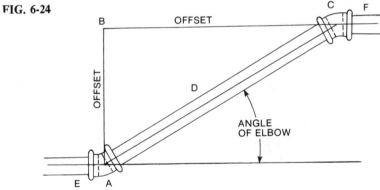

TABLE 6-20:
ELBOW CONSTANTS

Angle of elbow	Elbow centers AC	Offset AB
60°	1.15	0.58
45°	1.41	1.00
30°	2.00	1.73
22 ½°	2.61	2.41
11 ¼°	5.12	5.02
5 ⅜°	10.20	10.15

413

FIG. 6-25

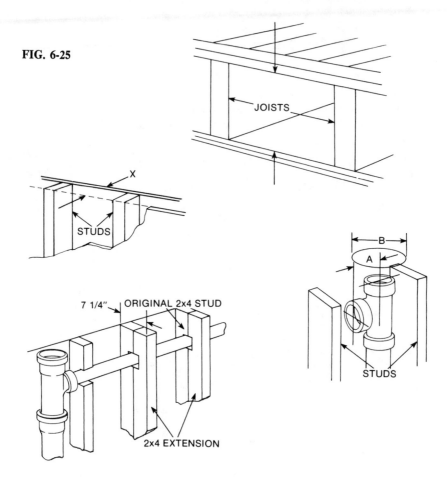

To find the length between centers of elbows, multiply offset by constant for the elbow used. That is, referring to **Figure 6-24.**

$$AC = \text{offset } AB \times \text{constant for } AC$$

$$BC = \text{offset } AB \times \text{constant for } AB$$

For example, if the distance between pipe lines E and F (offset AB) is 20 inches, what is length of offset BC and distance AC, between center of elbows, for 22 $\frac{1}{2}$-degree elbows? In **Table 6-20** the constant for AB with a 22$\frac{1}{2}$-degree elbow is 2.41. Substitute values into the equation:

$$BC = 20 \times 2.41 = 48.2 \text{ inches}$$

414

For distance AC, between centers of elbows, find AC in **Table 6-19.** It is 2.61. Substitute into the equation:

$$AC = 20 \times 2.61 = 52.2 \text{ inches}$$

Rigid copper tubing is usually measured face-to-face in the same manner as galvanized steel pipe; but add on the depths of the soldering hubs in the fittings to be used.

Plastic pipe is measured face-to-face in the same manner as galvanized steel pipe, but add on the depths the pipe will run into the fitting sockets. The procedure for measuring flexible copper tubing is the same as that used for the rigid type.

Planning Pipe Layouts

There must be sufficient space inside a partition or a floor (if there is a ceiling below) for the pipes to be run through them. Measure the clear (air) space inside (X in **Figure 6-25 top**). Space requirements for drainage pipes are shown in **Table 6-21.**

If you know the size of your studs (or joists), you can figure space as follows: A 2-by-4 stud partition has approximately $3\frac{5}{8}$ inches clearance inside it. It will not take even a 2-inch cast-iron pipe but will take a 3-inch copper or thin-walled plastic pipe (Schedule 30) with fittings. A 2-by-6 stud (or joist) has approximately $5\frac{1}{2}$ inches clearance. It will take a 2-inch cast-iron pipe. A 2-by-8 stud has approximately $7\frac{1}{2}$ inches clearance. It will take up to a 4-inch cast-iron pipe. Because plastic and copper pipes are easily cut to any length desired, and fittings can therefore be located as desired, you can run $1\frac{1}{2}$-inch pipe (without fittings) through a space as small as $1\frac{3}{4}$ inches, or 3-inch pipe

TABLE 6-21:
SPACE REQUIREMENTS FOR DRAINAGE PIPES

Pipe size	Plastic		Copper	Cast iron	Galv. steel
	Sched. 30	Sched. 40			
$1\frac{1}{2}$"	—	3"	2"	—	3"
2"	—	3 "	3"	4"	$3\frac{1}{2}$"
3"	$3\frac{1}{2}$"	$4\frac{1}{2}$"	$3\frac{1}{2}$"	$5\frac{1}{4}$"	—
4"	—	$5\frac{1}{2}$"	$4\frac{1}{2}$"	$6\frac{1}{4}$"	—

Wall thickness to accommodate vertical DWV pipes and fittings (without fittings) in a space of only 3¼ inches. Fittings are then planned to be where more space is available. Also, no turning space (for tightening) is required with plastic or copper as it is with any threaded pipe.

Planning a Bathroom

Assuming you have sufficient wall thickness to conceal the pipes, typical wall alterations are shown in **Figure 6-26.** The dimensions necessary for bathroom wall alterations are A = half the width of the tub, B = distance from the middle of the tub to the middle of the lavatory, C = distance from the middle of the lavatory to the middle of the toilet, D = distance from the finished wall to the center of the toilet-bowl outlet (usually 12 inches) plus 4 inches. When measuring from the face of the stud (not the finished wall), allow for the thickness of the wall finish (¾ inch for lath and plaster, ½ inch for gypsum board or ½-inch plywood, 1 inch for rock lath and plaster). For example, if rough-in is 12 inches and wall finish will be ½ inch, then D = 12 + ½ + 4 = 16½ inches. If the partition or wall must be thickened for pipe clearance, allow for thickening when measuring. E = distance from the floor to the top of the lavatory plus 2 inches (usually 33 inches), F = distance from the floor to the top of the tub, G = height of the shower (usually 5 feet), H = area needed to frame the medicine cabinet.

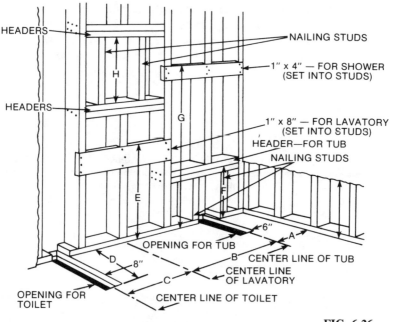

HEADERS

NAILING STUDS

1" x 4" — FOR SHOWER
(SET INTO STUDS)

H

HEADERS

G

1" x 8" — FOR LAVATORY
(SET INTO STUDS)

HEADER—FOR TUB

NAILING STUDS

E

F

6"

A

OPENING FOR TUB

B   CENTER LINE OF TUB

D

8"

CENTER LINE
OF LAVATORY

C

OPENING FOR
TOILET

CENTER LINE OF TOILET

FIG. 6-26

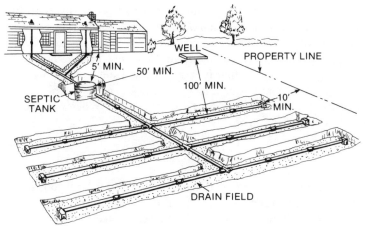

FIG. 6-27

Septic Tank Systems

In locations where a public sewer line is not available, a private disposal system must be provided. The most common way of accomplishing this is to use a septic tank. **Figure 6-27** shows a properly planned and laid-out septic tank system.

When planning a septic system, the first important question is how good is the absorption of the ground. The answer tells you how many square feet of drainage trench area you will need for each bedroom in the house. It is customary to figure drainage trench area on the basis of bedrooms because

TABLE 6-22:
ABSORPTION AREA REQUIREMENTS FOR INDIVIDUAL RESIDENCES
(PROVIDES FOR GARBAGE DISPOSAL AND AUTOMATIC
CLOTHES-WASHING MACHINES)

Percolation rate Per inch in minutes	Required absorption area, in sq. ft. per bedroom	Percolation rate Per inch in minutes	Required absorption area in sq. ft. per bedroom
1 or less	70	10	165
2	85	15	190
3	100	30	250
4	115	45	300
5	125	60	330

417

their number indicates the maximum number of people likely to live in the house. You can test the absorption of the ground by performing a soil percolation test (perk test). Do this by digging a 1-foot-square hole as deep as your drainage trenches will be, usually 18 to 24 inches. Fill the hole with water. Clock the time in minutes that it takes for the water to drop 6 inches. **Table 6-22** tells you how many square feet per bedroom each seeping time requires. In any event, you must have at least 150 square feet. When you know the area required you can lay out the system.

Planning a Septic System

This job begins with the selection of the tank. Your local code may tell you exactly what size and type you are permitted to have. Otherwise the basic facts are your guide. You have a choice between welded steel and cast concrete tanks unless you build your own. If you build your own, you should use solid (not hollow) masonry blocks, and "butter" the inside and outside of the job with a layer of cement to ensure watertightness. In general, you will save money or break even by buying a ready-made tank, and this will ensure it is tight at least initially. Metal tanks are cheaper than concrete. They last for decades in noncorrosive soil, but in other soils, their useful life may be considerably shortened. You can judge by the performance of metal tanks in the immediate area. If you want to cut costs and play it safe at the same time, coat your metal tank with a heavy metal-protecting preparation and let it dry thoroughly before setting the tank in the ground. Asphalt-base roof coatings are often used for this purpose. See **Table 6-23.**

The depth of the tank hole is particularly important. It should be such as

TABLE 6-23:
LIQUID CAPACITY OF SEPTIC TANKS (ALLOWS FOR USE OF GARBAGE GRINDERS, AUTOMATIC CLOTHES WASHERS, AND OTHER HOUSEHOLD APPLIANCES)

Number of bedrooms	Recommended minimum tank capacity (gals.)	Equivalent capacity per bedroom (gals.)
2 or less	750	375
3	900	300
4*	1,000	250

*For each additional bedroom, add 250 gallons.

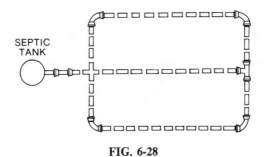

FIG. 6-28

to provide a downward pitch of the sealed pipe from the house to the tank of about $\frac{1}{4}$ inch per foot of run. A flatter pitch is likely to cause clogging. Too steep a pitch can cause the water-borne sewage to surge into the tank and churn the contents. Codes usually require cast-iron pipe at the start of the house-to-tank run.

The other factor involving the depth of the tank hole is the depth of the disposal field tiles—as this part of the system actually begins at the tank outlet. The outlet is usually 1 to 3 inches lower than the inlet, so the tank must be carefully leveled in the hole. Otherwise tilting endwise might cancel out the difference between inlet and outlet levels. The top of the tank should be at least 1 foot below sod level, but not more than 3 feet, as it must be accessible for servicing—lid removal and pump-out. Some tanks have a small removable lid in the top, others have a completely removable top. (Tank-cleaning people need an opening big enough to stir the contents with a shovel so that both solids and liquid are drawn out completely by the cleaning pump.)

The required absorption area, predicated on the results of the soil percolation test, may be obtained from **Table 6-22.** Note especially that the area requirements are per bedroom. The area of the lot on which the house is to be built should be large enough to allow room for an additional system if the first one fails. Thus for a three-bedroom house on a lot where the minimum percolation rate was 1 inch in 15 minutes, the necessary absorption area will be 3×190 square feet, or 570 square feet. For trenches 2 feet wide with 6 inches of gravel below the drain pipe **(Figure 6-28),** the required total length of trench would be $570 \div 2$, or 285 feet. If this were divided into five portions the average length of each line would be $285 \div 5$, or 57 feet. The spacing of trenches is generally governed by practical construction considerations, including safety and type of equipment. For serial distribution on sloping ground, trenches should be separated by 6 feet to prevent short-circuiting. **Figure 6-27** shows the various distances the system has to be kept away from wells, dwellings, and property lines.

419

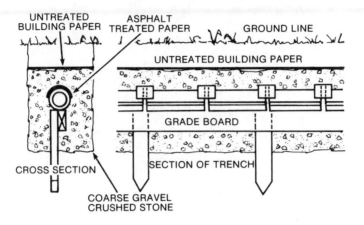

FIG. 6-29

Figure **6-29** shows the disposal trench construction. In cases where the depth of filter material (coarse gravel) below the tile exceeds the standard 6-inch depth, credit may be given for the added absorption area provided in deeper trenches with a resultant decrease in length of trench. Such credit is given in accordance with **Table 6-24,** which gives the percentages of length of

TABLE 6-24:
PERCENTAGES OF LENGTH OF STANDARD TRENCHES*

Depth of gravel below pipe (in.)**	Trench width					
	12 in.	*18 in.*	*24 in.*	*36 in.*	*48 in.*	*60 in.*
12	75	78	80	83	86	87
18	60	64	66	71	75	78
24	50	54	57	62	66	70
30	43	47	50	55	60	64
36	37	41	44	50	54	58
42	33	37	40	45	50	54

*The standard absorption trench is one in which the filter material extends 2 in. above and 6 in. below the pipe.
For trenches or beds having width not shown in **Table 6-24, the percentage of length of standard absorption trenches may be computed as

$$\frac{w + 2}{w + 1 + 2d} \times 100$$

where w = width of trench in feet and d = depth of gravel below pipe in feet.

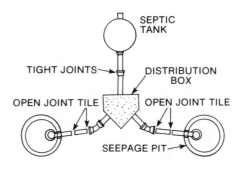

SEPTIC TANK

TIGHT JOINTS

DISTRIBUTION BOX

OPEN JOINT TILE

OPEN JOINT TILE

SEEPAGE PIT

FIG. 6-30

standard absorption trenches (as computed from **Table 6-22**), based on 6-inch increments in depth of filter material.

To use this table, consider the example given above. Using a trench 2 feet wide with 6 inches of gravel under tile, 285 feet are required. If the depth of gravel is increased to 18 inches, while the trench width is kept at 2 feet, only 66 percent of 285 feet is required, or 188 feet. If four laterals are used, the length would be 188 divided by 4, or 47 feet.

The space between lines for serial distribution on sloping ground is 6 feet × 3 spaces = 18 feet, plus 4 lines × 2 feet = 8 feet. Total land required is 26 feet in width × 47 feet in length = 1,222 square feet, plus the additional area required to keep the field away from wells, dwellings, and property lines.

Seepage Pits

In some states seepage pits **(Figure 6-30)** are permitted as an alternative when absorption fields are impracticable (as on very steep slopes) and where the top 3 or 4 feet of soil is underlaid with porous sand or fine gravel and the subsurface conditions are otherwise suitable for pit installations. But seepage pits, as with all soil absorption systems, should never be used where there is a likelihood of contaminating underground waters or where adequate seepage beds or trenches can be provided. When seepage pits are to be used, the pit excavation should terminate 4 feet above the ground water table.

Where circumstances permit, seepage pits may be either supplements or alternatives to the more shallow absorption fields. When seepage pits are used in combination with absorption fields, the absorption areas in each system should be prorated, or based upon the weighted average of the results of the percolation tests.

It is important that the capacity of a seepage pit be computed on the basis of percolation tests made in each vertical stratum penetrated. The weighted average of the results should be computed to obtain a design figure. Soil strata

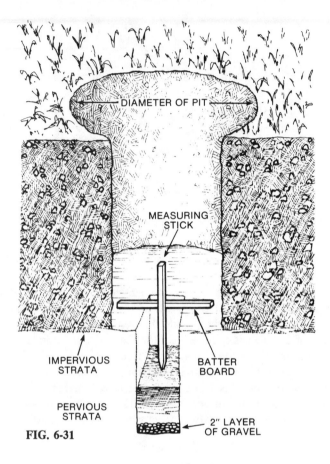

FIG. 6-31

in which the percolation rates are in excess of 30 minutes per inch should not be included in computing the absorption area. As will be apparent from **Figure 6-31,** adequate tests for deep pits are somewhat difficult to make, time-consuming, and expensive. Although few data have been collected comparing percolation test results with deep-pit performance, nevertheless the results of such percolation tests, while of limited value, combined with competent engineering judgment based on experience, are the best means of arriving at design data for seepage pits.

Table 6-22 gives the absorption area requirements per bedroom for the percolation rate obtained. The effective area of the seepage pit is the vertical wall area (based on dug diameter) of the previous stratum below the inlet. No allowance should be made for impervious strata or bottom area. With this in mind, **Table 6-25** may be used for determining the effective wall area of circular or cylindrical seepage pits.

TABLE 6-25:
VERTICAL WALL AREAS OF CIRCULAR SEEPAGE PITS IN SQUARE FEET

Diameter of seepage pit (ft.)	Effective strata depth below flow line (below inlet)									
	1 ft.	2 ft.	3 ft.	4 ft.	5 ft.	6 ft.	7 ft.	8 ft.	9 ft.	10 ft.
3	9.4	19	28	38	47	57	66	75	85	94
4	12.6	25	38	50	63	75	88	101	113	126
5	15.7	31	47	63	79	94	110	126	141	157
6	18.8	38	57	75	94	113	132	151	170	188
7	22.0	44	66	88	110	132	154	176	198	220
8	25.1	50	75	101	126	151	176	201	226	251
9	28.3	57	85	113	141	170	198	226	254	283
10	31.4	63	94	126	157	188	220	251	283	314
11	34.6	69	104	138	173	207	242	276	311	346
12	37.7	75	113	151	188	226	264	302	339	377

For example, assume that a seepage pit absorption system is to be designed for a three-bedroom home on a lot where the minimum percolation rate of 1 inch in 15 minutes prevails. According to **Table 6-22,** 3 × 190 or 570 square feet of absorption area would be needed. Assume also that the water table does not rise above 27 feet below the ground surface, that seepage pits with effective depth of 20 feet can be provided, and that the house is in a locality where it is common practice to install seepage pits of 5-foot diameter—that is, 4 feet to the outside walls, which are surrounded by about 6 inches of gravel. Design of the system is as follows:

Let d = depth of pit in feet, D = pit diameter in feet. Then:

$$\pi Dd = 570 \text{ square feet}$$

$$3.14 \times 5 \times d = 570$$

Solving for d:

$$d = \frac{570}{3.14 \times 5} = \frac{570}{15.7} = 36.3, \text{ or approximately 36 feet}$$

In other words, one 5-foot-diameter pit 36 feet deep would be needed, but since the maximum effective depth is 20 feet in this particular location, it will be necessary to increase the diameter of the pit, or increase the number of pits, or increase both of these. For example, a design for two pits, each with a 10-foot diameter, would be:

$$2 \times 3.14 \times 10 \times d = 570 \text{ square feet}$$

$$d = 9.1 \text{ feet deep}$$

Use two pits 10 feet in diameter and 9.1 feet deep.

Alternately, a design for two pits, each with a 5-foot diameter, would be:

$$2 \times 3.14 \times 5 \times d = 570 \text{ square feet}$$

$$d = 18 \text{ feet (approximately)}$$

Use two pits 5 feet in diameter and 18 feet deep.

Experience has shown that seepage pits should be separated by a distance equal to 3 times the diameter of the largest pit. For pits over 20 feet in depth, the minimum space between pits should be 20 feet. The area of the lot on which the house is to be built should be large enough to maintain this distance between the pits while still allowing room for additional pits if the first ones should fail. If this can be done, such an absorption system may be approved; if not, other suitable sewage facilities would be required.

MATH FOR ENERGY SAVINGS

SAVINGS ON HEATING AND COOLING

You don't need elaborate math to tell you that the cost of home heating and cooling has been rising steadily and sharply for years. Everyone knows this trend can be retarded through insulation, weatherstripping, storm windows, and so on. But which measures are most effective for *your* home, in *your* climate? Normally, it takes rather complicated math to answer that question.

To simplify things, however, we'll take shortcuts on the long, involved heat-loss calculations that professional heating engineers use. Instead, we'll use a far simpler method, adapted from the system in the US Government's energy-saving book *In the Bank or Up the Chimney*. The math will help you decide on the most cost-effective conservation measures for your own situation.

Your Heating and Cooling Bills

The first step in evaluating your situation is to find out how much you pay to heat and cool your home.

Oil or Coal

If you heat with oil or coal, your heating bill is simply the sum of your coal or oil bills for a full year. If you don't have your records on hand, phone your fuel dealer for the figures.

Note: If you use the same fuel for home heating and for heating your hot water, your actual expenses for home heating will be only about 80 percent of the total fuel bill.

In this case, multiply your total fuel bill by 0.8 for home heating costs.

Gas Heat or Electric Heat Without Central Air Conditioning

If you heat your home and your hot water with electricity or gas and want to isolate costs for home heating, the math involves a few steps. You'll need a couple of monthly fuel bills and some information from **Table 7-1**. Enter figures on the Home Heat Worksheet, as explained in the paragraph below. Here's how to fill in those blanks. If you have gas heat, or electric heat *without central air conditioning,* enter your January fuel bill on Line 1. Then refer to **Table 7-1** to find the city nearest you. Next to that city will be the name of a month. Write your gas or electric bill for *that month* on Line 2. Now subtract Line 2 from Line 1 and enter that number on Line 3. Return to **Table 7-1** and enter the number from Column A for the city nearest you on Line 4. Then multiply Line 3 by Line 4 for a rough approximation of your heating bill.

HOME HEAT WORKSHEET

Line 1	$_____	(January fuel bill)
Minus Line 2	$_____	
Equals Line 3	$_____	
Line 4	_____	
Line 4 × Line 3 =	$_____	(approx. annual gas/electric heating bill)

Electric Heat and Central Air Conditioning

If you have electric heat *and central air conditioning,* you must change the Home Heat Worksheet sequence slightly. Follow the steps outlined above, but instead of entering the multiplication factor from Column A on Line 4, use the factor given in Column B.

Record the approximate annual heating bill on Line 4 for reference later in this chapter.

Air Conditioning Costs

Finding air conditioning costs involves essentially the same processes as those needed to find your heating bill. Enter figures on the Air Conditioning Worksheet as explained in the paragraph below.

AIR CONDITIONING WORKSHEET

Line 1	$_____	(July electric bill)
Minus Line 2	$_____	
Equals Line 3	$_____	
Line 4	_____	
Line 4 × Line 3 =	$_____	(approx. annual cooling costs)

TABLE 7-1:
REFERENCE FOR HOME HEAT WORKSHEET

Location	Month	Gas or electric heat alone A	Electric heat with electric A/C B	Electric A/C alone C	Electric A/C with electric heat D
Alabama					
Montgomery	May	4.2	5.2	7.3	7.3
Alaska					
Anchorage	July	7.8	7.8	*	*
Arizona					
Flagstaff	July	6.4	6.6	*	*
Phoenix	April	4.4	5.1	5.1	6.3
Arkansas					
Little Rock	May	4.3	4.7	5.6	5.9
California					
Bishop	Sept.	5.2	7.5	3.5	5.1
Eureka	July	17.0	17.0	*	*
Los Angeles	Oct.	6.0	7.1	10.5	***
Bakersfield	April	4.8	5.3	4.9	8.0
San Francisco	Sept.	6.7	7.0	*	*
Colorado					
Alamosa	July	6.0	6.0	*	*
Denver	Sept.	6.2	6.3	3.5	*
Connecticut					
New Haven	Sept.	5.8	6.1	4.7	**
Nevada					
Elko	Sept.	6.8	6.8	2.2	*
Las Vegas	April	4.7	4.9	4.1	5.7
New Hampshire					
Concord	July	5.5	5.9	*	*
New Jersey					
Atlantic City	Sept.	5.4	5.7	5.1	8.2
New Mexico					
Raton	Sept.	6.3	6.5	3.7	*
Silver City	Sept.	4.7	5.3	5.7	5.9
New York					
New York City	Sept.	5.1	5.6	5.9	8.0
Rochester	Sept.	6.1	6.4	5.0	*
North Carolina					
Raleigh	May	4.9	5.2	5.3	6.9
Wilmington	May	4.3	4.8	7.0	5.9
North Dakota					
Bismarck	July	5.3	5.5	*	*
Ohio					
Youngstown	Sept.	6.1	4.8	5.2	*

(Continued)

TABLE 7-1:
REFERENCE FOR HOME HEAT WORKSHEET (continued)

Location	Month	Gas Electric Heat Alone A	Electric Heat With Electric A/C B	Electric A/C Alone C	Electric A/C With Electric Heat D
Delaware					
Dover	May	5.7	5.8	3.8	9.6
District of Columbia					
Washington	May	5.3	5.5	4.3	6.7
Florida					
Miami†	Feb.	†	†	9.6	9.6
Tallahassee	April	4.4	4.9	5.6	6.5
Georgia					
Atlanta	May	4.8	5.2	4.7	5.4
Savannah	April	4.6	5.1	5.3	6.5
Idaho					
Boise	Sept.	5.9	6.0	3.1	**
Illinois					
Chicago	Sept.	5.5	5.8	5.2	**
Springfield	May	5.4	5.5	3.6	**
Cairo	May	4.7	4.9	4.2	5.3
Indiana					
Indianapolis	Sept.	5.6	6.1	6.5	**
Iowa					
Des Moines	Sept.	5.1	5.4	11.8	**
Dubuque	Sept.	5.8	6.0	4.1	*
Kansas					
Wichita	May	4.9	5.0	3.5	5.8
Goodland	Sept.	5.7	5.8	3.4	9.8

Location	Month	Gas Or Electric Heat Alone A	Electric Heat With Electric A/C B	Electric A/C Alone C	Electric A/C With Electric Heat D
Cincinnati	May	5.4	5.4	4.0	10.0
Oklahoma					
Oklahoma City	May	4.5	4.8	4.9	6.1
Oregon					
Salem	July	6.1	6.5	*	*
Medford	May	7.4	6.3	3.3	11.3
Pennsylvania					
Philadelphia	May	5.7	5.8	3.8	10.5
Pittsburgh	Sept.	5.9	6.2	5.4	*
Rhode Island					
Providence	Sept.	5.9	6.1	4.7	*
South Carolina					
Charleston	April	4.7	4.9	4.9	6.2
Greenville-Spartanburg	May	4.6	5.0	4.8	5.4
South Dakota					
Rapid City	Sept.	6.3	6.3	3.2	*
Tennessee					
Knoxville	May	5.1	5.3	4.7	6.5
Memphis	May	4.3	4.8	5.2	5.6
Texas					
Austin	April	4.1	4.5	5.5	7.0
Dallas	April	4.6	5.0	5.0	7.7
Houston	April	4.0	4.8	5.9	7.0

Kentucky					
Lexington	May	5.6	5.6	4.0	11.4
Louisiana					
Baton Rouge	April	4.1	4.8	5.9	6.5
Shreveport	April	4.6	5.0	4.9	7.7
Maine					
Portland	July	5.7	5.7	*	*
Maryland					
Baltimore	May	5.5	5.6	3.9	9.0
Massachusetts					
Worcester	Sept.	6.2	6.4	4.4	*
Michigan					
Lansing	July	5.5	5.5	*	*
Minnesota					
Duluth	July	6.0	6.1	*	*
Minneapolis	May	6.2	6.3	2.8	*
Mississippi					
Jackson	April	4.9	5.3	5.0	7.7
Missouri					
St. Louis	May	4.8	4.8	3.4	5.9
Springfield	May	5.6	5.7	3.7	9.1
Montana					
Helena	July	5.8	6.0	*	*
Nebraska					
Omaha	Sept.	5.3	5.5	4.3	*
Scottsbluff	Sept.	6.1	6.2	3.1	*

Lubbock	May	4.7	5.2	6.8	9.3
Utah					
Salt Lake City	Sept.	5.6	5.7	3.2	6.4
Milford	Sept.	5.5	5.7	2.7	*
Vermont					
Burlington	July	5.6	5.9	*	*
Virginia					
Richmond	May	5.1	5.4	5.2	8.0
Washington					
Olympia	July	6.8	7.0	*	*
Walla Walla	Sept.	5.3	5.6	3.3	8.0
West Virginia					
Charleston	May	5.7	5.7	4.2	9.6
Elkins	Sept.	6.5	5.2	4.0	*
Wisconsin					
Milwaukee	July	5.7	6.2	*	*
Wyoming					
Casper	Sept.	6.7	6.8	2.8	*

*Air conditioning savings not significant.
**Your air conditioning bill is about ⅟₁₀ of your electric heating bill.
***Your air conditioning bill is about ⅟₄ of your electric heating bill.
†Heating savings not significant.

First enter your July electric bill on Line 1. Then on Table 7-1, find the city nearest you. Next to that city is the name of a month. Enter your electric bill for that month on Line 2 and subtract from Line 1. Enter the difference on Line 3. If you have electric heat as well as central air conditioning, enter the number from Column D on Line 4. But if you heat with oil, coal, or gas, enter the number from Column C on Line 4. Multiply Line 3 by Line 4 to determine your cooling bill.

Heating and Cooling Factors

Now that you have your heating and cooling bills, you can calculate your heating and cooling factors. These factors will then be used later in this chapter as constants in simple equations that will allow you to estimate potential savings offered by a variety of home improvements.

Heating Factors

Finding your heating factors is easy. To do that, determine the city nearest you in Table 7-2. Then find the heating multiplier for that city under the appropriate fuel column. You are now ready to compute your heating factor using this simple formula:

$$\text{heating multiplier} \times \text{fuel price} = \text{heating factor}$$

In this case, fuel price is the amount you pay for fuel in the following units:

Gas: ¢/100 cu. ft.
Oil: ¢/gal.
Electricity: ¢/kWh
Coal: ¢/lb.

Your heating factor will be a simple constant with no dollar value assigned to it. For example, if you live in New Haven, Connecticut, and heat with oil at $1.20 a gallon, your formula will read:

$$.0143 \times 120 = 1.716$$

Your heating factor is 1.716 with no dollar signs, no cent signs.

Cooling Factor

If you have central air conditioning, find your cooling factor using this formula:

$$\text{cooling multiplier} \times \text{electric price (¢/kWh)} = \text{cooling factor}$$

430

TABLE 7-2:
HEATING and COOLING MULTIPLIERS

		Heating multipliers				Cooling multiplier
		Gas	Oil	Elec.	Coal	
		J	K	L	M	N
ALABAMA	Montgomery	.0105	*	.2260	.0987	.0859
ALASKA	Anchorage	.0275	*	.5956	*	.0001
ARIZONA	Flagstaff	.0233	*	.5040	*	.0056
	Phoenix	.0081	*	.1741	*	.1430
ARKANSAS	Little Rock	.0147	*	.3176	*	.0769
CALIFORNIA	Bishop	.0163	*	.3515	*	.0414
	Eureka	.0212	*	.4580	*	.0001
	Los Angeles	.0078	*	.1682	*	.0367
	Bakersfield	.0097	*	.2093	*	.0941
	San Francisco	.0137	*	.2967	*	.0059
COLORADO	Alamosa	.0278	*	.6010	*	.0023
	Denver	.0168	*	.3640	*	.0231
CONNECTICUT	New Haven	.0192	.0143	.4155	*	.0312
DELAWARE	Dover	.0188	.0140	.4054	.1770	.0447
D.C.	Washington	.0161	.0120	.3473	.1517	.0559
FLORIDA	Miami	.0010	.0007	.0211	*	.1589
	Tallahassee	.0068	.0051	.1465	*	.0941
GEORGIA	Atlanta	.0113	*	.2435	.1063	.0612
	Savannah	.0083	*	.1794	*	.0892
IDAHO	Boise	.0166	.0124	.3582	*	.0330
ILLINOIS	Chicago	.0182	.0136	.3944	.1722	.0373
	Springfield	.0138	.0103	.2976	.1300	.0453
	Cairo	.0125	.0093	.2692	.1176	.0663
INDIANA	Indianapolis	.0163	.0121	.3514	.1534	.0398
IOWA	Des Moines	.0188	.0140	.4062	*	.0406
	Dubuque	.0210	.0157	.4548	*	.0257
KANSAS	Wichita	.0151	*	.3255	*	.0603
	Goodland	.0175	*	.3786	*	.0337
KENTUCKY	Lexington	.0153	.0114	.3300	.1441	.0423
LOUISIANA	Baton Rouge	.0071	*	.1539	*	.1046
	Shreveport	.0100	*	.2155	*	.0914
MAINE	Portland	*	.0161	.4631	*	.0138
MARYLAND	Baltimore	.0167	.0124	.3603	.1573	.0461
MASSACHUSETTS	Worcester	.0227	.0169	.4911	*	.0185
MICHIGAN	Lansing	.0197	.0147	.4260	.1860	.0200
MINNESOTA	Duluth	.0254	*	.5482	*	.0073
	Minneapolis	.0213	*	.4595	*	.0268
MISSISSIPPI	Jackson	.0102	*	.2209	.0964	.0918
MISSOURI	St. Louis	.0153	*	.3306	*	.0540
	Springfield	.0160	*	.3453	*	.0518
MONTANA	Helena	.0206	*	.4456	*	.0093

(Continued)

431

TABLE 7-2:
HEATING & COOLING MULTIPLIERS (continued)

		Heating Multipliers				Cooling Multiplier
		Gas	Oil	Elec.	Coal	
		J	K	L	M	N
NEBRASKA	Omaha	.0189	.0141	.4077	*	.0446
	Scottsbluff	.0169	.0126	.3658	*	.0232
NEVADA	Elko	.0188	.0141	.4075	*	.0128
	Las Vegas	.0103	.0077	.2228	*	.1114
NEW HAMPSHIRE	Concord	.0211	.0157	.4552	*	.0170
NEW JERSEY	Atlantic City	.0183	.0137	.3957	.1728	.0312
NEW MEXICO	Raton	.0203	*	.4388	*	.0391
	Silver City	.0121	*	.2611	*	.0391
NEW YORK	New York City	.0183	.0137	.3959	.1729	.0434
	Rochester	.0220	.0164	.4755	.2076	.0259
NORTH CAROLINA	Raleigh	.0155	.0115	.3347	.1462	.0500
	Wilmington	.0107	.0080	.2315	.1011	.0730
NORTH DAKOTA	Bismarck	.0224	*	.4852	*	.0171
OHIO	Youngstown	.0209	.0156	.4522	.1974	.0204
	Cincinnati	.0144	.0107	.3107	.1357	.0439
OKLAHOMA	Oklahoma City	.0121	*	.2625	*	.0705
OREGON	Salem	.0217	.0162	.4690	*	.0101
	Medford	.0229	.0170	.4940	*	.0283
PENNSYLVANIA	Philadelphia	.0183	.0137	.3959	.1729	.0448
	Pittsburgh	.0180	.0134	.3890	.1698	.0120
RHODE ISLAND	Providence	.0194	.0145	.4195	*	.0285
SOUTH CAROLINA	Charleston	.0087	.0065	.1888	*	.0869
	Greenville-Spartanburg	.0113	.0085	.2450	*	.0561
SOUTH DAKOTA	Rapid City	.0186	.0139	.4027	*	.0209
TENNESSEE	Knoxville	.0133	.0099	.2873	.1255	.0557
	Memphis	.0119	.0089	.2569	.1122	.0780
TEXAS	Austin	.0078	*	.1688	*	.1071
	Dallas	.0090	*	.1943	*	.1049
	Houston	.0061	*	.1319	*	.1000
	Lubbock	.0117	*	.2521	*	.0617
UTAH	Salt Lake City	.0197	*	.4264	*	.0371
	Milford	.0212	*	.4578	*	.0267
VERMONT	Burlington	*	.0176	.5098	*	.0178
VIRGINIA	Richmond	.0147	.0110	.3178	.1388	.0537
WASHINGTON	Olympia	.0239	.0178	.5165	*	.0035
	Walla Walla	.0137	.0102	.2963	*	.0357
WEST VIRGINIA	Charleston	.0146	.0109	.3154	.1377	.0388
	Elkins	.0185	.0138	.3999	.1746	.0208
WISCONSIN	Milwaukee	.0218	.0162	.4707	.2055	.0216
WYOMING	Casper	.0188	*	.4062	*	.0151

Find the cooling multiplier by referring to **Table 7-2** next to the city nearest you. As with computing the heating factor, above, the fuel price (in this case ¢/kWh) should be expressed without decimals. That is $.06, or 6¢, should read simply as 6 in your formula.

Determining Potential Energy Savings

Now, armed with your heating and cooling bills and your heating and cooling factors, you are ready to compare potential energy savings. Let's see how much you can save per year by making the following changes:

1. Changing thermostat settings
2. Caulking and weatherstripping
3. Adding storm windows
4. Insulating your attic
5. Insulating walls
6. Insulating crawl space, floor, or basement walls
7. Servicing furnace and air conditioner

If you calculate the savings for each of these improvements and determine how much each improvement will cost, you can then determine which are most cost effective and undertake them first.

Changing Thermostat Settings

Determine which zone you live in as shown in **Figure 7-1.** Then determine

	ZONE 1	ZONE 2	ZONE 3
5° turn-down	14%	17%	25%
8° turn-down	19%	24%	35%

FIG. 7-1

433

how low a thermostat setting would be realistic for your household during the winter. You should be able to remain comfortable at 65°F if you dress warmly. If you formerly kept your home at 70° and decide to drop down to 65°, you will have made a 5 degree turndown. A glance at the table accompanying **Figure 7-1** shows you the percent savings you will achieve for either a 5- or 8-degree turndown in your zone. Multiply that percentage by your yearly fuel bill to find your annual savings.

EXAMPLE: Let's say you live in Denver (Zone 2) and spend $1,800 a year to heat your home. A 5-degree turndown in Zone 2 is worth 17 percent. Here .17 × $1,800 = $306 savings per year. That's a good return on an investment equaling a heating season's wear and tear on a few sweaters.

Caulking and Weatherstripping

If your windows and doors are presently well stripped and caulked, with good tight seals all around and no unbroken beads of caulk, you can skip this section. Otherwise, step outside with a pencil and paper to assess your situation. If the caulking around your windows and doors is old, cracked, and missing in a few places, your caulking is *FAIR*. If there is no caulking, or very little of it, consider your caulking *POOR*. The same goes for weatherstripping around windows and doors. If you have it but it is worn or missing in spots, call it *FAIR*. If you have none, call it *POOR*.

CAULKING AND WEATHERSTRIPPING WORKSHEET

A.	YOUR WINDOWS		Multiply these two numbers		
	Caulking and putty:				
	in *FAIR* condition:	number of windows	× 0.3	=	_____
	in *POOR* condition:	number of windows	× 1.0	=	_____
	Weatherstripping:				
	in *FAIR* condition:	number of windows	× 1.0	=	_____
	in *POOR* condition:	number of windows	× 8.4	=	_____
B.	YOUR DOORS		Multiply these two numbers		
	Caulking:				
	in *FAIR* condition:	number of doors	× 0.3	=	_____
	in *POOR* condition:	number of doors	× 0.9	=	_____
	Weatherstripping:				
	in *FAIR* condition:	number of doors	× 2.0	=	_____
	in *POOR* condition:	number of doors	× 16.8	=	_____
C.	Add up all the numbers you've written in the boxes to the right and enter the total here:				
			SAVINGS FACTOR		_____

Count the number of windows and doors that fall into the *POOR* and *FAIR* categories for both weatherstripping and caulking. Enter those numbers in the spaces provided on the accompanying Caulking and Weatherstripping Worksheet. Multiply the numbers you have entered times the constants next to them, and enter the products in the boxes provided. Then add up all the boxed numbers to arrive at your savings factor for weatherstripping and caulking. You are now only a step away from finding your annual savings. To find how much you will save use this formula:

$$(\text{heating factor} + \text{cooling factor}) \times \text{savings factor} = \text{savings}$$

Your answer will read in dollars saved per season at present fuel rates.

Note: If you have no central air conditioning, eliminate the cooling factor from the equation.

Calculations for one home in New England with 12 poor windows and doors and with oil heat resulted in an estimated yearly savings that exceeded caulk and weatherstripping costs by 50 percent. So the payback occurred in less than one heating season.

Adding Storm Windows

Here's another common energy-saving measure. Assessing yearly storm-window savings is a simple matter. First, count the number of single-glazed windows in your home. Then use the number of windows in this equation:

$$\text{Number of windows} \times 7.9 \times \text{heating factor} = \text{yearly savings}$$

In this equation 7.9 is a constant. Then retrieve your heating factor, which you determined earlier in this chapter.

Your answer will be in dollars saved per year, and these savings will be in addition to any savings you achieve through improved weatherstripping or caulking.

Insulating Your Attic

This is one of the biggest fuel savers you can undertake. Current recommendations for adequate attic insulation vary from R-26 in the South to R-38 in the North. For the sake of convenience, we will compromise and make our calculations using R-30 as though it were the recommended level.

First step is to determine the area of your attic in square feet. When making your measurements, be sure to include only attic area that lies above heated

435

living space. Once you know the attic area, multiply that by 0.54 to determine the savings factor:

$$\text{attic area} \times .54 = \text{savings factor going from R-0 to R-19}$$

Multiply your savings factor by the sum of your heating and cooling factors, which you determined earlier, and you have approximate potential savings. If you do not have central air conditioning, simply multiply your savings factor by your heating factor.

Many attics already have six inches of insulation in them, providing an R-value of 19. How much can you save by adding enough insulation to bring the total to R-30? The savings here will not be nearly as great as if you had no insulation to start with, because there is a much greater gain in going from R-0 to R-19 than in going from R-19 to R-38, or in our case to R-30. Still, the extra insulation may be worth the bother and expense. To determine the savings factor, multiply and attic area by .048:

$$\text{attic area} \times .048 = \text{savings factor going from R-19 to R-30}$$

Again, multiply the savings factor for the area of your attic by your heating factor (determined earlier) to find savings for the heating season. If you also air condition your home, multiply the savings factor by the sum of your heating and cooling factors, determined earlier. Your answers will be in dollars saved per year.

Insulating Walls

Here's another way to save a lot of energy. Adding wall insulation only makes sense if you have no insulation in your walls at all. If there is any insulation in there at present, adding more will probably not make economic sense because of the expense involved in opening portions of interior or exterior walls.

Putting insulation into finished walls is a job for a contractor who will blow insulation into place. **Table 7-3** shows common types of insulation used for this purpose, each with a different R-value in the typical $3\frac{1}{2}$-inch stud wall.

To calculate the possible savings you can have after insulating your walls, you will first need to know the exterior wall area surrounding heated portions of your home.

First, determine the linear feet of exterior wall surrounding heated portions. If your house has one floor, simply measure the distance around the house to

436

TABLE 7-3:
R-VALUES OF HOUSE COMPONENTS

Material	Thickness	R-Value
Air Film and Spaces		
Air space, bounded by ordinary materials	¾″ or more	0.91
Air space, bounded by aluminum foil	¾″ or more	2.17
Exterior air film	—	0.17
Interior air film	—	0.68
Masonry		
Sand and gravel concrete block	8″	1.11
Sand and gravel concrete block	12″	1.28
Lightweight concrete block	8″	2.00
Lightweight concrete block	12″	2.13
Face brick	4″	0.44
Concrete cast in place	8″	0.64
Building Materials (General)		
Wood sheathing or subfloor	¾″	1.00
Fiber board insulating sheathing	¾″	2.10
Plywood	⅝″	0.79
Plywood	½″	0.63
Plywood	⅜″	0.47
Bevel lapped siding	½″ × 8″	0.81
Bevel lapped siding	¾″ × 10″	1.05
Vertical tongue and groove board	¾″	1.00
Drop siding	¾″	0.94
Asbestos board	¼″	0.13
⅜″ gypsum lath and ⅜″ plaster	¾″	0.42
Gypsum board	⅜″	0.32
Interior plywood panel	¼″	0.31
Building paper	—	0.06
Vapor barrier	—	0.00
Wood shingles	—	0.87
Asphalt shingles	—	0.44
Linoleum	—	0.08
Carpet with fiber pad	—	2.08
Hardwood floor	—	0.71
Insulation Materials (Mineral wool, glass wool, wood wool, etc.)		
Blanket or batts	1″	3.70
Blanket or batts	3½″	11.00
Blanket or batts	6″	19.00
Loose fill	1″	3.33
Rigid insulation board (sheathing)	¾″	2.10
Windows and Doors		
Single window	—	Approx. 1.00
Double window	—	Approx. 2.00
Exterior door	—	Approx. 2.00

find its perimeter. If it has more than one heated floor, combine the perimeters of all the heated floors. Do not count the basement.

Once you have the total linear feet of wall, refer to **Table 7-3** to find the total that most closely matches yours. Then read the column under that figure to determine the savings factor for the type of insulation you'll use.

Once you have the total linear feet of wall, multiply that times the appropriate figure for the type of insulation you'll use. Figures are as follows: *mineral wool is 1,* and *cellulose fiber is 1.1,* and *U-F foam is 1.15.* Plug the appropriate figure into the following formula:

$$\text{linear feet} \times \text{(insulation figure for mineral, cellulose, or U-F)} = \text{savings factor}$$

Once you determine your savings factor, compute your annual savings. Savings for heating only are equal to the savings factor times your heating factor, which you determined earlier. Savings for heating and air conditioning are equal to the savings factor times the sum of your heating and cooling factors.

Your answer—in dollars saved per year—can then be related to the price a contractor will charge you to insulate the walls. If his estimate is no more than about seven times your annual savings, insulation would be a good investment, giving you a gross seven-year payback.

INSULATING CRAWL SPACE, FLOOR, OR BASEMENT

This is one of the least effective insulation projects you can undertake. Still, if you have already performed the insulation jobs mentioned above, and if you live in a cold climate, basement or crawl space insulation may still result in dollar savings. If so, the savings is easy enough to determine.

Crawl Space

If you have a crawl space under your house, make your calculations like this: Measure the distance around the outside of any crawl space that is beneath heated living space. Do not include any crawl space over porches or other unheated spaces.

Once you've determined the perimeter of your crawl space, multiply it by 0.54. The result is your savings factor. Multiply that savings factor by your heating factor (determined earlier) and you'll arrive at the yearly savings you can expect after insulating your crawl space walls and a two-foot-wide band of floor around the perimeter using R-11 mineral wool. This type of insulation is best for a crawl space that can be sealed off to prevent air flow through it during the winter.

Floor

If your crawl space can't be sealed off—as in the case of a house standing on piers—you will have to insulate the underside of your floor instead. This will require a different calculation of savings. First step is to determine the area of the floor to be insulated in square feet. Multiply that by 0.29. The result will be your savings factor.

Once you determine your savings factor, multiply it by your heating factor, determined earlier. That will give you the savings you can expect per year if you insulate your floor with R-11 mineral wool. Most floors will have depth in floor joists for R-19 insulation if you want to spend the extra money. If you do use R-19 instead of R-11 insulation, multiply the yearly savings you have just computed by 1.7. That will give you a good idea of how much the extra thickness will save you per year.

Basements

What about fully heated basements? Still another means of computation is required. In this case, determine the linear feet of basement wall in your home that lies above ground level at least two feet. Write that number down. Then estimate to the nearest foot how far—on the average—this length of wall rises above the ground.

For example, say your basement has 60 feet of wall that lies at least two feet above grade. About 30 feet of the wall lies four feet above grade, and the other 30 feet lies only two feet above grade. That averages out to 3 feet above grade for the whole 60 feet.

Next, refer to the figures below to find the average height above grade that corresponds to your home. Beneath it will be a number, your intermediate savings factor. Multiply that number by the total length of basement wall. That will give your savings factor.

Average height above ground	2 feet	4 feet	6 feet	8 feet
Intermediate savings factor	.77	1.3	1.9	2.4

Now multiply your savings factor by your old friend, the heating factor (which you determined earlier). Your answer will be dollars saved per season by insulating your basement walls with R-7 insulation, down to a level 2 feet below grade. To achieve R-7 you can use 2 to $2\frac{1}{2}$ - inch mineral wool, or 1-inch plastic foam board.

Servicing Your Furnace and Air Conditioner

If you have a coal or oil burner that has not been serviced for a year or more, a service call can save you about 10 percent on your heating costs. To estimate your yearly savings, simply multiply your annual heating bill by 0.1. It's that

439

simple. Find your savings on air conditioning in the same way. Just multiply your annual cooling bill by 0.1 and the result is saving per season in dollars. If you have a gas furnace, service isn't as critical. A checkup every few years is enough. Don't expect gas-burner tune-up savings to be as large as for coal and oil burners.

HEAT LOSS CALCULATIONS

All of the techniques for estimating savings earlier in this chapter are quick and easy. But they employ assumptions, based on averages, that make them less than perfectly accurate. A more accurate way to evaluate possible savings is to make a heat-loss calculation. Here's a fairly simple way to make such a calculation:

We already know that the resistance to heat flow through a section of your home is equal to the sum of all the R-values for the components that make up that section. **Figure 7-2** shows the overall R-value for a section of typical wall, for example.

Table 7-3 gives a listing of the R-values for the major types of building components that you will find in most homes. To use these figures, analyze the

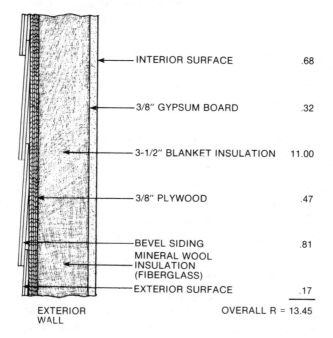

INTERIOR SURFACE	.68
3/8″ GYPSUM BOARD	.32
3-1/2″ BLANKET INSULATION	11.00
3/8″ PLYWOOD	.47
BEVEL SIDING	.81
MINERAL WOOL INSULATION (FIBERGLASS)	
EXTERIOR SURFACE	.17
EXTERIOR WALL	OVERALL R = 13.45

FIG. 7-2

440

construction of any section of your home you want to study. Find out what materials went into its construction. Then look up the R-values for those materials in **Table 7-3.** Add those R-values together to find the total R-value of that section of your home. Now you can make a quick calculation to find out how much heat you lose per year through that section of your home. Use this formula:

$$\text{Annual loss} = \frac{1}{R} \times 24 \times \text{area} \times \text{annual degree days}$$

In this formula, area is the area in square feet of the section of your home you are studying, and your annual degree days can be found in **Table 6-4** on page 361. Here's an example: Let's say you live near Minneapolis, Minnesota, and want to insulate the walls of your home. The walls presently have no insulation and are composed of the following materials: Inside is a layer of $\frac{3}{8}$-inch gypsum lath and $\frac{3}{8}$-inch plaster (R-0.42). Next comes a $3\frac{1}{2}$-inch air space (R-0.91). Then comes $\frac{5}{8}$-inch plywood sheathing (R-0.79). Finally there is $\frac{1}{2}$-inch lapped bevel siding (R-0.81). In addition to these building materials, there are inside and outside air films (R-0.68 and R-0.17 respectively) considered insulating-surface resistances. Add all these R-values together, and you get R-3.78 as your total for the wall.

Let's say that the total area of your walls is 640 square feet. On the heating-degree table (**Table 6-4,** page 361) Minneapolis has an annual degree-day total of 8,382. All this information plugged into our equation looks like this:

$$\text{Annual loss} = \frac{1}{3.78} \times 24 \times 640 \times 8,382$$

$$\text{Annual loss} = 34,060,181 \text{ Btu}$$

To compute your cost, refer to **Table 6-5** on page 372. First divide Btu per unit of fuel into the Btu loss you computed above. That result will be the units of fuel lost. Then simply multiply units of fuel times your current cost for each fuel unit.

So far so good. Now let's assume you are planning to have cellulose fiber blown into those same walls. Three and a half inches of cellulose will give you about R-11. Add that R-11 to the R-3.78 of your present wall. Total is R-14.78. Adding that insulation takes away the former insulating air space in your wall, so you have to subtract R-0.91. That leaves you with R-13.87. Now let's go through that heat loss calculation again, as we did two paragraphs earlier, using the R-value for our wall with the insulation in place.

$$\text{Annual loss} = \frac{1}{13.87} \times 24 \times 640 \times 8,382$$

$$\text{Annual loss} = 9,282,446$$

Adding that insulation would cut heat loss from over 34 million Btu down to a bit over 9 million. To be exact, that insulation would save you 34,060,189 minus 9,282,446 Btu or 24,777,743 Btu per year. Multiply that figure by your cost per Btu, computed above, to see how much money the insulation can save a year. For example, if that house were heated with oil yielding 91,000 Btu per gallon, you'd divide the 24,777,743 Btu lost per year by 91,000 for a result of 272.3 gallons lost. At $1.20 per gallon, that loss would cost you $326.76.

Once you have computed your possible savings, ask some contractors to give you estimates on the job. If the job costs no more than 10 times your annual savings, it is probably a good investment. Here's why: If the price of heating fuel stays the same, a job costing 10 times the annual savings would pay for itself in 10 years. But fuel prices will surely rise, so your payback time for dollars spent will be shorter. Even so, there are other factors such as real value of the dollar in relation to your income that may hold that payback time closer to 10 years.

HOME APPLIANCES

Too many people decide to buy a new appliance simply on the basis of price. In these days of rising energy costs, that can be a mistake. It's smarter to base your shopping decisions upon *price plus operating costs*. Ideally, these operating costs should include maintenance costs, but these are hard to forecast. For the sake of simplicity, evaluate an appliance in terms of initial cost plus energy costs.

At one time, this was a fairly complicated task. But it has been simplified by the advent of the EnergyGuide label. By law, these labels are now required to appear on seven categories of home appliances. Included are refrigerators and refrigerator/freezers, freezers, room air conditioners, automatic washers, dishwashers, water heaters, and furnaces. Central air conditioning will also be included.

Because of the differences between these various kinds of appliances, there are three different types of EnergyGuide labels to consider. These are the *energy cost* label, the *energy efficiency* label, and the *generic* label. Let's look at each.

Energy Cost Label

This label provides information on the probable yearly energy costs for running an appliance. Appliances covered include refrigerators, refrigerator/freezers, and water heaters. **Figure 7-3** shows a sample of this label. Outside

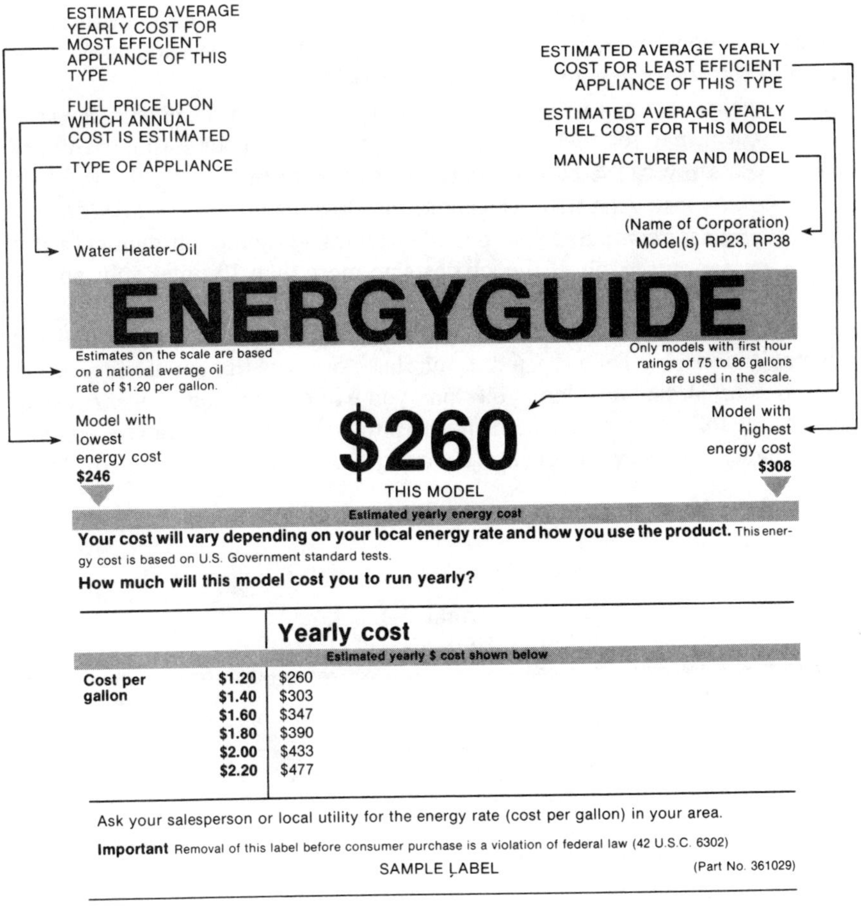

ESTIMATED AVERAGE
YEARLY COST FOR
MOST EFFICIENT
APPLIANCE OF THIS
TYPE

FUEL PRICE UPON
WHICH ANNUAL
COST IS ESTIMATED

TYPE OF APPLIANCE

ESTIMATED AVERAGE YEARLY
COST FOR LEAST EFFICIENT
APPLIANCE OF THIS TYPE

ESTIMATED AVERAGE YEARLY
FUEL COST FOR THIS MODEL

MANUFACTURER AND MODEL

Water Heater-Oil

(Name of Corporation)
Model(s) RP23, RP38

ENERGYGUIDE

Estimates on the scale are based
on a national average oil
rate of $1.20 per gallon.

Only models with first hour
ratings of 75 to 86 gallons
are used in the scale.

Model with
lowest
energy cost
$246

$260
THIS MODEL

Model with
highest
energy cost
$308

Estimated yearly energy cost

Your cost will vary depending on your local energy rate and how you use the product. This energy cost is based on U.S. Government standard tests.

How much will this model cost you to run yearly?

		Yearly cost	
		Estimated yearly $ cost shown below	
Cost per	$1.20	$260	
gallon	$1.40	$303	
	$1.60	$347	
	$1.80	$390	
	$2.00	$433	
	$2.20	$477	

Ask your salesperson or local utility for the energy rate (cost per gallon) in your area.

Important Removal of this label before consumer purchase is a violation of federal law (42 U.S.C. 6302)

SAMPLE LABEL   (Part No. 361029)

FIG. 7-3

the label itself, we've explained some of the most important factors. As you can see, a large number at the center of the label gives the estimated average annual energy cost. This energy cost is based on national averages for fuel costs, and it gives you a convenient way to compare the operating costs of various appliances of roughly the same capacities.

Beneath that large annual cost figure is a scale showing the estimated range of operating costs for all appliances in the same capacity class. At the left end of the scale you will find the operating cost for the most efficient appliance in this class, and at the right end of the scale, the cost for the least efficient appliance of this type. This scale lets you see where the appliance you are considering compares with its competition.

443

Note that both the large estimated yearly cost and the scale beneath it are based on national averages for fuel costs. Your fuel may cost you more or less. To get a better idea of your true operating costs, look at the table at the bottom of the label. There you will find a range of fuel prices. Pick the one closest to the price you pay for fuel and next to it you will find the estimated yearly energy costs you can expect at your current fuel price.

Life Costs

Once you know your specific yearly energy cost, you can make an intelligent shopping decision. Take the initial purchase price of the appliance you are considering. Decide how long you think you will own the appliance. A useful service life for major appliances is from 10 to 20 years, depending on the type of appliance and its overall quality. Refrigerators, for example, tend to be fairly

TABLE 7-4:
LIFE COST OF AN APPLIANCE

Life expectancy (years)	Life cost constant
10	15.93
11	18.52
12	21.37
13	24.51
14	27.96
15	31.76
16	35.93
17	40.52
18	45.57
19	51.13
20	57.25

Note: You can derive constants for inflation rates other than 10 percent if you like, using a lengthy technique, as described below. Using a 15 percent inflation rate (or 1.15) as an example, make a list for each year from 1 to 20 down the left margin of a paper. Enter the number 1 next to year 1. For the second entry, multiply 1 by the inflation rate, or 1.15. You'll get 1.15. For the third entry, multiply 1.15 by 1.15. You'll get 1.32. For the fourth entry, then multiply 1.32 by 1.15. You'll get 1.52. Continue in this manner until you have multiplied by 1.15 19 times, entering your product each time you multiply. Now you should have a column of 20 numbers running from 1 to 20.

Next, make a cumulative total, next to each entry. For example, next to the number 1 add 0 for a total of 1. Next to the 1.15 enter the sum of 1 plus 1.15 (2.15). Next to the number 1.32 enter the sum of 2.15 plus 1.32 (3.47). Next to the number 1.52 enter the sum of 3.47 plus 1.52 (4.99). Keep this up until you reach the end of the column. The numbers you have produced will be the life-cost constants for life expectancies from 1 to 20 years, assuming a 15 percent rate of increase per year. You can develop similar tables for any assumed annual inflation rate for fuel.

rugged and usually last longer than washers. For the purposes of life cycle costing, you can pick 15 years as a good compromise.

At any rate, the life cycle cost of any appliance you buy will be its initial cost, plus its fuel costs for the lifetime you select. But to find lifetime fuel costs, you can't simply multiply your current yearly cost by the number of years you expect the appliance to last. The reason? Fuel prices will go up, and this has to be taken into account.

Table 7-4 will make it easy to account for inflation. It lists life-cost constants for all the life expectancies from 10 to 20 years, assuming a 10 percent annual increase in the cost of fuel.

How Do You Use a Life-Cost Constant?

Simple. Just multiply it by the estimated yearly energy cost at present energy prices as listed on the Government's EnergyGuide label on the appliance.

For example, let's say you are considering a water heater. According to the sticker, the heater will cost you $150 to run for a year at current prices. You expect the heater to last 20 years. The life cost constant for 20 years at 10 percent annual increase in fuel cost is 57.25. Therefore 57.25 × 150 = $8,-587.50.

It's hard to believe, but over a period of 20 years you would spend over $8,500 to fuel that heater. Add that to the initial purchase price, and you have the life cycle cost. These calculations quickly show the importance of efficiency in an appliance with a long service life.

Say for example you are choosing between two heaters. One costs $200 and has an estimated annual energy cost of $150. The other costs $250 but will run for just $140 a year. On a life cycle basis, the first one will cost $200 plus (57.25 × 150) or $200 plus $8,587.50 or $8,787.50. The second heater would cost $250 plus (57.25 × 140) or $250 plus $8,015 or $8,265. Thus the more expensive heater will cost $522.50 less in inflated dollars over the course of 20 years.

You can do similar calculations with any other type of appliance covered by an energy cost label such as EnergyGuide label. This includes all refrigerators, refrigerator/freezers, and water heaters.

Note: This same type of label, and the same math procedures can be used to check costs for washers and dishwashers. The only difference is that the energy cost information on the label will be given in two tables instead of one. One table will show the costs for using the appliance with a gas water heater, the other for using it with an electric water heater. Just pick the table that corresponds to the type of heater you have in your home and ignore the other table. The same math outlined above will work with the information on this type of label (shown in **Figure 7-4**).

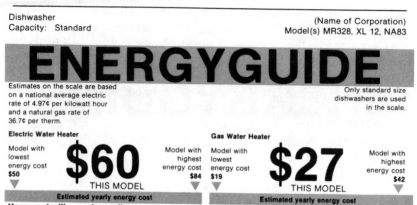

Dishwasher
Capacity: Standard

(Name of Corporation)
Model(s) MR328, XL 12, NA83

ENERGYGUIDE

Estimates on the scale are based on a national average electric rate of 4.97¢ per kilowatt hour and a natural gas rate of 36.7¢ per therm.

Only standard size dishwashers are used in the scale.

Electric Water Heater

Model with lowest energy cost $50

$60
THIS MODEL

Model with highest energy cost $84

Gas Water Heater

Model with lowest energy cost $19

$27
THIS MODEL

Model with highest energy cost $42

Estimated yearly energy cost

Estimated yearly energy cost

Your cost will vary depending on your local energy rate and how you use the product. This energy cost is based on U.S. Government standard tests.

How much will this model cost you to run yearly?

with an electric water heater

with a gas water heater

Loads of dishes per week	2	4	6	8	12
Estimated yearly $ cost shown below					
Cost per kilowatt hour 4¢	$15	$31	$46	$62	$92
6¢	$23	$46	$69	$92	$139
8¢	$31	$62	$92	$123	$189
10¢	$39	$77	$116	$154	$231
12¢	$47	$92	$139	$185	$278
14¢	$54	$108	$162	$216	$324

Loads of dishes per week	2	4	6	8	12
Estimated yearly $ cost shown below					
Cost per therm (100 cubic feet) 20¢	$5	$11	$16	$22	$33
30¢	$7	$14	$21	$27	$41
40¢	$9	$19	$28	$36	$55
50¢	$12	$23	$35	$45	$68
60¢	$19	$28	$42	$54	$82
70¢	$22	$44	$66	$88	$110

Ask your salesperson or local utility for the energy rate (cost per kilowatt hour or therm) in your area, for estimated costs if you have a propane or oil water heater.

Important Removal of this label before consumer purchase is a violation of federal law (42 U.S.C. 6302)

SAMPLE LABEL

(Part No. 73906)

FIG. 7-4

Energy Efficiency Label

This label is used on air conditioners. Direct cost information of the type provided in the energy cost label cannot be given for air conditioners. The reason? Annual use of an air conditioner depends upon the climate. A typical energy efficiency label is shown in **Figure 7-5,** complete with explanations of the label's important features.

You can use the information on this label in the same way as you used the information on the cost label described earlier. The only difference is that you must first estimate how many hours per year you will use the air conditioner. Obviously, the cooler your climate, the less you will use the air conditioner.

446

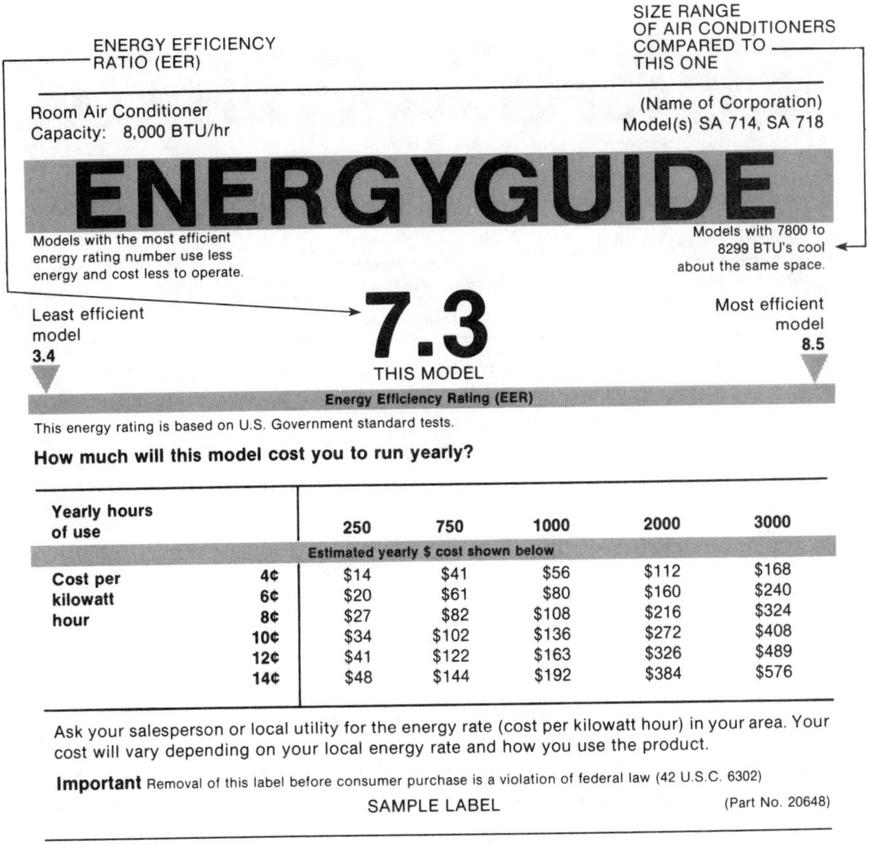

FIG. 7-5

Once you have estimated your yearly hours of use, you can read down the table to find your yearly cost at the electric company rates that most nearly correspond to your present rates. Then proceed with the math outlined earlier for the energy cost label.

Generic Label

This is the type of EnergyGuide label used on furnaces. As you can see by looking at the sample label in **Figure 7-6,** this label doesn't provide much information. To make a good decision when buying a furnace, you will have to ask your heating contractor for information on the relative efficiencies of these appliances. He will have the information on energy fact sheets.

(For Furnaces)

You can save substantially on home heating and cooling energy costs by following the simple steps outlined below:

1.	Weatherproof your house.
2.	Assure energy efficient heating and cooling equipment selection and installation.
3.	Operate and maintain your system to conserve energy.

Help conserve energy. Compare the energy efficiency rating and cost information for this model with others. Check the figures and spend less on energy.

Your contractor has the energy fact sheets. Ask for them.

Important Removal of this label before consumer purchase is a violation of federal law (42 U.S.C. 6302)

FIG. 7-6

Other Appliances

Not all home appliances are covered by EnergyGuide labels. When you shop for these you will have to base your decisions on other criteria. For example, if you are buying a new range, look for features that add to efficiency. Thick insulation in the walls of the oven will cut heat loss and ensure more efficient baking and broiling. Automatic spark ignition on a gas range will save energy when compared to pilot light ignition.

Even when you shop for appliances that have EnergyGuide labels, check for energy-saving features as well. For cxample, a dishwasher that has an air-dry switch will let your dishes dry naturally without the need for the current to supply a 600 to 900 watt heating coil to force-dry the dishes. A clothes dryer with a moisture sensing control to shut off the dryer when the clothes are dry can save money compared to a dryer that only has a timer. With the timer you have to guess at the proper drying time. If you overestimate, any energy used to run the dryer once the clothes have dried is simply wasted. A washing machine with a cold water cycle can save a great deal of energy. Nearly 95 percent of the energy used during a hot-water wash goes for heating the water.

When choosing lighting fixtures for your home, remember that fluorescents are about four times as efficient as incandescent bulbs. They also give off less heat, which can reduce cooling loads during the summer.

448

AUTOMOBILE FUEL EFFICIENCY

There are two main factors that determine fuel efficiency. The first is the efficiency of the car itself. The second is the driver—his driving habits and his maintenance of the car.

Buying an Energy-Efficient Car

The most important single factor for fuel economy is vehicle weight. All other things equal, the more a car weighs, the more fuel it will require. As a rule of thumb, fuel consumption increases about 1 percent for every 100 pounds added to the weight of a car. Weight is most important during stop-and-go driving, and least important at highway speeds. Once a car achieves cruising speed, air resistance becomes the primary force the engine has to overcome.

Since weight is so important, always try to buy the smallest or lightest car that can carry the passenger and cargo loads you'll have. Aim for *everyday* needs, not the occasional weekend when you need to bring home lumber or firewood. For those occasional big loads you can rent or borrow a truck or trailer, or perhaps buy a trailer. There is no point in paying for the fuel to move an oversize vehicle when that extra size is needed only a few times a year.

After weight, the next most important factor is engine size and type. The smaller the engine, the better its mileage. There are two reasons for this. First, small engines have to work harder than big ones, and engines tend to be most efficient when working near their full power outputs. Second, larger engines weigh more, and extra weight means lower mileage.

Since small engines save gas, it pays to buy the standard engine offered for the car you plan to buy. Standard engines in most cars have adequate power for normal driving and acceleration. You'll need a larger engine only if you plan to consistently haul heavy loads or pull a trailer.

What about diesels? According to the EPA, a diesel engine can deliver 40 to 70 percent better mileage than a comparable gasoline engine. This is partly because diesels have higher compression ratios than gasoline engines, and partly because there is more energy in a gallon of diesel fuel (about 137,750 Btu) than in a gallon of gas (123,500 Btu).

Of course, diesel engines cost more than gasoline engines, at least from most makers. GM diesels can cost as much as $850 more than comparable gas engines. VW diesels are about $170 extra. Mercedes, on the other hand, sells its diesels for less than its gasoline engines. You have to weigh the extra cost of the diesel—if any—against the possible savings it can give you. We'll cover such life-cycle costs later in this chapter.

Tires

Steel-belted radials are the best all-around buy in tires. Various studies have shown they can boost gas mileage from 3 to 10 percent, depending on the car and tire being tested, and upon the test. This increase in mileage is due to the radial's lower rolling resistance compared to ordinary bias-ply tires.

Radials cost more than other tires, but they provide longer tread life, and improved braking and handling. Over the life of the tire, a radial will more than offset its higher initial price and provide better handling and greater safety at the same time.

Even among radials, there are some significant differences. Steel belts are important. They significantly outperform other types of belts (glass for example). Among the steel-belted radials, the new P-metric types and ellipticals are designed to allow higher inflation pressures than other types, without a drop in ride comfort or tread life. Raising the pressure further reduces rolling resistance and therefore increases mileage. The increases are in the order of a few percent. Note that the benefit of any radial is greatest when you drive at a steady moderate speed, and lowest in city driving or very high speed cruising.

If you have standard steel-belted radials (not the newer metric type) you can still boost gas mileage by raising the tire pressure a few pounds (no more than four), but this will make your ride a bit harsher, and may change handling characteristics.

Transmissions

Even though the gas mileage provided by automatics has improved over the past few years, manual transmissions still give the best mileage. How much better are they? Best way to determine this is to check the EPA mileage figures for any car you are considering. The list will show mileage for both the manual and automatic versions of that car.

What about overdrive and five-speed gear boxes? Overdrive can cut gas consumption by about 10 percent at highway speeds. Other times it won't save anything at all. Since the option may cost you $135 or so, you have to decide whether you do enough highway driving to justify the extra cost. See the discussion on life-cycle costing later on.

Five speed boxes are a bit different. With some, the five speeds will be packed into the same range of gear ratios you would get with a four-speed transmission. With others, the fifth speed serves as an overdrive gear. The first type—the close-ratio transmission—would be a better choice than the overdrive type if you don't do a lot of cruising. But the overdrive type is better for long-distance driving.

Life Cycle Costing

Whenever you buy a car, you are faced with a variety of choices. Should you buy that oversized car with the low gas mileage at a very low price, or that more-expensive compact that gets double the mileage? Should you get the five-speed or the automatic?

The only way to make a sensible choice is to do some life-cycle costing. This means to combine the price of the car with the cost of the fuel it will require over the entire time you own that car. True life-cycle costing would also include costs for tires, oil, maintenance, insurance, and so on, but for the sake of simplicity, we will just deal with fuel costs.

Suppose that you are considering buying a car that gets an estimated 35 miles to the gallon on the highway and 20 miles to the gallon in the city. You know that you average about 20,000 miles per year, with 70 percent on interstate highways and the rest, more or less, in the stop-and-go conditions of the city. You plan to keep the automobile you buy for five years. Here's how to figure gas consumption over those five years:

Highway miles per year: 20,000 miles $\times$ 70 percent = 14,000 miles

City miles per year: 20,000 miles $\times$ 30 percent = 6,000 miles

Highway gas per year: $\dfrac{14,000 \text{ miles}}{35 \text{ miles to a gallon}}$ = 400 gallons

City gas per year: $\dfrac{6,000 \text{ miles}}{20 \text{ miles to a gallon}}$ = 300 gallons

Total gas per year: 700 gallons

If you know you would burn about 700 gallons of gas a year, how much will that much gas cost you? This will take a bit of guessing, because we don't know how fast the price of gas will increase over the next five years. But for the sake of our example, let's start with gas at $1.40 a gallon, and assume an annual 20 percent increase. At that rate:

$1.40 $\times$ 700 gal. = $980 for the first year

$1.68 $\times$ 700 gal. = $1176 for the second year

$2.02 $\times$ 700 gal. = $1414 for the third year

$2.42 $\times$ 700 gal. = $1694 for the fourth year

$2.90 $\times$ 700 gal. = $2030 for the fifth year

451

Total gasoline for all five years? $7,294. Add to that figure the price of the car and you have a rough idea of the life cycle cost. Go through the same procedure for any other cars you are investigating and compare life-cycle costs to see which is lowest. Or do the same for different versions of the same car. For example, EPA figures will be listed for different engine options, and transmission options. Compare the life cycle costs for the car with any of these engine or transmission options and you can quickly see how much you'll have to pay for the convenience of an automatic, or the extra power of a larger engine.

Once you know the lifetime fuel cost for a particular car, you can also make some rough estimates on the cost for fuel needed to run some other options, or the fuel dollar savings you can gain with others.

Let's say you can have overdrive for $135 extra. It will save you 10 percent on fuel for highway driving. From our earlier calculations, we determined that highway driving accounted for 400 of the 700 gallons consumed a year. Thus, four out of every seven gallons are used for highway driving, and four sevenths of your total gas bill goes for highway driving. Therefore $\frac{4}{7} \times$ $7,294 (total gas bill for five years) = $4,168 (spent on highway driving).

We estimate that overdrive will save you 10 percent of that money. So, $4,168 $\times$ .1 = $416.80. The overdrive will save you about $416, far more than its initial price of $135. That makes the overdrive a good buy.

Other Options

Some options are more difficult to cost out. Air conditioning is a good example. With modern aerodynamic cars, there is evidence that you can get better mileage cruising with the A/C on, than you can with the windows rolled down. That may be true, but at lower speeds, that advantage is lost. Meanwhile, your car carries that air conditioner around all the time. Just the weight of the unit (around 100 pounds) can cost you .4 mpg for a compact car or about .1 mpg for a large sedan. And you pay that premium even when the air conditioner is off.

When it is being used, at least during local driving, the air conditioner can cost around 2 to 3 mpg. If we assume hypothetical car discussed earlier loses 2 mpg with the air conditioner on at low speeds, and loses nothing at cruising speed, it would cost about $312 in fuel for air conditioning in a climate with high temperatures all year around, and about $100 in a climate that requires the air conditioner four months out of the year. Add to that the up-front price of the air conditioner (around $550 or so) and you get a rough idea of what it costs to keep cool while driving, excluding maintenance costs for the air conditioner.

The A/C is not the only accessory that uses fuel. In fact, any part of the car that uses electricity will do so by increasing the load on the alternator, which in turn drains energy from the engine. Keep this in mind when selecting options, and also when driving.

INDEX

456